THE COURT MARTIAL OF
ROBERT E. LEE

THE COURT MARTIAL OF ROBERT E. LEE

A Historical Novel

Douglas Savage

COMBINED BOOKS

Pennsylvania

For information, address:
COMBINED BOOKS, INC.
151 East 10th Avenue
Conshohocken, PA 19428

Library of Congress Cataloging-in-Publication Data
Savage, Douglas.
The court martial of Robert E. Lee / Douglas Savage.
p.   cm.
Includes bibliographical references.
ISBN 0-938289-26-8
1. Lee, Robert E. (Robert Edward), 1807-1870—Fiction.
2. Courts-martial and courts of inquiry—Southern States—Fiction.
3. United States—History—Civil War, 1861-1865—Fiction.
I. Title.
PS3569.A8223C68   1993
813'.54—dc20   93-24378
CIP

Combined Books Edition   1 2 3 4 5

First published in the USA in 1993 by Combined Books, Inc.
and distributed in North America by
Stackpole Books, Inc.,
5067 Ritter Road, Mechanicsburg, PA 17055

Printed in the United States of America.

Acknowledgments

The Court Martial of Robert E. Lee would have been impossible without the following publishers' generous permission or license to quote from the following materials:

From *The Wartime Papers of Robert E. Lee* edited by Clifford Dowdey and Louis Manarin. Copyright © 1961 by the Commonwealth of Virginia. Copyright © renewed 1989 by the Commonwealth of Virginia. By permission of Little, Brown and Company, Boston.

From *R. E. Lee*, Vol. I, Douglas Southall Freeman. Reprinted with the permission of Charles Scribner's Sons, an imprint of Macmillan Publishing Company. Copyright © 1934 Charles Scribner's Sons; copyright © renewed 1962 Inez Goddin Freeman. From *R. E. Lee*, Vol. II, Douglas Southall Freeman. Reprinted with the permission of Charles Scribner's Sons, an imprint of Macmillan Publishing Company. Copyright © 1934 Charles Scribner's Sons; copyright © renewed 1962 Inez Goddin Freeman. From *R. E. Lee*, Vol. III, Douglas Southall Freeman. Reprinted with the permission of Charles Scribner's Sons, an imprint of Macmillan Publishing Company. Copyright © 1935 Charles Scribner's Sons; Copyright © renewed 1963 Inez Goddin Freeman. From *R. E. Lee*, Vol. IV, Douglas Southall Freeman. Reprinted with the permission of Charles Scribner's Sons, an imprint of Macmillan Publishing Company. Copyright © 1935 Charles Scribner's Sons; copyright © renewed 1963 Inez Goddin Freeman.

From *Lee's Lieutenants*, Vol. I, Douglas Southall Freeman. Reprinted with the permission of Charles Scribner's Sons, an imprint of Macmillan Publishing Company. Copyright © 1942 Charles Scribner's Sons; copyright © renewed 1970 Inez Goddin Freeman. From *Lee's Lieutenants*, Vol. II, Douglas Southall Freeman. Reprinted with the permission of Charles Scribner's Sons, an imprint of Macmillan Publishing Company. Copyright © 1943 Charles Scribner's Sons; copyright © renewed 1971 Inez Goddin Freeman. From *Lee's Lieutenants*, Vol. III, Douglas Southall Freeman. Reprinted with the permission of Charles Scribner's Sons, an imprint of Macmillan Publishing Company. Copyright © 1944 Charles Scribner's Sons; copyright © renewed 1972 Inez Goddin Freeman.

From *To Markie: The Letters of Robert E. Lee to Martha Williams*,

For Sidney Savage
An Old Soldier
145th Infantry; Company B
37th Division, U.S.A.

MAPS

THE COURT MARTIAL OF ROBERT E. LEE

Introduction

*E*very character appearing in this story once lived and breathed in a place called the Confederate States of America, under a government which lasted barely four years. Although this is an historical novel, there are no fictional characters.

The Court Martial of Robert E. Lee is both fact and fiction. Robert E. Lee, Commanding General, Army of Northern Virginia, was not court martialed after the disaster at the July 1863 Battle of Gettysburg. But that is the story here. General Lee was indeed recalled to Richmond five months after Gettysburg. He remained in the Confederate capital from December 9th through the 21st. This fictional court martial takes place during that period.

All descriptions here of General Lee's private life, his stewardship of his beloved army, and all of the battles noted, including Gettysburg, are drawn entirely from fact. The citations to historians' treatises and eyewitness memoirs of these engagements are annotated in the Appendix.

Wherever possible, the historical characters portrayed speak in their own words as recorded in their own official reports, diaries, and recollections published after the war. While some documents are paraphrased for the sake of clarity and modern syntax, most appear in their original and sometimes rather stiff language. Overly formal dialogue reflects extracts from 19th century letters and dispatches.

A detailed bibliography and appendix of notes concludes this volume.

The sources in the references are limited. Devoting a lifetime to blowing the dust from old manuscripts, collections of family papers, and original military reports, is left to the professional historians. This is a novel and not a research dissertation.

With apologies to my memorable professor at the College of Wooster, Dr. John Gates, who labored mightily to teach me military history, my references are generally limited to secondary sources by historians who have already interpreted the events described here.

This book could not have been written without Clifford Dowdey and Louis H. Manarin's *The Wartime Papers of Robert E. Lee* (1961) from which most of General Lee's actual words are drawn. Without the generous permission to use this source by Little, Brown and Company, Boston, this project would have been impossible. I also cite General Lee's letters compiled by his son, Robert, Jr., *Recollections and Letters of General Lee* (1904), and John W. Jones' *Life and Letters of General Robert E. Lee* (1906). The Reverend Jones tended to leave in General Lee's pro-slavery remarks which both Dowdey and Robert Lee, Jr., judiciously edited out.

References to the weather in Richmond during December 1863 are generally drawn from John B. Jones' *A Rebel War Clerk's Diary* (1866).

The portrait painted here of General Lee's family, and especially of his three daughters, is drawn primarily from Mrs. Mary P. Coulling's elegant volume *The Lee Girls* (1987). Her work stands alone for its eminently readable history. I am also most grateful to Mrs. Coulling for her generous time and kindness in December 1988 when she escorted me through Robert E. Lee's tomb in the Chapel of Washington and Lee University at Lexington, Virginia. She graciously hosted my first pilgrimage to Lexington and to the graves of Lee, Stonewall Jackson, and Sandie Pendleton.

Robert E. Lee's life-long relationship with his cousin, Martha Custis Williams, known affectionately as Markie, is drawn primarily from the elegant little volume, *To Markie: The Letters of Robert E.*

Lee to Martha Custis Williams, by Avery Craven (1933). I gratefully acknowledge the generous permission of the Henry E. Hutington Library, San Marino, California, to quote extensively from these letters.

Permission to quote from the girlhood journals of General Lee's daughter, Eleanor Agnes, was graciously provided by the University of North Carolina Press, Chapel Hill, and the Virginia Historical Society, Richmond.

All study of General Lee begins with the monumental works of Douglas Southall Freeman (1886-1953). His seven volumes, *R.E. Lee* (4 volumes) and *Lee's Lieutenants* (3 volumes), are relied upon throughout this story. However, like the several historical narratives by Clifford Dowdey cited widely in this story, Professor Freeman takes pains to deify Robert E. Lee while exaggerating the alleged character flaws and military shortcomings of General James Longstreet—Lee's sturdy field commander and close personal friend.

Professor Freeman devoted 19 years to the creation of *R.E. Lee* and perhaps seven years to the writing of *Lee's Lieutenants.* He saluted the statue of Robert E. Lee in downtown Richmond every day he drove to his office. Dr. Freeman's genius and prejudices are reflected in his scholarship.

My rather revisionist assessment of General Longstreet owes much to William Garrett Piston's scholarship in *Lee's Tarnished Lieutenant: James Longstreet and his Place in Southern History* (1987).

The author's effort to pierce the public image of Robert E. Lee and to ferret out the genuine inner man is grounded in the controversial psychological study of General Lee by University of South Carolina history professor Dr. Thomas L. Connelly in *The Marble Man: Robert E. Lee and His Image in American Society* (1977). Professor Piston cited above dedicated his Longstreet text to Professor Connelly. Also useful is attorney Alan T. Nolan's *Lee Considered: General Robert E. Lee and Civil War History* (1991).

No scholarly treatment of the Battle of Gettysburg will ever displace the essential references used in this story's research: Edwin

B. Coddington, *The Gettysburg Campaign: A Study in Command* (1963) and Harry W. Pfanz, *Gettysburg: The Second Day* (1987).

This book's overview of the battles of Antietam, Fredericksburg, Chancellorsville, and Gettysburg is indebted to the Army War College's battlefield guides to these engagements by Professor Jay Luvaas and Colonel Harold Nelson. I am especially honored to pay tribute to Dr. Luvaas whose father, Dr. Morten Luvaas, was my mother's beloved professor of music at Allegheny College, Meadville, Pennsylvania. She would have approved.

For the three-day Battle of Gettysburg, the scholars cited here disagree on the number of troops engaged at any given moment and casualty figures. I have relied almost exclusively upon the epic study, *Regimental Strengths and Losses at Gettysburg* (1986) by John W. Busey and David G. Martin. Their scholarship will not be equalled.

I owe a special debt to Dr. Martin, co-author of *Regimental Strengths*. He combed through the historical details of this story with a surgeon's precision and with abiding good cheer. The historical accuracy of this work owes much to Dr. Martin's credit.

I am much indebted to Dr. Martin K. Gordon for his editorial insight and generous counsel. At his suggestion, I gave shoes to as many Confederates as I could.

John Cannan of Combined Books offered wise and expert counsel to keep my history honest.

It is difficult to express the strange attachment which a student of the war finds developing from one's study of these incredible men after 130 years. General Lee, Jeb Stuart, "Stonewall" Jackson, and their contemporaries who wore the blue or the gray, surely lived when there were giants on the earth in our bloodied country. Professor Freeman puts it best: "Lee the captain of the host, and his right arm, Jackson, are to be added to those of one's acquaintances, living or dead, real persons or the creation of literature, by whom one's personal philosophy of life is shaped beyond understanding."

But this author's fascination with Robert E. Lee does not exclude the darker aspects of Lee's temperament: his profound and nearly life-long depression, his tendency to feel unfulfilled by his pre-war army career, his desperate homesickness, and his overwhelming sadness. Very few authors have dared to dabble into Lee's thoughts.

The "real Lee" remains lost in myth and glorification. As Professor Connelly lamented:

> The real nature of Robert Lee has remained an enigma.... None of his biographies tells of the drives that shaped his life. Many writers have been content to describe Lee only in terms of his character traits, and have closed the book on his inner soul.

Through the artifice of historical fiction, I have labored to convey the character and the personality of these Confederate citizens who gave all they had for the "Lost Cause" in spite of its battlefield holocaust and its despicable cornerstone of human slavery which still haunts the country's collective mind. As is fitting, Professor Freeman laid down the challenge best in *Lee's Lieutenants*:

> A writer of biography can ask for nothing more interesting than to begin with a score of names on printed, military dispatches and then to work over the historical materials of many sorts until names become personalities, characteristics emerge, and reports take on the sound of a voice. At first, one had the feeling that these Confederates had ridden so far toward oblivion that one could not discern the figures or hope to over take them before they had passed over the horizon of time. In the end, there was the sensation of reaching their camp, of watching the firelight in their faces, and of hearing their brave and genial conversation.

Douglas Savage
Canton, Ohio
September, 1993

A soldier's heart, you know, is divided between love and glory.
— Robert E. Lee

Chapter One

Wednesday Morning, December 9, 1863

My heart and thoughts will always be with this army.
　　　　Robert E. Lee

*N*o louder sound had ever been made by men in North America.

Colonel Porter Alexander, age 27, returned his watch to his gray vest. It was seven minutes past one o'clock on a stifling hot Friday, the third day of July 1863. The youthful colonel barked an order and the massed batteries of the Army of Northern Virginia opened with a roaring cloud of sulfur. Along the two-mile front at Seminary Ridge, as many as 170 Confederate cannon lobbed six- and 12-pound shot across the valley of death toward the east.

Along the opposite ridge, artillerymen heaved powder and ball down Federal cannon. From Cemetery Ridge, over 200 Federal cannon replied. Red hot shot flew westward from the battlements of the Army of the Potomac.

Shot and shell whined across the valley criss-crossing the hot July sky with trails of smoke from hissing fuses. Batteries pounded each other across the one-mile wide valley. The ground trembled, dyed black with blood. Well over 30,000 men and boys wearing blue and gray had already fallen during two days of combat across the Pennsylvania countryside.

The cannonade rattled glass and cracked walls in the tiny village four miles north of the awful artillery duel. Citizens were huddled in damp stormcellars and beneath corn cribs as the bombardment uprooted their dead fathers and mothers. Ancient bones were unearthed where Rebel shot fell on the town graveyard atop Cemetery Hill on the far right center of the Federal line along Cemetery Ridge.

The stricken civilians caught between two armies and 170,000 men called their sleepy college town "Gettysburg."

On the field were 192 Confederate regiments of 55,000 men from 12 states facing 270 Union regiments of 75,000 Yankees from 18 states.

For over an hour the cannonade continued. Survivors would remain half-deaf all their days from the ungodly concussion. Farmers in rich Pennsylvania fields 140 miles away shook their heads. They could hear the distant thunder from Gettysburg and they looked to the sky for storm clouds. But the summer sky was clear.

Atop Seminary Ridge, the Old Man paced anxiously. All day he had watched for his troops in homespun uniforms dyed brown with butternut oil to assault the Federals across the valley. What could be delaying Lieutenant General Longstreet? Three times the white-bearded chief had trotted on his warhorse Traveller the full length of his lines for evidence of the advance. As was General Robert E. Lee's way when angry, his neck grew redder by the minute as Colonel Alexander's bombardment continued. The general's head and neck twitched nervously as always when struggling to control the temper so rarely seen.

One mile to the east, the hail of Confederate cannon landed long. Shot exploded behind Union breastworks down the far side of Cemetery Ridge. Rebel shells exploded well behind their targets: the batteries of Union cannon. Confederate cannon balls plowed into General Meade's headquarters at the Widow Leister's house. Federal chief of staff, General Daniel Butterfield, was slightly wounded. Instead of softening the enemy guns, the exploding artillery rounds fell upon the Federal reserves and upon the horse-drawn ambulances. From burning hospital tents pitched between piles of amputated limbs sawed off wide-eyed men, the cries of the twice-wounded rose into the sky full of sulfur clouds.

At 2:30 in the afternoon, Colonel Alexander ordered his gray batteries to cease fire in response to slackening enemy fire. After over an hour of the cannon barrage, the Army of Northern Virginia was nearly out of artillery ammunition.

In the valley between the armies where 300,000 eyeballs burned and watered from the stinking smoke, the sickly yellow clouds rolled silently toward the boulder-covered Round Tops. Colonel Alexander stood nervously by his cannon. He penned an urgent dispatch to General Pickett: "If you are coming at all, you must come at once or I cannot give you proper support."

Lieutenant General James Longstreet—"Old Pete" to his men—conferred with George Pickett well behind Alexander's cannon.

Between the ridges a strange stillness lingered in the smoky valley. Old Pete nodded to Rebel General George Pickett, one-time captain in the United States 9th Infantry. The absolute bottom man at West Point, class of 1846, George Pickett shined in his polished boots and gold spurs. George Pickett would never have gotten into West Point at all had not his uncle, Andrew Johnston of Quincy, Illinois, pulled strings with his close friend—a Springfield, Illinois, lawyer named Abe Lincoln. By Mr. Lincoln's influence, Virginia-born Pickett went to West Point on an Illinois appointment. Pickett and General Longstreet had known each other for many years. They had served together eight years earlier in the U.S. 8th Infantry at Fort Bliss. General Pickett's long hair was worn in perfumed ringlets and his curls bounced as he hurried to his division. The dandy was a 38-year-old major general. His hour had come at last.

At Seminary Ridge, General Lee—Number Two man at West Point, class of '29—remained edgy. He waited for his generals Longstreet, Pickett, and Hill to assault Cemetery Ridge. Neck red with anger, Lee was exhausted. A week of dysentery and acute diarrhea had left him weak, pale, and sorely irritable. Lee had been out of sorts since his first coronary attack only four months earlier when a serious sore throat was accompanied by severe chest pains. His face, always ruddy, had been even redder than usual during the week ending April 6th when he had been confined to an ambulance. The terrible chest pain lasted until April 16th, only two and a half months ago.

Along the slopes of Seminary Ridge, men in butternut began falling in. They formed two parallel lines, each over a mile long. The parade forming across Seminary Ridge warmed Lee's dull spirits.

Division commanders, Generals George Pickett, Dorsey Pender, and Johnston Pettigrew (substituting for wounded Henry Heth) straightened their troops. Men and boys stood shoulder to shoulder in the blinding sunshine.

On command, some 14,000 infantrymen rested their heavy rifles with the weapons' butts between their feet, many bare. With bayonets fixed, the Enfield, Springfield, or Mississippi rifles were longer than all but the tallest soldier. Regiment upon regiment executed the "Load in Nine Times" maneuver: (1) Take out a paper cartridge with its 120 grains of powder behind one, thimble-size .58 calibre bullet; (2) Rip open the paper cartridge with the teeth—hence the blackened lips on the swollen corpses; (3) Pour the black powder down the rifle barrel; (4) Drop the lead Minie ball into the barrel; (5) Drive the bullet down with the rifle's iron ramrod; (6) Reseat the ramrod into its sockets, called thimbles, along the barrel; (7) Ear back the hammer above the iron nipple at the breech; (8) Press a tiny percussion cap onto the hollow nipple; and, (9) Fire! The last step must wait until the infantrymen were closer to the enemy whom General Lee called "those people."

The weapons were primed. The men stood tensely under the terrible sun behind Seminary Ridge. Close by, Robert Lee looked on, tired, impatient, and proud.

Beyond the crest of Seminary Ridge, the valley was quiet. Across the valley, 40,000 blueclads waited. Their chief waited: Major General George Gordon Meade—"Old Snapping Turtle" to his Federals. Mounted astride his horse Baldy, which would be wounded in battle four times, General Meade—West Point, '35—may have been thinking of those days 70 years earlier when his father had ridden at the side of another General Lee to help George Washington crush the Whiskey Rebellion. That old Virginia patriot was General Henry "Light Horse" Lee. Now, Henry Lee's youngest son wore three gold stars on his gray collar and he paced Seminary Ridge in ill temper.

The Army of the Potomac crouched behind low stone walls. They tensely waited for the Rebel assault sure to follow the 90-minute cannonade. At the extreme Federal right, men lay low atop Cemetery Hill among the uprooted bones of the long-dead and the fly-covered cadavers of their newly dead messmates. Nervous boys wise-cracked about the ancient stone archway at the entrance to the Gettysburg town cemetery. The gate bore an inscription on the cold stone flecked with bullet and shrapnel holes: "ALL PERSONS FOUND USING FIREARMS IN THESE GROUNDS WILL BE PROSECUTED WITH THE UTMOST RIGOR OF THE LAW."

Along the Union line, eyes squinted into the afternoon sun high above the Confederate lines. Something was astir.

Behind the long brown line, General Pickett shouted to his regiments: "Up men! Don't forget that you are from old Virginia!" At the head of one brigade was Brigadier General Lewis Armistead from North Carolina. General Armistead set his gray hat atop the point of his uplifted saber so his men could see it and could follow him. Before going over the top, General Armistead took off his ring and gave it to his friend George Pickett. Armistead asked Pickett to give the ring to Sallie Corbell, Pickett's young and beautiful fiancee, should Armistead fall in the grim valley.

The ranks opened as they advanced between the line of cooling cannon. They closed up past the cannon and continued into the calm valley.

Thirteen hundred yards away, one long gasp rose from behind the low stone walls along Cemetery Ridge. The blueclads had never seen such a grand Confederate parade. In the valley, 14,000 Southerners were arrayed in two lines, each line one and one-half miles long. The two Rebel lines were separated by 150 yards.

In the blinding sun, the hot breeze filled 47 regimental battleflags from the Army of Northern Virginia. So quiet was the valley that the Federals could hear the snapping of the Confederate banners: 19 bearing Virginia regimental colors, 14 from North Carolina, 7 from Alabama, 4 from Mississippi, and 3 regimental ensigns from Tennessee. In the calm afternoon, the Federals could hear the clatter of 14,000 Rebel canteens, many made from cedar wood because the Confederacy had no tin.

They marched in two lines across the valley with three-quarters of a mile separating the opposing armies. On the Confederate right, the brigades of Generals Richard Garnett and James Kemper led the brigades of Generals Wilcox and Armistead. Back in the "Old Army," Brigadier General Cadmus Wilcox was a groomsman at the wedding of his old friend Ulysses S. Grant. Brigadier General Kemper's grandfather was a colonel on the staff of George Washington.

The lines wheeled slightly to their left to cross the quiet valley's diagonal en route to the Yankee entrenchments on the high ground. On the Confederate left were the four brigades led by Colonels Robert Mayo, J.K. Marshall, and Birkett Fry, and General Joe Davis (the President's nephew), all from Heth's Division. Behind them in the Confederate center were the brigades of General James Lane and Colonel W. Lee Lowrance from Pender's Division.

In the valley, both lines turned a quarter turn to the left to cross the dirt road running between Gettysburg to the north and Emmittsburg toward the south. This put the Confederate far right flank within the sights of the Federals on Little Round Top on the southern tip of Cemetery Ridge. Behind the Rebel lines, a brass band played as the brigades of Kemper, Garnett, and Armistead marched off.

For two hundred yards, the two lines of Southerners advanced in perfect parade order. Hardly a shot greeted them.

"Fire!" was the hoarse cry atop Cemetery Ridge, behind those low, stone walls.

A wall of white sulfur smoke rolled down from the Union line as Federal cannon opened along the mile-long crest.

The Southerners in front wavered and dropped. Union cannon-eers were firing double loads of the dread "canister": gallon size cans of iron marbles. But the bloodied butternut lines marched doggedly forward even though men were falling ten yards from where their severed arms and legs were bouncing upon the red earth.

Above the boom of cannon, 40,000 Yankee rifles opened with the *crack crack crack* of dry twigs snapping.

Every fourth Confederate dropped upon the wet field. Some rolled on the warm ground and clutched hysterically at emptied sleeves and at emptied trouserlegs.

In the iron hailstorm, the wavering lines closed up and marched up the hillside.

A roar of musketry plowed into the Rebel right flank. Men fell with thumb-size holes in their backs and exit wounds in their chests the size of a fist. They were raked by flanking fire from behind and from the side where riflemen had opened along the Round Tops.

Not since last December had so many men committed such a grand, mass suicide. Then, it had been Fredericksburg, Virginia, when Union Generals Burnside and Sumner had sent human waves up the bloody hill toward the Confederate entrenchments. In one afternoon, 13,000 Federals dropped like rows of bloody corn.

"Fredericksburg," a Federal whispered through a crack in the stone wall close to his powder-blackened mouth. He remembered. Down the line, another blueclad looked over the wall into hell and shouted, "Fredericksburg!"

By now, the two Rebel lines had merged into one line with great gaps where whole regiments of mothers' sons had been mowed down by canister as if by a red hot wind. The Confederates shrieked the ferocious Rebel Yell born of the Confederacy's Celtic heritage. They stormed Cemetery Ridge and the line of hot Federal cannon. Lead-ing them was old Armistead, his bullet-riddled hat now a gray rag atop his flashing saber. These men from the land of cotton were close enough to hear the blood-thirsty shouts from the Yankees behind their walls:

"Fredericksburg!"

"Fredericksburg!"
"Fredericksburg!"

Climbing up Cemetery Ridge, the Rebels took waves of canister and a wall of Minie balls directly in their faces. Federal flanking fire ripped them open from the Round Tops to their right.

Brigadier General Armistead led 150 survivors over the Yankees' stone wall as he shouted, "Give them cold steel, boys!" Then he dropped into a pool of his own blood and bowels between two enemy cannon. He and his boys had made it to the top of the Union position. Down the line somewhere, a solitary North Carolina boy stumbled over the wall to plant his regimental colors between the Federal cannon. The men in blue held their fire out of bloody respect and a terrible pity.

From his post 1,700 yards away, General Lee could barely see his men enter a mile-wide wall of smoke.

Gradually, General Lee was able to distinguish shadows of gray and butternut brown running from the smoking hill in the distance. They stumbled down the hill and fell over the torn bodies and the dismembered limbs of their fine parade.

Pickett's Charge was over.

The long gray line crumbled. Muskets were thrown to the red ground. Into the valley 14,000 men had marched gamely. Now, fewer than 7,000 ran or crawled back.

The survivors struggled back toward Seminary Ridge. They were met behind the ridge by Generals Pickett and Longstreet, and by the sick commanding general. There was no covering fire from Porter Alexander's Rebel cannon. The limber chests of shot were empty.

Across the valley, the firestorm of molten lead stopped. Along Cemetery Ridge, the Union guns ceased fire.

"Fredericksburg! Fredericksburg!" rang between the ridges.

The valley heard its own song. The wounded cried "Water, Water!" in the frenzied thirst which comes in nauseating waves from sudden hemorrhage. Other bodies were perfectly still with their thin faces tranquil and calm. Drying eyeballs looked to the July sky so far away. Around two years worth of campfires, how often had these eyes blinked back boys' tears when some grizzled Rebel veteran filled the night with the sad sweet melody "Lorena," the Confederate soldier's most beloved ballad:

> *The years creep slowly by, Lorena.*
> *The snow is on the ground again.*

Between the cooling Federal cannon, General Armistead lay dying. In the arms of a Yankee cannoneer, the bleeding Rebel asked that his pocketwatch and his spurs be given to his life-long friend Union General Winfield Hancock, to be sent south to the Widow Armistead. The Union man nodded. Armistead smiled and died among the bodies of 42 Rebels who had made the climb with him.

> *The sun's low down the sky, Lorena.*
> *The frost gleams where the flowers have been.*
> *But the heart throbs on as warmly now*
> *As when the summer days were nigh.*

The sweating survivors hobbled down the backside of Seminary Ridge. Old, old men would one day remember how the little stream behind the ridge flowed brown with blood where thousands of men and boys bathed fresh wounds in the cool water.

Across the valley, Northerners looked down their hill at 30 Rebel battleflags lying among 5,675 dead and dying Confederates cut down within thirty minutes. General Garnett's brigade lost 948 of 1,459 men who joined the charge. General Richard Garnett, West Point '41, died with his men, his riddled body being interred in an unmarked, mass grave. The 18th Virginia and the 47th and 13th North Carolina regiments were all but exterminated on the slopes of Cemetery Ridge.

These shattered bodies brought the number of Southerners to fall at Gettysburg within three days to at least 22,000 killed, wounded, and missing. Six Confederate generals were dead, 3 captured, and 8 wounded. Eleven colonels were dead with another 7 missing. Of 35 officers above the rank of captain who had gone over the top in Pickett's division, only one was not bleeding.

A hundred months have passed, Lorena,
Since last I held that hand in mine
And felt that pulse beat fast, Lorena,
Though mine beat faster far than thine.

Behind Seminary Ridge, George Pickett was devastated by his stunning defeat. General Lee, his red face stricken, comforted his general with the perfumed hair. Lee sadly mourned, "It's all my fault."

The shattered Confederate line braced behind its battlements for a countercharge sure to come. They dared not send the stretcher-bearers down the hillside to fetch their broken friends who still cried, "Water! For God's sake, water!"

Behind Cemetery Ridge, General Meade sat astride Baldy. He had no plans to attack the bloodied Rebels. He did not have to win at Gettysburg; he had only not to lose. Nearby, a Federal band struck up "Hail to the Chief" for General Meade. The brass band drowned out the pitiful cries which rose from the far side of the stone wall.

A hundred months 'twas flowery May,
When up the hilly slope we climbed
To watch the dying of the day
And to hear the distant church bells chime.

The following night in torrential rains and high water with mud up to the axles of the wagons, Robert E. Lee would lead his bleeding army out of Pennsylvania and the Confederacy's last invasion of the enemy's heartland. Confederate ambulance wagons would form a train of misery seventeen miles long between Gettysburg and Maryland.

Nothing would be left but a long retreat through 21 more months of ferocious bloodletting.

The pursuit would end in Virginia at an obscure widening in the dirt road called Appomattox.

★　　★　　★

"My heart and thoughts will always be with this army," General Lee scrawled in a long hand note to young Jeb Stuart, the brash, 30-year-old general of Confederate cavalry. He dated the dispatch Wednesday, December 9, 1863.

A freezing fog hugged the banks of the Rapidan River where the Army of Northern Virginia shivered in winter camp near Orange Court House, Virginia, 50 miles northeast of Charlottesville.

General Lee sat in his command tent with its spartan fixtures: a single wooden table, three chairs, a cracker box, and a cot with two blankets. He sat with Colonel Walter Taylor and Colonel Charles Marshall, his sole administrative staff.

No one could really be intimate with the commanding general other than his family in Richmond. Even 34 years ago at West Point, Cadet Lee was so elegant and so guardedly austere with his emotions that his classmates dubbed him "The Marble Model."

The exhausted chief was particularly fond of Walter Taylor from Norfolk. Only 25 years old, Taylor had been promoted to lieutenant colonel two months ago and was adjutant general for Lee's legion. Colonel Taylor's mission was to steer General Lee through the paper burden of administering an army of 70,000 men when all three corps were operating together.

General Lee sat quietly, his ruddy face dark with continuous grief. The last two months in Virginia had only added disappointment to his anguish after Gettysburg. The October 1863 campaign at Bristoe Station, the November debacle at Kelly's Ford, and the dry hole of the Mine Run operation just completed had accomplished nothing except to plant more hungry Confederates in unmarked graves by the side of the road. During the five months since fleeing Pennsylvania, General Lee had suffered his second and third heart attacks. His chest pain creased his dark face and was written in his brooding eyes.

On September 20th, the chest and back pains were so severe that General Lee was confined to an ambulance until October 10th. His sore chest was then free from angina pain for only three weeks. A third coronary seizure on October 31, 1863, had laid him up in an ambulance until November 5th, hardly a month ago. Four months ago to the day, General Lee had tendered his written resignation to President Jefferson Davis.

President Davis declined to accept the August resignation. But Robert E. Lee was now old at age 56. His hair and beard were completely white. The last two months of futile engagements and continuous chest pain had taken a terrible toll on the solemn general.

The Army of Northern Virginia had been pursued by General Meade who slowly pressed them out of Pennsylvania. The Federal army was spread out near Culpeper, Virginia. On October 9th, the Confederate's III Corps led by Lieutenant General Ambrose Powell Hill—"A.P." to headquarters, but "Little Powell" to his troops—marched from Orange toward Madison Court House. General Richard Ewell—"Old Bald Head" to his boys who loved their eccentric bug-eyed commander—joined the march with his II Corps.

Both Rebel corps reached Culpeper two days later as Baldy Ewell rode strapped awkwardly to his saddle. At Groveton in August 1862, a Yankee bullet had blown off Lieutenant General Ewell's leg. Jeb Stuart's cavalry covered the Confederate right flank. The cavalry of General Fitzhugh Lee, Robert Lee's nephew, provided the rearguard. General Meade and his blue columns were in motion northward just ahead.

By early afternoon, Wednesday, October 14, 1863, A.P. Hill was on the high ground at Bristoe Station. Little Powell could see the enemy regiments marching for the railhead at Manassas Junction.

General Hill saw his chance to cripple the Federals. He opened with his cannon. When III Corps saw their Little Powell wearing his familiar red "battle shirt," they knew it was time. Three brigades rushed the Union rear.

But Little Powell had been lured into a deadly trap. Concealed Federal guns opened along the railroad. The Confederate brigades of Generals Cooke and Kirkland were ripped into a bleeding heap. After a brief but fierce clash, 1,361 Rebels lay dead and dying upon the rail tracks. Generals John Cooke (a Harvard graduate engineer) and William Kirkland (a West Point dropout) fell with their men.

Another 520 Southerners were captured. Brigadier General Cooke was the brother of Jeb Stuart's wife.

By October 17th, the Army of Northern Virginia was back in winter camp along the banks of the Rappahannock. On October 31st, General Lee was abed with his third coronary attack. He could not take horse until November 5th. Then, in great pain, he inspected a grand cavalry review staged by Jeb Stuart at Brandy Station, six miles east of Culpeper.

General Lee knew Brandy Station. Here, five months earlier, his son Rooney Lee fell wounded in a June clash. Rooney, age 26, remained a prisoner of war. Rooney's beautiful young wife, Charlotte, was on her deathbed near Richmond. Rooney had married Charlotte Wickham, a distant cousin, at Shirley Plantation in March 1859 in the same great hall of the Lee ancestral home where General Lee's parents were married.

Saturday, November 7th, one month ago, a Federal force had been spied at Kelly's Ford five miles downriver from the Confederate camp along the frigid Rappahannock. III Corps and A.P. Hill were upriver to the west. Rappahannock Bridge downriver was held by Ewell's II Corps with grim-faced Jubal Early's troops dug-in at the bridge. "Old Jube" to his boys was 46, a confirmed bachelor, a Viking in battle, a former prosecuting attorney, and graduate number 18 from the Point's class of '37. Six feet tall, stooped by crippling arthritis, General Early was known for his habit of turning his perpetual tobacco chaw over and over in his mouth when he was agitated.

Old Jube had good reason to fuss with his chaw that bloody Saturday afternoon. A fierce Federal attack had crushed Early's position and both Rappahannock Bridge and Kelly's Ford had fallen to waves of blueclad infantry. By nightfall, the bloodied butternut columns were retreating south from the river toward Culpeper. They left 2,023 men behind. Of those losses, 1,674 were sacrificed by General Early at the bridge.

For two weeks, the graybacks shivered beside the freezing river. Then, on Thursday, November 26th, Union infantry columns were in motion along the Rapidan River. General Lee saw a chance to strike General Meade. II and III Corps advanced to cut the Federals off and to protect the Rebel right flank.

Next day, blood flowed all afternoon at Locust Church, 14 miles east of Culpeper. The fire did not slacken until darkness. Upon the cold ground were 545 Southerners, motionless.

On the 28th of November, Federals and Confederates were camped along Mine Run Creek north of Verdiersville in freezing rain.

When the Federals refused to climb out of their works on Tuesday, December 1st, General Lee said of General Meade to his field officers, "They must be attacked!" Two Confederate divisions then crunched upon frozen ground all night through the thickets to turn the Union left and to roll up the long blue line. During the nighttime march, it had been so cold that water froze in the cedar canteens of the Southern infantry. The grand offensive to crush General Meade once and for all was set for daybreak.

But dawn on Wednesday, December 2nd, found the Union entrenchments deserted. While the Rebels were marching all night, General Meade had been moving his troops northward.

General Lee had been sorely disappointed. The two months from Bristoe Station to Mine Run had cost 4,255 Confederate casualties. All for nothing.

General Lee sighed toward Colonel Marshall, "I am too old to command this army. We should never have permitted those people to get away."

"It was the weather, General," Colonel Marshall consoled his anguished chief.

"Perhaps," General Lee shrugged.

"At least, General, you will be home in Richmond for Christmas this year."

"Yes, Colonel." The officer rose painfully from his hard chair. He still had chest pain this December 9th.

In his blue greatcoat and slouch hat, General Lee led Colonel Marshall into the overcast morning by the river. Colonel Taylor joined them. Outside, an orderly had Traveller saddled and ready beside a mounted escort of cavalry. The two staff officers and their chief mounted.

The little caravan turned southeast toward Richmond. After a short ride, they planned to meet the train for the trip by rail to the capital city of the Confederate States of America. The Old Man called it "taking the cars."

As the escort and General Lee rode slowly through camp, little clusters of thin hungry men stood silently beside small fires where they huddled to keep warm. When General Lee passed, not a head remained covered. The weary general on the great gray horse belonged to them, and the ragged boys to him. The affection ran deep in these sunken, pale faces for their general whom they lovingly called Uncle Robert or Marse Robert behind his back.

Lifting his hat to his tattered men, the commanding general disappeared into the snowy trees. Battalions of homesick boys blinked wet eyes toward the back of their Uncle Robert, their Robert E. Lee, General, the Army of Northern Virginia.

Chapter Two

Wednesday Evening, December 9, 1863

But year after year, my hopes go out and I must be resigned.
Robert E. Lee

The most striking feature on the soldier's face was his eyes. Sad and worn, General Lee's brooding eyes blinked at the snowy Virginia countryside passing quickly outside the train's dirty window. His beard touched the window fogged by his breath. He had stopped shaving two years ago, in September 1861, during his first excursion into the field of the War Between the States. In the aborted campaign of Cheat Mountain in the new Unionist state of Western Virginia, General Lee's new beard came in dark gray. Now, the beard and his thinning hair were white.

The train was chilly. A single pot-bellied stove in the far corner kept the uniformed passengers from freezing. Although the winter camp of the Army of Northern Virginia at Orange Court House, Virginia, was only 75 rail miles from Richmond, the train ran only 20 miles per hour due to a shortage of firewood and coal for the steam engine.

General Lee and his party caught "the cars" at Orange Court

House for the seven-mile ride to Gordonsville on a short spur of the Orange and Alexandria Railroad. Major General Jeb Stuart of Lee's cavalry boarded the train at Gordonsville. From Gordonsville, the train made 42 miles southeast on the Virginia Central Railroad to Hanover Junction. At Hanover, Lieutenant General A.P. Hill, commanding III Corps, climbed on board. The train then clattered southward on the 24-mile leg of the Richmond-Fredericksburg-Potomac Railroad line from Hanover toward the center of Richmond an hour away.

Warming his hard and chapped hands on the sides of a tin coffee cup, Robert Edward Lee studied the heavy clouds full of snow. His weary mind wandered through the years and across many ghastly fields of hopelessly broken men.

By the time Abraham Lincoln had taken the oath to become the divided nation's sixteenth President on March 4, 1861, Jefferson Davis had been sworn in as first President of the Confederate States of America in Montgomery, Alabama, the seat of the new government before the capital was moved to Richmond. On Inauguration Day 1861, Lieutenant Colonel Robert E. Lee still accepted his pay from the army of the United States. General-in-Chief Winfield Scott—"Old Fuss and Feathers"—promoted Lee to full colonel on March 16, 1861. Twelve days later that commission was signed by Abraham Lincoln. When Virginia left the Union the next month, Colonel Lee resigned his Federal commission and went home to Virginia. His sister, Ann Lee Marshall, living in Baltimore, remained loyal to the Union.

To General Lee's ancestors, the age of Pilgrims in the New World was a matter of living memory. His great-great-great-grandfather had owned 16,000 Virginia acres by 1642—hardly half a lifetime removed from Plymouth Rock. Richard Lee had arrived in America from Worcestershire, England, in 1639. He served in the colonial Virginia legislature, was a colonel in the colony's militia, and was a leading slave-trader. Richard's son, Richard "The Scholar" Lee, also served in the legislature. Henry Lee II, Robert Lee's grandfather, was the third generation of Lees in the Virginia House of Burgesses and also served in the state senate. Thomas Lee, Robert's great-great-uncle, had served as Acting Governor of Virginia 25 years before the Revolution. During the decade before the Revolution, five Lees (three brothers and two cousins) were in the Virginia legislature at the same time.

General Lee's father, Henry Lee, had been a lieutenant colonel in a Virginia regiment during the Revolution. He managed to get himself court martialed twice.

Henry Lee embodied all the manly weaknesses which his son found repulsive. Henry was sufficiently picturesque during the Revolution to have earned his cherished wartime moniker "Light Horse Harry Lee." All of his son's 56 years were devoted to being better than Light Horse Harry and to driving from his soul the character flaws which terrified the chief of the Army of Northern Virginia.

The general struggled not to cave in to baser instincts which he feared were in his very bones, deposited there by his sire. Perhaps in Robert Lee's devotion to his troops was his dark recollection of his father. In 1781, Light Horse Harry had hanged a North Carolina deserter from his Revolutionary regiment and had sent the dead man's severed head with rope still attached to General Washington.

General Lee winced as he moved toward the cold window and toyed with his tin cup.

Robert Lee's entire homelife had been devoted from his earliest childhood to caring for sickly womenfolk—from his fragile mother to his now crippled wife. This too was more than one man's fireside duty. Perhaps it was atonement for his father's uncanny gift for using women.

Henry Lee's first wife was a Lee cousin, Matilda Lee, whom the Revolutionary hero married in 1782. After watching Light Horse Harry piddle away her family fortune, Matilda Lee retained an attorney to put her remaining assets into a trust for their two children to prevent Henry from squandering what money was left. After Matilda's sudden death which devastated Henry, the 37-year-old widower married 20-year-old Ann Hill Carter in 1793. Her father disapproved of his new spendthrift son-in-law.

The Carters were one of Virginia's wealthiest families and had owned the sprawling Shirley Plantation since 1610. Ann Carter Lee bore her husband a brace of children, the last of which came January 19, 1807: Robert Edward Lee, named for Ann's two brothers. But neither children nor "marrying up" for the second time could change Light Horse Harry. In April 1809, he went to prison for one year for failure to pay his debts.

Henry Lee was not above passing a bad check to George Washington. In 1806, he sold a parcel of Kentucky land to his own brother although Henry had already sold it to someone else. Henry's brother was sued over the land fraud.

When young Robert was six years old in 1813, his floundering father fled the country. The children never saw his face again. Light Horse Harry died on the voyage home in March 1818. His body returned no further than Cumberland Island, Georgia, where his old friend from the Revolution, General Nathanael Greene, provided a corner of the family cemetery plot for Henry Lee's destitute remains.

Despite Light Horse Harry's weaknesses for rich women and financial speculation, the Lee name remained an honorable part of civilian service. Robert E. Lee's uncle Charles Lee served President Washington as attorney general.

But there were other Lee men whose stock Robert Lee shared with mortification. General Lee's worn face became hard when his sleepy mind wandered to his half-brother, Henry Lee, Jr., the son of Light Horse Harry and Matilda Lee. If the elder Henry Lee managed to violate most of Southern manhood's sense of worth, then his son and namesake desecrated all the rest. Robert E. Lee looked down glumly at his raw fingers on the cold tin cup.

Henry Lee's son earned the nickname "Dark Horse Harry" for his 1820 indiscretion which tainted the Lee name for a generation. When young Robert Lee was 13 years old, half-brother Henry, Jr., bedded his wife's 19-year-old sister, Elizabeth. The tryst produced a child dead at birth. The scandal went public ten years later when President Andrew Jackson repaid his Virginia political debts by naming Dark Horse Harry United States emissary to Morocco. After a public airing of the story, the United States Senate defeated the nomination and a disgraced Dark Horse Harry left the country. In 1839, he died in France.

Only in his black-eyed mother, Anne Carter Lee, did Robert Lee find abiding love, integrity absolute, and the peaceful memories of childhood which would warm him on a lifetime of battlefields. A tight smile illuminated General Lee's face in the rickety train to Richmond. Even with his manly vigor sapped by war and by three heart seizures in two years, Robert Lee knew that all he was or hoped to be he owed to this long-gone and frail woman.

General Lee had adored his mother and she him. Always sickly, her great heart broke when young Robert went off to West Point in 1825 at age 18. He returned from the United States Military Academy after his 1829 graduation in time to repay her fidelity at her bedside. Anne Carter Lee refused to die until her Robert could be at her side. Family legend recalled that during her last weeks, she would turn the dark eyes in her thin, pale face toward the closed door whenever Robert had to leave her room. And she watched the door until it was filled again with her handsome broad-shouldered son of 22.

Anne Carter Lee looked at his face when she closed her eyes for the last time on July 10, 1829.

Swaying with the movement of the train, General Lee blinked up at the bearded face of A.P. Hill who stood silently beside his general's wooden bench.

Hill's grandfather, Henry Hill, 48 years dead by 1863, had been a soldier in the Revolution who served in Light Horse Harry's command. A.P. Hill was a seventh generation Virginian and perhaps even a direct descendant of King Henry II. At 38, A.P. Hill now commanded III Corps in General Lee's army. When he had made major general in May 1862, he was the youngest division commander in the Army of Northern Virginia and his division was the largest in the South. So impressive was his reckless bravery on the battlefield that he had advanced from colonel to major general in exactly ninety days.

The frail lieutenant general of III Corps sat down in the wooden seat which faced the commanding general.

"It will do you good, General, to see your children in Richmond," Hill smiled warmly.

"My heart aches to be with them," General Lee nodded with a weak smile.

"Yes, General. I am also anxious to see my family in Richmond."

General Lee thought of his children. He and Mary Custis Lee during their 32 years of married life had borne seven children. Sons William Fitzhugh (called "Rooney" or Fitzhugh), age 29, George Washington Custis ("Custis"), 21, and Robert, Jr., 20, all wore the gray. Unmarried daughters Mary, 28, Agnes, 22, and little Mildred, 17, were all waiting with Mrs. Lee in Richmond. Daughter Annie was one year dead; she would have been 24 now.

Staring out the window at the dismal landscape of wintertime Virginia, General Lee smiled when he thought of his eldest son Rooney. Perhaps General Lee loved Rooney most of his three sons only because he had to love Rooney the hardest. Almost from birth, Rooney was troublesome. Adventuresome and fearless, an eight-year-old Rooney managed to whack off two fingertips when the Lee family was stationed at Fort Hamilton in New York City's harbor. Before and since, the brawny child, who became a brawny youth, tried his father's patience sorely—not least of all when he had dropped out of Harvard College ten years ago to join the Army.

Now the problem son of General Lee lay gravely wounded in a Federal prison hospital, a prisoner of war. After falling wounded at the Battle of Brandy Station in June, just before Gettysburg, the invalid Rooney was carried bodily from his farm at Hickory Hill by Union cavalrymen. His crippled mother and his hysterical wife, Charlotte, had watched in horror as Rooney was hauled with his bloodied mattress into a wagon. Only one month before this frigid train ride to Richmond, Rooney had been transferred to the prison camp at Fort Monroe, Virginia, and then to Fort Lafayette. There was always the chance that Rooney Lee would be transferred again to the prison camp for Rebel officers on Johnson's Island in Lake Erie.

As Lee and Hill looked out the filthy window, General Lee's exhausted mind wandered to other family sorrows which lay so heavily upon the heart still sore from three coronary attacks since spring.

The commanding general thought of his daughter Annie. "My Sweet Annie" was the only name he had ever used for her. When Annie was two years old, she had nearly put an eye out with a scissors. She was self-conscious about her scared face after that and refused all her short life to allow her photograph to be taken. Because she always felt ugly around her attractive sisters, General Lee had lavished special affection upon her.

A year ago October, Annie suddenly took sick. Wasted from either typhoid fever or diphtheria, she had died at Jones Springs, North Carolina, on October 20, 1862, one month after the terrible battle beside Antietam Creek, Maryland.

On July 5, 1862, one year to the day before General Lee gave the order to retreat from Gettysburg, Rooney and his fragile wife, Charlotte, buried their first child dead from pneumonia in Richmond. The two-year-old infant was General Lee's first grandchild—Robert E. Lee III. Five months later, Rooney and Charlotte buried their month-old daughter, Annie, next to their son. Charlotte never recovered from her grief at losing two children within months of each other and from her terror at seeing Rooney dragged on his own bed to prison.

General Lee turned his anguished face toward A.P. Hill who rocked with the train in the wooden seat.

"It has been a wearisome year, General," Hill said with gentleness in his voice. Like his general, A.P. Hill took great care of his men and they loved him for it. A voice of compassion was not at all out of place on the green-eyed warrior from Culpepper, Virginia.

"Yes, General," Lee sighed. "I was thinking of the burdens that my poor wife has had to bear alone during the last two years." He faced the moist window. "She buried our granddaughter a year ago this week."

A.P. Hill lowered his head as his own family grief rushed over him.

"You know, General, that I can understand the loss of a child—or a grandchild." One year ago, Hill's wife buried their two-year-old daughter Henrietta who had died from diphtheria one week before the Battle of Fredericksburg.

General Lee spoke so softly about his dead granddaughter that Hill had to lean forward to catch his words over the rattle of the train.

"I have grieved over the death of that little child of so many hopes and so much affection and in whose life so much of the future was centered." Lee's subdued voice cracked and his sore chest heaved. "But God's will be done. It is a bright angel in heaven, free from the pains and sorrows of this world."

Hill could say nothing.

"You gentlemen are a happy lot!" a stocky man smiled broadly in the narrow car's aisle. Generals Lee and Hill looked up at the massive, black beard and smiling blue-gray eyes of Major General Jeb Stuart. James Ewell Brown Stuart looked much older than his 30 years. Two years in the saddle at the head of General Lee's cavalry had aged his face.

With a genuine smile, General Lee nodded for Major General Stuart to share General Hill's wooden bench. Hill scooted toward the window to make room.

Jeb Stuart had been most uncomfortable at the summons to join the army's high command in Richmond. He still stung from his dreadful performance at Gettysburg—the only time he had earned General Lee's censure. General Lee never publicly reprimanded anyone, least of all anyone as generally reliable and courageous as Stuart. But Jeb understood the message during the recent September reorganization of the cavalry service when the cavalry was made a two-division corps with Stuart nominated as corps commander.

By law, all corps were led by lieutenant generals. But when his promotion came down for corps command, he remained a major general—a typical Lee rebuke without a single word of recrimination. If Jeb Stuart of the dashing blade and plumed hat felt any twinge of acrimony toward his chief, it evaporated in his genuine affection for Lee. When General Lee was superintendent of West Point ten years earlier, Jeb was one of his favorite cadets and a favorite of all the Lee household. (He graduated 13th in the Class of '54.) He sat down beside Hill opposite General Lee.

"I am afraid we are not as cheerful a company as we would prefer, General Stuart," Lee smiled warmly. "We seem to have gotten sidetracked remembering the losses of our poor families at home without us."

Jeb Stuart's ruddy face darkened. His mind went back eleven months to the death of his first child, five-year-old Flora, named for Mrs. Stuart. The child died November 3, 1862, within one month of Annie Lee's death and the death of little "Netty" Hill.

The cavalryman sniffed and blinked at General Lee. "You lost your daughter when I lost my precious Flora."

General Lee nodded toward the steamed window.

"I have always counted," the commanding general sighed, "if God should spare me a few days after this civil war was ended, that I should have her with me. But year after year," General Lee was whispering now, "my hopes go out and I must be resigned."

"Ah, yes, General," Hill had to break the somber tension. "But the living endure as do our children old and new....My little Lucy waits for us in Richmond."

General Lee smiled. He knew that Hill's five-week-old daughter Lucy Lee Hill had been named for himself and for Hill's sister, Lucy, whom A.P. cherished as his beloved "Lute."

On the train to Richmond, only Lieutenant Generals James Longstreet and Richard Ewell were needed to complete the general staff of Lee's army. The one-legged "Baldy" Ewell was ordered to oversee the army during Lee's absence. Old Pete Longstreet would be arriving in Richmond in a day or two. Having spent the last several months with his I Corps detached in Tennessee, Longstreet had already departed Knoxville for the Confederate capital.

General Lee missed having Old Pete's solid presence. Although sometimes slow to deploy his divisions when his heart was not quite committed to an elaborate field maneuver, Longstreet was as dependable as comfortable shoes once he engaged the enemy. General Lee regarded James Longstreet as a friend. "My Old Warhorse" Lee had called Longstreet at Sharpsburg. Longstreet could also understand the father's grief which wounded Lee's sore heart. The January 1862 epidemic of scarlet fever which ravaged Richmond had killed three Longstreet children in a matter of days.

Jeb Stuart felt a little uncomfortable intruding into Lee and Hill's private moment. The object of every Southern girl's fondest dreams, Stuart did better in noise than he did in quietude. Jeb was a strange combination. He raised flirting with the ladies to a high art form, yet to his devoted wife he was faithful and loving. In camp, no day was complete until his personal banjo player, Sam Sweeney, had entertained the cavalry's mess. But Stuart never drank nor smoked. He had foresworn strong drink as a teenager for his mother.

Like Lee and A.P. Hill, Jeb Stuart was a Virginian and professional soldier. Stuart was the seventh child of Archibald Stuart who had represented Patrick County, Virginia, in the state senate and the United States House of Representatives during 1837-1839.

General Lee looked at Stuart, whose burly face made Hill appear even more diminutive than he was, and the commanding general had to smile. Jeb and Lee had soldiered together before this war. When Lieutenant Colonel Lee of the U. S. Army crushed John Brown's raid at Harper's Ferry in 1859, Lieutenant Stuart led the charge against Brown's armory hideout. When Virginia left the dividing Union on April 17, 1861, Stuart resigned his Old Army commission by May 3rd.

"You will be home soon, General," Lee said to Stuart. The familiar countryside outside was the outskirts of Richmond. He knew that Stuart had family in the capital.

"Yes," Stuart smiled. "Flora will be waiting at her sister's."

Lee nodded. "I know that Mrs. Lee also looks forward to seeing you. She remembers you fondly from your West Point years."

"Mrs. Lee was like a mother to me," Stuart smiled.

The train rumbled around the bend where the rail bed joined the Deep Run Turnpike entering Richmond from the west. On the north side of the pike, the railroad followed Broad Street into the center of town.

Freezing rain on the window took General Lee back to a kinder time. It had rained violently on the day of his June 1831 marriage to Mary Custis. One of his wedding party's groomsmen was young Joe Johnston. When General Joe Johnston was gravely wounded in May 1862, command of the army protecting Richmond fell upon Robert Lee. Like all the Lee men, Lee had married up, not just to wealth but into the family of the hero of his life, George Washington.

Lee and Mary Custis had played together as children and each had married a life-long friend on that long-ago June 30th. Mary's father was George Washington Parke Custis, the grandson of Martha Washington, the second wife of General Washington. Parke Custis always regarded himself as George Washington's stepson.

Mary Custis Lee had abandoned her pampered life as the "Child of Arlington" for the far, dismal outposts of a second lieutenant's life. Their first of 30 years of threadbare forts from New York harbor to Texas wilderness came only five days after their wedding when Lieutenant Lee took his bride to Fort Monroe, Virginia. Twenty-one years later, Lee was superintendent at West Point.

The officers gazed out the window as the train slowed along Broad Street in downtown Richmond. General Lee knew that Mrs. Lee would not meet his train when it stopped at the corner of Broad and Seventh Street. Crippled by arthritis, she had been a near invalid since the spring of 1856. The Lees' most delicately beautiful daughter, Agnes, was well on her way to suffering her mother's life of arthritis. Since 1856, Agnes had experienced swelling and pain in her hands and feet aggravated by bouts of rheumatic fever.

The train slowly rumbled down Broad Street in the late afternoon gloom of wartime Richmond. The chill from the freezing rain leeched into the cold cars.

"You will be home soon, General," an aide smiled from the aisle. "You'll see, Sir, you'll be back in the field by Christmas." The officer labored to sound cheerful.

"Yes, General," Stuart added from the opposite bench, "all will go well. Those people in the government will not hurt you."

"I agree, General," Hill offered, "this board of inquiry will end in the destruction of Wigfall and his whole band of fish-mongers."

General Lee was now uncomfortable. He never complained to junior officers.

"I deeply regret that you gentlemen are being dragged into this inquiry business on my account. I don't know whether you will be asked to give testimony. A subpoena from Senator Wigfall and Congressman Foote might just be sufficient to ruin everyone's career."

"We have been through worse than hearings, General." Stuart smiled behind his wild beard. He remembered the thrashing he took at Brandy Station where Rooney Lee had fallen.

"Yes," Lee spoke to the filthy window as the train slowed and the brakes squealed. "Politics," he sighed. "Politics. Now the memories of our brave dead up at Gettysburg will become a political side-show." He paused for a long moment and then spoke as if unaware that his general staff was listening. "I fear that my dear old friend, General Johnston, has fallen into bad company. Because of politics in our Congress, we are dragged down here from the field where we all belong."

Generals Stuart and Hill looked quickly at each other. Their commanding general had pulled back the veil for the first time since the terse order to pack their kits for Richmond 48 hours ago.

"General Johnston, Sir?"

"I'm afraid so, Jeb." Lee turned toward his cavalry chief. "I gather that Joe Johnston has become something of a crony of Senator Wigfall. You know that feelings are not quite cordial between General Johnston and the President. We are being drawn now into a political contest—a test of wills, while our country's independence hangs in the balance."

"Then it's true, General? About Tennessee?"

General Lee smiled at Hill. Containing military secrets was like juggling mercury.

"Yes," Lee spoke in a whisper. The rail car was full of ears. "President Davis wants me to leave Virginia and go west to command the Army of Tennessee. Senator Wigfall prefers General Johnston for General Bragg's old command."

Hill and Stuart exhaled together. Everything was suddenly clear.

Although Joseph E. Johnston had been theater commander of Tennessee and Mississippi for a year, he held no active field command where the real glory was to be had. General Pemberton commanded the garrison captured at Vicksburg and General Bragg commanded in Tennessee. Vicksburg fell the day Lee evacuated Gettysburg. Braxton Bragg's army was routed in a humiliating defeat only two weeks before the cold train ride to Richmond.

John Pemberton, West Point '37, had no army to command at all. Braxton Bragg, Pemberton's classmate at the Point, had resigned only seven days ago. President Davis brought his old friend Bragg to Richmond to serve as chief-of-staff to ease the pain of defeat. Davis had begged Lee to take theater command in the shattered west and Lee had gently declined within the week. Joe Johnston wanted that command in Tennessee desperately.

"Wigfall wants General Johnston?" Hill asked softly.

"Yes. So does Congressman Foote."

Hill shook his head.

"Why doesn't the President appoint him then? Johnston's a decent enough sort."

Robert Lee had to smile.

"Our President would rather have all his teeth pulled."

Stuart and Hill chuckled together.

The train slowed to a stop in the depot of downtown Richmond. Men began to shuffle about the car for their long greatcoats and sabers. Outside, mounted cavalrymen steadied their horses as the engine roared out the last of its head of steam from smokestack and brakelines.

"The army simply owes you better than this!" Hill argued.

With a look of exhausted care, Lee stopped him in mid-thought.

"I have no complaints to make of anyone but myself," General Lee said drily. "I have received nothing but kindness from those above me, and the most considerate attention from my comrades and companions in arms."

"Gentlemen," General Lee said as he heaved his thick body out of the seat, "our country must come before us all."

Hill and Stuart followed General Lee down from the car. Colonel Taylor and the rest of the entourage mingled in the depot's damp and sooty air. Each officer mounted a wet horse.

General Lee climbed into the saddle after stroking his animal's neck and affirming that he would rather be on his great gray Traveller. But the general's prize mount remained at Orange at the army's winter quarters.

Lee and Stuart said good night to Hill who went with his mounted escort east on Broad, four blocks down to the Powhatan Hotel opposite the capitol building and Capitol Square. Hill rode at an easy trot to see his wife and infant daughter.

General Lee and Major General Jeb Stuart rode slowly south one block to Grace Street, then five blocks west away from the capitol to Second Street.

Generals Lee and Stuart said their good nights at the corner before Stuart and a mounted escort headed five more blocks west on Grace to the home of Dr. Charles Brewer, Jeb's brother-in-law, on Grace between Second and Third Streets. Jeb's wife Flora waited at the window. The mounted squadron of cavalry stayed well clear of Main Street and its rows of saloons and whorehouses.

From Grace Street, General Lee, Walter Taylor, and their honor guard of cavalry rode north on Second Street one block to cross the railroad track which had brought them to Richmond. They continued up Second another three blocks to Leigh Street.

"Gentlemen, I know the way from here, thank you," General Lee smiled. His greatcoat's collar was pulled up around his neck and white whiskers against the damp chill.

The escort and Colonel Taylor saluted and General Lee rode to the right, east on Leigh for half a block. He stopped and dismounted between Second and Third Streets at a small, two-story frame house. He grimaced when his right boot touched the wet mud by the hitching post. His chest was still sore from his last angina attack.

Robert Lee walked alone up the gravel to the front porch. His spur heel chains jingled on the wooden stoop. Before he could knock on the door, it opened and a dark-haired girl rushed into his open arms.

"Father!" she shouted.

"Precious Life," General Lee murmured with his face close to 17-year-old Mildred's neck. "My Precious Life."

After their embrace on the landing, Mildred Lee stepped back at arm's length from her father. Their hands were still locked together. Her face darkened. She had not seen her father's hair and beard completely white before. She was startled by the age and care in his face.

"May an old soldier come in out of the cold?" General Lee smiled to ease his child's discomfort. Mildred led her father into the narrow hallway. She closed the door to the world tightly behind him.

He removed his wet gray hat as his oldest daughter, Mary, age 28, greeted him with open arms.

"Dear, dear Father," Mary said softly into his wet collar.

"Daughter," her father said as he stroked her dark hair.

"And my dear Wig!" the soldier stammered as daughter Agnes joined Mary and Mildred in a four-way hug.

He gently pushed his daughters to arm's length and he looked over their shoulders and wet cheeks toward the parlor.

"Where's the Mim?" he whispered.

The creaking of the hardwood floor sounded through the hallway. General Lee stepped past his weepy daughters as Mrs. Lee came around the corner. Too crippled to stand, Mary Lee sat in a rolling chair and she pushed herself along on wooden wheels toward her husband. Tears ran down the cheeks of the 55-year-old woman.

General Lee silently handed his hat to Mildred and his blue greatcoat to Agnes. He took the two steps to his chairbound wife, knelt down beside her, and embraced her.

"Molly," the general whispered into Mary Custis Randolph Lee's ear. "My Molly." Robert Lee had called his wife "Molly" since their courtship. "I am home at last."

When the general released his grip upon her shaking shoulders, he rocked back on his knee so the couple could look at each other's faces. After being married to a soldier for 32 years, Mary Lee had welcomed her man home from many distant posts. Through tear-dimmed eyes, she focused on the ruddy face and its sad black eyes.

Her voice caught in her throat. She searched for the words to welcome her husband to her borrowed home a lifetime removed from Arlington, which had already become a Yankee cemetery.

Mrs. Lee's pale hand gently touched the general's hard cheek. Her fingers touched his white beard by his sunburned ear and weary eyes.

"Dearest Robert. What have they done to you?"

Chapter Three

Thursday, December 10, 1863

You have no idea what a horrible sight a battlefield is.
    Robert E. Lee

*T*he two-horse carriage left narrow tracks in the powdery snow which had dusted clean the muddy ruts carved into Leigh Street. The morning air was brittle and cold.

A short round man in long frock coat kicked the snow from his shiny boots on the front porch of the small house. Two cold Confederate privates stood guard at either side of the doorway. Their long Mississippi rifles were propped against the wall. A fire in an iron pail warmed their gloved hands. The door opened after the visitor's firm knock.

"Good morning, Mr. Secretary," the beautiful young woman smiled to the cold guest.

"And to you, Agnes," the thick man said as he removed his hat.

"The general is expecting you."

Judah P. Benjamin, Confederate Secretary of State, entered the Lee residence. The young woman took his coat. With her thick black hair pulled tight in a bun, Eleanor Agnes Lee looked older than her

22 years. Her delicate and beautiful features were pursed into a look of sadness which darkened her lovely face. Agnes and her sister Annie had always been like twins. For years, they had shared the same bedroom at Arlington plantation. Agnes had not stopped mourning the death of Annie. Her heart was broken again when her childhood suitor, Orton Williams, was hanged five months ago as a spy by the terrible Yankees.

"You are looking well, Agnes," Secretary Benjamin smiled warmly.

"Thank you, Sir. My father is in the parlor."

The hallway door opened and General Lee entered. He extended his hand and warmly greeted his guest.

General Lee wore a knee-length Prince Albert coat of gray. On his collar were three gold stars surrounded by the gold braid of a general. On the regulation Confederate uniform, majors wore one gold star, lieutenant colonels wore two, and colonels wore three stars. Yellow braid around three stars marked a general officer without differentiating between brigadier general, major general, lieutenant general or general. In the case of General Lee, his stars and braid marked a full general—the highest rank the Confederate Congress could confer. The Federal Army had no rank above major general. George Washington was the last three-star lieutenant general.

"It is my pleasure, General," the 52-year-old statesman smiled. His voice carried a lilting British accent.

Judah P. Benjamin, born of English parents in the West Indies, immigrated to New Orleans in 1828 where he was admitted to the Louisiana bar for the practice of law four years later. During 1844 and 1852, lawyer Benjamin had attended the Louisiana Constitutional Convention. In 1852, he had been appointed to represent Louisiana in the United States Senate. He was re-elected to the Senate in 1858. He resigned to stand by the Confederacy three years later.

A brilliant lawyer and politician full of ambition, Benjamin declined an appointment from President Franklin Pierce to the United States Supreme Court. His nomination would have made Mr. Benjamin the first Jew on the high court. In the summer of 1858, President James Buchanan had offered Senator Benjamin the ambassadorship to Spain. But he refused this honor, too, in order to remain in the United States Senate.

Since casting his lot with the new country of the Confederate States of America, Judah Benjamin was the only man to hold three cabinet posts in the Jefferson Davis Administration: Attorney General (April 1861-August 1861), Secretary of War (August 1861-March 1862), and Secretary of State since 1862.

General Lee ushered Secretary Benjamin to a seat in the parlor. The general pulled a chair close to his visitor. When General Lee nodded toward Agnes, she knew that it was time to excuse herself and close the parlor door.

The little room was cozy in the morning light filtering through the windows and with the fire alive in the hearth.

"Can your reputation stand this most generous gesture, Mr. Secretary?" General Lee asked cheerfully.

"My dear general," Judah Benjamin chuckled, "my reputation is already made."

"So it would seem," the general smiled. It was impossible not to respond to the perpetual good cheer of the Secretary of State. Perfectly dressed and grand in his bearing, Judah Benjamin had the personality which made small dinner parties seem like large dinner parties. At table or in cabinet debates behind closed doors, the stout man never lost his amiable and cheerful disposition. He was described as a man who always seemed to enjoy whatever company he kept at the moment. It was hard not to regard the immaculate diplomat as a friend, unless politics made friendship impossible.

"But then there is your reputation, General Lee." Secretary Benjamin stroked his salt-and-pepper beard. His twinkling dark eyes were momentarily serious. "I refer, Sir, to the religion matter."

General Lee rocked back in his chair.

"Mr. Benjamin, that you are a Hebrew is of no matter one way or the other." General Lee spoke firmly and looked squarely into the secretary's face.

"Appreciated, General. But you know that the talk never stops in this town about the need to 'Christianize' the government." The stocky man narrowed his eyes. "They mean me, to be sure. I just think that you must consider that my representation of you before the board of inquiry may do more harm than good. You must understand the risk."

"I understand all of the risks well enough, Mr. Secretary ....I remain most honored that you would elect to defend me in this court martial affair. Besides, " General Lee looked grave, "I trust that the real risk will be one borne by Senator Wigfall and his kind." The general's haggard face betrayed the wisp of a smile.

"Indeed, General. But if I am to be your counsel of record, call me Judah."

"I am unaccustomed to such informality. Especially in matters of my superiors under the Constitution." General Lee looked uncomfortable. For thirty years in the "Old Army," and for the last two years in the army of his new country, he had regarded his constitutional "inferiority" to the civilian government to be an article of faith.

"Yes, General, I do understand. However, I am not here as an officer of this administration. I am here as your advocate."

"I shall try...Judah." The Secretary of State's name stuck in the soldier's throat. "And you, also, must dispense with formality with me."

"I regret, General, that this might be impossible."

General Lee understood.

"For what it's worth, General, this business is not quite a court martial. You are not going on trial before a military tribunal. It's a Congressional inquiry, really, by a joint House and Senate committee. But they have authority to call witnesses and cross-examine them."

"Yes, I understand. I presided over several courts martial in my early career. But this joint committee can relieve me of command, I believe."

"That is true, General. The Senate has final authority to confirm general officers. Or to relieve them, Sir."

"Then, Mr. Secretary...Judah...it is a court martial to me." The soldier's face was as hard as the stone masonry of the blazing hearth.

"Well, to get on with business....I must know your every thought on campaigns past, especially the Pennsylvania invasion."

"I had presumed as much, Judah." Informality was getting easier in the company of this cheerful little man with the round face and happy eyes.

"You are aware, General, that the press here has not been kind to you since Gettysburg?"

"I am overwhelmed with confusion when I hear of my name in the papers." General Lee was clearly distressed. "I believe it would be better to have no correspondents of the press with the army."

General Lee rose and paced the floor in front of the crackling fire which bathed his reddish face and white beard with light.

"Well, General, the Richmond papers have not been charitable about the Pennsylvania campaign. Wigfall and his people have certainly had their say in print over the last five months. Whether the press will have an impact on a military court of inquiry remains to be seen. The editors think themselves generals, you know. I very much doubt if the court martial can be kept secret very long."

"I am sorry," General Lee said into the fire light, "that the movements of the armies cannot keep pace with the expectations of the editors of papers. I know that they can regulate matters satisfactorily to themselves on paper."

"I suppose, General, that we shall both have to grow thicker skins by the time this court martial is terminated." Secretary Benjamin opened his brief case from which he pulled a folder full of documents. "The Congress, too, has been quite vocal. Senator Wigfall and Henry Foote may be the loudest voices against the administration. But Mr. Hunter is still rather moderate. With Congress convening this week, we can expect quite a clamor when the entire body learns about the court martial. At least Senator Hunter has enough influence to keep this inquiry confidential, for a week or so, anyway.

If we go into a second week, the whole Congress may want to subpoena witnesses."

Congress had reconvened after a recess on December 7th, two weeks after the loss of Chattanooga and General Bragg's disaster in the clouds atop Missionary Ridge. On December 9th, Congressman Henry S. Foote from Nashville, Tennessee, demanded a public hearing on the losses of Vicksburg and Chattanooga, the day Robert Lee came to Richmond. Foote had despised Jefferson Davis for twenty years. The loathing was mutual. Senator Robert M. Hunter from Virginia was President of the Confederate Senate, Secretary of State before Judah Benjamin replaced him, and only recently a member of the anti-Davis camp.

"One thing for certain, General, we can count on Wigfall, Foote and Hunter to be the most outspoken of the half dozen men on the Joint Military Affairs Committee when the inquiry—or court martial, as you call it—begins Monday." The Secretary of State smiled. "Dare I ask what you think about Congress?"

General Lee looked at the fire. The firelight dancing in his eyes resembled the peculiar light which had been seen in the eerily pale eyes of Stonewall Jackson when the air was full of the stench of gun powder. Men who had seen that strange light coined Stonewall's other nickname renowned throughout his Army of the Valley: Old Blue Light.

"What has our Congress done to meet this exigency, I may say extremity, in which we are placed?" General Lee gently pounded his right fist into his open left palm. "As far as I know, concocted bills to excuse a certain class of men from service and to transfer another class in service out of the service where they hope never to do service."

General Lee turned to face Benjamin.

"No man should be excused from service for any reason not deemed sufficient to entitle one already in service to his discharge. No man capable of bearing arms should be excused unless it be for some controlling reason of public necessity."

The soldier turned back toward the fireplace and he spoke softly through clenched teeth.

"Congress seems to be laboring to pass laws to get easy places for some favorites or constituents, or get others out of active service. I shall feel very much obliged to them if they will pass a law relieving me from all duty and legislating someone in my place better able to do it!"

Secretary of State Benjamin looked stricken by General Lee's anger toward the Confederate Congress.

"Forgive me, Sir, but I can assure you that some restraint on your part would go a long way toward securing your acquittal at the board of inquiry." The little man had to smile at the stern-faced general who paced the parlor's hardwood floor. "At least our people have rallied to the war for our independence. If—more like when—your court martial makes the press, we can certainly count on widespread popular support for you and for our cause."

General Lee turned a hard eye toward his defense attorney.

"Our people have not been earnest enough, have thought too much of themselves and their ease." General Lee's voice was dry and cold. "Instead of turning out to a man, they have been content to nurse themselves and their dimes and leave the protection of themselves and families to others. To satisfy their consciences, they have been clamorous in criticizing what others have done and endeavored to prove that they ought to do nothing. This is not the way to accomplish our independence!"

The lawyer needed to lighten the conversation.

"If I may change the subject, General, President Davis has inquired about your health." There was concern in the little man's Caribbean accent.

General Lee stood by the window. He squinted outside at the brilliant sunshine which pushed aside the gloomy clouds of winter.

"I have felt very differently since my attack of last spring from which I have never recovered." General Lee turned to face Secretary Benjamin whose merry face was dark with concern. "I am much better now, though still stiff and painful. I fear that I will never be better and I must be content."

"At least, General, you will be in out of the cold for the next two weeks. That should help, I am sure."

"Cold or no cold, Mr. Secretary," General Lee said gravely, "I have not the time to be sick."

"I suppose not, Sir. As former War Secretary, I can't help but ask about the troops in the field. The winter will be hard on them."

General Lee sat down in a deep chair close to the fire. With his hands resting on his knees, he lowered his face until his white beard touched his broad chest. He did not turn his face toward Judah Benjamin but continued to study the comfortable fire in the stone hearth.

"Thousands are barefooted," General Lee said softly. Secretary Benjamin had to lean slightly forward to catch the general's words which were barely audible over the crackling and popping firewood. "Thousands with fragments of shoes and all without overcoats, blankets or warm clothing. I could not bear to expose them to certain suffering."

"Yes, we are well aware in the cabinet of the privations facing the troops in the field, General. At least both sides have gone into winter quarters for the season. The commissary department will move mountains for the men if it can. But forage for the horses and mules is another matter, I'm afraid." Judah Benjamin had learned the awful burden of feeding tens of thousands of men during his brief stint as Secretary of War during the conflict's first year.

"Nothing prevents my advancing now but the fear of killing our artillery horses....Some days, we get a pound of corn per horse and some days more, some days none. Our limit is five pounds per day per horse. You can judge of our prospects."

"I can understand," Benjamin interrupted, "but really, we must get on to your defense."

"The army is in great distress for shoes and clothes," General Lee continued into the fire. His reddish face looked sorrowful as his mind wandered back to brigades of starving men shivering beside the frozen river near Orange Court House. "Every inspection report painfully shows it: artillery, cavalry, and infantry. The requisitions sent in are unanswered." He shook his head. "The want of the supplies of shoes, clothing, overcoats, and blankets is very great." The anguished soldier turned his wornout face toward Judah Benjamin who studied the general thoughtfully. "The Commissary Department proposes to issue sugar to the army in lieu of part of its meat ration!"

Robert Lee looked hard at Benjamin as if the little man still controlled the military commissary.

"You know, Sir, that we do have other armies to feed outside Virginia," Benjamin stated.

"Mr. Secretary, I was the President's military adviser for nearly thirteen months before I took the field last year. I am aware of the logistical burdens. I meant no disrespect to you, Judah."

"General, let's just move on. I am concerned about your sentiments regarding the whole political issue of secession. Clearly, the constitutional question of a state's right to withdraw from the Union is being settled by force of arms. Obviously your Southern loyalties are beyond reproach—even by Senator Wigfall. But your politics might come up at the trial. Wigfall will stop at nothing to discredit the President."

"Secession is nothing but revolution," Lee said firmly. "A Union that can only be maintained by swords and bayonets, and in which strife and civil war are to take the place of brotherly love and kindness, has no charm for me. I shall mourn for my country and for the welfare and progress of mankind."

"General, if you are opposed to secession, how and why did you go South and take up arms against your colleagues from the Old Army?"

General Lee shrugged as if pushing a great weight from his wide shoulders.

"With all of my devotion to the Union, and the feeling of loyalty and duty of an American citizen, I was not able to make up my mind to raise my hand against my relations, my children, my home."

General Lee looked into Secretary Benjamin's face. "Though opposed to secession and deprecating war, I could take no part in an invasion of the Southern States."

"But, General, you seem to have changed in a most fundamental way in just a matter of days, hours perhaps, from a pro-Union officer in the Federal army to a citizen—a willing citizen—of a section in open rebellion against that Union."

Robert Lee measured every word in his slow answer.

"True patriotism sometimes requires of men to act exactly contrary, at one period, to that which it does at another. The motive which impels them—the desire to do right—is precisely the same. The circumstances which govern their actions change. Their conduct must conform to the new order of things."

"Then, General, you have no regrets?"

"I could have taken no other course without dishonor. And if it all were to be done over again, I should act in precisely the same manner."

"Good. At least your fundamental loyalties cannot be impugned at the court martial. You know that Foote and Wigfall, and especially Senator Reade, are rabidly pro-slavery. Your thoughts on the institution might also be fair game to them."

General Lee shook his head in disbelief before he spoke to the floor which glistened in the fire's light.

"In this enlightened age, there are few, I believe, but what will acknowledge that slavery as an institution is a moral and political evil in any country." General Lee had to smile. "Are you glad you asked, Judah?"

Secretary Benjamin did not smile.

"Well, General, I certainly sense some abstract opposition to slavery on your part."

"It's not abstract at all, Judah. I am indeed opposed to slavery. But this hardly means that I am an abolitionist. I fully accept that African slavery may be the natural order of things in our country."

"Your family owns slaves still?"

"Yes. I have been laboring mightily to honor the bequest in my father-in-law's will which emancipated his slaves over several years. He died, you know, in '57 and nominated me executor."

"Mr. Custis' will, General, bequeathed his slaves to you and Mrs. Lee?"

The General frowned. "He has left me an unpleasant legacy."

"But nothing you cannot administer should time permit?"

"I suppose not. After all, I do have experience with the people, you know. My man Perry is still with me in the field. Don't know what I would do without him in fact. And when my mother died 34 years ago, she bequeathed her people to me. I was barely 22 at the time. I remember them well. When I shipped out to Mexico 17 years ago, I still owned them: Nancy and her children. But I now recognize the difficulty in maintaining that institution for our country."

"Believing that, Sir, are you not something of an abolitionist after all?"

Robert Lee was losing patience.

"Considering the relation of master and slave, controlled by humane laws and influenced by Christianity and an enlightened public sentiment, as the best that can exist between the white and black races while intermingled as at present in this country, I would deprecate any sudden disturbance of that relation unless it be necessary to avert a greater calamity to both."

"Then you do see situations where the relation might be changed out of necessity?"

"I think measures should be taken at once to substitute Negroes for whites in every place in the army or connected with it where the former can be used." General Lee's dark eyes narrowed. "It seems to me that we must choose between employing Negroes ourselves and having them employed against us."

"Employing Negroes! Come now, General, you can't believe that Negroes can become working men! What would you tell the committee if they went down this road? Wigfall and Senator Hunter are both appalled at the prospect of employing slaves for wages."

"I have always observed that wherever you find the Negro, everything is going down around him, and wherever you find the white man, you see everything around him improving." The soldier shrugged. "I know their place, Mr. Secretary."

"And yet, General Lee, you are not a believer in Negro servitude as a permanent way of life?"

"Judah," Lee argued, "I think it would be better for Virginia if she could get rid of them!"

"So you are not an abolitionist, but you advocate employing Negroes like white men and you wouldn't mind if Virginia had no Negroes at all?"

For some reason, Judah Benjamin was smiling. Cross examination with him was a blood sport, even with his own client.

"Mr. Secretary, I am sworn to defend the Constitution of the Confederate States of America. That instrument expressly recognizes the right of citizens to own chattel slaves and the right of the government to expand slavery into the unincorporated, western territories of the land. I shall defend that Constitution!"

General Lee was angry.

"Yes, General. You speak, I believe, of Sections Four and Nine of Article One. Very good. Does that mean you endorsed President Buchanan's amendments in '60?"

In December 1860, one month after Abraham Lincoln's election, President James Buchanan attempted to avert civil war by proposing three constitutional amendments. The amendments would have recognized a property right in Negro slaves, would have required the Federal government to enforce the fugitive slave laws, and would have extended slavery into the western territories until such time as the territories became states and elected to abolish slavery by popular vote.

"I remember my reaction to President Buchanan's proposals vividly," the general replied more calmly. "The three propositions of the President were eminently just, were in accordance with the Constitution, and ought to have been cheerfully assented to by all the states." General Lee frowned. "But alas, Mr. Secretary, they were not and now our country is a caldron of blood and bitterness."

"Well, General, if I can keep you from making any public

speeches, I may still be able to have you back with your army by New Year's. At least this war should be over by spring and your unusual politics won't matter."

"Spring?" General Lee asked with a raised eyebrow. "The war may last ten years."

"Ten years? Are you prepared to endure another decade of this struggle?"

"I shall endeavor, Sir, to do my duty and fight to the last." The fire glistened in the soldier's eyes.

"Well, General, on the field of battle you are in your element. The history of your grand army surely proves that. My job will be to convince the joint committee. I shall do my best to send you back there."

"Please, Mr. Secretary, do not confuse my devotion to my men and to my country's independence with a love for war." General Lee looked at his knees as his mind returned to a lifetime of ghastly fields. "You have no idea what a horrible sight a battlefield is."

"I am sorry, General. I did not mean to imply...."

"I am gradually losing my best men," General Lee continued softly. "Jackson, Pender. There was no braver soldier in the Confederacy than Deshler. I see he is numbered among the dead." General Lee faced his defender. "My heart bleeds at the death of every one of our gallant men." His weather-worn face sagged.

"Yes, General....The court martial, as you know, deals mainly with the Gettysburg campaign. What are your thoughts on that engagement?"

General Lee rose and paced the floor.

"Had I had Stonewall Jackson at Gettysburg, I would have won a great victory." General Lee blinked his moist eyes at the mention of the name of the fallen captain whose iron men called their eccentric Lieutenant General Thomas Jonathan Jackson "Old Blue Light" or plain "Old Jack." General Lee could not speak of General Jackson without the words sticking in his throat. He still grieved for both the man and the soldier. "It had not been intended to deliver a general battle so far from our base unless attacked. But coming unexpectedly upon the whole Federal army, to withdraw through the mountains with our extensive trains would have been difficult and dangerous. At the same time, we were unable to await an attack as the country was unfavorable for collecting supplies in the presence of an enemy who could restrain our foraging parties by holding the mountain passes with local and other troops. A battle had therefore become, in a measure, unavoidable."

The tired chief looked out the window for a long moment before he spoke to Secretary Benjamin.

"What of General Longstreet?"

"As of today, General Longstreet should be in Bristol, Virginia. I would expect him in Richmond by tomorrow."

"Good, good. I miss General Longstreet greatly."

Benjamin put aside his file of field reports and dispatches. He spoke softly when he walked dangerous ground with his client.

"You do understand, General, that our defense regarding Gettysburg may be to hold Generals Longstreet and Stuart responsible for the unfortunate results. Stuart allowed you to collide with the Federal army without warning and Longstreet delayed his deployment on that terrible field. That may be our only defense, Sir."

Robert Lee stood straight as a Springfield rifle ramrod, straight as if he were again The Marble Model on the plain at West Point.

"Never, Mr. Secretary. Never."

★   ★   ★

The afternoon sun shone brightly through the windows of the capitol building of the Confederate States of America at Capitol Square, Richmond. The narrow room was comfortable where Texas Senator Louis Wigfall visited with his colleagues from the newly seated Confederate Congress. The burly Texan was chairman of the Senate Military Affairs Committee. Forty-seven years old, the big man was a lawyer. In 1859, he had taken his seat for Texas in the United States Senate only to be expelled from that body in July 1861 with the coming of war.

"Has it ever occurred to you," Wigfall fumed, "that Davis's mind is becoming unsettled? No sane man would act as he is acting! I fear that his bad health and bad temper are undermining his reason."

"Davis is becoming a dictator," Senator Reade nodded.

Senator Wigfall enjoyed two great passions: his profound hatred for Jefferson Davis, and his dislike of Robert Lee. The court martial of General Lee was Senator Wigfall's idea.

Wigfall had started his Confederate career on Jefferson Davis' good side. In December 1860, Wigfall drafted an anti-Republican, pro-secession proclamation which Davis signed. When the Confederate government moved from Montgomery, Alabama, to Richmond in June 1861, Mr. and Mrs. Wigfall rode the train to Richmond with Jefferson and Varina Davis as friends. The new Confederate President appointed Wigfall first as a presidential aide and then to a brigadier generalship. Wigfall resigned his commission in February 1862 to enter the Senate in Richmond.

Suspicious of Davis' efforts to expand his presidential powers, Wigfall fought Davis daily and bad-mouthed him in Richmond saloons when the senator had a little too much Kentucky bourbon in him. By October 1862, Wigfall was calling for congressional action to limit the President's power to nominate military officers.

Henry Stuart Foote, Senator Edwin Reade of North Carolina and Virginia's Senator Robert M. Hunter listened impassively to the leader of Davis' opposition. Before the war, Hunter had been speaker of the United States House of Representatives in 1839-1841 and a senator from 1847 until Virginia left the Union.

"His blunder at Gettysburg," Louis Wigfall continued with a fist pounding the table, "his wretched handling of his troops, and his utter want of generalship, have only increased Davis' admiration for him!"

The falling-out between Wigfall and President Davis had erupted into public hostility when the President removed General Joe Johnston from command after the general's wounding at Seven Pines in May 1862. The genial General Johnston was a favorite of the senator.

"Davis and Lee, a pathetic combination," Congressman Foote agreed.

Foote's distemper toward Jefferson Davis dated to May 1844 when lawyer Foote defended the man accused of murdering the husband of Davis' sister. Foote and Davis were Mississippi's two United States senators in the '40s. They agreed on little. Only the intervention of Senate friends prevented Davis and Foote from fighting a duel to the death in the spring of 1848 after a heated debate on the Senate floor. Fourteen years later in 1862, Congressman Foote, now living in and representing Nashville, sponsored a no-confidence resolution in the Confederate House of Representatives against Judah Benjamin, then Secretary of War. The resolution failed but Davis felt the sting.

"It's no wonder Davis ordered that little Jew to defend General Lee. What a perfect combination: our befuddled President, that incompetent Virginian, and that smiling Hebrew Englishman."

The Texan felt a shadow cross his face. Turning toward the door, he saw the tall figure of President Davis.

"Senator," Jefferson Davis said drily, "that little Jew, as you put it, happens to be my dear friend. We have yet to reach a verdict as to General Lee."

Now the tall sickly President and his Secretary of State were close friends. Benjamin and Davis shared the same presidential office in the old U.S. Customs House. But in June 1858, Louisiana Senator Benjamin challenged Mississippi Senator Davis to a duel after angry words in floor debate. Davis had to apologize to avoid gunplay.

President Davis was thin as a rail, sickly-looking, and aged well beyond his 55 years.

Jefferson Davis was born in Christian County, Kentucky, within one year and one hundred miles of another Kentuckian who had also made something of himself: Abraham Lincoln. Like his most trusted general, Robert Lee, Jefferson Davis knew how to "marry up." His first wife had been the daughter of President Zachary Taylor. His bride died from malaria within three months.

Now remarried with young children, President Davis suffered

from physical pain and a legendary restlessness. A chronic insomniac, the President would take a horse and ride alone through the streets of sleeping Richmond all night long. His physical pain was real and lingering. He endured constant and severe facial pain and spasms, complicated by daily stomach discomfort. Since 1858 he had been blind in his left eye from glaucoma and herpes.

The President had known General Lee since they were cadets together at West Point a lifetime ago.

"If I could take one wing and Lee the other," President Davis chided Wigfall and his cohorts, "I think we could, between us, wrest victory from those people."

Senator Wigfall winced. Like many in Richmond, he regarded the President's sense of military affairs as evidence of his delusions of grandeur. But the embattled President was not without credentials: before his 1861 resignation from the United States Senate, Davis had been chairman of the Senate's Military Affairs Committee. He had also been U.S. Secretary of War under President Franklin Pierce while Robert Lee was superintendent at West Point. Davis also saw action in Mexico when he was colonel of the First Mississippi Volunteers regiment. He resigned from the U. S. House of Representatives to serve in Mexico where he was seriously wounded in the right foot at the Battle of Buena Vista in February 1847.

"Well, Mr. President," Senator Wigfall said acidly, "we shall whip those bloody Yankees no matter who leads our armies. The enemy cannot prevail on the field."

President Davis regarded the Texas senator sourly before he responded coldly.

"Our maximum strength has been mobilized, while the enemy is just beginning to put forth his might." President Davis looked tired and his bad eye twitched in painful spasm.

"Time will tell," Wigfall argued softly in the stuffy room. "But, Sir, nothing can change the public record of your General Lee's sorry performance at Gettysburg five months ago."

President Davis lingered in the doorway leading to the capitol corridor.

"To some men," the President answered, "it is a given to be commended for what they are expected to do and to be sheltered when they fail by a transfer of the blame which may attach. To others, it is decreed that their success shall be denied or treated as a necessary result, and their failures imputed to incapacity. General Lee seems to me to be an example of the second class." The President's pained eyes narrowed and his voice sounded like dry leaves underfoot. "My confidence has not been diminished."

★   ★   ★

The crackling fire in the stone hearth warmed the parlor of the little house on Leigh Street. Beyond the frosted windows, Richmond was dark and the nighttime sky was brilliant with starlight.

General Lee stood beside the fireplace. He rubbed his hard hands close to the fire. The general looked over his shoulder toward the sound of light steps upon the hard wood floor. Daughters Mildred and Agnes approached the cozy fire. The weary soldier smiled warmly at the lights of his life.

"Where's Daughter?" General Lee smiled toward Mildred, the youngest Lee daughter at 17.

"Mary is upstairs with mother." Daughter Mary Custis, 28, had been "Daughter" since girlhood, just as little Mildred had always been "Precious Life" and the beautiful Agnes, 22, had always been "Wig" to their father who had a pet nickname for all of his seven children. There were now six Lee children. Sons Robert, Jr., 20, and Custis, 21, were soldiers, Robert in artillery and Custis an aide to Jefferson Davis in the War Department. Son Fitzhugh, "Rooney" since he had outgrown his boyhood nickname of Mr. Boo, remained a prisoner of war.

General Lee looked toward the three baskets of knitting in the corner. Mother Lee's basket overflowed with socks for freezing Confederate soldiers. The baskets of Mildred and Agnes were nearly empty. Lee smiled at the empty baskets and then toward his two daughters.

"I fear," the father grinned warmly, "my daughters have not taken to the spinning wheel and loom as I have recommended. I shall not be able to recommend them to the brave soldiers for wives."

"Oh, Father!" Agnes said with mock indignation.

"Daddy!" Mildred blushed.

Agnes stepped toward her tall father and hugged him. "How I have missed you these last two years!"

The soldier kissed his fragile daughter's cheek and he pushed her to arm's length.

"If you have missed me," he sighed, stroking her black hair from her forehead, "how much more must I have missed you?"

The general looked past Agnes toward Mildred, his "Precious Life."

"I think of you," he said toward Mildred, "long for you, pray for you. It is all I can do." The general sighed and turned toward the fire. He spoke into the flames with his children standing behind him.

"I wish indeed that I could see you more," he said softly toward the fire, "be with you, and never again part from you. Only God can give me that happiness. I pray for it night and day."

Agnes held her sore hands toward the fire. Already her hands and feet were prone to swelling and pain from the arthritis which had crippled her mother.

"You girls have no time to be sick. You have a sacred charge: the care of your poor mother."

To lighten the somber atmosphere, General Lee invited his daughters to join him on the back porch. Mildred and Agnes threw shawls over their shoulders and followed their father outside. The night was cold as they stood in the dark and admired the sky full of stars which hardly twinkled in the still air.

"We studied astronomy at St. Mary's," Mildred said toward the sky, with her father and sister on the back steps. Mildred was home on Christmas vacation from her second year at St. Mary's Academy in Raleigh, North Carolina.

"Me too, Life," the general smiled toward Mildred. "I studied the stars and planets at West Point. One of my first assignments as an engineer was as an astronomer, you know." Six years out of the Academy in 1835, Lieutenant Lee had been an assistant astronomer surveying the disputed border between Ohio and Michigan.

"I think it afforded me more pleasure than any other branch of study." The soldier paused, looked down at his shivering daughters, and then returned his gaze toward the brilliant sky. "How unerring is the course and periods of the heavenly bodies and how sure are the calculations of science....I would that our course were as true and our calculations as sure."

"It's all so beautiful." Mildred exclaimed. General Lee put his strong arm around her shoulders.

When the girls had enough of the biting cold, they turned toward the warm glow of the doorway. They saw Mrs. Lee at the steamed window. She sat in her rolling chair and only her face and white hair were visible.

"Mama," Agnes whispered. General Lee turned, smiled at his wife, and followed his daughters inside. The two girls continued upstairs to join their sister Mary Custis. The general and his lady were alone in the back room overlooking the dark yard. They were warmed by an iron stove in the corner.

"I tried to keep the girls from bothering you, Robert."

"Bother?" the general smiled. "They are a joy, Molly."

"They are that," the woman smiled, "and full of life in spite of the wicked war going on around them. Bless their hearts."

"Yes, Molly," General Lee said warmly as he laid his hard hand upon hers. "Our young people, as is natural, I suppose, seem to look at what is agreeable. I fear they will meet with disappointment."

"I hope to get over to see Charlotte tomorrow," Mother Lee said sadly. "If I can manage the carriage. The dear girl is doing so poorly, I'm afraid." Mary Lee worried about her daughter-in-law, slowly wasting away from grief after the deaths of her two infant children and the June capture of her husband.

"It has been a hard year for us all," Mary Lee said sadly. "The loss of our precious Annie was hardest of all." Tears welled up in Mrs. Lee's gray eyes.

"I cannot express the anguish I feel at the death of our sweet Annie," General Lee sighed softly. "To know that I shall never see her again on earth, that her place in our circle, which I always hoped one day to enjoy, is forever vacant, is agonizing in the extreme." The father grieved for his dead child, named for his mother and buried at age 23 far from home.

"And our big Rooney, kidnapped from his very bed where he lay wounded!" Mary Lee choked back tears.

General Lee's face became hard and his voice was angry.

"I had not expected that he would have been taken from his bed and carried off." He reached for his shaking wife's hand. "I saw him the night of the battle—indeed, met him on the field as they were bringing him from the front. He seemed to be more concerned about his brave men and officers, who had fallen in the battle, than about himself."

"What will become of our boy?" Mary sobbed.

"Fitzhugh has been sent to Fort Lafayette," General Lee consoled his wife. "Any place would be better than Fort Monroe with Butler in command. It is probable he will be sent to Johnson's Island where the rest of our officers are." The general did not mention that Confederates were freezing to death at the Johnson Island prison compound on frozen Lake Erie just off Sandusky, Ohio.

"Will he be paroled?" Mary Lee asked through her tears. "Charlotte cannot wait for him much longer."

"I have no idea when Fitzhugh will be exchanged. The Federal authorities still resist all exchanges because they think it is to our interest to make them." The general shrugged. "Any desire expressed on our part for an exchange of an individual magnifies the difficulty. They at once think some great benefit is to result to us from it. If you want a person exchanged, the best course is to keep quiet about it." He touched his wife's face. "His detention is very grievous to me."

Robert Lee patted his wife's hand.

"Oh, my Molly," he sighed toward the iced window. "What a cruel thing is war. To separate and destroy families and friends and mar the present joys and happiness God has granted us in the world. To fill our hearts with hatred instead of love for our neighbors and to devastate the beautiful face of this world."

Mary Lee studied her husband's anguished face.

"How many happy homes have they destroyed," General Lee shook his head slowly, "and turned the occupants adrift in the world with nothing. From how many hearts have they expelled all hopes of happiness—forever."

Lee's worn-out face was close to Mary's.

"Nights are the hardest, Molly," he said softly. "In the quiet hours of the night when there is nothing to lighten the full weight of my grief, I feel as if I shall be overwhelmed."

"God will see us through, Robert. He always has."

"There is a just God in heaven who will make all things right in time."

"Yes, Robert. But as long as you are home with us, you can share your terrible burdens with me and your children. We are here for you."

"I know that. And I'm grateful." He labored to smile. "But I am accustomed to bearing my sorrows in silence."

The soldier shrugged.

"I cannot feed my army, Molly. Our state governors are little help to the President. They seem to regard each state as their own country and they are reluctant to share men or material for the defense of other states. If I allowed myself, I would fear the worst."

"Yes, Robert. I fear for the way this inquiry affair is weighing on you."

"I'm fine, Mother. I have borne more. We both have. Our Charlotte has, poor girl. And Agnes, too." His dark eyes narrowed. "It's this matter about the west, too. The President still wants me to go to Tennessee to replace General Bragg. But the court martial's leaders seem to want Joe Johnston, which is fine with me. Just fine. If only the President could suffer Johnston to be appointed."

"He's that set against him?"

"Worse, I think. I understand that our old friend, who stood by

me at our wedding, has fallen into bad habits and worse company."
Johnston was a groomsman at the Lees' marriage. "He has shared
confidential dispatches from the field with Senator Wigfall, maybe
even with the press. To deflect criticism for Vicksburg, they say. The
President will not forgive him for that."

"And if you succeed in this inquiry business and the President can
have his way with Congress?"

The general sighed deeply.

"Tennessee, Molly. I would probably never see my brave men
again."

"Who would replace you, Robert?"

He looked down into her soft face.

"I don't think it would even matter to me."

"Things will go better for all of us, Robert, if England takes up
our side."

General Lee slowly shook his head. He spoke with resignation in
his quiet voice.

"We must make up our minds to fight our battles and win our
independence alone. No one will help us."

"Then we shall rely upon each other and upon God," Mary Lee
said firmly.

Mary Custis Lee looked toward the window.

"The Yankees may cross the James one day," she sighed.

"I begrudge every step he makes towards Richmond."

"They cannot have Richmond!" Mary protested.

General Lee looked into her gray eyes before he spoke gently.

"I do not think Richmond will be permanent."

"What more can we do?" the general's lady demanded softly in the
lamp light.

"It is plain," he said, "we have not suffered enough, labored
enough, repented enough, to deserve success."

"Oh, Robert! You do sound sometimes like an old preacher."
Mary was at last her cheerful self. "You cannot take upon your own
shoulders the burdens of the entire country."

"When I reflect upon the calamity pending over the country, my own sorrows sink into insignificance."

Mary Lee nodded. "It's time we went upstairs."

General Lee took his place behind her to push her to the stairs. He called to daughters Mary and Agnes to help him get Mother Lee up the steps.

"Tomorrow will be a better day, Robert."

"Of course it will, Molly."

Chapter Four

Friday, December 11, 1863

I find too late that I have wasted the best years of my life.
          Robert E. Lee

The two, bearded men rode slowly on horseback beneath a brilliant, morning sky. A squad of mounted cavalry followed quietly behind.

The two riders in the lead rode past the few citizens of Richmond who braved the biting cold on Leigh Street. Townsfolk silently raised their hats in salute to the familiar figures of General Lee on the gray stallion, Traveller, and General James Longstreet at his side. Fourteen years younger than General Lee, Lieutenant General Longstreet looked muscular and vigorous beside his exhausted, sickly chief.

During the night, cavalrymen from Stuart's command had managed to secure a rail car for delivering General Lee's favorite horse to the Lees' stable behind the rented house. At daybreak, General Lee had greeted Traveller like an old friend from many campaigns. Old Pete Longstreet had also found his way to Richmond during the night.

The mounted men rode peacefully through the frozen dirt streets, south down Second Street for six blocks to Main Street where they turned right for another three blocks. They then turned left onto Adams which they followed for the two blocks leading to Canal Street. Turning right on Canal, the horses puffed clouds of steam into the cold air for the two-block climb up the slope of Oregon Hill where Canal became Cumberland Street. After three blocks on Cumberland, they turned left for three blocks ending at the corner of Albemarle.

Generals Lee and Longstreet paused at the gate of Hollywood Cemetery. With a wave of his gloved hand, General Lee halted the cavalry escort. Lee and Longstreet rode through the gate alone.

Hollywood Cemetery was deserted under the purple sky of early morning. Lee had taken breakfast with Mrs. Lee at daybreak before General Longstreet had climbed the steps to the front porch. When the two men mounted their horses, General Lee's daughters were still asleep.

Generals Lee and Longstreet tied their horses to a hitching post. The animals were skittish from the cold. Each pawed the hard earth. Leaving their mounts behind, the two men walked on through the marker-covered field.

Old Pete Longstreet was half a head taller than Lee. Born in South Carolina, he had lived his first eight years in Gainesville, Georgia. Upon the death of his father when Longstreet was 12 years old, he was raised by his uncle, Judge Augustus Longstreet, in Augusta, Georgia.

With three heart seizures in one year behind him, General Lee walked slowly. His chest hurt in the cold air, and he was tired. But Longstreet never appeared tired. He was the picture of robust middle-age: strong and hardy with clear blue eyes, full black beard, and a taste for both poker and whiskey between battles. He had entered West Point in 1838. His close friends at the Academy included George Pickett whose division Longstreet saw destroyed at Gettysburg, Ulysses S. Grant now wearing the blue, and Confederate generals-to-be Lafayette McLaws and Daniel Harvey Hill (Stonewall Jackson's brother-in-law). Longstreet's roommate at the Point was

Will Rosecrans, now a Federal general. Longstreet had destroyed his old roommate's command only three months ago at the Battle of Chickamauga near Chattanooga, Tennessee.

The two officers stopped beside three narrow graves covered by a dusting of snow. Longstreet distractedly reached into his gray greatcoat and retrieved his pipe. Fumbling awkwardly, he put the cold pipe back into his pocket. General Lee stood close to Longstreet so he would not have to speak loudly: a life-time in the company of cannon had left Longstreet slightly deaf.

"It is a sad place, General," Robert Lee said softly into Longstreet's good ear. Longstreet nodded and blinked hard.

They stood in the cold before the graves of Longstreet's three young children who had died within days of each other. Hundreds of children perished when an epidemic of scarlet fever swept Richmond in January, 1862. Three of them were Longstreet's.

"Strange," Lee said gently, "how we can see the horrors of a hundred battlefields, but nothing is as sad as a child's grave." General Lee thought about his own daughter Annie.

"Yes," Longstreet mumbled toward the little mounds of earth. "A hundred battlefields."

Longstreet was no stranger to grim battlefields. Like Lee, he had apprenticed in the Mexican War sixteen years earlier. Longstreet was severely wounded there during the siege of Chapultepec. During that conflict, Lee had been an engineer on the staff of General Zachary Taylor. Taylor would become President of the United States, his daughter would be Jefferson Davis' first wife, and Taylor's son would ride as a general in the Valley Army of Stonewall Jackson.

On Taylor's staff, Lee had worked with young Lieutenants George McClellan and George Gordon Meade. Lee worked, too, with Captain Joe Hooker on General Pillow's staff. It would be McClellan whom Lee engaged in 1862 during the spring Battle of the Seven Days and in the fall along Antietam Creek. Lee's greatest victory would be at Chancellorsville in May 1863 when Stonewall Jackson defeated General Joe Hooker. General Meade would hold the rugged little mountains around Gettysburg when Lee retreated under cover of darkness from his worst defeat.

During the Mexican War, Lee was an engineer with General Winfield Scott. Fourteen years later, Scott would be General-in-Chief of the United States. To him in 1861, Lee tendered his resignation to go with the South. In Mexico, General Scott used Lee to reconnoiter the Cerro Gordo front. For his bravery, Lieutenant Lee received three temporary field commissions or "brevets" to the rank of major.

Longstreet's great day at Chapultepec in September 1847 marked many future careers of merit. Engineer Lee scouted the ground for a commanding position where young Lieutenant Tom Jackson, later Stonewall, could place his cannon. The whole assault was led gallantly by Lieutenant James Longstreet whose color bearer was Lieutenant George Pickett, one year out of West Point and the bottom man of the Class of '46. Lee was slightly wounded at Chapultepec and was brevetted colonel.

The Mexican War was not the only tie binding the boys of the Old Army with the graybeards of the new in blue and gray. There were ties also of family. Federal General Grant was married to Longstreet's cousin, Julia Dent. Grant and Longstreet had always regarded themselves as kin. When Ulysses Grant married Julia in 1849, in St. Louis, Longstreet was a groomsman, as was future Confederate General Cadmus Wilcox who played a key role in Lee's victory at Chancellorsville.

Julia Dent Grant was herself an example of the family conflicts aggravated by the bloody strife between the nation's sections. Her husband, General Grant, was a poor Ohioan reared in an anti-slavery state, but Julia Dent grew up in slave-state Missouri where her father owned 18 slaves. As a teenager, Julia had her very own slave called "Black Julia" to prevent confusion with her young, white mistress.

"I am glad you came with me, General," Longstreet muttered at last. "I know you understand my grief." The tall, corps commander looked down at Lee by his side.

General Lee sighed down at the little graves.

"Coming here certainly puts all things in proper perspective." Longstreet raised his face to the bare trees. "How can so much sorrow sleep in such peace when the world is full of guns and madness?" He paused, reached into his pocket, and fiddled with his pipe without pulling it out. "I suppose we do have something else to show for our lives beyond the graves of our children," Longstreet said softly on a cloud of steam.

General Lee thought for a moment and shrugged. "How great is my remorse at having thrown away my time and abused the opportunities afforded me." The weary soldier looked up into the full, firm face of General Longstreet. "I find too late that I have wasted the best years of my life." General Lee looked back down at the three headstones of Longstreet's children.

"Nonsense," Old Pete said firmly. "All that we have to be proud of has been accomplished under your eye and under your orders."

General Lee looked uncomfortable at Longstreet's sudden kindness standing over the graves of his children. The commanding general shrugged inside his blue greatcoat under the cold sunshine. The two old soldiers were genuine friends. Since the retreat from Gettysburg, blame had fallen equally upon Lee for his failure to exercise closer command and upon Longstreet for slowness of engagement on the battle's second and decisive day. But the abiding friendship between the two men was too strong to be diverted by the quibblings of fireside generals in the press and the Confederate Congress.

General Lee meant it when he had called James Longstreet "the staff of my right hand." Although Stonewall Jackson received the lion's share of public glory, it had always been to Longstreet that Lee looked for rock-solid dependability and courage under fire. When the Army of Northern Virginia was reorganized after its staggering losses at Sharpsburg in the fall of 1862, Longstreet's I Corps was given five divisions while the much lauded Jackson in command of II Corps was entrusted with only four divisions.

Since the death of his three children two years earlier, the usually jovial and outgoing Longstreet had become withdrawn and quiet.

No longer a happy man of many words and many friends, Old Pete showed his love for General Lee without words. Longstreet had named his now two-month old son Robert Lee Longstreet. The baby's mother, Maria Louisa, was the daughter of the Old Army's General John Garland.

"I suppose we can go, General," Longstreet said as he returned his hat to his thick, dark hair. General Lee did likewise, covering his white and thinning hair.

Robert Lee's tired mind was elsewhere—south where his "Sweet Annie" slept beneath the snow in North Carolina. Speaking to the three new graves at his cold feet, General Lee mumbled softly the inscription from a favorite hymn which he had requested for the stone marker above Annie's grave at Warrenton, North Carolina's Jones Springs Cemetery: "Perfect and true are all His ways whom heaven adores and earth obeys."

James Longstreet looked down at his weary chief.

"I do hope so," Old Pete said as he walked away from his children.

Lee and Longstreet mounted their impatient horses under a dazzling sky. Their cavalry escort kept pace discreetly behind as the little column rode at a walk back along the route they had come. They headed north up Second Street, crossing the railroad track laid along Broad. Continuing past Broad, they rode past Leigh Street after three blocks. Six blocks north of Leigh on Second Street, the caravan of mounted men stopped at another iron fence which separated Richmond from its other burial ground, Shockoe Hill Cemetery.

They dismounted at the fence along Second Street, the cemetery's west side. On the far east side of Shockoe Hill was City Hospital on Fourth Street. The county poor house stood on the cemetery's north side. Way over the hill, at the cemetery's northeast corner was the Hebrew Cemetery for Richmond's few Jews. Generals Lee and Longstreet handed their animals' reins to a cavalry trooper and the two men went into the cemetery. There were still more dead babies to visit.

General Lee led Longstreet to the graves of his only grandchildren who laid side-by-side. Longstreet looked truly pained as he stood before a small stone marker which bore the inscription "Robert E. Lee." General Lee's imprisoned son Rooney and his sickly wife Charlotte had named their first child for his grandfather in the spring of 1860, the last year the country had been one nation. Robert E. Lee, III, had died of pneumonia in early July 1862.

"I would have wished him a better name and hoped he might be a wiser and more useful man than his namesake." General Lee frowned at the frozen ground.

Beside the little grave of General Lee's grandson was another tiny mound of frozen earth. There, Rooney's second child, a daughter named for General Lee's mother, was laid in December 1862 after living less than eight weeks.

Robert E. Lee, the grandfather, stood bare-headed in a cold wind. "Only old people should be allowed to be sick," he said with a dry voice which sounded almost angry to General Longstreet's good ear.

"That would surely be more fair," Longstreet said softly.

After leaving Shockoe Hill, the two generals rode down Second Street in silence until they parted for the morning at the corner of Leigh Street. Longstreet continued into town to his hotel as General Lee slowly took the steps of his home.

★   ★   ★

Jeb Stuart on the streets of the capital city evoked cheers and hoots. Young General Stuart responded with a jaunty wave of his famous yellow gloves holding his more famous plumed hat. The most popular cavalry commander to date in the war, Major General James Ewell Brown Stuart was seven weeks shy of his 31st birthday.

General Stuart was greeted on the noontime street with immediate cheers when he left the home of his brother-in-law, Dr. Charles Bower, on Grace Street. People on Richmond sidewalks waved and cheered him during his ride on horseback down Grace for the four blocks to Second. He and two cavalry guards made the left, north on Second for the four blocks to Leigh Street and the Lee quarters.

Stuart had come to Richmond from his cavalry's "Camp Wigwam," winter quarters near Orange Court House, Virginia.

Hats were waved and shouts raised when Stuart halted his mount at the Lee house. The small group of townspeople who kept vigil outside General Lee's home warmly greeted General Stuart. Young Jeb waved back with genuine gratitude. He took pleasure in his fame and days of glory commanding the cavalry corps of the Army of Northern Virginia. When Stonewall Jackson fell wounded at Chancellorsville, Jeb Stuart had taken temporary command of II Corps when the ranking officer on the field, General A.P. Hill, was temporarily disabled.

Stuart handed his animal's reins to a cavalry trooper under early afternoon sunshine. Stuart had contemplated a career in the law as a young man ten years earlier. He had even clerked in a Wytheville, Virginia, law office for a short time. But soldiering was what called him. After his father had been defeated in a campaign for a seat in the United States Congress from Patrick County, Virginia, the candidate who defeated Archie Stuart appointed Jeb to West Point in 1849. After graduating number 13 in his class, Lieutenant Stuart tasted battle fighting Indians in Texas. There he met Major James Longstreet and became a second lieutenant in the U.S. First Cavalry at Fort Levenworth, Kansas, in July 1855.

During 1856 and 1857, Jeb rode against Indians in Kansas under the command of then-colonel Edwin Sumner in June 1856, and one year later joined the command of Major John Sedgwick fighting the Cheyenne. Sumner and Sedgwick had become Federal generals. General Sedgwick was loved by his troops who called him Uncle John. The Army of Northern Virginia had locked swords with old Sumner (the Union's oldest corps commander of the war at 66) at Sharpsburg along the Antietam in September 1862 and at Fredericksburg in December 1862. General Sumner was now six months dead from pneumonia. Uncle John Sedgwick felt Robert E. Lee's hot lead at Sharpsburg where he was seriously wounded, and again at Gettysburg. Sedgwick now had six months to live.

Indian fighting taught young Jeb all he knew about making war.

In July 1857 at Solomon's Fork on the Smoky Hill River in northwest Kansas, a Cheyenne bullet struck him in the chest. Though badly wounded, he led his cavalry column 120 miles back to Fort Kearny.

Stuart advanced quickly with the coming of civil war. One month after Fort Sumter, he was commissioned a lieutenant colonel in May 1861 in the Provisional Army of the Confederate States of America. By September 24, 1861, he was a brigadier general of cavalry in command of 1,500 troopers in six regiments. He was not yet 29 years old and only one year past being a first lieutenant in the U.S. Cavalry. In July 1862, he was promoted to major general. Rank and glory had come to Jeb Stuart with dizzying speed after dazzling successes in the field. He had not failed General Lee until Gettysburg.

For a moment, Jeb Stuart stroked the nose of his horse. He had gambled his life on a trusted mount many times. The first lesson he taught new cavalry recruits was the difference between the gaits of the trot and the gallop. He forbid his troopers to employ the faster pace whenever their backs were toward the bluecoated enemy. He lectured his men that "A good man on a good horse can never be caught. Cavalry can trot away from anything and a gallop is a gait unbecoming a soldier, unless he is going toward the enemy. We gallop toward the enemy and trot away. Always."

Major General Stuart patted his mount before taking the steps toward the Lee home.

Stuart was always where the bullets were thickest. He enjoyed more than one near miss. On November 10, 1862, near Culpeper, Virginia, a Yankee Minie ball had shot off half of his massive mustache.

Jeb had great affection for General Lee, and for Mrs. Lee in particular. He took much pleasure from flirting with the Lee daughters. He had abiding admiration for General Lee both as a soldier and as something of a father figure. He had first met Lee when Lee was superintendent at the Point. But it was Stonewall Jackson whom Stuart worshiped. Only Stuart could make the dour Jackson laugh.

Stuart's knock on the front door summoned Lee's daughter Mildred. The youngest Lee child was wide-eyed in the presence of the "Beau Saber of Dixie." Jeb's smile melted every female heart that dreamed of his figure on horseback.

"General Stuart, do come in out of the cold," Mildred said breathlessly.

"Now, Mildred, I shall always be Jeb to you, please." He smiled broadly. Little Mildred blushed. They had known each other since West Point where Jeb was dubbed "Beauty" Stuart by his brother cadets from the first day. When her father approached, Mildred tore her eyes from Stuart's rugged, wind tanned face and wild beard.

"General," Stuart nodded to his chief.

"Jeb," General Lee smiled warmly as he reached for Stuart's hard hand. "You are looking rested."

"Thank you, General. It's amazing what one night in a real bed will do for an old horsesoldier." Stuart's billet with his brother-in-law and Jeb's wife, Flora, were a welcomed vacation after two years of sleeping on the ground or in the saddle.

The two men took chairs beside the blazing hearth in the parlor. Mildred leaned quietly against the doorway. When her dark eyes met her father's, General Lee smiled his permission for the youngest Lee woman to enjoy her fill of the dashing Stuart. Mildred smiled sweetly and her gaze drifted from her father to his commanding general of cavalry, young enough to be Lee's son. Jeb was only two years older than Lee's eldest daughter, Mary Custis Lee.

"It feels as if you and I have been together since the first shot of this cursed war," General Lee said.

"We have been," Jeb Stuart nodded.

General Lee and Stuart were present together for the true first shots of the war which echoed through Harper's Ferry during the aborted slave revolt known as John Brown's Raid. When Brown seized the fire engine house at Harper's Ferry in October 1859, then-lieutenant Stuart, U.S.A., was dispatched by the War Department and President James Buchanan to Arlington, Virginia, to summon Lieutenant Colonel Lee, United States Army. On October

18th, Lee led the assault by United States Marines against Brown and his hostages. John Brown was hanged in December 1859.

The two warriors, like father and son, sat before the blazing fireplace. For several warm minutes, the soldiers said nothing. Watching the fire in the stone hearth, they might have been remembering the blazing ruins of the Chancellor House which culminated General Lee's greatest single victory in the thickets of Chancellorsville seven months earlier. Had that battle not cost General Lee the sturdy presence of Stonewall Jackson, reflections on Chancellorsville and the rout of "Fighting Joe" Hooker's bluecoats might have given Lee pleasure. But Lee's memory of that May evening was now draped in black crepe and muffled drums.

"I have always done my duty," Jeb said softly, "as best I could."

General Lee was startled. He turned his ruddy face toward his major general of cavalry.

"Of course you have."

Lee's faith in Jeb had not abated after Stuart's failure to adequately screen the Rebel army's march to Gettysburg in late June 1863. Stuart's orders were to guard the flanks of Lee's legions and to locate the unseen Army of the Potomac under its new commander, General Meade. Stuart's failure to keep Lee appraised of Meade's whereabouts was largely responsible for the two great armies stumbling into each other amid the rocky hills and alleyways of Gettysburg. The accidental encounter cost the Army of Northern Virginia nearly 28,000 casualties. Jeb Stuart's pride was on the list of wounded.

"This whole court martial thing," Stuart said softly, "causes me great personal pain. You deserve so much better than this from those sawdust men in the Congress. I shall help in any way I can. You know that, General."

"Now, Jeb," Lee said firmly. Rarely, if ever, did he use first names with his general staff. "Your glories on the field will live forever in the annals of this army." The commander smiled. "However this war ends, old soldiers will one day bounce their grandchildren on their knees and tell them of Jeb Stuart's Ride Around McClellan. That's a fact, Jeb." The weathered face which inspired hungry men to call him their Uncle Robert looked kindly at Jeb Stuart. The 30-year-old general of cavalry had to smile. Lee had a way of putting other men at ease.

In the cozy firelight, Stuart's mind wandered back to June 1862 when his little band of horsesoldiers gave the new Confederacy its first great exploit to lift waning spirits. His Ride Around McClellan had inspired the new nation and had solicited grudging admiration even from his enemies across the Potomac.

"Those were indeed the days, General," Stuart smiled.

In June 1862, Federal General McClellan's huge army crawled like a 25-mile long snake toward Richmond. When General Lee summoned Stuart to headquarters in the Dabb House on the Nine Mile Road near High Meadows, Virginia, on June 10th, Lee had been in command of the Army of Northern Virginia for exactly nine days. Lee advised Stuart of his desire to attack the Yankees north of the Chickahominy River in eastern Virginia. Lee had stressed the need to reconnoiter the Federal lines to locate McClellan. Stuart chose for his daring raid the cavalry brigades of Rooney Lee, Fitzhugh Lee (Robert Lee's bawdy nephew), and John Mosby— 1,200 troopers in all.

The smile which spread across Jeb's face confirmed that in his mind he heard the stirring bugle call "Boots and Saddles" and jingling spurs, rattling sabers, and hoofbeats clattering upon rocky country roads.

At 2 o'clock in the morning of Thursday, June 12, 1862, Stuart and his three mounted brigades broke camp at Kelly's Station just north of Richmond. They covered 22 miles before camping near Taylorsville on the South Anna River. At dawn on the 13th, they headed east toward Hanover Courthouse. They defeated a Yankee column at Haw's Shop, 13 miles northeast of Richmond, confirming how close the bluecoats were to the Confederate capital. Federal prisoners recognized cheerful, burly Fitz Lee from the Old Army and called him "Hey! Lieutenant!" from his old cavalry days when Confederate Colonel Fitz Lee had worn the blue himself. Fitz Lee, 26 years old in 1862, was an 1856 graduate of West Point and had been an instructor at the Point in '61 when war came. His chest-length beard put even Stuart's mighty whiskers to shame.

Stuart pushed his weary column all night on June 13th and 14th. By morning on the 14th, the exhausted Rebels reached the Chicka-hominy River at Forge Bridge near Sycamore Spring. The river was high and violent from spring rains. Rooney Lee nearly drowned when he swam out to test the current before construction of a pontoon bridge. After dragging Rooney from the rapid water, Stuart built a bridge from felled trees. The cavalrymen walked across the crude bridge while their weary horses swam beside them on long reins. They crossed 35 miles from Richmond, having ridden com-pletely around the Federal army. Stuart put Fitz Lee in command of the cavalry detachment and Jeb galloped toward Richmond in search of General Lee.

Stuart and his exhausted horse reached Richmond at dawn on June 15th to report to Lee the location of McClellan's bluecoats. In addition to riding the full, 100-mile course around the Federal divisions while Yankees nipped at his heels, Stuart had whipped a unit of Yankee cavalry on the 13th. The bluecoats were commanded by his own father-in-law, Union General Philip Cooke. Stuart hated his wife's father for staying with the North.

The day Stuart's exhausted troopers crossed the flooded Chicka-hominy with Yankees in close pursuit, a fellow Southerner stood at Stuart's side and asked Jeb what he would have done had the Federals attacked the Rebels when their backs were at the river. Would Jeb have surrendered? the trooper inquired afterward. There was an alternative to surrender, Stuart had smiled: "To die game."

"Well, General," Jeb said to General Lee who sat quietly at his side by the fire, "We were surely on our game that week!"

"I suppose we taught George McClellan a thing or two," Lee smiled. He had always respected the deposed General McClellan. Lee and McClellan made war in June 1862 during the Battle of the Seven Days and at bloody Sharpsburg in September '62 beside Antietam Creek. Until his fall from favor, McClellan had been dubbed the

Union's "Little Napoleon" for his bluster and his stocky demeanor. "He was an able general," Lee added, "but a very cautious one."

General Lee had soldiered with George McClellan in Mexico when McClellan was an engineer with then-captain Lee. They worked side by side with then-lieutenants Pierre Beauregard, George Gordon Meade, and Captain Joe Johnston. Beauregard later captured Fort Sumter and McClellan's grand army wounded Joe Johnston in May of '62 which sent Lee into the field for his first real command.

"And," Lee continued, "McClellan is a gentleman."

Little Mac, relieved from command last year by President Lincoln, waged war during the first half of the Civil War before "total war" had been invented. He had taken care to protect Southern civilian property from destruction. During his Seven Days retreat, McClellan had given specific instructions to spare the estate of Rooney Lee when his defeated blue army burned two square miles of southland while destroying Federal supplies which could not be evacuated to the James River. Despite General McClellan's orders, an angry Yankee torched the Lee farm anyway.

"Well," Jeb said as he stood at Lee's side, "I only came by to pay my respects, General. Do give my love to Mrs. Lee. I remember her fondly from my West Point years. And to the girls." Jeb smiled over his shoulder at Mildred who blushed. General Lee stood on cracking knees by the hearth.

Mildred in the doorway looked over her shoulder at the sound of footsteps on the hardwood floor. She cast a quick look toward Jeb, standing by the hearth with her father.

"Mary!" Mildred said with a broad grin. "Jeb's here." Mildred's eyes twinkled and the impish gleam there was the kind which speaks between sisters.

"Mildred!" her older sister said with soft harshness in her voice. Mildred grinned as General Lee came up behind her.

"Now, Life," the general said with a smile beside his youngest daughter.

"Oh, daddy," Mildred sighed with exasperation in her voice. "Everyone knows about Mary and General Stuart."

"Mildred!" Mary Custis nearly shouted. General Lee put his arm around tall Mary Custis.

"Daughter," General Lee said cheerfully, "I believe you may remember General Stuart from old West Point?" Lee smiled behind his white beard. Mary Custis faced Jeb Stuart. Mary had celebrated her 28th birthday in July when her father was three days down the road retreating from Gettysburg.

"Nice to see you, General," Mary Custis said to the broad cavalryman.

"And you, Mary," General Stuart grinned.

In many ways, Mary Custis was the least attractive Lee daughter. Little Mildred had been full of life since birth and had always deserved her father's loving nickname "Precious Life." Mildred filled a room with cheer. Eleanor Agnes, the middle daughter at 22, was the most beautiful Lee with her long, black hair and fine features. Mary Custis, the eldest daughter, was very much like her mother when she was young: rather selfish, self-centered, and not very tolerant of weakness in others. Her round face, prominent nose, and humorless ways made her appear severe. But once Mary Custis Lee warmed to another person, she revealed the keenest and most intelligent mind of the three surviving Lee girls. For nine years, Jeb Stuart had very much enjoyed Mary's directness and intelligence.

Like her mother, to Mary Custis the family homestead of Arlington was the world itself. The eldest Lee daughter was born at Arlington House in 1835. As a little girl, Mary Custis slept in the Lafayette Bedroom, named in honor of the French hero of the American Revolution who visited Mary's grandfather, Parke Custis, in 1824. Of all the Lee children, Mary Custis was most intimate with Arlington history. Before starting school, she lived with her grandparents at Arlington while her parents were posted on the far frontier at St. Louis. Grandfather Custis conducted daily tours of the estate and its piles of George Washington memorabilia. Like her mother for whom she was named, Mary Custis was home only at Arlington which was now in Federal hands with dead bluecoats buried in her mother's cherished gardens.

"You know, Jeb, that you and Flora are welcome at our table anytime," General Lee said warmly as he excused himself from the hallway. With his foot on the stairs, he paused and waited for Mildred.

"Come, Life," the general ordered. "These young people have some catching-up to do."

Mildred reluctantly followed her father up the stairs.

"See you again, Mildred," Jeb called behind her.

Major General Stuart followed Mary Custis into the parlor. She took her father's chair by the hearth as Jeb added a log to the fire. He sat beside her.

Mary Custis knew of Jeb Stuart's happy marriage to Flora Cooke. But Mary and Jeb were old friends. Mary's firm face softened in the fire light which warmed her spirits.

"Good to see you, Marielle," Jeb Stuart smiled broadly.

"It has been too long, Jimmy," Mary Custis smiled.

While General Lee had been superintendent at West Point, Mary Custis went off to Pelham Priory, a girls' school in Westchester County, New York. It was there that the worldly Mary began using the appellation "Marielle" for her signature. She still used it for personal correspondence. To Jeb Stuart, who was Jimmy when he first met Mary Custis, the smartest Lee daughter was still Marielle.

"It's been nearly two years, Marielle."

"Yes, I remember. You and cousin Fitz saved my old copybook. Lucky for the cause that you two are soldiers and not poets!" Mary Custis smiled.

Jeb laughed. He loved her first cousin, Fitz Lee, West Point '52, the son of General Lee's close brother, Sidney Smith Lee. In March 1862, Jeb and Fitz Lee managed to discover Mary Custis' childhood copybook on a Lee farm ravaged by the Yankees. The old book was a scrapbook of clippings and diary entries kept by a young Mary Custis. Jeb and Fitz had returned it to Mary after first penning their handwritten verses onto the book.

"Do you remember your poetry?" Mary Custis asked.

"I try to forget my poetry," Jeb laughed.

"Well, Major General Jimmy Stuart, I remember your literary efforts."

"Please spare me," Jeb begged half seriously.

"Never!" Mary laughed. Turning to the fire and closing her dark eyes, her fine mind recalled Jeb's words written in air heavy with sulphur clouds from artillery: "In gazing on this precious token/ Fond mem'ry links a chain of pleasure/ Back to those days, unbroken;/ Each page discloses some dear treasure —/ Love off'rings to the darling one —/ That graced West Point and Arlington." Mary Custis opened her eyes and looked at the young cavalryman. "You and Fitz signed it March 19, 1862." She paused. "I remember."

"So you do, Marielle."

Jeb Stuart stood up for the second time.

"Now, I really must see to Flora and the children. She has been a little fragile since little Flora died."

Stuart's daughter, Flora, named for her mother, died 11 months earlier at age 5. Little Jimmy was almost 4 and baby Virginia Pelham Stuart was only 2 months old. Virginia's name honored the state her father so loved. Her middle name remembered Stuart's 23-year-old aide, John Pelham, whom Jeb loved like a brother and over whose body Jeb had cried like a woman when he was killed in action nine months earlier.

"Yes," Mary Custis said, rising. "I heard about your loss. I am truly sorry."

Jeb flushed. He was unaccustomed to public displays of emotion.

"Thank you, Mary. It has been hard enough watching good men die....But a child." He choked on the last words.

"I know, Jimmy. Maybe this war will be over by spring. How I do hope so."

Jeb stood close to his friend, Mary Custis Lee, two years his junior. When he spoke, she could feel a strange tingling at the back of her neck.

"This war," said the 30-year-old major general, "is going to be a long and terrible one. Very few of us will see the end." Before Mary Lee's eyes could fill with tears, Jeb Stuart walked into the hallway, retrieved his greatcoat and plumed hat, and walked outside. Across the street, the little crowd cheered.

Standing in the hallway, Mary Custis leaned against the parlor door frame. She wiped a tear from her eye as she watched Jeb Stuart ride slowly away. General Lee descended the stairs and he saw his daughter's moist eyes. Gently he laid his firm hand upon her shoulder. He spoke passionately.

"A more zealous, ardent, brave and devoted soldier than Stuart, the Confederacy cannot have."

★　　★　　★

The night air was bitter cold. Bright stars illuminated the darkened porch.

The two freezing sentries argued with the woman who labored to make her way to the Lee front door. The commotion outside roused General Lee who sat with daughter Eleanor Agnes at the dining room table. Mildred, Mary Custis, and Mrs. Lee were upstairs as the general enjoyed the gentle company of his middle daughter.

"Let me go, Father," Agnes insisted as General Lee rose from the table for the front door. "It may not be safe."

The general turned toward his 22-year-old daughter.

"Now Wig," he smiled, "those people over the way haven't hurt me yet. I think I am safe in my own home." His cheer was revived by his quiet day, the visit from Jeb Stuart, and as good a dinner meal as Mrs. Lee and the girls could forage from Richmond's meager resources of fresh food smuggled past the Federal blockade of the James River. The girls did the best they could to fill the pantry with the fruits of nearly worthless Confederate money. This 1863 Christmas season, Confederate paper money was worth four cents on the dollar and a single one-dollar gold coin was worth 28 Rebel dollars.

"You can boss around your troops, Father, but not me." Agnes smiled and pushed gently past her father toward the voices on the front porch. She opened the door to the frigid night air.

"Martha!" Agnes said breathlessly.

The woman outside was restrained by the guards who held her arms.

"Cousin Agnes," the visitor said in a cloud of steam, "are you going to keep all of the young men for yourself?"

"It's alright, Corporal. Let her pass. She's family." Agnes shivered in the cold as General Lee came up behind her.

With the general's nod, the sentries released their grip on the woman who stepped over the threshold into the house warmed by the blazing hearth and the stove in the kitchen.

"Martha," Agnes said as she helped the woman remove her heavy coat. "How did you get through the enemy lines?"

"Dear cousin, they are your enemy. I'm from New York, remember?" The visitor laughed and her softly drawling voice was pure Tidewater Virginia although she did keep an apartment in New York City.

General Lee stepped between the women. He embraced his cousin by marriage, Martha Custis Williams.

"Markie," General Lee sighed into her cold hair. "My dear, dear Markie. You found us after all!" Martha Williams hugged the general firmly.

"Of course I did."

General Lee released his cousin when he heard Agnes begin to sniffle behind him. He turned to see Agnes' lovely face streaked with tears.

"I'm sorry, Martha. But I just can't right now...." Agnes cried freely as she turned and ran up the stairs.

The soldier looked deeply pained as he turned back to Martha.

"It's alright, Cousin Robert. I suppose it's just too soon for Agnes. I was afraid that coming to Richmond would remind her of my brother." Martha Williams handed her coat to the general who hung it on a wall peg.

"Yes," General Lee stammered. "Too soon."

"I'll talk to Agnes later. How is Mother Lee?"

"Upstairs. She is in much pain and quite debilitated," the weary soldier sighed. "But how she does manage to bear up for the rest of us."

"That would be her way," Martha said warmly. She rubbed her raw hands together.

"You must be freezing, Markie. Come in by the fire." General Lee escorted the 37-year-old woman to the parlor hearth where she sat close to the fire. General Lee pulled his chair close to hers until their knees almost touched before the hearth.

"That's better," Martha said. The firelight twinkled in her eyes. General Lee studied the new lines around her eyes, the only telltale signs of approaching middle-age on an otherwise youthful face.

Martha Custis Williams was the great granddaughter of Martha Washington. Born in 1826, she was the orphaned daughter of Mrs. Lee's first cousin. She had spent her life as part of the Lee clan. When visiting Arlington House, Martha Williams lived in Lee's daughter Mary's room. Her younger brother Orton had courted Agnes before the war. Agnes had loved her cousin Orton and he, her. But a Yankee rope had snapped Orton's neck six months before this December evening.

"I heard you were in Richmond with the family. So I just took my chances that it was true." Martha spoke toward General Lee's kind face.

"Yes. I am here for some rather nasty business." The General turned to the fire.

"Politics?" the woman asked.

"Perhaps. I am to be court martialed for our failure in Pennsylvania." The words caused him physical pain. "It is supposed to be confidential as not to demoralize our brave men in the field. But secrets in Richmond have a way of growing wings, you know. I expect to see this affair on the front page of the *Sentinel* any day."

"Court martialed!" Martha nearly shouted with disbelief. "But you *are* the army of Virginia!"

"Other men wiser than I will determine if I am worthy."

Martha Williams held her hands toward the fire.

"This war, Cousin Robert, has made monsters out of good men. And so much sadness."

"Yes, Markie. It has broken many ties among families and between old friends."

Martha's life, too, was touched by the ironies of fraternal warfare. Her brother had been hanged by the Yankees in June as a Rebel spy. General Ulysses Grant who had captured Chattanooga only three weeks before this night had a personal connection to Martha Williams. During the Mexican War in September 1846, Martha's father was mortally wounded while he served like Robert Lee in General Zachary Taylor's Corps of Engineers. While Martha's father lay dying thousands of miles from home, young Lieutenant Grant sat by his bedside to comfort the dying soldier.

"Oh, my Markie," Lee sighed, "I have thought of you constantly." Robert Lee had loved his cousin Martha Williams since she was in her teens. From dozens of nameless outposts and God-forsaken wastelands, he had poured out his heart to her by mail. His affection and intimacy with Martha, 20 years his junior, was none the less for never having touched her. He loved her as another daughter, as secret confidant, as trusted friend.

"I have missed you too, Cousin Robert. I have written when I could. But who knows what letters have gotten through to you these last two years? But I have tried." She smiled at him.

"The pleasure of your company is even better than your letters!" the soldier said firmly with his face aglow by the fire.

"Thank you, Robert. But with me in New York City and you and the girls—my only living family now—being chased by the Yankees all over Virginia, the distance between us seems overwhelming. And with Annie gone now, I fear that I am an orphan all over again." Her parents were 20 years dead. Martha Williams wiped a tear from her eye. "It is Christmastime, and the whole world seems ugly and full of suffering." She turned her red eyes toward the general. "Oh, Cousin Robert, will we ever be together in peace again? A family again? Will the new year end the madness?"

"With the return of a new year," General Lee smiled, "my mind reverts to you with fresh pleasure. Although so distant, you are often present in my thoughts and you always come to brighten reminiscences of the past."

"I'm glad I could do something for you," Martha said softly. "But it all seems so little now. Orton is dead and cousin Rooney is a prisoner."

"Cheer up, Markie, your favorite second cousin will return loaded with honors. Nor is there any danger of him exchanging the laurels of the North for the willows of the South."

Martha Williams nodded with a grave expression upon her fine face.

"I pray that be so, Cousin Robert."

General Lee studied Martha's face for a long moment. In the firelight, new lines of care creased at the corners of her eyes. Her always cheerful face was newly darkened by the war which had touched her so closely. In a single moment, both she and Agnes Lee had been wounded grievously. But Agnes, at age 22, and 15 years younger than her cousin Martha, had been less strong to bear the sudden losses of both sister Annie and cousin Orton Williams. Upstairs, Agnes sobbed softly into her pillow while her father and Orton's sister quietly grieved before the hearth.

Annie had been 20 months older than her sister Agnes. They were like twins growing up. At Arlington House, they had shared a bedroom and to their father they were always "the girls," spoken of in the same breath. They were especially close during General Lee's tenure as superintendent at West Point, ten years earlier. Just entering their teens then, Annie and Agnes shared treasured moments of gossiping about which thin, youthful cadet was the handsomest. They knew as boys Jeb Stuart, distant cousin Stephen Lee now a Rebel major general fighting in the deep south, John Pegram now a brigadier general in Lee's army, General William Dorsey Pender who died at age 29 from wounds received at Gettysburg where he wore the gray and was loved by all, and Oliver Howard who was now a

Yankee major general who saw action at Chancellorsville. Part of Agnes was buried 14 months earlier with sister Annie.

During 1857, when Agnes was 16, the first love of her life was Martha's brother Orton. They had courted on horseback through the Virginia hills. When war came, Orton returned when duty permitted to continue his courtship of the beautiful Agnes Lee. On their happiest furlough, he had managed to spend Christmas 1862 at the Lee farm, Hickory Hill, north of Richmond.

That was exactly one year ago. Then, perhaps to impress his Agnes, on June 8, 1863, Orton went behind Union lines where he wore a Federal uniform to conceal his identity. He and another Confederate rode into the camp of the 85th Indiana Infantry near Franklin, Tennessee. He was discovered, tried by a midnight military court, convicted of spying at three in the morning, and hanged four hours later. The death sentence was ordered by Ohio's Brigadier General Rutherford B. Hayes, a future President. Orton Williams died at age 24. He was executed the same day Rooney Lee fell wounded at Brandy Station.

Hours before his death, Orton was allowed to pen a farewell letter to his older sister, Martha. He wrote of his father's death during the Mexican War: "I will meet my death with the same fortitude becoming the son of a man whose last words to his children were: 'Tell them I died at the head of my column.'" Markie had given the treasured letter to her cousin Agnes.

A tear rolled down Martha's face. She did not brush it away. General Lee studied her sad face.

"Dearest Markie."

"Oh, God," Martha sniffed, "how could those barbarians have killed my brother like that? Like an animal, not like a soldier!"

General Lee's reddish face hardened. His hands came down hard upon his knees when he spoke with anger in his deep voice. "My blood boils at the thought of the atrocious outrage against every manly and Christian sentiment which the great God alone is able to forgive!"

Martha turned toward the general. She looked startled at his sudden display of his famous temper.

"Cousin Robert, I know now that I shall never marry. I can see no point in it when either death by nature or by cruelty is the only certain end to love." There was physical pain in her quivering voice.

"You must not say you will never marry. It may be proper as well as becoming in you to marry one of these days. If you determine now 'never to marry,' it may make it difficult to you to do so." Robert Lee smiled with his eyes full of love for his treasured Markie. "I am certain that no one would make a better wife than you, Markie."

The woman smiled at her white-haired cousin, aged well beyond his years. She returned his love in kind and had done so freely for twenty years.

"Now, Markie, I must go up to Agnes. Her poor heart is broken and there is so little I can do for her." The father looked tired and anguished. He rose and his knees cracked with the effort. "She loves you, I know. But seeing you is like seeing Orton. Her pain is intense."

Martha Williams rose and she looked up into her cousin's weary eyes. Without words, she took the step into his arms and hugged him for an instant.

"Old age and sorrow are wearing me away," he whispered into her hair.

"If there were anyone in this world I would do anything for, it would be you and Mother Lee." She smiled as best she could with her heart full of love for Robert Lee and grief for her dead brother Orton.

"There is nothing, my dear Markie, that I want except to see you; and nothing that you can do for me except to think of me and love me."

Markie Williams watched Robert Lee walk slowly from the parlor past the darkened window. Tears were streaming down her face as she listened to his heavy footsteps upon the stairs in the hallway.

Chapter Five

Saturday, December 12, 1863

The contest must be long and severe, and the
whole country has to go through much suffering.
Robert E. Lee

*R*ichmond was more than the capital city of the Confederate States
of America. It was also the South's greatest brothel.

Lonely, ragged men by the tens of thousands marched daily
through the dirt streets of Richmond. Far from the little farmsteads
of home, separated from hearth and kin for the first time, all aware
of the weekly casualty lists posted on newspaper bulletin boards,
these hungry doomed men found their way to seedy Locust Alley and
its legendary cathouses. Johnny Worsham's saloon and whorehouse
was within spitting distance of the Confederate capitol building.

General Lee and his honor guard of four troopers steered clear of
Locust Alley as they rode at a walk down Broad Street at noon. With
the national and state governments shut down for the weekend, the
streets were nearly deserted. Soldiers on furlough raised their hats
when the general passed. General Lee nodded warmly to the lean
men who were either on leave from his army, were part of the
Richmond home guard, or were wounded convalescents from the

city's dozens of makeshift hospitals. Not until the general was well out of sight did many of the men make their way to Locust Alley and its welcome relief from war in the form of cheap whiskey, called "Oh Be Joyful," and painted women. The teenagers in gray called the ladies' work "horizontal dancing."

When General Lee dismounted, he handed Traveller's reins to a trooper, exchanged pleasantries with his escort, and walked quickly into the Powhatan Hotel.

In the large lobby, General Lee was greeted by Lieutenant General A.P. Hill, commander of III Corps. General Hill looked thin and his hazel eyes were deeply sunken behind his red beard. He wore one of his famous calico "battle shirts" sewn by his wife Dolly. When at ease, Hill enjoyed a good pipe and he transferred the warm briar to his left hand as he reached out with his right hand for General Lee's firm grip.

"Good morning, General," Hill smiled warmly.

"And to you," Lee nodded. He enjoyed the thin general who had saved the army at Sharpsburg beside Antietam Creek at the last possible minute.

"I appreciate your courtesy call," Hill said as he escorted Lee to a secluded corner of the spacious lobby. The few guests and uniformed men milling about gave the two officers wide privacy for their chat.

"Well, I want my staff to know how much I appreciate their support here next week." General Lee seemed uneasy as he shifted his gray, slouch hat from one knee to the other where he sat stiffly. "I just hope the Federals continue to permit us to have so much of the general staff away from the field."

"It is our pleasure, General," Hill nodded. "Believe me."

The corps commander was pale and tired. He looked much older than his 38 years. Hill's birthday had been four weeks earlier. A lifetime of illness had weakened him gravely. When at his peak of personal strength, he could be a vigorous fighter. But when disease haunted his gaunt face, he seemed to fade away as he had done at Gettysburg where he played little part in the last two days of battle.

The diseases so much a part of soldiering lingered long in his frail body.

In 1855 during his career in the Old Army, he had been stationed in the disease ridden tropics of Florida. He suffered grievously from an outbreak of yellow fever. He had to be sent home to Virginia to recover. The fever severely complicated the chronic prostatitis from which he had suffered since he was 18 years old. During a furlough from West Point in 1844, Hill contracted gonorrhea during a young cadet's weekend lark. He suffered for twenty years for his momentary respite from the dreary Point.

Hill made friends at West Point whose names would become household words. During his first year 1842-1843, his roommate was a 16-year-old boy from Philadelphia, George McClellan. His other close friends at the Point included George Pickett and Jesse Reno from Wheeling, western Virginia. When war came, Reno stayed with the Union and advanced to a generalship commanding IX Corps of McClellan's army. During the opening skirmishes of the Antietam campaign in the mountains three days before the Battle of Sharpsburg, Jesse Reno was killed in action and was mourned as a good soldier by friend and foe alike.

Another classmate was Ambrose Burnside who led his battered regiments in blue upon a daring assault against a bloody bridge at Sharpsburg. From that September 1862 afternoon, the bridge would be known forever as Burnside's Bridge.

Hill became the only member of the Point's class of '47 who saw action in Mexico during that dirty, little war where so many future generals won their spurs. He suffered miserably during an 1847 outbreak of typhoid fever. After Mexico, young Hill had courted beautiful Ellen Marcy. But he lost her hand to his West Point classmate and close friend George McClellan.

Having lost at love once, Hill did not lose again. Ten years after Mexico, he met a red-haired girl who was a widow at the tender age of 23, Kitty McClung. Ambrose Powell was in love instantly. Two years later, in July 1859, he married his beloved Kitty whom he adored as his "Dolly." She was eight years his junior.

When the Union came unglued two years after his marriage, Hill stayed with his native Virginia. In May 1861, he became a colonel in the 13th Virginia Infantry, leading 700 raw recruits. The young colonel enjoyed the full support of his Dolly—she made the regiment's first battleflag out of her wedding dress.

No officer took better care of his men than A.P. Hill and his troops were grateful. During the war's opening skirmishes along the Virginia peninsula in the spring of 1862, Hill led his new brigade into action. In April, at Louisa Court House, Virginia, Hill had reached into his own pocket and bought a welcomed shot of whiskey for every soldier in his command to warm them after a rain-soaked march through cold mud.

"You look tired, General," Hill now said gently to his weary chief in the comfortable lobby.

"I have suffered a good deal of pain in my chest, back and arms. The doctors are very attentive." General Lee smiled at A.P. Hill. "They have been tapping me all over like an old steam boiler before condemning it."

Hill smiled back. It was good to see General Lee's cheer creep over his wornout face.

"Well, General," Powell Hill nodded, "with Christmas just about upon us, our thoughts can turn for a while to better times. We can only pray that the war will end this spring."

General Lee shrugged.

"The contest," Lee said with resignation upon his dark face, "must be long and severe, and the whole country has to go through much suffering."

"Perhaps," Hill nodded. "Much depends upon the will of the Southern people. Their spirit of sacrifice will determine the success of our forces in the field."

"Indeed," General Lee said firmly. "Our people are so hard to control that it is difficult to get them to follow any course not in accordance with their inclinations." He shook his white head as if his thoughts disappointed himself.

"Yes, General. And the cost in blood among the officers and men cannot be paid forever." Hill's thin face darkened behind his reddish beard. "I am thinking of the deaths of Generals Cobb and Gregg."

A promising Georgia lawyer, Thomas Cobb was killed at age 39 at Fredericksburg. General Maxcy Gregg, the staunch secessionist from South Carolina, was wounded at Sharpsburg under Hill's command but lived to die at Fredericksburg in December 1862. He was 49.

General Lee thought about Cobb and Gregg. "The Confederacy has lost two of its noblest citizens and the army two of its bravest and most distinguished officers. The death of such a man as General Gregg is a costly sacrifice."

"Yes, General," Hill sighed. "And Dorsey Pender, too. I know what you thought of him."

"The loss of Major General Pender," Lee sighed heavily, "is severely felt by the army and the country. He served this army from the beginning of the war and took a distinguished part in all its engagements." Lee looked at the floor. He keenly felt the loss of the 29-year-old officer, mortally wounded at Gettysburg. "His promise and usefulness as an officer were only equaled by the purity and excellence of his private life."

When General Lee rose slowly, Hill followed. Lee looked much larger than his subordinate who shuffled and appeared thin to the point of being fragile.

"At least you know," Hill said, "that your general staff is behind you and with you to the last man."

"I cannot tell you how much that means to me," General Lee smiled.

The two men shook hands and General Lee walked from the lobby of the hotel. Only when the white haired chief stepped into the sunshine did conversation again buzz through the foyer. Hill turned and headed upstairs. He walked slowly like a man with pain deep in his belly.

In the cold air, General Lee stroked Traveller's black mane. The tall horse rubbed its nose against Lee's shoulder. Lee smiled at his faithful warhorse. When the general's orderlies approached, General

Lee waved them off. He had one more stop to make in downtown Richmond.

General Lee walked across Capitol Street toward the Virginia statehouse, now the seat of the government of the Confederate States of America. With pain in his chest, Lee climbed Capitol Hill and entered the imposing building beneath great marble pillars.

On a cold Saturday afternoon, the statehouse was nearly empty of government workers. Lee entered the deserted chamber of the Confederate House of Representatives. All about him were the somber portraits of Virginia's founding fathers and the sons of Virginia who had become Presidents of the now ruptured Union. He removed his gray slouch hat, stood quietly, and thought about his ancestors. They included three governors of Virginia, three members of the foundling nation's Continental Congress 80 years earlier, three United States congressmen, and five of Virginia's seven signers of the Declaration of Independence.

General Lee's mind wandered through the whirlwind of the last 32 months.

In February 1861, Lieutenant Colonel Lee bivouacked with the United States Cavalry in distant San Antonio, Texas. With disunion looming, Lee was summoned to Washington. He arrived across the Potomac at his Arlington House on March 1st. The day he was ordered home, February 13th, the Virginia Constitutional Convention had taken its first test vote on secession. By one vote, the Convention voted to remain loyal to the Union.

Struggling to avoid civil war, Virginia sent three delegates to Washington to meet the new President on April 9, 1861. They went secretly to discuss avoiding war by political compromise. They met President Lincoln April 12th. "You are too late," the sad face of the doomed President reported. The Rebels had fired on Fort Sumter that very dawn. Three days later, President Lincoln called for 75,000 volunteers to bring the seceded Southern states back into the Union at bayonet point. On April 17th, Virginia voted for secession. Robert Lee then began the most anguished three days of his life.

On April 17, 1861, Lee received a secret note from Federal

general-in-chief, Winfield Scott. Lee was summoned to meet the next day with Francis Blair, Sr., Mr. Lincoln's private emissary to Lee.

On April 18th, Lee left Arlington House for Washington and the Blair residence at 1651 Pennsylvania Avenue, across from the State, War, and Navy Building a block from the White House. Blair offered Colonel Lee command of the Union armies taking the field to crush the rebellion. Lee declined and went to pay his respects to his lifelong friend and mentor, 75-year-old General Scott, who had held the post of general-in-chief for 20 years. When Lee informed General Scott of his decision to resign from the Army to return to Virginia, Scott sadly informed Lee that the Virginian was making the worst mistake of his life.

The next day, the new Provisional Army of the Confederate States of America laid siege to the vital Federal arsenal at Harper's Ferry, Virginia. An eccentric Rebel commander named Tom Jackson took command of the Harper's Ferry garrison on April 30th. Joe Johnston took command of the garrison three weeks later.

On April 19th, Lee drafted his formal letter of resignation from the Old Army which had been his home and his life for thirty years. The letter was hand-delivered to General Scott the next day. On the 22nd, Lee had gone to Richmond where Virginia Governor John Letcher offered Lee a commission as major general in the new Virginia Militia. The next day, Major General Lee was introduced to the Virginia Constitutional Convention. By May 10, 1861, Lee also had a commission as brigadier general in the Provisional Army of the Confederate States. To the soldier standing alone in the House chamber, it all seemed like a lifetime ago.

"Good afternoon, General Lee."

Lee was startled. He turned to see President Jefferson Davis standing tall and thin in the doorway. Holding the President's hand was his son, Joseph, almost five years old. The little boy had five months to live. In his free hand, little Joseph held Stonewall, his sister Margaret's kitten.

"Mr. President...I was just...."

"I know, General. Me too."

The two men smiled as the child fidgeted with the kitten.

"We have all come a long way," Davis said softly, "from our days at West Point." The President's facial muscles twitched with chronic pain. But his smile was genuine as his face warmed to memories of his troubled youth at the Point.

General Lee and President Davis had been students together at West Point.

Cadet Davis had arrived at West Point in 1824 at age 16. That same year—his plebe year—he was arrested for frequenting Benny Haven's—the Point's legendary and off-limits saloon. Two years later, Cadet Davis was arrested again on Christmas Eve for drinking and partying. Barely escaping court martial and expulsion, Davis managed to graduate in 1828, number 23 in a class of 32 cadets.

Cadet Davis was court martialed at West Point at least three times. He once spent six weeks under arrest. When he finally graduated, he ranked 163rd in conduct out of the entire cadet corps of only 208. His trouble with regimentation never stopped. He resigned from the Army in 1835 after being acquitted of insubordination at still another court martial.

Cadet Lee's record at West Point had been different. Lee was the first cadet in the Point's 27-year history to graduate with zero demerits. In his senior year, 1828-1829, he was appointed corps adjutant, the Point's highest academic honor.

"A long way from the Point," General Lee smiled warmly.

"I know, General, that casting your lot with us was no easy decision. And I am grateful, indeed thankful, that you did." The President's faith and affection for Robert Lee was abiding and constant.

General Lee turned his back upon the President and the soldier studied the great hall all around them. He spoke toward the ceiling in a deep and somber voice.

"You cannot imagine the struggle it has cost me to separate myself from a service to which I devoted all of the best years of my life and all the ability I possessed. During the whole of that time, more than

30 years, I had experienced nothing but kindness from my superiors and a most cordial friendship from my companions." Lee sighed deeply. "Save in defense of my native state, I never desire to again draw my sword."

"I understand, General." Davis looked into Lee's dark eyes. "Would you do Varina and me the honor of joining us for dinner?"

"I would love to, Mr. President, but I must continue on my way. I shall not have much time next week, I fear. I must still stop by Charlotte's, my daughter-in-law's." Lee's voice choked. "She is quite frail and very ill with sickness and with grief."

"I understand that, too, General." When President Davis spoke, his painful face showed deep anguish. He knew that Charlotte's husband, Lee's son Rooney, was a Federal prisoner. And the President knew about grief. When Davis' first wife died after three months of marriage, Davis mourned for eight bitter years. After marrying again to Varina, they waited seven years for a child. Their son Samuel was born in 1852 only to die from yellow fever or measles at age two. President Pierce had come to the funeral of his war secretary's child. Davis still mourned. "I know, General, what it is like to grieve for a child."

The President cleared his throat as if he had something else on his tired mind.

"General Lee, you know very well what a near mutiny I had on my hands in Tennessee last month. A dozen of General Bragg's general officers begged me to relieve him even before Missionary Ridge. Your General Longstreet was among them."

Lee nodded gravely, disappointed that Old Pete had joined the disarray of Bragg's disintegrating command. Longstreet had been detached to Tennessee when Bragg begged for reinforcements to fight Grant.

"General, if you would consent to taking over the Army of Tennessee, a great weight would be lifted from me. I do not want to send General Johnston. I have my reasons. General Beauregard is even more objectionable to me as a substitute for General Bragg. Could you go west? I would not send you without your approval."

Robert Lee scanned the walls where portraits of his forefathers glared down at him and Jefferson Davis.

"Mr. President, unless it is intended that I should take permanent command, I can see no good that will result, even if in that event any could be accomplished. I also fear that I would not receive cordial cooperation. I have not the confidence either in my strength or ability as would lead me of my own option to undertake the command in question."

The officer sounded as if he had rehearsed the reply more than once.

"Well, General, let's just hope that Wigfall, Foote and company leave us both the option to choose such things freely."

Lee nodded.

When little Joseph laughed happily, Lee and his President were grateful to have the boy break the sudden gloom of memories and of burdens to come.

General Lee excused himself, bowed to Davis, and shook the happy child's hand.

Outside in the brilliant sunlight of afternoon, Lee mounted Traveller. The cold horse was anxious to break into a trot but General Lee reined him into a walk.

★　　　★　　　★

General Lee and his escorts did not ride far through the deserted streets of Richmond. Cold, damp weather kept citizens huddled snugly in their homes. As the small party of mounted men rode slowly from the capitol building, the only activity in town was marked by billowing, black smoke rising from the narrow finger of land between the Kanawha Canal and the James River south of Richmond. There, only half a mile east of Hollywood Cemetery, sat the great stone fortress of the Tredegar Iron Works.

The massive structures of Tredegar covered five acres. Twenty percent of Richmond's laborers worked there side by side with 1,200 slaves at the Confederacy's only smelter of artillery pieces. All of the

South's cannon came out of the great forges and furnaces of Tredegar which blackened the sky seven days a week.

The column stopped at one of Richmond's houses where weary civilians took what solace they could from the grim resolve of war. Dismounting, General Lee handed Traveller's reins to an orderly who stamped his feet on the frozen ground to keep his toes from freezing.

Lee climbed the steps to the landing of the home where his daughter-in-law lay near death. After a brief exchange of pleasantries, the owner led the general to Charlotte's room. The mistress of the house left the soldier alone at Charlotte's door.

"Papa!" The fragile woman in bed smiled weakly when General Lee entered softly.

"Child," he stammered. He pulled a chair close to the bedside. Charlotte Wickham Lee's pale face filled with color when General Lee held her bony hands tightly. For a long moment, they held hands in silence.

General Lee had known Charlotte since she was a child. Her grandfather was General Lee's uncle. General Lee had privately objected to Charlotte's marriage to his son Rooney, then only 22 in 1859. "They are both mere children," the worried father had written to his wife. But now, he had taken Charlotte into his heart where his own daughters lived. Charlotte was always particularly close to her sister-in-law Agnes Lee. At 23, Charlotte was only one year older than Agnes.

Charlotte stirred and opened her eyes.

"Your face, Papa? I have missed it so very much."

"I now have a beautiful white beard," General Lee labored to smile cheerfully. "It is much admired. At least, much remarked on."

"Oh, I like your whiskers," the thin woman smiled. "If only our Fitzhugh could be here with us now," she sighed. "All would then be well." She closed her moist eyes but did not let go of her father-in-law's hands.

Lee smiled and his voice was a whisper when he looked down at the sickly woman.

"I cannot bear to think of you except as I have always known you: bright, joyous and happy. You may think of Fitzhugh and love him as much as you please. But do not grieve over him or grow sad."

So desperate was Charlotte's fading health that General Lee's eldest son, Custis, 31, had offered the Federal authorities to take his brother Rooney's place in prison for 48 hours over Christmas so Rooney could be at Charlotte's deathbed. But the Yankees had refused the exchange.

Rooney had first been imprisoned at Fort Monroe, Virginia, on Chesapeake Bay. General Lee helped build it and his eldest son Custis had been born there in September 1832 when his father was with the Corps of Engineers after West Point.

"How I grieve for my Rooney—my sweet Fitzhugh." Charlotte did not open her eyes. A tear rolled down her ashen cheek. General Lee struggled to keep his iron composure.

"I can see no harm that can result from Fitzhugh's capture, except his detention," the general said cheerfully. "I feel assured that he will be well attended to. He will be in the hands of Old Army officers and surgeons, most of whom are men of principle and humanity."

Charlotte's hot tears fell freely. She pulled the general's hands to her chin and her tears rolled down his wrists.

"My dear husband—gone. And my babies—gone. It has been exactly a year since my little girl was taken from us....Oh, Papa!" Charlotte was whimpering like a child for her own child.

"I was so grateful at her birth," the grandfather sighed, blinking hard. "I felt that she would be such a comfort to you and such a pleasure to my dear Fitzhugh." General Lee squeezed her small hands in his. "But you have now two sweet angels in heaven. May God give you strength."

General Lee released her deathgrip on his hands. He gently stroked her damp forehead. Charlotte Lee closed her eyes and the oil lamp light flickered upon her white skin pulled tightly over bone.

For many minutes, the weary soldier stroked Charlotte's face, brushing the matted hair from her eyes.

"It's so cold, Papa," she whispered from the edge of sleep.

The old man pulled the blanket up to her chin. The woman was sleeping before he could speak.

"Summer returns when I see you," General Lee wept softly.

Outside the little window above the bed, snow fell lightly in the gray shadows of late afternoon.

★   ★   ★

The pale winter sun was low in the west by the time General Lee handed the reins of Traveller to an orderly. The windows of the house on Leigh Street glowed from fire light when General Lee entered the front door. Mildred greeted her father with a long hug. He handed her his coat and wet flakes of snow chilled her fingers.

"Mama is in the kitchen," Mildred smiled.

"I missed you, Precious Life." His face carried the sadness of Charlotte's bedside.

"You saw Cousin Charlotte, Papa?"

"Yes. She is very weak."

"Oh. Perhaps Christmas will cheer her?"

"I hope so, Life."

Mildred took her father's coat. The general entered the front parlor to warm himself by the fireplace. He saw Agnes sitting alone beside the cozy hearth.

"Evening, Wiggie," the general bowed to kiss the top of her head.

"Papa," Agnes smiled. Eleanor Agnes Lee was named for the older sister of Mrs. Lee's father.

General Lee pulled a chair close to Agnes. They sat together close to the warm fireplace. Agnes was silent and pensive. Her beautiful face rarely had smiled since Orton's June execution.

"What are you thinking about?" the general asked gently.

"Home," she said softly.

"Yes."

"I long for Arlington," Agnes whispered. "My precious Arlington, my own dear home."

"Perhaps, one day, we shall all see Arlington again, Wig." General Lee's ruddy cheeks above his white beard reflected the crackling fire.

"Dear, dear Arlington," Agnes said in a voice so soft the general could hardly hear her. "How I miss it. How I miss it."

"I know, child. We do have our wonderful memories of the place. And remember, we had perfect times at other homes." The soldier nodded toward the fire. "Do you remember West Point? You were only 14 when we left."

"Dear West Point," Agnes smiled, "the beautiful mountains, the deep rocky Hudson with its pure dark waters, the fresh mountain air, the buildings, the band, the parades," Agnes closed her eyes as vivid memories flooded into her mind, "the people—down to the very flagstaff and sidewalk."

"That's better," General Lee smiled. His teenage daughters especially had loved the dinners when Superintendent Lee would have a few handsome cadets over on Saturday nights. Those happy evenings ten years ago were called "he dinners." When the Lees' posting to West Point ended in the spring of 1855, the Cadet Corps chorus had serenaded the Lee home with the sadly sweet melodies of "Home Sweet Home" and "Carry Me Back to Old Virginy."

"I had no idea," Agnes smiled, "I would regret leaving it so much....If I could only hear the band once more."

"I know, Wig."

A crash of china from the dining room startled the general who rose quickly. His first thought was that wheelchair bound Mrs. Lee had taken a fall.

In the small dining area, General Lee glared at a broken glass and rumpled napkins.

"Life!" the general called to Mildred.

Mildred Childe Lee ran downstairs and into the dining room. She was breathless when she arrived at her father's side.

"Papa! What is it? Is Mama alright?"

General Lee pointed his hard hand toward the window sill. On the sill sat a red-tailed squirrel. The renegade rodent was Mildred's long-time pet pirated from Arlington. She called the animal Custis

Morgan in honor of her brother Custis and General John Hunt Morgan, one of the South's great cavalrymen.

"I'm sorry, Papa," Mildred laughed.

"I fear that he will give some of the family a terrible bite before he is dispatched." The general struggled to remain angry at Mildred's side. "It is their nature and they become more vicious with age. I recommend he be confined to his cage or be dismissed." A faint smile broke within the white beard while Custis Morgan scratched at the dirty window and the evening shadows beyond.

"Mama is in the kitchen," Mildred pleaded. "Please don't tell her about the broken glass. I'll clean it up. Oh, please Papa."

"Keep Custis Morgan out of her sight!" Lee said firmly. "If you would immerse his head under water for five minutes in one of his daily baths, it would relieve him and you of infinite trouble."

"Oh, Papa," Mildred laughed. She retrieved the squirrel from the window and the little animal cuddled in her arms. "He's so sweet. You know you don't mean that!"

"Just keep him away from your mother. I know you will make the correct decision about that little beast."

"But that is not always easy, Papa." The girl was sullen as she stroked Custis Morgan's neck.

"You have only always to do what is right," General Lee said softly. "It will become easier by practice." He had to smile.

Mildred held the squirrel in one hand while she scooped up the broken glass with the other hand. She carefully put the pieces of glass into the pocket on her frock.

"The squirrel! Again!" called Mrs. Lee as she wheeled herself from the kitchen into the dining room. "What will our daughters do next?" Mildred quickly made her escape with Custis Morgan in her arms and her pocket full of glass. General Lee watched her retreat and a smile lighted his weary face.

"Our precious girls," Mother Lee smiled to her husband.

"Mildred has it in her power," the old soldier smiled, "to give them a great treat: squirrel soup thickened with peanuts!" The general touched his wife's hand. "Custis Morgan in such an exit from the stage would cover himself with glory."

"Glory indeed," Mrs. Lee laughed. "Push me back to the kitchen and dinner will be ready directly....Glory."

In the tiny kitchen where the woodburning stove sputtered, the general and his lady shared a private moment. The window was now dark with December night.

"How is Agnes?" Mother Lee inquired softly.

"Sad. She spoke again of Arlington."

"I know, Robert. I think she misses that place as much as I do." Mrs. Lee laid her head against General Lee's waist where he stood beside her wheelchair. She blinked back a tear as the Arlington house filled her own thoughts.

Mother Lee was raised at Arlington. All of its history and beauty were her childhood memories. Now, it was gone, perhaps forever. When she was 15 years old, the Revolutionary hero Lafayette had stayed overnight at Arlington as her father's guest. As a young woman, she was courted there briefly by a young Congressman from the new state of Texas, Sam Houston. After marrying her handsome Lieutenant Lee, Mrs. Lee remained at Arlington for much of her childbearing years while her soldier-husband was at his distant outposts with the army. The rose gardens she tended at Arlington were famous throughout eastern Virginia and Washington City just down river.

General Lee felt a warm tear upon his hand.

"I know, Molly," he said softly as he stroked her white hair by his side. "Our Arlington memories are happy and sad, all at the same time."

"Yes, Robert. And now the Federals are burying their dead beside my parents." She clutched the soldier's hand to her face. "Beside my mother's grave."

Mary Lee's mother had died in Arlington house in April 1853. The Lee children adored their Grandmother Custis. When the old lady died, the Lee daughters, little Mary age seven and Annie age nine, were cuddling in bed with her. General Lee remembered Grandmother Custis like a mother.

"Her illness was short: one day in the garden with her flowers, the next with her God," the general said sadly of his mother-in-law. "Her lamp was always brightly burning and she breathed her last repeating the Lord's Prayer....We have lost a dear friend."

"And dear, dear father," Mary Lee sighed. General Lee was also very close with his father-in-law who was the father Lee never had as a boy.

"He had been to me all a father could," the general remembered of George Washington Parke Custis.

"All gone," Mother Lee wept. "All gone."

Federal troops had seized Arlington plantation during the first month of the war, on May 23, 1861, when some 13,000 Yankees under General Irvin McDowell invaded the estate. At the time, Mrs. Lee and her daughters had fled to the Lee homestead of Ravensworth. From there, Mrs. Lee penned an angry protest to Federal General-in-Chief Winfield Scott. She wrote that she had abandoned Arlington only to keep Robert from worrying about her if she fell into Yankee hands. "Were it not that I would not add one feather to his load of care, nothing would induce me to abandon my home." Mother Lee signed her letter to family friend General Scott, "Yours in sorrow and sadness."

One week after Arlington fell to the Federals, Mrs. Lee demanded by letter that she be permitted to return unmolested to Arlington to gather her personal effects and family relics of George Washington. She was furious when she wrote to General Charles Sandford, Arlington's occupier, on May 30, 1861: "It never occurred to me, Gen'l Sandford, that I could be forced to sue for permission to enter my own house and that such an outrage as its military occupation to the exclusion of me and my children could ever have been perpetrated."

Ever a gentleman, General McDowell responded instantly to Mrs. Lee's letter with a reply signed the same day as Mrs. Lee's protest to General Sandford. McDowell wrote Mrs. Lee that "When you desire to return, every facility will be given you for doing so. I trust, Madam, you will not consider it an intrusion when I say I have the most sincere sympathy for your distress, and, so far as compatible with my duty, I shall always be ready to do whatever may alleviate it."

"It is better to make up our minds to a general loss," the Robert Lee said sadly. "They cannot take away the remembrance of the spot, and the memories of those that to us rendered it sacred....That will remain to us as long as life will last, and that...we can preserve."

The old couple said nothing for many minutes while they listened to the crackling of the stove.

"How I grieve for sweet Charlotte," Mother Lee said.

General Lee added softly. "And particularly for our dear son whose sorrow under the circumstances will be inexpressibly grievous." He trembled with anger at Rooney's imprisonment. "I now long to see him more and more and wish I could communicate with him without affording to his jailers the opportunity of rejoicing in his misery." The father spoke through clenched teeth.

"Yes, Robert. Last year we lost our dear Annie. And now, God will take another daughter from us. At least Charlotte has always had our love." Mother Lee looked up into her husband's anguished face. Tears welled in General Lee's eyes.

"I feel for her all the love I bear Fitzhugh....I loved them as one person." He could hardly get out the words.

General Lee knelt down in the cramped kitchen, a world removed from the palatial splendor of Arlington house.

"We have each other, Robert. Now and forever," Mother Lee said firmly.

When Robert Lee spoke, his soft voice was a terrible mixture of grief and anger. His moist eyes glistened with helplessness.

"I spend many anxious hours reflecting on your suffering condition and my inability to aid or tend you and my dear daughters."

Lee was down on one knee in front of Mrs. Lee who sat between the wooden wheels of her rolling chair. Her husband laid his wind-burned face in her lap and she stroked his thinning white hair.

The kitchen and the popping stove filled the house on Leigh Street with the sweet smells of home and of another time and place.

Chapter Six

Sunday, December 13, 1863

We are in a state of war which will yield nothing.
Robert E. Lee

Sunday morning dawned with a hint of warming in the air. Snow melting from the eaves of the house sounded like rain on the windows. A trace of clouds rose into a clear sky on the first anniversary of the Battle of Fredericksburg where the Army of Northern Virginia nearly decimated the Army of the Potomac.

At mid-morning, General Lee stood beside Agnes on the front porch. Most of the light snow melted during the night and the air felt like springtime 12 days before Christmas 1863.

Father and daughter turned their heads toward the corner of Leigh and Second, half a block to the west. They were distracted by the distant rumble of wooden wagons creaking slowly through the layer of melting mud atop the frozen dirt streets.

At the corner, thin draught horses pulled a train of wagons northward along Second. Agnes knew what the wagons meant: ambulances making their way five blocks north toward Shockoe Cemetery. Four wagons were packed with crude wooden boxes bearing the shattered bodies of Southern mothers' sons and husbands for burial. The burial details could not even rest on the Sabbath.

Although the lines on the distant battlefields of Virginia were fairly quiet when both sides went into winter camp, soldiers still struggled with death in Richmond's 34 field hospitals. Perhaps some of the dead men being dragged past the corner were just now dying from long bouts of disease or from wounds long festering since the battles at Sharpsburg, Fredericksburg, Chancellorsville, or Gettysburg.

The city's hospitals filled the capital with horse-drawn ambulances. When the wind was right, the air carried the stench of rotted bandages. The amputated limbs were piled man-high outside the squalid surgery tents. Winder Hospital managed 4,300 beds. The greatest field hospital of the entire war was Chimborazo Hospital on Richmond's outskirts beside the James River. It had 8,000 beds among 120 tents and shacks. Chimborazo's bakery turned out 10,000 loaves of bread every day when flour was available. By war's end, some 78,000 men passed through Chimborazo and 16,000 of them were buried at Oakwood Cemetery.

Jackson Hospital had another 6,000 beds. The city was so desperate for hospital space that many of Richmond's tobacco warehouses were pressed into service to house the ghastly wounded. Moore Hospital at the corner of Main and 23rd Street had been a warehouse. Robertson Hospital had the distinction of being run by a woman, Captain Sally Tompkins—the only female commissioned officer on either side during the war.

Agnes Lee's beautiful face was sadder than usual as her dark eyes watched the funeral procession disappear past the end of the street. "It is so solemn to realize the presence of death," she said softly toward her stone-faced father.

"Do not grieve for the brave dead," Robert Lee said as he thought of the thousands of men who had already died under his own command. "Sorrow for those left behind: friends, relatives, and families. The former are at rest; the latter must suffer."

"I do wish I was a better Christian," she thought aloud with a sigh. "But it is so hard to be one."

"You are just fine, Wig," the soldier smiled as the last wagon went out of sight. "I would not have you any other way." He smiled at the sweet face looking up at him on the porch.

"I am happy for the pride you take in me, Papa," Agnes said gravely. "But alas, it is far, far from being merited."

"Nonsense, child! When Mother, you, and your sisters labor to knit socks and sweaters for our troops in the field, you are doing your fair share indeed."

"Oh, Papa....If I were married to a soldier, I would go off with him to fight the Yankees myself!"

Lee smiled warmly at his dutiful daughter. He placed his firm hands on her thin shoulders and he spoke softly.

"I want all the husbands in the field and their wives at home encouraging them, loving them, and praying for them."

Their warm moment was interrupted by the clatter of wagon wheels again. A second line of wagons rolled slowly toward Shockoe's freshly turned soil.

When Agnes shuddered, her father pulled her close. He wrapped his arms firmly around her. "One of the miseries of war," he sighed in the Sunday morning sunshine, "is that there is no Sabbath."

When the front door creaked open, Martha Williams stepped into the sunshine. A light shawl was wrapped around the 37-year-old spinster's shoulders. Her clear eyes regarded General Lee closely. The look in her eyes went beyond admiration and familial respect. Like the three living Lee daughters, Martha "Markie" Williams could not marry until she met the likes of Robert Lee. The Lee daughters would never marry; Markie would not as long as her cousin Robert lived.

Markie Williams had been part of the Lee household for a lifetime. As a teenager, she had visited young Lieutenant Lee and his bride when the Lees were stationed at Fort Hamilton in New York harbor.

Agnes excused herself, kissed the general on the cheek, and went into the house.

General Lee and Martha Williams stood side by side on the narrow porch. Together, they watched the two sentries marching slowly back and forth in the mud. Markie could not remember a time when she did not love the soldier in the knee-length gray waistcoat. Fifteen years earlier when General Lee was a captain of engineers in Mexico, Markie had sent him dried violets pressed in a letter.

Another wagonload of dead clattered up Second Street. Unconsciously, General Lee rubbed his sore chest where his weary heart ached with angina and grief.

"This cursed war is too much for your heart, Cousin Robert," the woman said softly and sadly.

"If it was not for my heart, Markie," he whispered, thinking of his life as an engineer and builder of bridges, "I might as well be a pile or stone myself, laid quietly at the bottom of the river. But that has no hardness for you and always returns warmth and softness when touched with a thought of you." Robert Lee looked down at the brown sod where the night's rain had melted the snow.

Markie watched the death train disappear half a block away. She thought of all the widows who did not know yet that the loves of their lives were about to be buried in shallow graves. Their widows, children and mothers would go to their windows every day to watch for a thin-faced man or boy to come home down the lane. Forever.

"There is no place for love now." Her voice was cold.

Robert Lee looked into her face for a long, silent moment. She blinked up at the sad eyes which creased at their corners when he smiled lovingly.

"Love is all-powerful," said the commanding general of the Army of Northern Virginia.

The soldier and his cousin turned toward the street when an orderly led an unsaddled horse into the sunshine. The orderly led Traveller by a rope cinched to the tall gray animal's halter. It was

Traveller's morning walk to stretch the horse's legs. General Lee smiled at his trusted mount.

Traveller was four years old when General Lee bought him for $200 in 1861 from Major Thomas Braun of South Carolina. The tall horse was once named Jeff Davis. By the time General Lee bought him, he was named Greenbrier for a county fair race he had twice won as a colt. Lee then named him Traveller.

"If I were an artist like you, I would draw a true picture of Traveller—representing his fine proportions....Such a picture would inspire a poet whose genius could then depict his worth and describe his endurance of toil, hunger, thirst, heat, cold, and the dangers and sufferings through which he passed....He might even imagine his thoughts through the long night marches and days of battle through which he has passed. But," the soldier smiled, "I am no artist. I can only say he is Confederate gray. I purchased him in the mountains of Virginia in the autumn of 1861, and he has been my patient follower ever since—to Georgia, the Carolinas, and back to Virginia. He carried me through the Seven Days battle around Richmond, the second Manassas, at Sharpsburg, Fredericksburg, the last day at Chancellorsville, to Pennsylvania at Gettysburg, and back to the Rappahannock." General Lee smiled down at Martha. "You must know the comfort he is to me!"

Martha and her cousin watched a rider rein in his horse beside the sentries on the street.

The front door burst open with a clatter. Mildred ran into the warm sunshine. Her face brimmed with cheer.

"Chudie!" she called toward the muddy street.

A giant man with a massive black beard dismounted at the curb. Just one month past his 28th birthday, Major General Fitzhugh Lee handed his animal's reins to the orderly. Mildred bounded into the yard and jumped into Fitz Lee's open arms.

"Oh, Chudie!" she called happily. "I knew you would come!"

With his arms around Mildred's shoulders, Fitz Lee mounted the steps and exchanged a warm handshake with his uncle Robert Lee. Fitzhugh Lee was the son of General Lee's brother Sidney Smith Lee who served the Confederate Navy. Fitz was an intimate member of the Lee family circle.

Major General Fitz Lee had always been "Chudie" to his female cousins. Fitz had been a cadet at West Point while General Lee was superintendent during 1853-1855. Chudie Lee had been a major general since August and he led half of Jeb Stuart's cavalry, having seen action at Sharpsburg, Chancellorsville, and Gettysburg. Fitz Lee, West Point '56, was also a close friend of Jeb Stuart and they shared a mutual fondness for good fun.

Cousin Fitz followed Mildred into the house as another rider stopped on the dirt street: Lieutenant Colonel Walter Taylor, adjutant general of the Army of Northern Virginia, arrived after Fitz.

Colonel Taylor greeted General Lee and Martha Williams in the noontime sunshine. He came to wish his general well before the proceedings opened tomorrow. Colonel Taylor, 25, attended Virginia Military Institute at Lexington during 1852-1855. While at VMI, Taylor's professor of artillery was Thomas Jackson who would be the great Stonewall within seven years. Before the war, Taylor was an officer with the Bank of Virginia where he mastered the administrative arts which served him brilliantly as General Lee's primary aide. He had entered the Confederate service in May 1861 and was elevated to lieutenant colonel in October 1863.

"Well, Colonel," General Lee smiled warmly, "it will be my pleasure to entertain such a full and famous table this Sabbath day." General Lee followed Markie into the parlor which was full of happy voices.

With the exception of Annie and Rooney, the Lee family circle was complete on a comfortable Sunday afternoon. Even 32-year-old Custis Lee was released from the service of the President long enough to enjoy an hour with his family. George Washington Custis Lee had graduated first in his class at West Point in 1854 while his father was superintendent. A newly minted brigadier general since June, Custis was denied all of his requests to be relieved from his administerial duties as military aide to President Davis. He itched for the battlefield, but he remained a clerk. Around the table in the small dining room were three General Lees: Robert, his son Custis, and cousin Fitz.

Robert Lee, Jr., sat next to his father. Young Rob was only 20 and had left school to enlist in the Army of Northern Virginia as a private in the Rockbridge Artillery. During the first year of the war, Rob served in Stonewall Jackson's ranks. At the battle of Second Manassas during the summer of 1862, Rob's powder-blackened battery of cannoneers bumped into General Lee and his staff on the battlefield. The general had not recognized the hungry, filthy face of his own son.

At bloody Sharpsburg, General Lee ordered his son's gunners to hold the crumbling gray line at all costs. Rob asked his tired father if the battered artillerymen must go into action again. The general faced his son and answered sadly: "Yes, my son. You must all do what you can."

Shortly after Sharpsburg, Private Lee was promoted to lieutenant in Stonewall Jackson's corps. In June 1863, six months earlier, young Rob was part of the melee at Brandy Station where he saw his brother Rooney gravely wounded. When Rooney was kidnapped by Federals in late June, Rob watched from a hiding place in the bushes while the Yankees dragged his injured brother away under the tearfilled eyes of his own mother and a hysterical Charlotte.

"How do you manage so, Molly?" General Lee smiled across the table to his wife. She had fed her family their Sabbath dinner from pitiful rations and over-priced food. The Federal blockade, the winter, and rampant devaluation of Confederate money all conspired to render shopping almost impossible. Butter was $4 per pound, flour was $37 per barrel, corn was $15 per pound, and the turkey in the middle of the table had cost an outrageous $40. Ordinary apples were $80 per bushel.

The genial conversation turned to politics.

"There just does not seem to be sufficient determination among our people," Lieutenant Colonel Taylor remarked.

"Our people are opposed to work," Robert Lee said with anger rising in his voice. The telltale flush colored the back of his neck.

"Our troops, officers, community and press all ridicule and resist it. It was the very means by which General McClellan advanced. Why should we have left to him the whole advantage of labor? Combined with valor, fortitude, and boldness of which we have our fair proportion, it should lead us to success." With each phrase, the soldier's voice rose in pitch. His right hand tapped the table with each statement. "What carried the Roman soldiers into all countries but this happy combination? The evidences of their labor last to this day. There is nothing so military as labor!"

The general looked sheepishly around the table. Silverware was poised before open mouths.

"I did not mean to cause you distress, General," Walter Taylor smiled weakly. "Politics, I fear, has no place at a Sunday table."

"Colonel Taylor," General Lee smiled warmly, "when I lose my temper, don't you let it make you angry."

Walter Taylor nodded. Perhaps more than anyone on the general staff, Taylor's close work with General Lee exposed him to his commander's sharp temper which often came over the general in fits of rage which passed just as quickly.

"Sunday is not for politics," Mother Lee said softly. "Sunday is for family and for Bible."

"Yes, Mother," General Lee smiled with his composure restored. "I prefer the Bible to any other book. There is enough in that to satisfy the most ardent thirst for knowledge." For some reason, the general looked Mildred straight in the eyes when he spoke.

Agnes helped her mother by bringing rice pudding to the table. The talk returned to words of family and peace. The troops shivering in the cold along the Rappahannock River and the court martial set to begin tomorrow were far away from the comfortable fireside.

By early afternoon, the company broke. One by one, the friends and family with other duties to attend excused themselves. Custis Lee left for the Confederate capitol and the War Department with Fitz Lee close behind. Young Rob and Walter Taylor followed.

While Mildred, Mary, Agnes, and Martha Williams helped Mrs. Lee clear the table, General Lee sat alone in the parlor close to the fire. Toward 3 o'clock in the afternoon, a steady procession began as aides and well-wishers came to pay their respects before the court martial on Monday.

Secretary of State Judah Benjamin arrived first. The jovial man had one thing in common with his client: an abiding love of family. Far from home in Richmond, Benjamin had been adopted by the Davis family in general and by Mrs. Davis in particular. He had become Varina Davis' close friend and confidante over the last two years. Although he longed for family, Benjamin's history was one of disappointment.

In 1492, Benjamin's ancestors had been expelled from their native Spain with the rest of Spain's Jews during the Inquisition. His ancestors settled in Holland. His parents were later married there. Then they left Holland for London and wound up in St. Croix, British West Indies, where Judah Benjamin was born. His father was thoroughly Anglicanized and even owned three slaves.

By the time he was 10 in 1821, Judah's family had settled in the New World at Charleston, South Carolina. He attended school at the Hebrew Orphan Society which was also open to poor children. In 1825, he entered Yale University at age 14 and left two years later under a quiet cloud of scandal which haunted him all his political career. From Yale, Benjamin settled in New Orleans and studied law.

Benjamin, the Jewish Englishman, married a French Catholic in New Orleans. Natalie St. Martin became Mrs. Judah Benjamin in 1833. Her baby brother, nearly 20 years younger than Judah, became like a son to him. During the 1840s, Benjamin built Natalie a virtual palace near New Orleans called Bellechasse plantation. The land was worked by 140 slaves. But even a plantation could not satisfy Natalie Benjamin's extravagant, French tastes. In 1844, she took the Benjamins' one-year-old daughter, Ninette, and fled to Paris. During the 19 years between that heartbreak and a sunny afternoon in Robert E. Lee's parlor, Benjamin saw his wife and daughter only once each year. After his wife and child abandoned him, Benjamin's family became his widowed older sister Rebecca and Rebecca's daughter.

They moved into Bellechasse and Rebecca became the plantation's permanent mistress.

Benjamin's adopted family watched him enter the United States Senate from Louisiana as that club's first elected Jewish member. With the election of Abraham Lincoln as 16th President, Louisiana seceded from the Union in January 1861. Senator Benjamin resigned from the Senate on February 4th.

Beside the fireplace, Secretary Benjamin and General Lee reviewed the inquest set for the next morning. The womenfolk tended to the dining room and kitchen and left the two men alone.

"The contest could be bitter this week if it turns into a battle between the President and Henry Foote."

"I don't understand, Judah."

"Well, Sir, their hostility goes back a long way in Mississippi politics. Before Mexico even."

"I didn't know."

"Yes, General. As I understand it, the last time they saw eye to eye was 1844 when they were both delegates from Mississippi to the Democratic National Convention in Baltimore. The President went to Congress in '45 and the Senate three years later. The President was in Mexico, as you know. He came home with his foot wound. On crutches over three years, they say." Judah Benjamin smiled. "Foote knows about the crutches. On Christmas Day 1847, in Washington, Mr. Davis attacked Foote after a political argument. Pounded him senseless with his crutch!"

The brawl occurred at Gadsby's Hotel on Pennsylvania Avenue where Davis boarded. Friends prevented a duel afterwards. That made two aborted duels between Foote and Davis. Their mutual hatred ran deep.

"Mr. Davis ran for governor of Mississippi in '51." Benjamin paused for the effect. "Ran against Henry Foote. Foote won. They've each waited eleven years to destroy and humiliate the other."

Robert Lee frowned.

"Nice to know that I can be in the middle."

"Squarely in the middle, General."

The general nodded his head without saying a word.

"General," Benjamin said into the blazing hearth, "there is talk that President Lincoln offered you command of the Federal armies taking the field against us in the spring of '61. Wigfall will surely mention this point to impugn your Confederate loyalties. I must ask you, Sir, to elaborate on this and other matters if I am to defend you effectively."

The general thought for a long moment.

"I never intimated to anyone that I desired the command of the United States Army. Nor did I ever have a conversation with but one gentleman, Mr. Francis Preston Blair, on the subject, which was at his invitation, and, as I understand, at the insistence of President Lincoln. After listening to his remarks, I declined the offer he made me: to take command of the army that was to be brought into the field. I stated as candidly and as courteously as I could that, though opposed to secession and deprecating war, I could take no part in an invasion of the Southern states." General Lee sighed deeply. "On the second morning thereafter, I forwarded my resignation to General Scott."

"Then, General, you were opposed to secession?"

"Mr. Secretary," the general said firmly, "as an American citizen, I prize the Union very highly and know of no personal sacrifice I would not make to preserve it...save that of honor."

"Are you still fundamentally opposed to the dissolution of the Union, General?"

"I only see that a great calamity is upon us and fear that the country will have to pass through for its sins a fiery ordeal. I am unable to realize that our people will destroy a government inaugurated by the blood and wisdom of our patriot fathers." Anger rose in the soldier's deep voice and the flush returned to his face and the back of his neck. "I wish to live under no other government. There is no sacrifice I am not ready to make for the preservation of the Union save that of honor."

"What do you feel on the matter at this moment?" Judah Benjamin looked into General Lee's eyes.

"Now," the general said firmly, "we are in a state of war which will yield to nothing."

"What about the country, Sir? Are the Confederate people up to the challenge at hand?"

"It has occurred to me that the people are not fully aware of the danger, nor of the importance of making every exertion to put fresh troops in the field at once. If the fact were presented by those whose position best enables them to know the urgency of the case, they and the State authorities would be stimulated to greater efforts." General Lee was slowly pounding his right fist into his left palm. "The success with which our efforts have been crowned should not betray our people into the dangerous delusion that the armies now in the field are sufficient to bring this war to a successful and speedy termination."

"Not sufficient? You mean other than the shortage of food, forage and shoes?"

"Our army would be invincible if it could be properly organized and officered. There never were such men in any army before! They will go anywhere and do anything if properly led." The general's eyes were glistening in the fire light. "But there is the difficulty: proper commanders. Where can they be obtained?" General Lee looked over to the Secretary of State.

"No one, General, can say that you do not share the privations of your troops in the field."

General Lee shrugged.

"I am willing to starve myself, but cannot bear my men and horses to be pinched. I fear many of the latter will die."

"Well, General," the Secretary said as he rose to his feet. "Tomorrow we take on the Wigfall faction. It will be good to return to the courtroom....We shall have our day." The jovial man smiled warmly as he walked with the general toward the door.

In the narrow hallway, General Lee handed Secretary Benjamin his coat.

Secretary Benjamin paused, looked up, and spoke softly.

"You gave up much, General, to side with us. I fear that your army career is becoming something of a disappointment to you."

General Lee looked for a long moment at his defense attorney before he spoke in a slow and subdued voice.

"I can advise no young man to enter the Army. The same application, the same self-denial, the same endurance, in any other profession, will advance him faster and farther."

"Tomorrow morning, General," Judah Benjamin smiled as he turned and stepped into the sunshine. His carriage waited to take him to the Davenport house on West Main Street where he lived with his estranged wife's younger brother, Jules St. Martin. After twenty years of separation from his wife, Natalie's little brother, now in his late 20s, remained the son which Judah Benjamin never had. Benjamin had pulled strings with President Davis to secure a clerkship in the War Department for young Jules. They now shared the Davenport house with Confederate Congressman Duncan Kenner, the man Judah P. Benjamin had defeated in 1852 for the Louisiana seat in the Senate of the United States.

Secretary Benjamin lifted his hat in salute toward the broad horseman who dismounted at the curb beside Benjamin's carriage. The rider doffed his broad-brimmed hat with its long feathery plume. Jeb Stuart's hat was as famous throughout the South as was its young owner. General Stuart handed the reins of his horse Virginia to an orderly. Virginia had been Stuart's horse since before Gettysburg after his famous mount Skylark had been captured by the Yankees.

"Did you bring Sam?" the smiling orderly asked the general of the cavalry.

"Gave him Sunday off," Major General Stuart laughed. His banjo player, Sam Sweeney, was as much a part of Stuart's personality as the swaggering cavalryman's famous hat and cape. Sweeney's brother Joe had actually invented the American banjo. Wherever Stuart camped in the field, Sam Sweeney would become the minstrel of the mounted wing of the Army of Northern Virginia. Stuart's camps were filled with young men enjoying the excitement of the cavalry and the music of Sweeney's banjo.

General Stuart marched up the walk toward General Lee who waited patiently at the door. Though sorely stung by the criticism which Gettysburg had brought down upon him, Stuart was devoted to General Lee and to the South. When Stuart's father-in-law, Philip Cooke (a year behind Robert Lee at the Point) had remained loyal to the Union, Jeb changed his baby son's name from Philip Stuart to James Stuart, Jr. There was no room in Jeb Stuart's command for disloyalty or for malingering. Jeb set aside a special detachment for tired or slightly wounded troopers who could not keep pace with the mounted arm of the service. He called it "Company Q" or "Cripple Company." Men would drag themselves into the saddle rather than be branded members of Company Q.

"Good afternoon, General," Jeb Stuart saluted his commander.

"And to you, General Stuart," Robert Lee smiled. "What brings you away from your lovely family on a Sunday?"

"Just wanted to wish you well for tomorrow, Sir," Stuart said.

"You are always welcome," Lee nodded. "I know the girls will be glad to see you."

"Daughter," General Lee called as he escorted Jeb Stuart into the Parlor. "It's General Stuart come to call."

"Jeb!" Mary Custis called as she entered the parlor from the kitchen. "Good to see you."

Mary wanted to visit with Jeb, but her father made it clear that it was time for man-talk. So Mary excused herself and returned to the kitchen. Stuart and General Lee sat beside the hearth in the parlor.

To Stuart, the war from the saddle was like living the legend of King Arthur. Jeb saw the cavalry as a body of knights fighting the way real men fight: from horseback. There would be no slugging through mud and blood on the ground for Jeb Stuart. Like his strange friend, Stonewall Jackson, Stuart regarded camp life as an Elizabethan madrigal complete with court minstrel, Sam Sweeney, and camp squires.

Stuart's squire had been John Pelham, known to every Southern girl's fluttering heart as "the boy major." Major Pelham served brilliantly in Stuart's mounted artillery.

Beside the fire at the Lee home, Stuart spoke emotionally of Major Pelham. At Gaines Mill during the Battle of the Seven Days on June 27, 1862, young Pelham, then 23, held off eight Federal cannon with but one Rebel gun. Stuart described it as "one of the most gallant feats of the war." Stuart was drawn to the shy, unassuming hero. Pelham was as quiet and plain as Stuart was loud and gaudy.

"Major Pelham was the best," Jeb Stuart sighed into the fire at General Lee's side.

"Yes, my boy," Lee said sadly.

On March 17, 1863, nine months ago, Stuart's 800 cavalrymen charged a force of 1,200 Yankee cavalry at Kelly's Ford, 14 miles from Culpeper Courthouse, Virginia. Major Pelham took a shell fragment in the brain and died the next day in the arms of his fiancee, Bessie Shackelford. Jeb Stuart wept over the body and ordered the cavalry artillery corps to wear mourning badges for 30 days. Stuart wrote to his wife that he wanted his son, James Stuart, Jr., to grow up to be just like Major Pelham. When Stuart and Flora's third child was born, he named his daughter Virginia Pelham Stuart.

Jeb Stuart and General Lee spoke softly about comrades and enemies who had left the grim stage.

When Stuart spoke of Stonewall Jackson, General Lee leaned toward the fire and said in a low voice, "the indomitable Jackson."

A professor at Virginia Military Institute in Lexington before the war, Professor Thomas Jonathan Jackson labored to teach himself concentration. He would sit alone in a dark room atop a high stool and try to stay awake. Jackson was a quiet man who spoke in a very soft voice and who was slightly deaf from years in the artillery service of the United States Army.

On the battlefield, his trademark was the lemon he sucked incessantly. Eccentric and almost a mystic, the stern Presbyterian deacon made no effort to conform to the army's rituals of social conduct. "I have no talent for 'seeming,'" he would say to others who wanted him to be something other than what he was. While a teacher at VMI, Jackson taught Sabbath school to slave children. Agnes Lee had done the same back at Arlington when she was only 12 and 13.

Jackson entered the war in April 1861 as a colonel of Virginia volunteers and he was a major general within six months. By the time of his death in May 1863, Jackson was a lieutenant general and led half of Lee's army with Longstreet leading the other half.

Stonewall could slay thousands of men while he sucked his lemon, yet weep like a woman when a single loss touched his heart. The story of little Janie Corbin had moved quickly through the ranks until it became the stuff of legend.

After Fredericksburg in December '62, Jackson made his winter headquarters with the Corbin family at their Moss Neck farm. He instantly made friends with Janie Corbin who was five years old with blonde hair and blue eyes. The quiet general gently taught the child how to make paper dolls. When the little girl had no ribbons, Jackson took the gold braid from his officers' hat and fashioned a ribbon the same color as Janie's hair. Jackson left Moss Neck in March of '63 for the spring offensive which would take his life. In the field on March 18th, General Jackson received word that Janie Corbin was dead of scarlet fever. Old Blue Light bowed his head and cried. The fever also killed two tiny cousins of Janie Corbin who lived at Moss Neck.

Sitting beside the hearth, Jeb Stuart and the general watched the fire. Lee and Jackson had shared a mutual confidence absolute. Of General Lee, Stonewall had remarked, "I am willing to follow him blindfolded."

Jeb Stuart sadly noted that the loss of Jackson during the army's stunning victory at Chancellorsville severely diminished that achievement.

"Any victory," Lee nodded, "would be dear at such a price."

The momentary sadness was broken by Mildred's call from the hallway that General Hill had arrived.

"I'll move on, General," Stuart smiled. "Little Powell will be good company."

Jeb Stuart flirted briefly with Mildred and Mary who was at her side.

"I shall assume whatever blame for Gettysburg might be mine tomorrow," Stuart said firmly as he offered his hand to General Lee at the doorway.

"Not necessary," Lee smiled warmly as Jeb stepped off the porch. "I was in command in Pennsylvania. Responsibility stops there."

Stuart took the reins of Virginia as A.P. Hill handed his gray stallion Champ to the orderly. Hill had ridden Champ into battle since August of '62 when he picked up the tall horse at the battle of Cedar Mountain in western Virginia, now part of the Union as West Virginia. Hill had been in Champ's saddle when Stonewall slumped in the darkness at Chancellorsville after taking two bullets accidently fired by his own men. When Jackson was disabled, command of Jackson's divisions fell first upon A.P. Hill and then upon Jeb Stuart. The memories of Stonewall bound together the robust Stuart and the sickly General Hill who greeted Stuart in the sunshine.

"Good afternoon, General," Hill said to Robert Lee. "Just dropped by to wish you well tomorrow."

"With pleasure," General Lee smiled to the red-bearded general of the army's III corps.

Hill took Stuart's seat by the hearth at General Lee's side.

There would be little talk of Jackson with Hill. Although he had admired Jackson's record, there had also been much strain between Hill and Stonewall. Hill led a division under Jackson's command before Chancellorsville.

Hill often locked horns with Jackson, who had a habit of giving orders in a soft taciturn voice without giving his subordinates counsel or reasons. Hill's diplomatic problems with Jackson finally came to blows in the fall of '62. Stonewall placed Hill under arrest on the road which ended beside Antietam Creek.

Beside the Lee hearth, Hill and his general exchanged idle pleasantries. They could not speak of Jackson. Nor could they speak genially about their comrade Longstreet or their old friend and mortal enemy General McClellan. So they spoke instead about the weather.

The terrible war had many ironies. McClellan's cavalry was led by General Philip Cooke, Jeb Stuart's father-in-law. General McClellan's first cousin, Henry McClellan, was a trusted aide to Jeb Stuart and adjutant general for Stuart's cavalry command. Three of the Rebel McClellan's brothers wore Union blue.

So, too, were the twists of fate which entwined the lives of A.P. Hill and George McClellan. After West Point, George McClellan as a new lieutenant was assigned to a Texas exploration expedition under the command of Captain Randolph Marcy in 1852. Marcy was so pleased with his young officer that he named a newly discovered Texas stream McClellan Creek. McClellan worked hard to earn Marcy's respect. Captain Marcy had something else that George McClellan wanted: his daughter Ellen. McClellan proposed marriage to Ellen in 1854 but she rejected him.

Ellen Marcy had other suitors. In 1856, she announced her engagement to a dapper young solder—Ambrose Powell Hill. Somehow, Ellen's parents were informed secretly about Hill's venereal disease contracted during his West Point days. The sordid intelligence had not come from McClellan. In July 1856, Ellen broke her engagement with Hill and returned his ring. Hill gave the ring as a gift to his sister, Lucy, whom he called Lute. The ring had been engraved "Je t'aime."

When McClellan had first proposed to Ellen, she was 18 and he was 27. After breaking her engagement with Hill, she finally gave in to McClellan's years of devotion by accepting his proposal in 1859. They were married in May of 1860. For the rest of his life, George McClellan wrote to Ellen every day that his military duties kept them apart.

The eldest Lee daughter, Mary Custis, entered the parlor. She informed Generals Lee and Hill that Lieutenant General Longstreet had arrived outside.

"Thank you, Mary," General Hill smiled. "It's time for me to be on my way, General."

"All will be well, General," A.P. Hill said with a firm shake of General Lee's hand.

"We'll see, General," Lee nodded. "Thank you for coming."

On the sidewalk, General Hill of III Corps passed General Longstreet of I Corps. Without a word, each man raised his hat in salute. There was nothing for them to say to each other. They were not friends.

Like Stonewall, Longstreet had placed the hot-tempered Hill under arrest back when the Army of Northern Virginia had time for such things. From the doorway, General Lee watched two of his three corps commanders exchange chilly glares. General Lee waited for Longstreet as Hill mounted Champ and turned the tall stallion toward the Powhatan Hotel.

In July 1862, Richmond newspapers had competed with each other to sing the praises of then-Major General Ambrose Powell Hill during the Seven Days Battle of June around Richmond. Angered at Hill's sudden glory, Longstreet penned a protest to the newspaper which Longstreet felt had slighted other commands. Outraged, Hill asked General Lee to be removed from Longstreet's corps. Longstreet approved of the requested transfer. On the same day as Longstreet's endorsement on the transfer demand, Hill refused to expedite some paperwork for Longstreet. Old Pete promptly arrested Hill. On July 26th, Lee restored Hill to division command and dispatched him to Jackson's wing of the army. Stonewall would arrest Hill later.

"Good of you to come," Lee smiled as he warmly greeted Longstreet.

"Just to wish you well tomorrow," Longstreet nodded.

In front of the parlor hearth, Longstreet sat at his general's side.

"Mind if I smoke, General?" Longstreet inquired of Robert Lee who neither smoked nor drank.

"Not at all," Lee smiled. Old Pete pulled a pipe from his pocket and lit up. He puffed peacefully. Lee enjoyed Longstreet's company as a friend.

The press had been hard on both Longstreet and Lee after Gettysburg. Editors who never smelled a battlefield condemned Longstreet for dallying at Gettysburg rather than moving his I Corps quickly to execute Lee's instructions. But Longstreet tended to be slow when he opposed General Lee's tactics. During the three days at Gettysburg, Longstreet had bitterly opposed Lee's frontal assaults against the entrenched Union lines on the high ground. But General Lee wanted to meet General Meade's bluebacks head-on. Well over 22,000 Southern casualties were left on the field under the blistering Federal guns.

Longstreet's occasional slowness and his opposition to policy had never dampened Lee's faith in the officer whom Lee had embraced as "my old warhorse" at Antietam. After Longstreet's September 1863 victory at Chickamauga when I Corps had been detached to Tennessee, General Lee had sent Longstreet a heartfelt letter of high praise: "If it gives you as much pleasure to receive my warmest congratulations as it does me to convey them," Lee had written, "this letter will not have been written in vain. My whole heart and soul have been with you and your brave corps....Finish the work before you, my dear general, and return to me. I want you badly and you cannot get back too soon."

Lee and Longstreet had much in common during their days in the Old Army. Neither had seen much action between the Mexican War and the War Between the States. Longstreet's largest command before 1861 had been leading 240 cavalrymen in pursuit of Mescalero Apaches in Texas during 1855. No action was seen then. Lee's Texas command had been of similar size, also without exchanging fire.

General Lee said very little as Longstreet puffed slowly on his pipe.

"Well, General," Longstreet said as he tapped his pipe on the hearth stones. "I shall leave you with your family."

The two men rose.

At the doorway, the two generals stood awkwardly.

"You know that I am with you, General," Longstreet said firmly.

"I am confident," Lee said, "that at all times and in all places, you will do all that can be done for the defense of the country and the advancement of the service."

"Thank you, General," Longstreet smiled with emotion cracking in his voice.

"Until tomorrow, General," Robert Lee smiled.

"Tomorrow," Longstreet said as he tipped his hat to Mrs. Lee whose rolling chair creaked across the floor behind her husband.

As Longstreet mounted and set off toward the American Hotel, Mrs. Lee reached for her husband's hand.

"Robert, might we take some fresh air?"

"Of course, Molly." Lee pushed her rolling chair onto the porch.

Outside, the Sunday evening air was still comfortable and unseasonably warm. In the darkening twilight, the sentries on the street were lighting fires in iron pots to warm their fingers when night brought December chill.

"It is so beautiful," Mother Lee said softly. Her husband stood behind her wheelchair and he laid his right hand gently upon her shoulder. He looked up at the bright stars before he spoke in a low voice.

"What a glorious world Almighty God has given us....How thankless and ungrateful we are, and how we labor to mar His gifts....May He have mercy on us."

General Lee looked down when he felt his wife's hand reach up and touch his on her shoulder.

Under the stars, the couple said nothing as their hands touched. The sentries paced in the mud of Leigh Street as Richmond went to sleep on the eve of the court martial of Robert E. Lee.

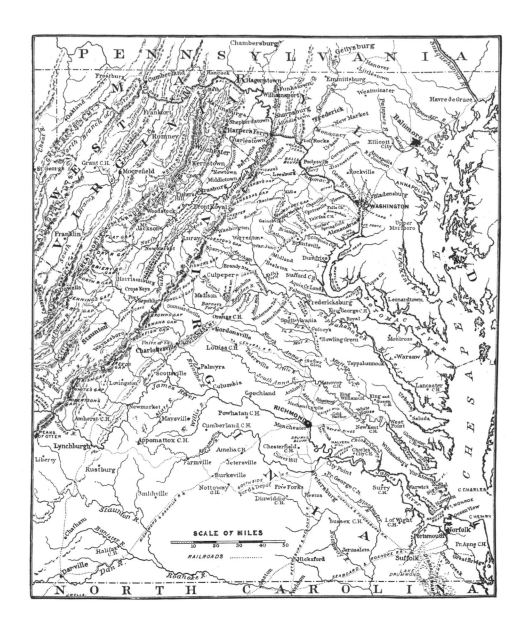

Area of Lee's Campaigns

Chapter Seven

Monday Morning, December 14, 1863

*I would have much preferred had your choice
fallen on an abler man.*
        Robert E. Lee

General Lee paced anxiously in the hallway. He wore his blue greatcoat over his dress grays. He held his slouch hat as he watched the clock on the mantle above the parlor's stone hearth. The brass hands of the clock showed 8:30 on a cold morning.

"Our carriage is waiting," the general said firmly toward the kitchen.

Robert Lee's wife of three decades had two reputations within her family: she grew the finest garden along the Potomac, and she was always late.

Mary Custis pushed her mother's rolling chair through the parlor to the hallway.

"It takes me a little longer, Robert," Mrs. Lee smiled cheerfully.

"I know, Mother," the general smiled down at her.

"Now we can go," she said. Mary and Agnes helped their mother stand and climb into her heavy coat.

Agnes braced the frail woman's left arm. General Lee held Mrs. Lee's right arm.

Gently, General Lee and Agnes helped Mother Lee step off the front porch and take each of the stairs slowly.

At the doorway above them, Mary Custis and Markie Williams stood quietly.

"We will have supper ready," Martha called.

"Yes, Markie. Thank you," Mrs. Lee answered over her shoulder.

"I love you, Father," Agnes called.

The general and his lady slowly walked toward the street. Orderlies assisted Mrs. Lee into the waiting carriage. Two thin horses pawed the hard dirt of Leigh Street. Four armed sentries were mounted around the carriage atop even thinner cavalry horses.

General Lee sat beside Mrs. Lee in the open carriage. The uniformed driver draped a pile of heavy blankets over the knees of his passengers. The carriage was worn and dirty. Every available wagon in Richmond had been appropriated long ago for the war effort.

The driver jerked the reins and the carriage jolted forward for the ride to the capitol. The sentries rode along side as their sabers clattered.

"Not much of a ride for the granddaughter of George Washington," General Lee said without smiling.

Along the Monday morning streets of Richmond, people raised their hats in salute as the Lees rode down Leigh Street three blocks to Broad Street. There, the procession turned left for the dozen blocks to the capitol building. The entire city was buzzing about the unusual meeting of the general staff of the Army of Northern Virginia. General Lee, Lieutenant Generals Longstreet and Hill, and the dashing Major General Jeb Stuart had all been seen on Richmond streets over the weekend.

Hopes ran wild that the conference could only mean one thing: President Lincoln must be suing for a ceasefire before the '64 election. Surely General and Mrs. Lee riding to town meant that peace was in the air along with the sweet, warm scent of pine logs in a thousand chimneys.

A large crowd stood shivering at the War Department building on the corner of Broad and Ninth Streets, between the Baltimore and Potomac Railroad depot and the Broad Street Hotel. They waved and smiled warmly as the Lee carriage passed for the final two blocks to the capitol. These men in uniforms and business suits all knew General Lee well. The War Department had been Lee's office during the first 14 months of the war while Lee served as military adviser to President Jefferson Davis.

The Lee entourage stopped on Capitol Hill behind the building. Sentries secured the carriage horses at hitching rails along Bank Street where the capitol looked down upon the Customs House.

Teetering on General Lee's arm and with a tall orderly on her other side, Mrs. Lee painfully climbed the hill to the capitol of the Confederate States of America.

General and Mrs. Lee entered the building at 9:30. They were met by their son Custis Lee, of President Davis' staff.

As General and Mrs. Lee entered the chamber of the Senate Military Affairs Committee, they passed four armed sentries at the doorway. Two guards on either side of the door carefully inspected formal passes. To enter the chamber, each pass had to be signed by President Davis and countersigned by Co-Chairman Louis Wigfall. All of Richmond heard only the rumors about Mr. Lincoln suing for "Peace by Christmas." No one but the bearers of the official passes knew that the closed session of the Military Affairs Committee was not a spectacular meeting of the Confederate cabinet with the general staff of the Army of Northern Virginia.

The Lees went up the center aisle between five rows of seats. Mary Lee eased herself into a chair in the first row. An orderly took the Lees' coats. The white-haired soldier wore his magnificent sword in the sash slung over his shoulder and he held onto his hat. General Lee kissed Mary Lee's hand before he went forward to one of two tables set before a raised platform. Upon the platform were a long table and seven high-backed chairs of leather. Seven politicians stood as General Lee entered and came forward.

Beside the lower table, Secretary of State Judah Philip Benjamin stood looking dapper and merry. Secretary Benjamin reached out his hand and gave General Lee a firm handshake. The general nodded with a cold hardness set upon his wind burned face. Secretary Benjamin directed General Lee to a chair at the table upon which were piled stacks of documents. Judah Benjamin stood at General Lee's side with their backs toward the noisy gallery.

At the front of the chamber, Texas Senator Wigfall stood like a round, black-bearded bear in front of the center chair. Three grave looking men on either side of Senator Wigfall stood like somber undertakers in their black frock coats which hung to their knees. Senator Wigfall waited for the gallery to fill. One of the sentries pulled the door tightly shut. Milling guests shuffled to their seats. Between the raised platform and Lee's table, a single wooden chair waited for subpoenaed witnesses.

"We will come to order," Senator Wigfall's voice boomed over the din. His heavy gavel pounded a block of wood atop the massive raised table.

When the six men surrounding Louis Wigfall sat down, a hush fell upon the room. For a long moment, only the crackling of two fireplaces, one in each opposite wall, filled the committee chamber.

"We will come to order!" the burly 47-year-old Texan called. The former brigadier general of the 1861 Provisional Army of the Confederacy knew how to bark an order.

Senator Wigfall sat down and looked at Secretary Benjamin who stood round at General Lee's side. The general stood stiffly in his formal gray coat. Each collar held three gold stars. Robert Lee was a full general of which the Confederacy had but five living: General Lee, ranking from August 1861; General Pierre Beauregard of Louisiana, West Point '38, ranking from August 1861; General Braxton Bragg, West Point '37, ranking from June 1862; old General Sam Cooper, now 65, West Point '15, ranking from August 1861 and since then Inspector General of the Confederate Army; and Joe Johnston, West Point '29, ranking from July 1861.

One other full general had been Albert Sidney Johnston, West Point '26. During the two, bloody days of the terrible Battle of

Shiloh in April 1862, Sidney Johnston was mortally wounded. Jefferson Davis had loved Sidney Johnston like an older brother since their teenage years together at Transylvania University, Lexington, Kentucky.

General Lee stood rigidly. Senator Wigfall did not look at the white-haired chief of the Army of Northern Virginia. He looked instead squarely at Judah Benjamin.

"Secretary Benjamin, are you ready to proceed?"

Judah Benjamin smiled and bowed when he spoke clearly and with a touch of Old England in his West Indies and Carolina accent.

"The defense is ready, Mr. Chairman."

"Thank you, Sir. Please be seated."

Secretary Benjamin nodded and sat down. But General Lee paused for an instant. The assembly held its collective breath. While the twin hearths crackled and no one breathed, Robert E. Lee silently laid his slouch hat upon the table. Then, without a word, General Lee lifted his formal sash and saber over his head. He laid the sword upon the table. The cold metal clanged upon the table top. In the space between heartbeats, General Lee looked Senator Wigfall in the eye. Not until the big Texan had to blink did General Lee take his seat at Judah Benjamin's side.

"General Lee," Senator Wigfall began reading from notes, "Secretary Benjamin, invited guests, members of this tribunal. From this moment on, we shall be on the record. Although Representative Foote of Tennessee and I are co-chairmen of this Joint Select Committee on Military Affairs, I shall preside since I chair the Senate Military Affairs Committee." A clerk in military uniform furiously scribbled notes at a small table off to the side of the defense table. "Everyone here is sworn to maintain absolute secrecy regarding these proceedings. I remind everyone that our troops in the field in the East will be without many of their commanding officers during this hearing. Revealing why we are here to our enemies would guarantee a disaster in the field. Southern blood will be thick upon the hands of anyone of you who speaks about this hearing beyond the walls of this chamber.

"General Lee and Secretary Benjamin, this Joint Select Military Affairs Committee thanks both of you for responding to our subpoena to appear here. I remind everyone that we are very much different from our neighbors across the Potomac in Washington. They have suspended civil rights and habeas corpus among their own people. Our government has not. Our enemies have suspended the freedom of the press; our government has not. Although I must caution all participants and observers to scrupulously observe the secrecy of this hearing, I also remind General Lee and his learned counsel, Mr. Benjamin, that your rights to confront the witnesses against you and to enjoy your full protections at law and in equity will be observed here in all ways and at all times.

"On matters of evidence, Virginia law will be followed. This is not a military court martial. Since this hearing was convened by a joint House and Senate resolution, the civil law will control in matters of evidence and impeachment of hostile witnesses.

"This proceeding is essentially a hybrid between a Congressional hearing and a court martial. As such, this entire committee and the Co-Chairs will inquire of the various witnesses called to testify. Upon completion of the testimony, we will make a formal recommendation to the entire Senate on the issue before us: Is General Robert Lee fit to command the Army of Northern Virginia during the present national emergency? In effect, this committee will serve as inquisitor.

"Mr. Benjamin, are there any preliminary questions?"

Judah Benjamin rose, grabbed the lapels of his Prince Albert coat, and spoke slowly.

"Chairman Wigfall, Chairman Foote, gentlemen, on behalf of General Robert Lee, the instant respondent, I ask this committee to dismiss the pending secret indictment in that this committee does not have jurisdiction over military matters which are the exclusive province of the Executive branch of the national government. Likewise, gentlemen, criminal and quasi-criminal indictments are the exclusive jurisdiction of the judiciary, not of the legislative branch of our national government."

The Confederacy had no national Supreme Court since any centralization of the Richmond government offended the rabid States Rights men in Congress.

Judah Benjamin stood beside his seated client as Senator Wigfall responded with firmness in his voice but not a trace of malice.

"Mr. Secretary, in that the Constitution of the Confederate States of America gives the national Senate the power to confirm the appointment of all officers of general rank and in that this committee in particular has jurisdiction to review military matters for the entire Senate, I shall overrule your motion. Your exception will be duly noted for the record."

"So excepted, Senator," Benjamin nodded before sitting.

"Noted, counselor," the bearded Texan replied courteously.

"If we may now proceed, the clerk will read the Bill of Particulars which constitutes the indictment against General Lee." Senator Wigfall looked sideways.

The clerk at his paper-cluttered table stopped writing. Fumbling under the intense eyes of the gallery, the committee, and the defense, the young man rose on shaking knees. His voice piped out high and trembling as he read from a sheet of paper. The corners of the paper shook in his clammy hands.

"May it please the committee....*Be it resolved by the Joint Select Military Affairs Committee of the Congress of the Confederate States of America, meeting in closed session this Wednesday, the 18th of November in the year of our Lord 1863 and in the third year of our sovereign independence, that Robert Edward Lee, General, shall be summoned to appear before us within forty-five days to show cause why he should not be relieved of command for the exercise of his discretion and orders upon the field of battle at Gettysburg, Adams County, Pennsylvania, during his invasion of the country of the United States of America during June and July 1863.*

"*Be it further resolved that said Robert Edward Lee of Virginia shall respond to the following indictment issued by Bill of Particulars, to wit: first, that he did invade the country of our enemies without sufficient resources to sustain a protracted campaign; second, that he did engage a superior force of the enemy on the enemy's own soil without sufficient reconnaissance of the enemy's superior position of terrain; third, that he did fail on the first day of that engagement, 1 July 1863, to adequately pursue the enemy upon the breaching of the enemy's lines; fourth, that he did launch an offensive assault on the second day, 2 July 1863, without acquainting himself adequately with significant changes in the enemy's entrenchments and personnel so as to occasion great and wanton loss of life on the part of his force engaged; and, fifth, that he did launch a second, frontal offensive on the third day, 3 July 1863, with exhausted commands which were poorly coordinated for an assault upon entrenched enemy positions which were superior in both personnel and field position: specifically, an assault up-hill and over open ground against a superior force protected by field fortifications.*

"Be it further resolved that Robert E. Lee, General, be summoned to appear on Monday, 14 December 1863, to respond to the foregoing Bill of Particulars with benefit of counsel and all protections of the civil law. Signed, Senator Louis T. Wigfall, Co-Chairman, and Representative Henry S. Foote, Co-Chairman."

The youthful clerk stopped and blinked. He was completely breathless as if he had read his pleading from beginning to end with one breath. The youth returned to his seat and picked up his pen.

"Thank you," Louis Wigfall said dryly. "The clerk has read the Bill of Particulars. Secretary Benjamin, is the reading of this committee's indictment a correct statement of the same?"

"It is correct, Mr. Chairman," Judah Benjamin said.

"Thank you, Sir....General Lee, the committee will hear your plea. Since this is not a criminal proceeding, you need not plead Guilty or Not Guilty. The correct plea in this quasi-court martial will be an admission or a general denial. By counsel, how do you plead, General?" Chairman Wigfall leaned slightly forward.

General Lee rose with Secretary Benjamin.

"Mr. Chairman," Secretary Benjamin said in a clear voice, "respondent asks leave to enter his own plea."

"Leave is granted," Chairman Wigfall said with a twinge of

irritation in his voice at the deviation from procedure. "General Lee, have you read the indictment?"

General Lee's hands were clenched into fists at his side. His voice was deep and perfectly clear.

"I have, Sir."

"Have you had benefit of counsel to your satisfaction?"

"I have, Sir."

"Then, General Lee, how do you plead to the charges at bar?"

"Mr. Chairman....The allegations are denied, one and all."

When General Lee and Judah Benjamin sat down simultaneously, the gallery let out one great breath.

"Duly noted," Chairman Wigfall said. "The record will show a denial of all counts in the Bill of Particulars. All charges are therefore placed in issue." The Texan shuffled his papers. "General, in order to expedite matters, the Chair waives opening statement. The Bill of Particulars speaks for itself....Secretary Benjamin, you may make an opening statement if you wish."

Judah Benjamin rose and clasped his hands behind his back. He was the only figure standing in the chamber except for two sentries in uniform at the closed door.

"May it please the committee," Judah Benjamin said slowly. "Respondent waives opening statement. Let us proceed." The confident attorney sat down.

Senator Wigfall sat back in his tall chair. He blinked for a moment at Secretary of State Benjamin. The chairman had anticipated a two-day oration from Judah Benjamin who had spent 30 years in public life cultivating his reputation as one of the foremost speakers in national politics.

"In that case," Senator Wigfall droned impassively, "this committee calls as its first witness General Robert Edward Lee to testify as upon cross examination."

Judah Benjamin whispered to General Lee. The soldier rose and stood quietly. Chairman Wigfall nodded to the boyish clerk who left his cluttered desk to stand close to General Lee. The clerk carried a large Bible which he held out at General Lee's chest level. The

General raised his right hand and placed his left hand upon the closed book.

"Do you," the clerk said softly, "swear to tell the whole truth to the best of your recollection and belief, so help you God?"

"I do indeed."

The youth backed away from General Lee who sat down. The chairman waited for the clerk to return to his little desk before he spoke.

"Let the record indicate that General Robert Lee has been duly sworn....General Lee, would you kindly identify yourself for the record."

"Robert Edward Lee, General, commanding the Army of Northern Virginia."

"Thank you, General. Your background is well known to this committee and to your embattled country. We shall not belabor the matter here except very briefly to review your military vitae."

General Lee nodded.

"You are a graduate of the United States Military Academy, are you not?"

"Yes, Mr. Chairman. Class of 1829."

"And thereafter you entered service in the Army of the United States?"

"I did, Sir, in the Corps of Engineers."

"Kindly tell us your early promotion history."

"Mr. Chairman, I was commissioned a lieutenant in 1834 and captain in 1836."

"And you served in the Mexican War?"

"I did."

"And you were brevetted for gallantry?"

"I was brevetted colonel in August 1848."

"After Mexico, did you remain with the army?"

"Yes, Mr. Chairman. I returned to Washington the last week of June 1848 and was stationed in Baltimore from September 1848 to April 1852."

"And you were superintendent at the United States Military Academy at West Point, New York, during this period?"

"I was, Sir, from 1852 to 1855."

"During this period, did you have contact with President Davis?"

"I did, Sir. In March 1853, Mr. Davis became Secretary of War under President Pierce. As superintendent at West Point, I had occasion to work with Secretary Davis often."

"Was your well earned brevet for gallantry—at General Scott's recommendation, I might add—the high point of your distinguished record in Mexico?" Senator Wigfall seemed truly interested. His voice was free of any trace of rancor.

"No, Sir," the witness said slowly. "I can remember the high point of that dreary time like it was yesterday. On one occasion, my brother, Sidney Smith Lee, then a lieutenant in the United States Navy, met me at Vera Cruz. We fought the enemy of our country together. I am very proud of my brother, Commodore Lee of our country's navy."

"With good cause, General," Senator Wigfall nodded.

Robert Lee and his older brother, Smith Lee, had been close since childhood. Smith and Robert Lee were both lieutenants during the Mexican War: Robert in the Corps of Engineers, Smith in the Navy. When the Union dissolved in 1861, Colonel Robert Lee, U.S. Army, and Captain Smith Lee, U.S. Navy, both cast their lots with the Confederacy. Smith Lee was immediately commissioned a captain in the Confederate Navy to be followed by flag rank as Commodore Sidney Smith Lee. During the spring of '62, Captain Lee was executive officer at the Norfolk Navy Yard, abandoned by the Federals. Under Captain Lee's stewardship, the Confederacy's first "ironclad" battleship was launched as the C.S.S. *Virginia*.

General Lee looked up beside Judah Benjamin. The general's black eyes locked into Senator Wigfall's eyes.

"To continue, General. Let us skip to your career immediately prior to our present national circumstances. You were with the United States Cavalry in the late '50s I believe?"

"Yes, Mr. Chairman. I was assigned to Camp Cooper in Texas in April 1856. In July, my nephew, then-Lieutenant Fitzhugh Lee, West Point '56, and Lieutenant John Bell Hood, joined my command. As you know, Mr. Chairman, Fitz Lee is now a major general in Stuart's cavalry and Hood is a major general leading a division in I Corps of the Army of Northern Virginia."

"All well and good, General Lee." The Texan's round face hardened and his eyes concentrated on the witness. "Tell this committee, General, during your Texas assignment in '56 with the cavalry, did you lead troops in the field?"

"I did, Sir."

"And how large was your largest command?"

"Mr. Chairman, I led perhaps 300 troopers on a 40-day expedition in pursuit of renegade Indians."

"General, did you find any Indians during those 40 days?"

"I did not, Sir."

"Prior to your resignation from the army of our enemies, was that Texas command of 300 men the largest field command of your entire 30-year military career?"

"Mr. Chairman, my command of 300 men in June 1856 was my largest command prior to offering my sword to Virginia."

"And after Camp Cooper, General?"

"In July 1857, I was placed in temporary command of the United States Second Cavalry at San Antonio, Texas."

"And how many men were in your command then?"

"Precisely 739 troopers."

"But the earlier command of some 300 men was your greatest field command prior to secession?" The Chairman glared hard at Robert Lee.

"That is correct, Sir."

"Yes, General." The trace of a smile crossed Senator Wigfall's bearded lips. "And now you are in command of over 75,000 men...when your only other field experience was seven years ago, commanding a force something like—let me see—a force less than one-half of one percent of your present command?"

"I would agree with your calculation, Mr. Chairman." General Lee had to smile. "You know, Senator, when I was a cadet at the United States Military Academy, I was Acting Assistant Professor of Mathematics."

When the gallery muttered a subdued chuckle, Senator Wigfall laughed aloud.

"I am pleased, General, that you approve of my mathematical skills. Did you remain in active military service between your Texas command and your resignation from service in '61?"

"No, Senator. In October 1857, I was granted a furlough to my wife's home at Arlington upon the death of her father."

"When did you leave Virginia to return to active duty?"

"I returned to Texas in February 1860 to the Second Cavalry at San Antonio."

"And your mission at that time?"

"We patrolled a 135-mile long frontier along the Rio Grande River west of Brownsville."

"So, while the struggle for independence was just beginning here, you were mucking about in the wilderness in search of Indians who never showed their faces?"

"I would say, Mr. Chairman, that I was in the middle of that sad spectacle as it developed in the West. On December 22, 1860, I arrived at Fort Mason, 100 miles northwest of San Antonio. Barely six weeks later on February 1st, Texas seceded from the Union." General Lee's voice was cold and slow. "I wore Federal blue in a state which chose to leave the Union....Three days later, on February 4th, I was ordered back to Washington."

The tension in the closed committee chamber was intense. The Senator at Chairman Wigfall's left elbow leaned forward and spoke quickly to defuse the momentary ill temper.

"If I might intrude, Mr. Chairman." Senator Robert Hunter of Virginia said softly. He glanced quickly at Judah Benjamin. Hunter was Confederate Secretary of State from July 1861 until February

1862. He resigned when Jefferson Davis told him to be quiet at a cabinet meeting. Benjamin then replaced him at State. "General Lee, it is a fact that within weeks of your return to the East, you did resign from the Federal Army and you were promptly commissioned in late April '61 as commander of the Virginia Militia."

"Yes, Senator Hunter. My commission dates from April 23rd."

"And, General, with the Chairman's permission, no better choice could have been made. I voted to affirm your confirmation." As a murmur rose in the gallery, the Senator glanced sideways toward Chairman Wigfall who sat stone-faced.

"I would much have preferred," General Lee said softly, "had your choice fallen upon an abler man."

"Thank you, Senator," Chairman Wigfall said dryly. "But, General Lee, is it not also a fact that your support for secession came both late and, shall I say, rather luke-warm?"

"I must object," Judah Benjamin said as he rose at his place beside General Lee. "I fail to see the relevance of any discussion regarding Respondent's political beliefs. I would add that regardless of his private convictions, General Lee did take the oath of allegiance to this government." Benjamin's rosy face was stern as he stared at Senator Wigfall.

"Your objection is overruled, Mr. Benjamin, and your exception duly noted of record." Chairman Wigfall's eyes left Secretary Benjamin who sat down.

"To repeat, General: Did you or did you not endorse with all your heart the dissolution of the old Union?"

General Lee paused and looked up toward Wigfall. The general's words were calm and soft.

"Sir, the Constitution of the United States was intended for perpetual union so expressed in the Preamble, and for the establishment of a government, not a compact, which can only be dissolved by revolution, or the consent of all the people in convention assembled."

"Your exposition into constitutional law—about which you know nothing—is noted, General," Wigfall argued coldly. "You are rather out of your element on such matters."

"May I note," the witness said with strain in his voice, "that during my third year at the Military Academy, I read Hamilton's *The Federalist* nine times. It was in early '28. I remember the book vividly and have grounded my concepts of Federalism in that noble volume ever since."

"General Lee," Wigfall said firmly, "I apologize to you and counsel for my intemperate remark."

"Accepted, Mr. Chairman," Robert Lee said acidly.

"To continue, General...I shall note for the record your counsel's continuing objection to this line of questioning...I understand that you are also less than zealous in your defense of chattel slavery—an ancient system sanctioned in Scripture and necessary to our agrarian economy."

Senator Hunter on the platform nodded. Although generally a moderate politician, he was a vigorous advocate of slavery.

General Lee shrugged.

"As far as I have been able to judge," the general said looking up at Chairman Wigfall, "this war presents to the European world but two aspects: a contest in which one party is contending for abstract slavery and the other against it. The existence of vital rights involved does not seem to be understood or appreciated. As long as this lasts, we can expect neither sympathy or aid."

"Europe, General?"

"Yes, Senator. Winning our independence will be most difficult without assistance from abroad. Recognition of our statehood by Europe is also important. Negro slavery will hurt our chances for diplomatic recognition and military aid."

"You seem to have a good deal of affinity for Negroes, General." There was a sneer in the Chairman's voice.

General Lee's response was completely calm, almost casual.

"I have great consideration for my African fellow citizens, but I must have some for their white brethren. All must do their part in this great emergency."

"African fellow citizens!" Wigfall laughed loudly. "Need I remind you that even in the Constitution of our abolitionist enemies, Negroes are regarded as but two-thirds of a human being!"

"I am aware of the Federal Constitution, Sir."

"That may be, General, but I ask you for my own understanding of your position on this matter: What have you done about your own family servants—your own household's African fellow citizens?"

"First, Senator, any Negro servants in my household were property bequeathed to Mrs. Lee by her father upon his death in October '57. They were never my property. I have labored mightily to expedite their gradual emancipation within five years which is expressly required by my father-in-law's will of which I am the named executor."

"Are you releasing these servants, General?"

"Yes, Senator. I am emancipating our people as best I can."

"These people, as you call your father-in-law's Negroes, what will become of them?"

"As regards the liberation of the people, I wish to progress in it as best as I can." General Lee spoke calmly as if describing ordinary business affairs. "Those hired in Richmond can still find employment there if they choose. Those in the country can do the same or remain on the farms. I hope they will do well and behave themselves. I should like if I could attend to their wants and see them placed to the best advantage. But that is impossible."

"But, General, you do have your own servant in the field, do you not?"

"I do, Senator. My man Perry has been with us for years as was his father. Perry is like family."

"And you will give him his free papers, too?"

"Indeed, Mr. Chairman." General Lee looked up at Senator Wigfall. The soldier's face softened when he thought of his longtime servant Perry. "Perry is very willing and I believe does as well as he can. He is slow and inefficient and moves much like his father, Lawrence, whom he resembles very much. He is also very fond of his blankets in the morning—the time I most require him out." The general smiled. Perry remained behind in the cold, winter camp of the army. "I hope he will do well when he leaves me and get in the service of some good person who will take care of him."

"But, General," Senator Wigfall scowled, "the gripping issue of criminal abolition seems to have missed you."

"Not at all, Sir. Quite the contrary. You may recall that it was I who crushed the John Brown insurrection in '59—with the help of the very able Jeb Stuart. I saw with my own eyes the violent side of the issue and the risk to life and property occasioned by misdirected, abolitionist fervor."

John Brown had seized the Federal arsenal at Harper's Ferry, Virginia, on October 16, 1859. While still home on leave settling the estate of his father-in-law, Lieutenant Colonel Lee was ordered to suppress the Brown revolt. Lee had been summoned to action by then-lieutenant Jeb Stuart, U.S. Cavalry. Lee and a squad of Marines surrounded the fire engine house taken by Brown where 13 civilian hostages were being held. Lee sent in a written demand for Brown's surrender. The demand was hand delivered by Jeb Stuart. When Brown refused, Lee sent in the Marines on October 18th at dawn. All of the hostages were saved, one marine was killed, and John Brown was wounded and captured. Brown was hanged on December 2nd.

"I understand that, General. But I believe that you did not see action in the field after secession for perhaps five months. Is that correct, Sir?"

"That is correct, Mr. Chairman. I devoted every waking moment during the first summer of this war to serving President Davis as military adviser and to raising, equipping, and training the Virginia Militia. Thereafter, my immediate task was integrating that militia into the armies of the Provisional Army of the Confederate States." General Lee hesitated. "We created an army second-to-none...out of nothing."

Looking down upon General Lee and Judah Benjamin from his

raised platform, Senator Wigfall's dark eyes were cold when he questioned the witness.

"Virginia's first great victory on the field of honor was at Manassas Junction in July of '61. But you took no part in that campaign, did you?"

The flush of anger rose upon the back of Robert Lee's neck as he reflected upon commanding a desk at the War Department in Richmond while blood flowed along Bull Run Creek at Manassas.

"That indeed was a glorious victory and had lightened the pressure upon our front amazingly. I had wished to partake in the struggle, and was mortified at my absence. But the President thought it more important I should be here." The witness paused and his stony glare made Chairman Wigfall blink. "I could not have done as well as had been done....But I could have helped and taken part in the struggle for my home."

"Well," Wigfall smiled, "at least one hero emerged from Virginia at Bull Run!"

The chairman's remark drew laughter from his colleagues of the committee and hearty nods from the gallery. Everyone knew he meant the now dead General Jackson. It was at Bull Run that Rebel General Bernard Bee looked across the bloodied field at Brigadier General Jackson's command and muttered, "There stands Jackson like a stone wall." The name stuck instantly. Before the day was out, "Stonewall" Jackson was the stuff of legend and Bernie Bee was dead on the battlefield.

"So, General, you remained at your desk here through the spring of 1861?"

"I did, Sir."

"And how long did you remain in Richmond as adviser to President Davis?"

"Until late July."

"And thereafter?"

"Mr. Chairman, I went to western Virginia to oversee operations on that frontier."

"Well, General, I certainly wish to review those operations in detail. But first, perhaps everyone could use a brief recess while the fires are stoked. If the orderlies would be kind enough to tend the fireplaces, we shall reconvene in ten minutes....Gentlemen."

As Senator Wigfall rose, the entire chamber came to attention— except for General Lee's crippled wife. Robert Lee turned around and walked slowly to his wife.

"Molly," General Lee said gently.

When two orderlies opened the rear doors of the committee chamber, the gallery herded into the hallway. In the corridor outside, armed guards kept civilians and newspapermen from the gallery. The invited guests of the Joint Military Affairs Committee silently paced, smoked, or chewed and spat into the spittoons.

Newsmen swarmed toward the gallery. The reporters hungered for details on the closed hearing thought to relate to the Tennessee debacle two weeks earlier or to Yankee peace prospects. The journalists had howled when Jefferson Davis accepted General Braxton Bragg's resignation after Missionary Ridge only to bring him to Richmond as chief-of-staff.

Robert Lee did not leave the chamber since walking was too painful for Mary Lee.

"I cannot believe that your father's household servants would be fit subject of a Senate inquisition!" General Lee's whisper at his wife's side was hoarse. "I directed Mr. Collins, as soon as he could get in the small crop this fall, to obtain from the county courts their free papers and to emancipate them. They can then hire themselves out to support themselves. I do not know what to do better for them."

"Yes, Robert," Mary Lee added. "You have done for my father's last wishes all that a son could do."

"I much prefer their receiving their free papers and seeking their fortune," General Lee said firmly. "It has got to be done and it was in accordance with your father's will....I do not see why they cannot be freed and hire themselves out as others do."

"General," Judah Benjamin interrupted. "Your domestics are the least of our concerns at the moment. Wigfall and Foote will work diligently to paint your western Virginia campaign as a fiasco."

"Fiasco!" Robert Lee frowned. "The soldiers everywhere were sick! The measles were prevalent throughout the whole army." The general shook his head. "What could I have done with a sick army?"

"I know, General," Judah Benjamin said. "We shall have our day in court."

"Court, indeed," the tired soldier said. He looked over toward the doors.

Light flooded the Senate committee room when the doors opened. The noisy gallery filed into the drafty chamber. Orderlies busily stoked the hearths with fresh wood and the flames crackled back to life.

Through the doors, General Lee saw Henry Foote surrounded by a rabble of tobacco-chewing newspapermen. They all looked fit and fat in starving Richmond. Lee knew that the closest these men ever got to a battlefield was when they walked past one of the city's military hospitals and held their noses.

Representative Foote spoke to the press. He did not mention the subject of the closed-door hearing. Foote advocated the appointment of Joe Johnston to Bragg's command in Tennessee. Then he announced his newest resolution to be introduced in the Confederate House. He proposed relieving all officers of command who had lost public support. This would strip Jefferson Davis of his presidential authority to appoint officers. The newsmen scribbled furiously as Foote held court in the hallway.

General Lee patted Mrs. Lee's hand and he followed Secretary Benjamin back to their table in front of the gallery. Mingling with the gallery, Senator Wigfall entered the chamber. The gallery rose in silence as Senator Wigfall, Foote and his committeemen mounted their raised platform. With a nod of his beard, Senator Wigfall commanded the audience to take their seats.

"Ladies and gentlemen, General Lee, Secretary Benjamin, we shall convene where we recessed....Back on the record. General Lee, you were dispatched to western Virginia in August of 1861?"

"I was, Sir, at the President's request."

"When did you arrive in western Virginia?"

"About August 3rd, Senator."

"General, what is your recollection of that expedition?"

"Rain, Senator. By August 10th, the area had endured twenty consecutive days of rain."

"During this period, General, were you still an officer in the Virginia Militia?"

"Probably not. I was there representing President Davis. Also, on August 31, 1861, my commission as general in the Provisional Army of the Confederate States was confirmed by the Senate."

"What did you do on that expedition?"

"Primarily, I conferred with Brigadier General W.W. Loring who commanded some 10,000 Virginia troops in the region. Also, I had to deal with the genuine antagonism between two gentlemen, Henry Wise and John Floyd."

"Both former governors of Virginia?"

"Both, Senator."

"And the Federals in the region?"

"The Union troops were led ably by my old friend John F. Reynolds, who held the Cheat Mountain area. This important region commanded the Parkersburg-Staunton highway into the Valley of Virginia and the critical Virginia Central Railroad."

"Did you camp in the field, General?"

"Of course, Mr. Chairman. I tented with my friend, Colonel John Washington, President Washington's great-nephew. We camped on Valley Mountain."

"You mentioned the weather, General."

"Rain, rain, rain," the general sighed. "There had been nothing but rain. The cold, too, had been greater than I could have conceived. This state of the weather had aggravated the sickness that had attacked the army: measles and typhoid fever."

Henry Foote at Louis Wigfall's elbow leaned forward and spoke in a raspy voice.

"General Lee, precisely how widespread was disease among the Confederate commands?"

"Congressman," Lee shrugged, "the sick list would have formed an army!"

"But rain and sickness aside," Senator Wigfall interrupted, "attack orders were issued, were they not?"

"Yes, Senator. General Loring issued Special Order 28 on September 8th. His orders required a coordinated assault against the Federals at dawn on September 12th at Cheat Mountain Pass and along the Tygart Valley River."

"I believe, General Lee, that the official records of that engagement speak for themselves." Senator Wigfall glared over his spectacles.

At daybreak on September 12th, the proposed attack did not come until noon. The attack was delayed by more rain. Confederate General Albert Rust aborted a critical, opening barrage of artillery when he determined the Federal line to be impregnable. Former Governor Floyd's command was routed by Federals under William Rosecrans.

"Yes, Senator. It was during a cavalry clash led by my son, then Major Fitzhugh Lee, that Colonel Washington was killed in action."

"And this defeat you blame on rain, General?"

"I fix no blame, Sir." General Lee's voice was hoarse. "It had been raining in those mountains for about six weeks." Lee sighed. "It rained there all the time, literally. The ground had become so saturated with water that the constant travel on the roads had made them impassable."

"And you lost Cheat Mountain, General Lee, did you not? Your first field command of more than 750 men and you lost Cheat Mountain."

"I was not in command of that field, Sir. I was essentially the President's representative to General Loring."

Foote leaned forward when Wigfall took a breath.

"Sir, you were the ranking Confederate officer on the field."

"I was, Mr. Foote." The witness glared at the co-chairman. "I cannot tell you my regret and mortification at the untoward events that caused the failure of the plan. I had taken every precaution to ensure success...and had counted on it." General Lee bowed his head. He spoke softly toward his folded hands. "Our greatest loss was the death of my dear friend Colonel Washington....The colonel fell pierced by three balls. My son's horse received three shots." Colonel John Washington who fell on Cheat Mountain in the knee-deep mud was the last bearer of the Washington name to own Mount Vernon.

"Yes, General," Chairman Wigfall stammered in the sudden silence. "Colonel Washington and many good men died in western Virginia two years ago. But I cannot accept rain and poor coordination of subordinate officers as much of an excuse."

"It is fact, Sir, not an excuse." General Lee was more tired than angry.

At General Lee's side, Judah Benjamin stood and looked hard at Chairman Wigfall.

"Senator," Secretary of State Benjamin demanded, "if you persist at going over old ground instead of reviewing the Pennsylvania campaign which is at issue here, then I demand to proceed out of order. I demand the privilege of calling an immediate defense witness out of order."

"Your request, counselor, is overruled." Chairman Wigfall was loud and impatient.

"May I remind the chair that calling Respondent-Lee as on cross examination is also out of order." Judah Benjamin's rosy cheeks flushed. He was clearly enjoying his momentary confrontation.

Senator Wigfall leaned to his right to consult softly with Foote who nodded. North Carolina Senator Reade nodded on Wigfall's other side. The two other senators on the right side of the platform nodded in unison.

"Your motion is granted, Mr. Secretary. Will this take long?"

"Ten minutes, Mr. Chairman." Benjamin suppressed a smile behind his short beard.

"Very well, Mr. Benjamin. Call your first defense witness."

"Thank you, Mr. Chairman." As Judah Benjamin spoke, General Lee watched his advocate closely. "Respondent calls Colonel Walter Taylor."

Colonel Taylor in the packed gallery looked startled. He had half dozed in the warm glow of the crackling fireplace. Gathering his wits, the young banker from Norfolk rose and walked stiffly toward the defense table. Judah Benjamin motioned for Colonel Taylor to take his place at the witness chair beside the table shared by Benjamin and Lee. Colonel Taylor stood uncomfortably in front of General Lee.

"State your name, Sir," Senator Wigfall demanded coldly.

"Walter H. Taylor, lieutenant colonel and adjutant general of the Army of Northern Virginia."

"The clerk will please swear in the witness."

The clerk of the committee administered the oath to Walter Taylor who then sat down and fidgeted with his hands. Only 25 years old, Taylor had been an officer of the Bank of Virginia before the war.

"Colonel," Senator Wigfall said impatiently, "you are on General Lee's official staff?"

"I am, Sir. I have been on the general's staff since May of '61. My commission as lieutenant colonel dates from October 7th of this year."

"Thank you, Colonel Taylor. Your witness, Mr. Benjamin."

Judah Benjamin rose, grabbed his wide lapels, and spoke softly toward the young officer sitting beside him.

"Colonel, were you at Cheat Mountain?"

"I was, Mr. Secretary."

"And did you personally observe the workings of the western Virginia command of Confederate forces?"

"I did, Sir."

"What is your recollection of the state of affairs—shall I say 'diplomacy'—among Generals Floyd and Wise?"

Colonel Taylor looked away.

"Brigadier Generals Floyd and Wise were operating under great disadvantages: each having an independent command and neither being disposed to act a part subordinate to the other."

"And disease, Colonel? Have you a recollection of the health of the western Virginia commands?"

"Commands were seriously reduced by disease. It is no exaggeration to say that one-half of the army was ineffective."

"Tell us, Colonel, of your overall impressions regarding the Cheat Mountain operations in the fall of 1861." Judah Benjamin looked down at the perspiring officer at his side. Colonel Taylor's moist face looked very young. When Taylor spoke, his soft voice became firm and slightly hostile. He looked up at the brooding face of Louis Wigfall.

"It is useless to attempt to recount all the difficulties this little army encountered in that most impractical, inhospitable, and dismal country. Only those who participated in that campaign can ever properly estimate the disadvantages under which commanders and troops operated." Taylor glared at Wigfall whose round face flushed as anger rose in Walter Taylor's voice. "For weeks it rained daily and in torrents. The condition of the roads was frightful. They were barely passable. In other words, the wagons were hub-deep in mud. At the same time, and doubtless as a result of the rains, the troops were sorely afflicted with measles and a malignant type of fever which prostrated hundreds of each command." He paused, sighed, and looked hard at Chairman Wigfall. "Never did I experience the same heart-sinking emotions as when contemplating the wan faces and the emaciated forms of those hungry, sickly, shivering men."

"Colonel," Benjamin asked firmly, "did General Lee command the field at Cheat Mountain to the best of your personal recollections?"

Taylor's voice was clear as he looked up at Wigfall.

"He never assumed immediate personal command of the army."

Senator Wigfall leaned forward and his loud voice filled the Senate chamber.

"Then what precisely was General Lee's position at Cheat Mountain, Colonel?"

"Senator, I would have to say both diplomat and observer for President Davis. Nothing more, Sir."

"Diplomat?" Senator Hunter inquired.

"Yes, Sir. General Lee was not in direct command and he had the difficult task of keeping peace among general officers who regarded their commands as independent of each other and independent of General Lee."

"How did General Lee manifest this effort to deal with Generals Floyd and Wise?" The Senator ignored Chairman Wigfall's eyes.

"I discovered," Colonel Taylor said firmly, "that character of him that always marks his intercourse and relations with his fellow men: scrupulous consideration for the feelings and interests of others. The more humble the station of one from whom he received appeal or request, the more he appeared to desire to meet the demand if possible, or, if impracticable, to make denial in the most considerate way as if done with reluctance and regret."

"Thank you, Colonel." Judah Benjamin smiled. His round pink cheeks glowed. "I have nothing further of this witness for the moment, Mr. Chairman."

Senator Wigfall avoided Colonel Taylor's intense eyes.

"You are excused, Colonel. Thank you."

"Thank you, Mr. Chairman." Walter Taylor rose, and without glancing at General Lee, he marched back to his seat in the gallery.

Senator Wigfall waited for Taylor to take his seat. "May we now return to General Lee's testimony, Mr. Secretary?"

"No objection, Senator," Judah Benjamin replied without standing.

"Very good, Sir." Senator Wigfall adjusted his spectacles, pushing them up on his nose. "General, how long did you remain in western Virginia after Cheat Mountain?"

"Late fall, as I recall, Mr. Chairman."

Lee had returned to Richmond from the rain soaked mountains on October 31, 1861.

"And thereafter, General?"

"I was dispatched by President Davis on November 6, 1861, to the southeast coast of our country. My duties required inspection of our coastal defenses in South Carolina, Florida, and Georgia—all of which I inspected personally."

"How long were you in the deep South?"

"From November 1861 to early March 1862."

General Lee frowned. His four months in the malaria infested regions of the Confederacy were a daily grind of inspection and fortification. He prodded weary troops to do what they most hated: work in the hot sun and debilitating humidity to build entrenchments and breastworks. So hard did the men dig and so dogged was Lee's determination that he soon won the nickname of "King of Spades." His constant prodding of the men also earned the gray-bearded engineer the title of "Granny Lee."

"General, when did you officially take your place as military adviser to President Davis?"

"That would have been March 13, 1862. The President then issued General Orders Number 14 which put me in charge of—in the President's words—'the conduct of military operations in the armies of the Confederacy.'"

"So, General Lee, you left the field essentially to push paper in Richmond?" A low murmur growled through the gallery.

General Lee looked up at the chairman and their eyes met for a cold instant.

"Senator," the soldier frowned, "I did not see either advantage or pleasure in my duties."

"Well, General, how long were you the primary, military adviser to President Davis here in Richmond?"

"Sir, until the first day of June 1862."

"And then, General?"

"On June first, with the tragic wounding of General Joe Johnston, President Davis tendered to me the honor and the privilege of commanding the combined forces operating in Virginia. This was done pursuant to the President's Special Orders Number 22."

"Do you recollect your first actions as you took the field in General Johnston's stead?"

"I do indeed, Senator."

"And what did you do first, General Lee?"

"First, Senator, I renamed the Virginia Militia in the eastern sector of the state. I called the assembled forces the Army of Northern Virginia."

A low murmur reverberated through the gallery after the witness stated the new name of his divisions and massed batteries. Perhaps it was the way General Lee had said "The Army of Northern Virginia." He lingered upon each word as if tasting the phrase as he exhaled it. His firm, deep voice sounded like a benediction.

"There will be order!" Senator Wigfall called as his wooden gavel pounded the desk atop the raised platform. "This is a Senate chamber and there will be order....I shall have silence!"

The gallery quickly hushed. General Lee looked up toward Senator Wigfall.

"Ladies and gentlemen, General Lee, if there is no objection, perhaps it is time for a luncheon recess. We shall adjourn for ninety minutes during which absolute silence will be observed toward the gentlemen of the press."

When Wigfall rose, his colleagues at his sides and the entire gallery rose. The Texan left the chamber first, followed by the members of the Joint Committee. Slowly the gallery filed stiffly into the chilly hallway.

Halfway to Mrs. Lee, General Lee's black eyes scanned the emptying gallery. His gaze stopped at a tall, thin soldier who stood awkwardly with his back against the far wall by the guarded doorway. Lee nodded warmly toward the youthful officer. The long face and blond hair belonged to Lieutenant Colonel Sandic Pendleton.

Chapter Eight

Monday Noon, December 14, 1863

*His face was calm and granitelike. His blue eye
was restful and cold, except when now and then it
gave, for a moment, an ominous flash. His right
hand lay open and flat on his thigh, but now and
then was raised into the air as was his habit—a
gesture which the troops learned to believe was as
significant as the extended arm of Aaron.*
> Henry Kyd Douglas, Headquarters Staff,
> II Corps, describing Stonewall Jackson

*T*he galley emptied for the noon recess. Robert Lee stopped ten
paces in front of Mary Lee. The general blinked back tears as he saw
Sandie Pendleton. Alexander Swift "Sandie" Pendleton was the son
of Brigadier General William Pendleton who commanded the reserve artillery batteries of Lee's army. Sandie's youthful face brought
a flood of painful memories to General Lee. The younger Pendleton
was known throughout Lee's army as "Stonewall Jackson's man." To
see young Sandie was to remember Stonewall. Lee's heart ached.

"Mother," General Lee said softly in the nearly deserted chamber,

"Sandie Pendleton is here. I would very much like to spend a few moments with him."

Lee looked down at Mrs. Lee. As if reading his chief's mind which was often his job, Walter Taylor stepped forward toward the Lees.

"General," Taylor smiled, "might I entertain Mrs. Lee for a while?"

Mary Lee smiled up toward Walter Taylor.

"If you have no objection, Robert, to my being seen on the arm of a handsome young man?"

"Not at all," General Lee said.

"Then, with the general's permission," Walter Taylor grinned as he extended his arm which Mrs. Lee clasped firmly. Her husband helped her to her painful feet. Secretary Benjamin stepped forward and offered his arm for her other twisted hand. Benjamin and Taylor on either side of Mary Lee escorted her from the chamber. With their departure, only General Lee, Sandie Pendleton, and the two sentries beside the door occupied the Senate chamber.

"Hope you don't mind, General, that I snuck away from camp yesterday?"

"Are you deserting?" the general smiled as he clasped Sandie's right hand in both of his.

"I have a pass signed by General Ewell," Sandie said firmly.

"I never doubted that," Lee laughed softly. "Thank you for coming."

General Lee ushered Sandie Pendleton to a seat in the first row of the empty gallery. The two men sat down beside a cozy fire.

Pendleton looked very young beside his white-bearded chief. The assistant adjutant general of the army's II Corps—Stonewall's old corps—had turned 23 not quite three months earlier. Sandie looked pale from slim winter rations and periodic bouts of camp fever.

General Lee knew the close bond which had existed between the youthful soldier and Stonewall Jackson. It was said that Sandie was the only staff officer whom General Jackson had routinely called by his first name. To sit beside him was like opening a half-closed wound in General Lee's heart. Stonewall's death created a void in command which was not filled between the bloody ridges at Gettysburg.

"I grieve much over the death of General Jackson," General Lee said softly at Pendleton's side. "For our sakes, not for his. He is happy and at peace. But his spirit lives with us."

"Yes, General," Sandie Pendleton said sadly. "I can't believe he's gone."

"It is a terrible loss," General Lee nodded, "I do not know how to replace him."

Sandie had been in the Chancellorsville brambles that dark night when southern troops accidently fired upon Stonewall. Sandie had arrived at the makeshift field hospital shortly after Stonewall's wounded arm had been added to the piles of limbs stacked outside the surgeon's tent.

"Poor General Jackson!" Sandie thought aloud. "It was sad, sad to see him with his arm amputated."

"I can only imagine, Sandie," General Lee said gravely. "No one was more convinced of his worth or more highly appreciated him than myself."

"You know, General, that I met General Jackson in Lexington before the war."

"Oh?"

Sandie and his parents had moved to tiny Lexington, Virginia, in October 1853. The boy immediately entered Washington College when he was only 13 years old. The now-dead Jackson was already teaching at Virginia Military Institute just up the road. Always a lover of books, Sandie joined the college's Graham Literary Society in 1854. The strangely eccentric and dour Professor Jackson from VMI was an honorary member of the society. Although younger than most of his classmates, Sandie graduated with highest honors in July 1857. At commencement, Sandie gave the Cincinnati Oration reserved for the outstanding graduate.

For two years after graduation from Washington College, Sandie taught mathematics and Latin at his alma mater. In the fall of '59 as his country teetered on the brink of annihilation, Sandie entered the

University of Virginia to work on his masters degree. When Virginia left the Union in April of '61, Sandie joined a student regiment of volunteers as a private. By May 1861, he was unofficially brevetted lieutenant in the engineer corps of the Virginia Militia. On June 11, 1861, he left school for the last time for the garrison at Harper's Ferry. But he remained a lover of books more than war. At the little skirmish at Romney in the Shenandoah Valley in January of '62, Sandie managed to rescue several books from a burned out, local literary society building.

In June of '61, Professor Jackson—by then a colonel—was promoted to brigadier general in command of the five regiments of the First Virginia Brigade. Eight days later, General Jackson named Sandie Pendleton the brigade's ordnance officer. By November 30, 1861, Sandie's commission to lieutenant was confirmed. By January of '63, Sandie was a major and received permanent appointment to the post of Assistant Adjutant General (AAG) for the half of the Army of Northern Virginia commanded by Stonewall Jackson. After Jackson's death in May of '63, Stonewall's corps came under the command of Richard Ewell. General Ewell kept Sandie as his AAG. By August 1863, Sandie was a lieutenant colonel, the highest rank permitted for a corps-level AAG.

Pendleton saw action in virtually all of Stonewall's battles beginning with First Manassas (called Bull Run by the Yankees) in July '61. Stonewall's battle report cited him for rendering "valuable service" under fire. In the Shenandoah Valley at the Battle of Kernstown, Sandie joined a gun crew when a cannoneer was wounded. During the Battle of the Seven Days around Richmond in June of '62, Sandie was at Stonewall's side. At Cedar Mountain in August '62, Stonewall Jackson defeated Federal General Pope's forward divisions. Again, Jackson's battle report cited Sandie for giving "great assistance" to the cause.

When General Lee looked disaster in the eye at Sharpsburg beside Antietam Creek, Pendleton was with Jackson on the left flank of the army. At Fredericksburg three months later, a Yankee bullet struck Sandie in the side with a potentially fatal wound. But a lucky pocketknife prevented the hot lead from crashing into his chest. He received a bruise instead of a death blow. (Next time, his luck would run out.)

"So tell me, Sandie, did you bring Miss Kate with you to Richmond?"

Sandie smiled, "Not this time, General."

During the war's first months, Sandie had written his sister that when the fighting was finally over, he planned to "hunt me a wife and get married." Sandie's hunt ended earlier than planned, exactly one year ago. When Jackson's corps went into winter camp in December '62, Old Jack set up winter quarters at Moss Neck, the Corbin plantation. While camped at Moss Neck, Sandie met 23-year-old Kate Corbin, the sister of plantation owner Richard Corbin. Sandie's hunt for a wife ended swiftly and he became engaged to Kate in March of '63.

Their wedding day was to be October 23, 1863. But Kate's brother Richard was killed in action on September 13th. Richard's only child was dead by then too: little Janie whom Stonewall had loved. The wedding had been reset for November 25th—two weeks before the court martial of General Lee. But the wedding was again postponed when Lee canceled all leaves pending his aborted Mine Run campaign through the snow and ice. The general felt so badly about ruining Sandie's plans that Mrs. Lee wrote Kate a letter of consolation. When the wedding date of December 16th was set, Sandie could not get a furlough. But now, he was set to take the plunge four days after Christmas—in only 15 days. Sandie's preacher father, General William Pendleton, would officiate.

"I surely hope, Sandie, that nothing will prevent the happy day this time—not even General Meade." Robert Lee smiled.

The two soldiers sat silently for a long time.

"Are you alright, General?" Sandie asked softly.

"Yes." Lee looked down at his hands folded in his lap. "It's just that having you drop by these sorry proceedings is like having our General Jackson back." His voice stuck in his throat and his sore heart pained him.

"God knows," Sandie Pendleton nodded, "I would have died for him."

General Lee sat quietly beside Sandie Pendleton. Two rigid sentries guarded the closed doorway behind the general and Pendleton. In the peace of the empty gallery, Lee let his beard touch his gray waistcoat. His gold buttons reflected the flickering flames from the fireplace just as they had done when the Chancellor house burned behind him at Chancellorsville.

Sandie's elbow touched Lee's arm. After a long moment, the blond soldier glanced at his general. He saw Robert Lee close his eyes. The weary chief seemed to doze peacefully.

Behind General Lee's closed eyes, his mind wandered back over the two bloody years which had followed the election of Abraham Lincoln. Moved by the company of Sandie Pendleton, Lee remembered the pale blue eyes of Stonewall Jackson.

★   ★   ★

Lieutenant General Richard Ewell—Old Bald Head to his troops—had been a division commander under Old Jack during the Valley Campaign of spring '62. Early in that Shenandoah warfare, General Ewell had called Jackson "that enthusiastic fanatic." A monumental cusser, the little man tilted his head to speak, lisped mightily, and refused to eat real food. Ewell ate only a concoction of boiled wheat, milk, sugar, and egg yolk which he called "frumenty."

In May of '62, General Ewell said to Colonel James Walker of the 13th Virginia that Old Jack was "as crazy as a March hare." If Walker learned to admire Jackson, too, his respect was late in coming. When Walker was a cadet at Virginia Military Institute, Old Jack was his professor, then known among the cadet corps as Tom Fool Jackson. Walker had challenged Tom Fool Jackson to a duel to the death. Professor Jackson had Walker expelled rather than shoot him dead.

Jackson understood early that the war was for killing. At the little battle of Cross Keys in the Shenandoah Valley in June 1862, Confederate riflemen refused to shoot a particularly heroic Yankee officer. Jackson was livid. "The brave and gallant Federal officers are the very kind that must be killed," Jackson raved. "Shoot the brave officers and the cowards will run away and take the brave men with them."

Graduating from the Point in '46, Second Lieutenant Jackson in the artillery corps went off to the little war in Mexico. In March of '47, Jackson was under fire for five days during the attack on Vera Cruz where he was commended officially for "gallant and meritorious conduct."

In May 1851, Jackson had resigned from the United States Army and won an appointment to the faculty of the Virginia Military Institute in Lexington.

When Virginia left the Union, Governor Letcher placed Professor Jackson in command of a unit of VMI upper-classmen ordered to the Richmond garrison. Jackson was quickly promoted to colonel in the Virginia Militia. Colonel Jackson was dispatched to Harper's Ferry to take command there.

Jackson arrived at Harper's Ferry on April 30, 1861. During his hitch at Harper's, he found a new little horse named Fancy, soon dubbed Little Sorrel by the troops. Sorrel was yellowish and small and would lie down like a puppy to sleep on his front legs. Fancy quickly became Jackson's favorite mount. Riding Little Sorrel, Stonewall Jackson received his mortal wounds at Chancellorsville.

On October 7, 1861, Stonewall was promoted to major general. He was three months shy of his 38th birthday.

On November 4th, Major General Jackson was detached from eastern Virginia and was given command of the Shenandoah Valley district. The Shenandoah Valley was Virginia's breadbasket of rich farmland between the Allegheny Mountains to the west and the Blue Ridge Mountains to the east.

On March 23, 1862, Jackson's Valley Army of 3,000 weary men engaged General James Shields' blue legions of 12,000 troops at Kernstown in the Valley. Fighting was ferocious. Brigadier General Richard Garnett led the old Stonewall Brigade until ammunition was exhausted. Under withering fire, General Garnett pulled his brigade off the line to avoid extermination. The Rebels left 718 men bleeding on the field beside 590 Federal casualties. Outraged, Old Jack had General Garnett arrested for withdrawing without orders. Garnett would spend the next two years laboring under fire to prove his mettle. General Garnett would die at Gettysburg in Pickett's Charge.

On April 1st, McClellan landed 121,500 men on Virginia soil together with 44 cannon, 1,150 wagons of supplies, and 15,600 horses. But Jackson had bought time for Richmond. On April 4th, McClellan's offensive was temporarily crippled when President Lincoln ordered McClellan to detach General Irvin McDowell's entire blue corps to the Blue Ridge and Nathaniel Banks' division into the Valley to find Stonewall's wily and ragged army.

On the 21st while General McDowell threatened Fredericksburg, General Lee wrote a fateful letter to General Jackson in the Shenandoah. Lee suggested that Jackson's and Ewell's divisions distract General Banks in the Valley. Banks and Shields had some 20,000 men between them. Another 10,000 blueclads were detached from General McDowell to Winchester. In all, the massing Federals had some 70,000 men. General Lee authorized Jackson to strike the Federals anywhere Stonewall might choose. Jackson only had 10,000 men, yet General Lee counted on Stonewall to detain these divisions.

Immediately, Stonewall Jackson began his Valley Campaign. Jackson's hungry men covered 16 miles of mountains in two days. If Jackson could link up with Ewell's division at Swift Run, the entire Valley Army would muster only 17,000 men among 17 Virginia regiments, 5 Louisiana regiments, 2 Georgia regiments, and one regiment each from North Carolina, Alabama, Mississippi, and Maryland.

By May 5th, McClellan's divisions were at West Point, Virginia, only 37 miles from Richmond.

On the 7th, Stonewall was in motion to join General Edward "Allegheny" Johnson's brigade in pursuit of Brigadier General Robert Milroy's Federals near the hamlet of McDowell. General Milroy was an Indiana lawyer. Generals Milroy and Robert Schenck (an Ohio lawyer) were under the command of Major General John Fremont, a Georgian by birth and Union loyalist.

Near dawn on the 8th, Stonewall's division marched quickly from Staunton toward Allegheny Johnson's brigade. Jackson arrived in mid-afternoon after covering 20 exhausting miles over the Shenandoah Mountains to Bull Pasture Mountain. Confederates held the high ground above the tiny town of McDowell. Union General Milroy was reinforced by General Schenck's brigade.

The 3,000 graybacks held off assaults by 2,500 Yankees. General Johnson was severely wounded, but Milroy's Yankees were driven from the field in orderly retreat. By dark, Stonewall held the field while the Federals withdrew overnight.

The Confederate President met with his cabinet and General Lee on May 14th at the presidential mansion. One question had to be resolved: Would Richmond be evacuated or stand a siege until starved into surrender? Lee passionately urged the defense of Richmond to the last drop of blood. "Richmond," General Lee pleaded, "must be defended. Richmond shall not be given up!" Before the meeting broke for the night, the decision was made to hold the capital.

On the 17th, General Shields' blueclads numbering at least 6,000 men dragged 36 cannon over the Blue Ridge Mountains on their way to Fredericksburg.

Stonewall knew that he had to keep the Federals in the Valley from joining McDowell at Fredericksburg or McClellan on Richmond's doorstep. Stonewall's men already called themselves Jackson's Foot Cavalry in honor of their exhausting marches. In the preceding twenty days, they had covered 230 mountainous miles on bare and bleeding feet. Jackson had to hurry to prevent the Federals ahead of him from joining the Richmond offensive: General McClellan was now only 12 miles from Richmond at Bottom's Bridge.

On May 21st the divisions of Jackson and Ewell linked up near the town of Luray. Their combined force numbered 17,000 men and 50 cannon. Ahead of them lay the Federal garrison at Front Royal.

The Confederates deployed at daybreak on May 23rd. Only 1,063

Federals held Front Royal on the road which led to the strong Federal position at Strasburg on the Valley Pike to the west. Ewell's division stormed the town. The out-numbered Yankees crumbled.

On May 24th, General McClellan's army captured Mechanicsville, only five miles from Richmond. Little Mac had 35,000 men straddling the Chickahominy River close to the Mechanicsville Turnpike leading straight south to Richmond.

Stonewall's weary troops marched all night on May 24-25. At 2 o'clock in the morning of the 25th, the graybacks were given a one-hour rest. Regiments dropped where they stood and slept on the road. When the entire division collapsed in their own tracks, only Stonewall Jackson stayed awake while his army rested. Old Jack watched over his weary men as their solitary sentry.

Stonewall's division stirred before the sun on May 25th. Jackson's division deployed southwest of Winchester. General Ewell's division deployed southeast of town.

With the spring sun just at treetop level, Old Jack saw the Union line half a mile long. As the sweating Confederates marched past General Jackson, a column let loose a cheer. Jackson instantly ordered silence so close to the Yankees. So without a sound, regiment after regiment lifted their hats in silent and awful tribute to their dour chieftain with the pale blue eyes. As the files marched into position with their caps raised, Old Jack silently raised his own tattered VMI cap to return the silent salute.

Stonewall's two divisions fell upon the Federals from two sides at breakfast time on a calm Sunday morning in the Shenandoah. The Rebel attack on Winchester was led by Brigadier General Richard Taylor and his 6th Louisiana Brigade. He was son of President Zachary Taylor and the brother of Jefferson Davis' first wife. Taylor's men executed a line-charge upslope into the Federal riflepits. Taylor charged from west to east. Jackson's division followed from the southwest while Baldy Ewell's division charged Winchester from the southeast. The Union line collapsed.

By 7:30 in the Sunday morning sunshine, General Banks was in full retreat. Rebel infantrymen pursued for an hour and a half. Old

Jack's ferocious fighters ran after the Federals for five miles until they dropped from exhaustion. They had marched 100 miles in a single week while waging a running battle for 30 hours between Front Royal and Winchester.

Since Jackson had to do battle on Sunday, the former Sunday School teacher from Lexington issued orders that Sunday Sabbath would be observed on Monday.

Late on May 28th, stunning news arrived in the Confederate capital: General McDowell's division bound for Richmond had suddenly reversed course and was marching not toward Richmond but back toward the Shenandoah Valley. Abraham Lincoln had learned of General Banks' defeat at Winchester. Richmond could not be taken until Stonewall Jackson was annihilated. From the Valley of Virginia 120 miles to the west, Stonewall Jackson had saved Richmond from standing a siege on the 29th of May 1862.

Stonewall's two divisions were scattered between Winchester in the Valley and Harper's Ferry on the Potomac. Before dawn on the 31st, Old Jack's command was abandoning Winchester for the march toward Strasburg to stay clear of Generals John Fremont and Shields. Honest Abe's plan called for Generals McDowell and Shields to send their divisions against Stonewall from the east over the Blue Ridge toward Front Royal with General Fremont to strike over the Alleghenies through Harrisonburg.

The race of Generals Shields, Banks, McDowell, and Fremont to corner the Valley Army continued on June 2nd.

By June 3rd, Stonewall was near New Market on the Valley Pike, having crossed the North Fork of the Shenandoah before burning the bridge. Just behind them, General Fremont was laying a pontoon bridge across the North Fork to link up with General Shields for the final assault into Jackson's rearguard.

On June 7th, Baldy Ewell camped at Cross Keys, a hamlet four miles northwest of the Stonewall Division's bivouac at Port Republic. Ewell counted 5,000 Rebel rifles and Jackson mustered 3,000 down the road.

On June 8th, General Ewell engaged General Fremont on the

ridge line overlooking Cross Keys. From the superior position of the high ground, Ewell battered the Federals severely. Holding his line to the end, Baldy Ewell all but destroyed the 8th New York regiment of Fremont's command. The Union men left 557 dead and wounded along the green slopes.

After only five hours of fitful sleep on the morning of the 9th, Jackson's division assaulted General Shields' division at Lewiston Coaling on the South Fork River, two and one-half miles east of Port Republic. Fighting raged nearly four hours. Fifteen Yankee cannon pounded the hungry and tired Confederates. Toward 11 o'clock in the morning, the Confederate line was in serious trouble.

Even the famous Stonewall Brigade under General Winder crumbled and was nearly routed. They were saved from panic only when Old Jack himself trotted over and cried above the fire, "Follow me!" The brigade rallied and endured hand-to-hand butchery with the determined Federals. By noon, Baldy Ewell's division arrived from Cross Keys. With Ewell's support, the Rebels beat back the Federals who executed an orderly withdrawal. The little Valley Army of hardly 16,000 men held their ground against 60,000 bluecoats.

Stonewall held the field at Port Republic by noon. But he had suffered his worst casualties of the Valley Campaign: 800 men were dead or wounded. The retreating Federals lost 500 men killed or wounded, 500 prisoners, 800 small arms, and 5 cannon. In 48 hours the Stonewall Division and Baldy Ewell had defeated both Fremont and Shields.

On June 16th while the Valley Army licked its wounds, General Lee ordered Jackson's command to come quickly to the defense of Richmond. McClellan had been put on hold for the two weeks since Jackson had terrorized the Federals at Front Royal.

On June 17th, the Valley Army left the Port Republic area and headed east toward Staunton, arriving there on the 18th. On that day, the Valley Army of Stonewall Jackson crossed the Blue Ridge for Richmond and left behind the Valley of Virginia forever.

Jackson boarded a train to Gordonsville, Virginia, on the 21st.

Stonewall, already beyond worn out, took the last 52 miles to General Lee's headquarters on horseback. After 14 hours in the saddle non-stop, Stonewall arrived on June 23rd at General Lee's side near Nine Mile Bridge at the Dabb's House at High Meadows outside embattled Richmond.

Stonewall's meager Valley Army of 17,000 raw recruits had kept 175,000 Yankees off balance both in the Valley and out on the Peninsula between the Atlantic and Richmond.

Between May 30th and June 5th, Stonewall had driven his "foot cavalry" 104 miles. Between March 22nd and June 9th, Jackson had marched 676 miles during 48 days on the road. His barefoot troops had defeated four Yankee armies totaling 62,000 men under Generals Fremont, Shields, Banks, and McDowell. Jackson had left 3,500 bluecoats dead or wounded and he had captured another 3,500. He brought with him to the defense of Richmond some 10,000 captured small arms and 9 cannon with "USA" stamped on their muzzles. His victories cost 2,500 Confederates killed and wounded with another 600 marching north to Yankee prison camps.

Fourteen months earlier, Stonewall Jackson had been Old Tom Fool, the laughing stock of Virginia Military Institute.

★   ★   ★

General Lee at Sandie Pendleton's side touched his finger to the corners of his dark eyes. His gesture roused young Sandie in the empty committee chamber.

"I was thinking of our General Jackson," Lee shrugged wearily.

General Lee took a deep breath. His voice cracked.

"Such an executive officer the sun never shone on. I had only to show him my design, and I knew that if it could be done, it would be done." Robert Lee pounded a tight fist into his open palm. "No need for me to send him or watch him, straight as the needle to the pole he advanced to the execution of my purpose."

"Oh for the presence and inspiration of Stonewall just for one hour!" Sandie Pendleton said softly.

"We shall not see his like again," Robert Lee sighed with a terrible resignation in his deep voice.

Chapter Nine

Monday Afternoon, December 14, 1863

It was not war. It was murder.
> Daniel Harvey Hill, Major General,
> Army of Northern Virginia,
> Malvern Hill, July 1, 1862

General Lee and Sandie Pendleton rose when the doors to the chamber creaked open. The sentries entered first with the milling throng behind them. Mrs. Lee hobbled in on the arm of Walter Taylor.

"Excuse me, Colonel," General Lee smiled politely to Sandie Pendleton. "It was my pleasure visiting with you. Your support means much to me. Do give my warm regards to your father."

"Yes, Sir." Sandie shook the general's hand.

General Lee walked to Mrs. Lee's side. Taylor released his grip on Mrs. Lee's arm. The general helped his wife walk to her seat in the first row of the gallery.

"You did not eat, Robert?" Mary Lee asked softly.

"No, Molly. Sandie and I shared a quiet moment reflecting upon General Jackson."

Mother Lee nodded. She could take nothing from her husband's grief over the mere mention of Stonewall's name. As they walked slowly, the general glanced at his pocket watch which read 1:30.

"We may be here another three hours, Mother."

"I'll be fine, Robert."

"Of course you will."

Mrs. Lee sat down and the gallery filled behind her.

Major General Jeb Stuart arrived in the crowd directly behind Mrs. Lee. Jeb and General Lee exchanged cordial greetings.

Among the last of the gallery to enter the chamber was A.P. Hill, who looked thin and sickly.

When the assembly of spectators was full, the armed sentries at the door snapped to attention. Senator Louis Wigfall entered and led his colleagues to their raised platform. The gallery rose except Mrs. Lee.

"Please be seated," Senator Wigfall's voice filled the chamber as the sentries closed the double doors and rested their rifle butts at their heels.

"General Lee, Secretary Benjamin, may we proceed?" Chairman Wigfall asked courteously.

Judah Benjamin nodded.

"Thank you. Back on record....General Lee, I believe we were up to events of June 1862 and your assumption of command in the field of Virginia forces. I remind you that you are still under oath."

General Lee nodded from the witness table.

"What were your duties commencing June 1st?"

"For the first three weeks of June 1862, I directed the construction of field fortifications around Richmond as General McClellan approached the capital from the east," Lee said dryly.

"Yes, General. And you took the field in late June for the so-called Battle of the Seven Days?"

"I did, Mr. Chairman."

When Lee replaced Joe Johnston on June 1st, General McClellan's massive army was within five miles of the Confederate capital. Little Mac was poised to strike with 105,000 troops in Union blue.

George McClellan was only 35 when he camped on Richmond's

doorstep. In April 1862, Little Mac formally assessed his Peninsula adversaries, Generals Lee and Joe Johnston, in a letter to President Lincoln. "I prefer Lee to Johnston—the former is too cautious and weak under grave responsibility—personally brave and energetic to a fault," Little Mac wrote bravely, "yet he is wanting in moral firmness when pressed by heavy responsibility and is likely to be timid and irresolute in action."

"General Lee," Chairman Wigfall continued, "what were your intentions during late June of '62?"

"Sir, I knew that the Union force was prepared to invest Richmond from the north and east, having marched almost unmolested from Aquia Creek on the Atlantic to Richmond. I resolved to bring General Jackson's command from the Valley of Virginia and to strike the Federals with our combined armies before General McClellan could lay siege to the capital."

"Were these plans formulated prior to the sequence of battles known in the press as the Seven Days?"

"Fairly so, yes, Senator. However, I waited to meet in the field with my division commanders to formally put the plan into operation."

But unknown to General Lee, by June 21st a Confederate deserter had already alerted McClellan to Lee's planned offensive.

"General, were you acquainted with General McClellan's position in late June?"

"Indeed, Mr. Chairman. General Stuart's illustrious Ride Around McClellan in mid-June provided most useful intelligence on the Federal positions."

A murmur rose in the gallery which quickly broke into applause for Jeb Stuart who enjoyed the ovation.

Senator Wigfall did nothing to quiet the outburst of good will toward the general of cavalry whose Ride Around McClellan was legend. When the dour Chairman leaned back in his chair to let the clapping continue, Jeb could not resist standing with mock gravity to attempt to quiet the gallery. With his large hands, he urged the gallery to quiet.

"I had been to the Chickahominy to visit some old friends of the United States Army," Stuart smiled behind his massive beard, "but they, very uncivilly, turned their backs on me."

When Jeb sat down, the laughter and applause began again. Senator Wigfall gaveled the gallery to silence.

"I met with my field commanders," the witness continued, "on June 23rd just outside Richmond at the Dabb's house at Nine Mile Bridge near High Meadows. With me were Generals Longstreet, A.P. Hill, Harvey Hill, and Jackson—all division commanders."

While Lee held his council of war, General McClellan had four Union corps with 75,000 men camped only six miles east of Richmond south of the Chickahominy River. Federal General Fitz-John Porter bivouacked another corps near Mechanicsville, along Beaver Dam Creek six miles northeast of the Confederate capital and north of the river.

"We conferred throughout the afternoon of the 23rd, Mr. Chairman, from 3 to 7 o'clock."

"Did you leave that meeting, General, with a plan at hand?" Senator Wigfall inquired.

"Yes, Senator. General Stuart's Ride Around McClellan two weeks earlier had found the Federal right flank to be in the air on the north side of the Chickahominy. General Jackson's force was at Beaver Dam, 15 miles northwest of Richmond. We resolved to strike the Federal right flank, cut off as it was from the larger Union force south of the river. It was agreed that General Jackson would take the road south across Totopotomoy Creek to capture the bridges across the Chickahominy. Generals Jackson and A.P. Hill were to join forces to seize Mechanicsville and McClellan's supply trains at Cold Harbor. I left it to my generals to work out the details."

"Isn't it a fact," Senator Edwin Reade asked with a twinge of hostility in his voice, "that General Jackson was given the longest route for assembly of your combined forces on the 25th and 26th?"

"That was the case, Senator."

"And in view of General Jackson's fatigue after his Valley campaign, was that a wise decision, General?"

Robert Lee shrugged.

"I presume it was not, upon reflection, Sir."

After the June 23rd conference, Stonewall Jackson rode all night to rendezvous with his two divisions at Beaver Dam. The all-night ride was through rain and mud. Stonewall slept in the rain under his rubber poncho. In 96 hours of marching out of the Valley for Richmond, Jackson had slept but ten hours. During the 24th of June, Jackson's divisions slogged through mud for the 40-mile march from Beaver Dam Station to the exposed Union right flank near Hundley's Corner along Totopotomoy Creek.

By the 25th, Jackson was near Hanover Court House. His footsore divisions covered 20 miles on the 25th. On the 26th, he broke camp at 8 o'clock in the morning. He arrived at Hundley's Corner by 5 o'clock in the afternoon while Generals A.P. Hill and Harvey Hill were being bloodied at Beaver Dam Creek.

"Did General Jackson arrive in time at the appointed concentration point at Ashland on the 25th of June?" Chairman Wigfall leaned forward.

General Lee's voice sounded resigned.

"In consequence of unavoidable delays, the whole of General Jackson's command did not arrive at Ashland in time to enable him to reach the point designated on the 25th. His march was consequently longer than had been anticipated."

"Were there inherent problems which were not anticipated, General?"

"Yes, Senator. Among the very serious handicaps borne by our army was the lack of credible maps, even of the countryside around Richmond. When the war began, the entire Confederacy had only

13 engineers with prior experience in the U.S. Corps of Engineers. The Provisional Army of the Confederate States had only 93 engineers drawn from the civilian sector."

While Stonewall Jackson plowed without sleep through knee-deep mud on June 24th toward the Richmond front, General Lee issued his first great plan of battle, General Orders Number 75. Orders delivered on the 24th to dispersed field commanders called for concerted and complex action against General McClellan on the 26th.

General Orders 75 required not less than nine massive movements of the Army of Northern Virginia's 80,760 men. Within 48 hours, General Lee expected accurate deployment of 39 infantry brigades, three battalions of mounted cavalry, and 16 batteries of artillery.

"General Lee, can you summarize G.O. 75, since its text will be read into the record later?" Senator Wigfall shuffled his pile of documents.

"General Jackson," the witness swallowed hard on the words. "General Jackson was to march from Ashland on the 25th in the direction of Slash Church, encamping for the night west of the Central Railroad, and to advance at 3 o'clock a.m. on the 26th and take Beaver Dam. General A.P. Hill was to cross the Chickahominy at Meadow Bridge when Jackson's advance beyond that point could be known, and move directly upon Mechanicsville. As soon as the Mechanicsville Bridge could be uncovered, Longstreet and D.H. Hill were to cross the river, the latter to proceed to the support of Jackson and the former to that of A.P. Hill."

On June 25th, Stonewall's bedraggled divisions marched 20 miles through the mud to find A.P. Hill's command. That night, Stonewall's men rested at Ashland, seven miles from the Virginia Central Railroad checkpoint. After a few hours sleep with rifles in hand, Jackson's divisions planned to move out by 2:30 in the morning of the 26th. But profound exhaustion delayed their march past daybreak.

Stonewall Jackson's command left Ashland at 8 o'clock in the morning of the 26th. By 9:30, his men crossed the Virginia Central Railroad line, at least six hours behind schedule. Early in the morning, General Lee left his Dabb's House headquarters and headed down Nine Mile Road for the Mechanicsville Turnpike. Lee stopped on a hill overlooking Mechanicsville.

By 8 o'clock with Stonewall stalled at Ashland, Generals Longstreet and Harvey Hill were assembled east of the Chickahominy River where they impatiently awaited Jackson's signal cannon which would send their divisions against the Yankees. A.P. Hill's division waited at Meadow Bridge. For the first time, Hill wore his red "battle shirt" sewn by his beloved Dolly. The red shirt would become his trademark.

At 11 o'clock, Stonewall's brigades stopped their forced march at the Chickahominy to fill their dry canteens. While the ragged men knelt at the riverbank, Brigadier General Lawrence Branch's regiments skirmished with Federals at Atlee's Station, one mile east of the river where Stonewall slumped exhausted and nearly comatose. While Generals A.P. Hill, Daniel Harvey Hill (no relation), and James Longstreet waited anxiously for Jackson's signal, Stonewall rested his men from noon until 1 o'clock at the Shelton homestead, one and a half miles east of Totopotomoy Creek. Between 2 o'clock and 3 o'clock, Jeb Stuart's cavalry regiments arrived at Jackson's position.

At 3 o'clock in the afternoon, Jackson skirmished with Federals along Totopotomoy Creek. A.P. Hill never did hear Stonewall's signal guns because the cannon were never fired to hail Jackson's advance into the exposed Federal rearguard. Stonewall was supposed to dislodge General Porter's bluecoats from their trenches, but Jackson never reached his appointed position.

"When, General Lee, did the primary assault against the Union works commence? I understand that Major General Hill engaged on his own without direct orders from you."

In the back row of the gallery, the red-bearded A.P. Hill looked uncomfortable and his gaunt face flushed. Lee did not look over his gray shoulder when he spoke of his devoted and hot-tempered subordinate.

"General A.P. Hill did not begin his movement until 3 p.m., when he crossed the river and advanced upon Mechanicsville. After a sharp conflict, he drove the enemy from his entrenchments."

Out of patience and spoiling for a fight, A.P. Hill had enough of waiting for Stonewall by 3 o'clock. Hill had crossed the Chickahominy and five brigades had deployed in a mile-long line north of Mechanicsville along Beaver Dam Creek. Hill decided to engage the Yankees himself, without any idea where Jackson's divisions were.

By 4 o'clock in the afternoon, Stonewall moved slowly southward near Pole Green Church. Hill opened with his cannon against the dug-in Federals while Generals Longstreet and Harvey Hill prepared to cross the Chickahominy at Mechanicsville Bridge.

When Hill began the great battle to save Richmond virtually on his own initiative, the Federals were entrenched one mile east of Mechanicsville. The bluecoats numbered some 30,000. Two-thirds of the Army of Northern Virginia were still north of the Chickahominy and out of the picture as Hill's brave division walked calmly into the hailstorm of Union bullets and cannon fire.

"General," Chairman Wigfall sniffed, "weren't Brigadier General Dorsey Pender's men cut to pieces as the Confederate army engaged superior numbers and superior positions?"

The gallery murmured as the weary witness collected his thoughts.

"D.H. Hill's leading brigade under General Ripley advanced to support the troops engaged, and at a late hour united with General Pender's brigade of A.P. Hill's division in an effort to turn the enemy's left. But the troops were unable in the growing darkness to overcome the obstructions. After sustaining a destructive fire of musketry and artillery at short range, they were withdrawn."

Toward 5 o'clock in lengthening shadows, General Lee on his hill watched A.P. Hill deploy against overwhelming Union numbers. For two hours, Hill's men were pinned down under murderous fire. At 7 o'clock, A.P. Hill was joined by part of Harvey Hill's division and together they attacked the Federal right flank. The Rebels were driven back, leaving 1,400 casualties upon the bloodied fields around Mechanicsville. The 44th Georgia regiment of Dorsey Pender's brigade, A.P. Hill's division, lost 335 of 514 men in the bloodbath.

In the fading light of day, the Federals slowly pulled back from their Mechanicsville lines. Gunfire continued until well after dark, lighting the sky with artillery fuses until 9 o'clock. There still was no word from Jackson who was bogged down by mud, Yankees, and fatigue at Walnut Grove Church, two and a half miles northwest of the hamlet of Gaines' Mill. In the dark, the battered Confederates finally captured Mechanicsville at the end of the first of the Seven Days. Two thousand Rebels had been sacrificed during Hill's day of ferocious fighting along Beaver Dam Creek with Stonewall Jackson lost somewhere over the smoky horizon.

At 10:30 on the night of the 26th, General Lee met for a war council with Major Generals Longstreet, A.P. Hill, and Daniel Harvey Hill. Stonewall's whereabouts remained unknown.

"General," Congressman Foote demanded, "what percentage of your combined forces were actually brought to bear upon the enemy on the evening of June 26th, as compared to what was planned?"

"Mr. Co-Chairman, we concentrated perhaps 25 percent of our force."

"That's all, General?"

"Yes, Sir."

Although the Confederates carried the field, General Lee had managed to collect only 14,000 of his 56,000 men on the contested hillsides around Mechanicsville. Mechanicsville was nearly a disaster.

An intense whisper of voices spread through the back row of the gallery. A thin officer had risen and pushed his way past seated spectators. A.P. Hill glared at the Select Committee as he made his way toward the closed door of the stuffy chamber.

"Permission to step outside for a breath of air, Mr. Chairman?" Hill piped with an anguished voice.

"Are you well, General?" Chairman Wigfall asked courteously.

"Yes, Sir. I just need some air....The general's testimony brings up so many memories. Forgive me, Sir." Hill paused at the doorway where a young sentry stood ready to open the door.

"General Hill," Senator Wigfall asked with a kindly voice, "might I ask your reflections on the Battle of Mechanicsville?"

"Objection!" Judah Benjamin shouted as he jumped from his seat at General Lee's side. "You cannot interrogate an unsworn witness out-of-order!"

Hill stood stiffly at the doorway. Perspiration beaded on his forehead. In the middle of the chamber, Judah Benjamin's round face was red with anger.

"Now, Secretary Benjamin, this is a board of inquiry, not a court of law. You may call General Hill for direct testimony later. I am only asking General Hill for a brief statement of his impressions of that engagement. After all, General Hill did bear the brunt of the fighting during General Jackson's inexplicable absence. Your objection is overruled and your exception is duly noted of record."

Judah Benjamin sat down at General Lee's side.

"Now, General Hill," Senator Wigfall repeated gently, "kindly give us your very brief assessment of the Mechanicsville engagement."

Hill looked hard into Senator Wigfall's face and he spoke firmly.

"It was never contemplated that my division alone should have sustained the shock of this battle...but such was the case." Hill's voice carried a trace of sadness.

"Sergeant, you may allow General Hill to leave." Chairman Wigfall sat silently as Hill pushed into the hallway and the doors closed behind him.

Chairman Wigfall quickly arrested the murmur of the gallery which accompanied the departure of General Hill. The burly senator's gavel directed everyone's attention back to the raised platform at the front of the chamber.

"General Lee, if you please, the Federals were engaged on the day after Mechanicsville, were they not? We are speaking now of June 27, 1862, and the second day of the Battle of the Seven Days."

"Yes, Senator." Lee's weary face became animated. "Long lines of dead and wounded marked each stand made by the enemy in his stubborn resistance. The field over which he retreated was strewn with the slain." When he spoke, a strange light fired his black eyes. General Lee's face betrayed the ferocity which gentlemen warriors labor to deny.

"What was the disposition of the Union force on June 27th?"

"The principal part of the Federal army was now on the north side of the Chickahominy. General Hill's single division met this large force...." Lee paused for a breath as he thought of his sickly lieutenant who had to leave the chamber rather than walk again those ghastly fields. "Hill's single division met this large force with the impetuous courage for which that officer and his troops are distinguished." The witness allowed a soft flurry of whispers to subside behind him. "Three regiments pierced the enemy's line and forced their way to the crest of the hill on his left, but were compelled to fall back before overwhelming numbers. Though most of the men had never been under fire until the day before, they were rallied and, in return, repelled the advance of the enemy."

General Lee waited for Senator Wigfall's follow-up questions on the Battle of Gaines' Mill along the Chickahominy River, barely nine miles northeast of Richmond.

"I might add, Senator, that General McClellan's headquarters that day was at White House, my son Fitzhugh Lee's farm."

"Yes, General. This committee certainly extends to you and to your family our sincere hopes that your son will soon be paroled and exchanged from captivity at the hands of our enemies. Now, Sir, if we may continue, did General Jackson participate in the Gaines' Mill operation on the 27th of June?"

"Yes, Mr. Chairman, General Jackson's division finally arrived on the field in the evening—after General Hill's brave men had engaged the enemy."

Stonewall arrived at the Gaines' Mill battlefield five hours after A.P. Hill's bloodied division had plunged into the Union lines. Jackson forced march into the thick of the Battle of the Seven Days was not less than 34 hours behind the schedule dictated. Hill did battle with the Yankees so ferociously that one of Hill's cannon actually melted after launching 239 hissing artillery shells into the Federal lines.

Robert Lee spoke softly as he glossed over the slowness of the exhausted Stonewall's progress. Jackson's division had been expected to draw the Federal fire away from A.P. Hill's division. But he did not arrive on the field until dusk, although Richard Ewell of Jackson's command had arrived earlier.

"The arrival of Jackson on our left was momentarily expected," General Lee said gently. "It was supposed that his approach would cause the extension of the enemy's line in that direction. The attack on our left being delayed by the length of Jackson's march and the obstacles he encountered, General Longstreet was ordered to make a diversion in Hill's favor by a feint on the enemy's left."

As General Lee shuffled his battlefield reports and hand-drawn maps, he saw in his mind a bloody field covered with the 2,688 casualties from Hill's division. He resumed his testimony and remembered the smell of fields and streams running with blood.

Near dawn on June 27th, General Lee paced the body-strewn battlefield of Mechanicsville. General Fitz-John Porter was pulling his bloodied Union division out of Mechanicsville.

By 9 o'clock in the morning, George McClellan was being pursued by four Confederate columns of 56,000 men. By 10 o'clock, Stonewall Jackson's division was near Walnut Grove Church at the intersection of the roads from Hundley's Corner and Cold Harbor. General Lee met there with A.P. Hill and a completely exhausted Stonewall Jackson. The commanding general expected McClellan to make a stand at Gaines' Mill, a rise along Powhite Creek. Lee ordered Generals Longstreet and A.P. Hill to move their divisions toward the creek while Jackson and Harvey Hill deployed their divisions north of Gaines' Mill.

Harvey Hill's division was at Old Cold Harbor by 11 o'clock. By noon, heavy firing erupted at Gaines' Mill. Lee trotted in the direction of the rising musketry where he took council with A.P. Hill. An artillery dual rattled above the thickets of Boatswain's Swamp where the Federals had dug-in. Battle was beginning but Stonewall's divisions were again missing somewhere in the mud and blood.

Toward 1 o'clock, A.P. Hill was heavily engaged and was falling back under the wall of hot lead from Federal muskets and cannon. General Lee delayed a countercharge until Stonewall's divisions could form on the extreme left of the Confederate line. But there was no word from Jackson, lost on the fringes of the dismal swamp.

So desperate was the need for Stonewall's two divisions that General Lee dispatched Walter Taylor into the firestorm to search for Jackson. Colonel Taylor found Stonewall four miles northeast of Old Cold Harbor. Taylor prodded Jackson to deploy on the left flank of the embattled Army of Northern Virginia. But Jackson stumbled through the underbrush for another five hours in a state of stupor from weeks of warfare.

Finally, by 3:30, Ewell's division from Stonewall's command managed to form on A.P. Hill's left with not a minute to spare. The famed Louisiana Brigade had been driven from the field for the first time in its heroic history. Jackson arrived near Harvey Hill's command fighting in the miserable swamp near New Cold Harbor. But Jackson was still not on the Gaines' Mill battlefield.

While waiting for the lost Stonewall to find the battlefield, General Lee sent direct orders to Major General Longstreet to do battle at A.P. Hill's side. This marked the first direct order given by General Lee under fire during the war.

Heavy fighting continued from 3:30 until dark. Between 4 and 5 o'clock, General Ewell's division fought on the Rebel left flank in the swamplands. Baldy Ewell had to tell General Lee that Stonewall's division was still missing somewhere in the rear. While Lee paced and watched the smoky horizon for Jackson's powerful division, the commanding general ordered the brigades of Generals John Hood and Evander Law forward on the Confederate right flank where Longstreet was engaged heavily.

Jackson did not appear on the field until 5 o'clock and did not deploy his weary division until 6 o'clock in the lengthening shadows. As dusk darkened the countryside, Longstreet fought fiercely on the Rebel right. General Hood's brigade of Texans plugged a dangerous gap in the Confederate line on Longstreet's left. Hood's 4th Texas regiment and the 18th Georgia charged the Union line along Powhite Creek in the darkening twilight. The 4th Texas suffered 25 percent casualties.

Stonewall's division did not take the field until darkness. In bitter fighting, his division lost 3,700 men. The Federal army was in retreat. Gunfire continued until 9 o'clock.

The weary witness paused and drew a breath. "The enemy," General Lee continued, "were driven from the ravine to the first line of breastworks. These were quickly stormed, fourteen pieces of artillery were captured, and the enemy driven into the field beyond."

The cool darkness covered a battlefield littered with the dead and dying. The Confederates lost 8,358 men including at least eight colonels killed. General George Pickett was gravely wounded, but would recover to charge up Cemetery Ridge at Gettysburg. The retreating Federals left 6,837 men behind on the field together with 22 cannon.

In the dark of June 27th, General Lee conferred with Stonewall and Longstreet at the Hogan farm. As they spoke, General McClellan's plans for laying siege to Richmond went up in smoke. Little Mac was beaten and his only grand strategy now was to save his retreating divisions from annihilation at the hands of the man he had contemptuously called "Bobby Lee."

"Very well," Chairman Wigfall nodded. "Was McClellan engaged on the 28th after Gaines' Mill?"

"No," Robert Lee said wearily. "On the morning of the 28th, it was ascertained that none of the enemy remained in our front north of the Chickahominy."

During the day, the Confederates paused to tend the wounded. In the morning, Lee was at New Cold Harbor where he learned of the Federal withdrawal during the night. All of the invading Federals were now south of the Chickahominy River. McClellan was fleeing for his life down the Peninsula after abandoning his precious supply line on the York River Railroad.

"So, General," Senator Wigfall droned with fatigue in his voice, "after your forces regrouped on the 28th of June, I believe that General McClellan was then engaged on the 29th?"

"That is correct, Mr. Chairman. We met the enemy at Savage's Station, some 11 miles due east of Richmond on the Williamsburg Road. Major General John Magruder met the Federals in something of a rearguard action."

"Did General Jackson engage the enemy on the 29th?"

"He did not, Mr. Chairman."

"Had you intended to attack and destroy the Yankees on the 29th?"

"I did, Sir."

"How many miles did the Confederate army cover on the 29th in pursuit of the Federals?"

General Lee hesitated, gathering his tired thoughts.

"Five, Senator."

"Five miles only, General?"

"Five miles," the white-haired chief replied curtly. "Over roads watered with Confederate blood, Sir!"

"Indeed, General. What was the condition of the retreating, Federal army on the morning of the 29th?"

"General McClellan was in full retreat toward the James River. He abandoned his camp with the tents still standing."

"Tell us, General, did you intend to have Stonewall Jackson engage the fleeing Federals on the 29th?"

"I did, Sir."

"But you just testified that General Jackson took no part in the action of the 29th of June."

Robert Lee wiped perspiration from his flushed forehead. Then he spoke dryly and wearily.

"General Jackson was directed to cross the Chickahominy at Grapevine Bridge and move down the south side of the Chickahominy. Jackson's route led to the flank and rear of Savage's Station. But he was delayed by the necessity of reconstructing Grapevine Bridge. Late in the afternoon, Magruder attacked the enemy. A severe action ensued and it continued about two hours, then it was terminated by night."

"But only five miles were covered on the 29th, isn't that correct, General?"

"Sir, the troops displayed great gallantry and inflicted heavy loss upon the enemy." General Lee's voice was angry. "The result was not decisive and the enemy continued his retreat under cover of darkness."

"How long was Major General Jackson delayed at Grapevine Bridge while General Magruder's division met the enemy?"

"All day, Senator."

June 29th dawned hot and humid. At daybreak, General Lee crossed the Chickahominy and took the Nine Mile Road to Fair Oaks. He met there with 55-year-old Major General John Magruder, "Prince John" to the Old Army he had faithfully served since his

1830 graduation from West Point. He had ranked 15th in his class. Lee's West Point classmate (one year behind Lee), Magruder had served gallantly in Mexico.

Lee had outlined to General Magruder plans to attack McClellan over the next two days when the retreating Federals were stalled passing through White Oak Swamp. The plan was complex, like the mangled plan before Mechanicsville.

"General Lee, once you explained your order of battle to your field commanders, did you follow-up with supplementary orders or coordination from general headquarters during the 29th?" Representative Foote's expression suggested that he already knew the answer.

"No, Congressman, I did not."

At noon on the 29th of June 1862, Major General Magruder followed the retreating blue columns into a forest east of the hamlet of Fair Oaks. General Magruder stopped his pursuit and waited for the arrival of Stonewall Jackson who never showed. Magruder also waited for Major General Ben Huger, West Point '25, who had been brevetted to the rank of colonel during the Mexican War. Magruder's delay in waiting for Huger to form on the Confederate right flank was an error in Magruder's understanding of General Lee's complicated, but unwritten, orders for the day's action.

General Magruder sent an aide, Major Brent, to General Lee to inquire about Ben Huger's position. Lee sent Huger to Magruder's exposed right flank.

"General, did you ask Major Brent if General Jackson had joined General Magruder as planned?"

"No, Mr. Foote. I regret that I did not so inquire."

At 2 o'clock in the afternoon, General Huger withdrew from Magruder's flank when Huger thought that he was not needed there. But he neglected to inform Magruder that he was leaving with his division. With his line crumbling from poor command coordination, Magruder panicked in the face of Federal resistance. He ordered his division to attack the Yankees at will.

An inconclusive skirmish continued until dark. Stonewall never did come up from the bridge. When darkness put an end to the wasteful slaughter, a violent storm broke and raged until daylight.

Magruder took 11,000 men into the woods east of Fair Oaks at the battle of Savage's Station. But only half of them saw action. The disorganized Confederates suffered between 354 and 441 casualties while the retreating Yankees abandoned 2,500 wounded under rain and thunder.

"General Lee, were you satisfied with General Magruder's performance on the 29th?"

"Senator Hunter, I felt that General Magruder might have pressed the Federals to greater advantage. I communicated that regret by confidential communications directly to him."

The senator shuffled through his pile of papers. He pulled a document and handed it to the clerk who stopped his furious writing.

"The clerk will kindly mark this exhibit and hand it to General Lee and counsel, please."

The clerk marked the paper and handed it to Judah Benjamin. The secretary scanned the document and gave it to General Lee who frowned as he read it.

"General, can you identify this document?"

"Yes, Senator. It is my dispatch to Major General Magruder. It bears date 29 June 1862."

"Kindly read the dispatch, General."

Robert Lee hesitated and glanced sideways at Secretary Benjamin. The general's advocate nodded. The witness shook his head before reading the dispatch dictated 18 months ago.

"*I regret very much that you have made so little progress today in pursuit of the enemy. In order to reap the fruits of our victory, the pursuit must be most vigorous. I must urge you, then again, to press his rear rapidly and steadily. We must lose no more time or he will escape us entirely.*"

Senator Reade took over the questioning.

"Did the coming of night end the action on June 29th?"

"Not quite, Senator." General Lee glared hard at his interrogator. "Before his retreat from the field on June 29th, the enemy burned White House plantation, my son's home. This was more than a grievous, personal loss to my son Fitzhugh. The destruction of that grand old house was a loss to our sad country. On that site in a home destroyed some 30 years ago, George Washington married Martha Custis Washington. Now that historic place has been defiled by our enemies."

"We are all touched by our country's present difficulties," the Senator said softly. "The engagements continued on June 30th at Frayser's Farm?"

"Yes, Senator. Our forces fought bravely in the continuing effort to uncover Richmond."

"Yes, General. But on June 30th, were your efforts not again undermined by a failure to coordinate your combined forces?"

Lee toyed with his stack of documents for a moment before looking up.

"The superiority of numbers and advantage of position were on the side of the enemy. The battle raged furiously until 9 pm. By that time the enemy had been driven with great slaughter from every position but one."

"Yes, General," Senator Wigfall interrupted, "but the enemy was not destroyed at Frayser's Farm on the 30th of June. Was he? And Generals Jackson and Huger again failed to appear on the appointed field of battle. Wasn't that the case again?"

"Could the other commands have cooperated in the action," General Lee said passively, "the result would have proved most disastrous to the enemy."

"It would seem to me, General, that we have a clear picture of your failure to exercise sufficient control over your junior officers, the same failure which seems to have occurred at Gettysburg."

A murmur rumbled through the gallery.

"That is a judgment your committee will have to decide, Senator."

General Lee's orders of June 29th for pursuing the Federals on the 30th were again complicated for moving vast masses of battle-fatigued men through poorly mapped countryside. Lee's plans called for Jackson to continue repairing Grapevine Bridge and to cross the Chickahominy by the 30th to attack the bluecoats in White Oak Swamp with the assistance of the divisions of Generals Ewell, Whiting, and Harvey Hill. John Magruder was to advance from Savage's Station 11 miles down Williamsburg Road to support James Longstreet while Ben Huger advanced east on Charles City Road through White Oak Swamp.

The divisions of Longstreet and A.P. Hill were to move six miles down the Darbytown Road from Atlee's Station to Ben Huger's right flank. General Hunter Holmes, Robert Lee's classmate in the West Point class of 1829, was to march his brigade nine miles down New Market Road. The Rebel line placed General Holmes on the far right, with Longstreet and A.P. Hill (backed up by Magruder) in the near right and center, with Ben Huger on the left and Stonewall positioned in the Union rear to push the Federals into the combined strength of the Confederate line.

The Battle of Frayser's Farm (sometimes spelled "Frazier") also known as the Battle of Glendale, began in clear hot weather. Early in the morning, General Lee was anxious to trap the Federals at Glendale and he rode down the Williamsburg Road to find Stonewall near Seven Pines where Joe Johnston fell four weeks earlier. By noon, firing was heard between Old Pete Longstreet's grayclads and the Federals along the Darbytown Road, one and one-quarter miles from Glendale. Joining Longstreet and A.P. Hill, Lee could see lines of Federal supply wagons jamming the Willis Church Road. The retreating Federals were bound for the high ground of Malvern Hill. Longstreet and A.P. Hill deployed at the Wilcox farm to wait for General Ben Huger to open the attack.

When Robert Lee met Stonewall Jackson at Seven Pines in the

morning, Jackson was a shadow of the triumphant Viking of the Valley. The bone-tired Jackson had spent a fitful night sleeping in wet clothing under dripping skies. Jackson's 20,000 men were the only gray force behind the Yankees. Only Stonewall could prod the retreating Federals into Lee's elaborate trap downriver. Stonewall had worked all morning in the oozing mud to cross White Oak Swamp on June 30th. Harried by the Federals, Jackson opened a cannonade against the nearby Yankees at 1:45 in the hot afternoon. But while his cannon boomed and the Federal artillery replied, Jackson simply fell asleep against a sodden tree.

Stonewall stirred in a stupor of exhaustion when Rebel scouts reported a hidden path on dry ground through the dreadful swamp. Months of war and mud marches had made mush of Jackson's brain. Word of the path could not penetrate and mighty Stonewall slid back against his tree. He became nearly comatose under a sky full of hissing artillery shells. While Stonewall slept against his tree, Longstreet and A.P. Hill fought the Yankees without him.

By 2:30, Ben Huger's Rebel cannon opened fire along the Charles City Road. Then Huger's big guns stopped firing. As if to complicate General Lee's already muddled plan of battle, President Jefferson Davis rode to Lee's headquarters. Davis wanted to see his enemies destroyed.

After half an hour of silence on Ben Huger's front, there was still no sign of Stonewall Jackson's planned attack upon the Federal rear by 3 o'clock. Jackson was still two miles north of Glendale.

"General Lee, while you waited to learn why General Huger's cannon were silent and why Jackson was not heard from at all, did you send couriers to those fronts to investigate why your offensive was stalled?"

"I did not, Senator."

At 4 o'clock in the afternoon, Colonel Tom Rosser of the Rebel cavalry (West Point '61), reported to General Lee that the Yankees were retreating toward the James River down the New Market Road, also known locally as the River Road. Lee accompanied Rosser to the base of Malvern Hill. They could see the fleeing Federals nearing the safety of their gunboats on the James. The last possible hour for destroying General McClellan was approaching quickly.

Jefferson Davis was on the field with the troops. He had slept in bivouac with Lee's army for several days. At Frayser's Farm, he rallied stragglers while exposed to an enemy artillery barrage.

General Lee rode to Longstreet on Long Bridge Road at 5 o'clock. He ordered Huger and Jackson to attack the Yankees after Longstreet opened the assault. Longstreet and A.P. Hill attacked 40,000 Federals with half that strength. There was no support from Ben Huger or Jackson. Huger was strung out on the Charles City Road and Jackson's division was up to their knees in White Oak Swamp. The enemy escaped the last perfect trap the Army of Northern Virginia would ever set.

"General Lee, what were your casualties on June 30th?"

"Thirty-three hundred and five, Mr. Chairman," the witness said after a brief shuffle of papers on the table.

"So another day passed, General, without the Federals being destroyed?"

"Senator," the witness sighed, "Huger not coming up and Jackson having been unable to force the passage of White Oak Swamp, Longstreet and Hill were without the expected support."

By nightfall, Stonewall Jackson's mortal body was spent. When he tried to take a cold dinner in the darkness, he fell asleep with food unchewed in his mouth. The battered army had little to show for the Battle of Frayser's Farm other than the capture of a Union field hospital with 2,400 wounded at Savage's Station.

In the darkness, the Yankees were digging in along the superior high ground atop a rugged little mountain called Malvern Hill.

Robert Lee knew the rocky knoll called Malvern Hill, 18 miles southeast of Richmond. His maternal grandfather, Charles Carter, once owned a farm there. In the six bloody days since Mechanicsville, the Confederates had pushed the Federals back from the capital nearly 20 miles. President Lincoln's quest for Richmond had failed, but the invading army still lived to fight another day. With Yankee gunboats only eight miles further south on the James River, time was quickly running out to destroy McClellan's surviving divisions.

"General, July 1st marked essentially the end of the Seven Days with the Battle of Malvern Hill?"

"Yes, Senator."

"And your assessment, General, of the conduct of operations there?"

"Mr. Chairman, the general conduct of the troops was excellent, in some instances heroic."

The night before Malvern Hill, Stonewall Jackson enjoyed his first night of real sleep in weeks. Before daylight on the first of July 1862, Jackson had his division in a forward position, ready to lead the assault against Malvern Hill from the lowlands of Western Run Creek underneath the enemy cannon on the high ground.

July 1st was another hot, clear morning. By now exhausted himself, General Lee had to face McClellan's army with three Rebel failures commanding divisions: John Magruder, Ben Huger, and even Jackson. At least Jackson seemed more awake than he had since his harrowing ride from the Valley the week before.

"General, you did not seem to rely heavily upon your most able, division commanders at Malvern Hill: Generals Longstreet and A.P. Hill."

"No, Mr. Chairman. I was mindful that Longstreet and Hill had already borne the brunt of the battle and of our casualties during the preceding week."

"Can you describe, General, the overall disposition of the Federal position on the morning of July 1st?"

The witness did not hesitate to detail the superior Federal placement of men and arms.

"Immediately in his front, the ground was open and was completely swept by the fire of his infantry and artillery. To reach this open ground, our troops had to advance through a broken and thickly wooded country traversed nearly throughout its whole extent by a swamp. The whole was within range of the Federal batteries on the heights and the Federal gunboats in the river."

General Lee had ordered General Magruder's division to follow Stonewall's division down the Willis Church Road to deploy. But now Magruder had replaced Stonewall as the officer too tired to function. Magruder had only two hours of sleep during the preceding 72 hours. When Stonewall was ordered down the Willis Church Road toward the Yankee position, the division was led by William Whiting's brigade. Meanwhile, Ben Huger on the Charles City Road had dispatched the brigades of Ransom Wright and Lewis Armistead on patrol along Long Bridge Road. Willis Church Road quickly became a massive traffic jam of Confederate divisions.

"General, did you actively deploy cavalry detachments to scout the Federal positions prior to your July 1st attack?"
"I believe not, Senator."

Early in the day, Lee rode down Willis Church Road with James Longstreet to inspect for himself the Union position. They stopped at a small rise along the lane between the Crew house and the West house which stood on opposite sides of the dirt road. Western Run Creek crossed the road half a mile from Malvern Hill. The Poindexter farm was toward the north. General Lee deployed Daniel Harvey Hill's division on the right and General Whiting's two brigades from Stonewall's division on the left near the creek in dense thickets. Federal cannon opened along the crest of Malvern Hill. Lee sent Longstreet to examine Malvern Hill one and one-half miles from the Crew house to scout for a proper placement for Rebel artillery to answer the Yankee cannonade.

Longstreet inspected the Confederate left flank. He returned to advise Lee that 100 Confederate cannon could be placed in position to cover a frontal assault against the high ground. But Stonewall, who had joined Lee, suggested a safer flank attack from the Rebel right. Lee chose Longstreet's plan of a cannonade to precede a frontal attack. But instead of 100 Rebel cannon firing together, the batteries were engaged piecemeal, never more than 20 guns at a time. The Yankee cannoneers on the ridge 150 feet higher had no trouble lobbing shells into the Confederate artillery position.

As had been the case all week, Confederate troop placement suffered from poor maps and inadequate leadership in the field. At 1 o'clock in the afternoon, poor John Magruder took the wrong road to his assigned position. Magruder had been sent down the Quaker Road. Unfortunately, there were two lanes with that name. The locals also called Willis Church Road "Quaker Road" and Magruder followed the lane which went nowhere. Lee sent direct orders to Magruder to change course to find the right path to the front.

At 1:30, General Lee instructed Longstreet to deploy cannon on a hill opposite the higher Malvern Hill. Then Lee had his chief of staff, Lieutenant Colonel Robert Chilton, draft an attack order.

"General, do you have in your documents the order penned by Colonel Chilton?"

"I do, Mr. Chairman."

"Would you kindly read that order into the record?"

"Yes, Senator....*Batteries have been established to rake the enemy's lines. If it is broken as is probable, Armistead, who can witness the effect of the fire, has been ordered to charge with a yell. Do the same.*"

"And that rather nebulous order was deliv to your field commanders, General?"

"It was."

When the Army of Northern Virginia deployed at the foot of Malvern Hill, some 400 yards of open country separated the Rebel line from the Federal high ground. The 1 o'clock artillery duel lasted four hours.

"Were all Confederate cannon brought to bear upon the enemy?"

"Senator, I believe that perhaps 20 batteries—or some 90 artillery pieces—remained in General Pendleton's reserve and were not engaged that afternoon."

Stonewall Jackson contributed two artillery batteries to the cannonade at about 2:30. While Brigadier General Armistead waited near the Crew farm for the Yankee line to break under the disjointed artillery barrage, Stonewall was at the Smith farm with his troops deployed along Western Run Creek.

At 3 o'clock, General Armistead attacked Malvern Hill pursuant to Colonel Chilton's memorandum from Lee.

"When did the general assault finally commence?" Senator Wigfall glanced at his own stack of documents.

"Owing to ignorance of the country," General Lee replied, "the dense forests impeding necessary communication, and the extreme difficulty of the ground, the whole line was not formed until a late hour in the afternoon."

John Magruder did not reach the field after his Quaker Road detour until 4 o'clock. He found Confederate brigadiers Armistead and Wright pinned down by heavy Union fire. Magruder dispatched Captain Dickinson to General Lee for instructions.

"And what did you tell Dickinson, General?"

"I presumed that Brigadier General Armistead had advanced per my orders conveyed by Colonel Chilton issued at 1:30. Therefore, I instructed Captain Dickinson to order General Magruder to follow General Armistead in the advance."

Between 5 and 6 o'clock, Magruder let only two brigades—5,000 men—trickle into the fight for Malvern Hill. This increase in action led Major General Harvey Hill to believe that the entire Confederate line was advancing. Hill attacked with his division at 6:30 and was slaughtered for the next 30 minutes. Stonewall Jackson's division did not fight at all.

From his little hill on Willis Church Road, General Lee watched his troops near the Crew farm get massacred by the commanding Federal fire from the high ground. As dusk shadowed the growing heaps of dead Confederates, Harvey Hill removed his riddled division from the field. By dark, the firing had subsided as evening provided cover for the Federals to make good their final retreat to the James River and the protecting fire of Yankee gunboats.

Harvey Hill's division had marched against Malvern Hill with 6,500 men. He came down the hill with 4,500.

Little Mac had escaped again.

"Your assessment, General?"

General Lee looked up at Senator Wigfall. Both men were too tired that late in the afternoon for another meeting of their iron wills.

"For want of concert among the attacking columns, their assaults were too weak to break the Federal lines. After struggling gallantly, sustaining and inflicting great loss, they were compelled successively to retire. The firing continued until after 9 p.m., but no decided result was gained. The lateness of the hour at which the attack began gave the enemy the full advantage of his superior position and augmented the mutual difficulties of our own." General Lee sighed so deeply that Mother Lee in the front row of the gallery leaned forward. Her pale face showed the fear for her husband's failing heart. "Under ordinary circumstances," the witness continued with passion in his voice, "the Federal Army should have been destroyed."

"But it wasn't, was it, General?"

"No, Senator."

With darkness mercifully covering the slaughter along the slopes of Malvern Hill, another thunderstorm broke. The downpour washed the sweat from the dead or wounded bodies of 5,590 Confederates on the hillside.

During the rainy night of July 1st and the gray gloom of July 2nd, General McClellan escaped to Harrison's Landing on the James River. On the 2nd, General Lee set up field headquarters near Malvern Hill at the Poindexter farm. He conferred with Longstreet and Stonewall Jackson who were joined by President Davis, trailing the army like a camp follower. During the day, Jackson personally supervised the many burial details.

On July 3rd, Lee began making leadership changes. He began by relieving John Magruder of division command.

With McClellan safe at Harrison's Landing, the Battle of the Seven Days was over. The week before, Richmond faced siege and starvation; now the capital was breathing freely again. But the cost had been immense: the Seven Days left 3,286 Confederates dead, 946 missing, and 15,909 wounded. Half of the wounded would die of their wounds or would become permanently unfit for service. Within the battered command structure, 14 colonels were dead or would die of wounds, 1 general was dead, and 7 generals wounded. A.P. Hill's division suffered grievous losses with 5,500 casualties including 6 colonels and 3 majors dead, and 2 brigadier generals, 11 colonels, and 6 lieutenant colonels wounded.

Although not destroyed, McClellan was also badly hurt during his withdrawal from the doorstep of Richmond. Union casualties included 1,734 killed and 8,062 wounded with another 6,083 missing. Little Mac had abandoned at least 4,000 of his wounded to the advancing Confederates and left 52 cannon in his wake which would be turned against the Federals on other fields.

After the Seven Days, General Lee reorganized his cumbersome division structure into two "wings." Confederate law did not yet permit the formation of corps under the command of lieutenant generals. Major General James Longstreet would command the divisions of David Jones, Lafayette McLaws, Daniel Harvey Hill commanding Longstreet's old division, and Richard Anderson. Stonewall Jackson was given command of the divisions of Baldy Ewell, A.P. Hill, and Charles Winder. General Lee's cavalry was to be led by Major General Jeb Stuart commanding the brigades of Wade Hampton and Fitzhugh Lee (Robert Lee's nephew).

Lee's disappointment with the exhausted Jackson's performance during the Seven Days may account for entrusting Longstreet with four divisions and Stonewall only three.

Mr. Lincoln made some changes too after the Seven Days: Eight days after Malvern Hill, George McClellan was stripped of his laurels as general-in-chief although he retained command of the Army of the Potomac which he had managed to save from extermination during the retreat to Harrison's Landing.

"So, General Lee," Chairman Wigfall said, leaning back in his seat, "the army was reorganized and the battle for Richmond ended, at least for '62."

For a long moment, Robert Lee studied the bearded face of the heavy Texan.

"On Thursday, June 26th, the powerful and thoroughly equipped army of the enemy was entrenched in works vast in extent and most formidable in character within sight of our capital. By July 2, 1862, the remains of that confident and threatening host lay upon the banks of the James River, thirty miles from Richmond, seeking to recover under the protection of his gunboats from the effects of a series of disastrous defeats." As he continued, General Lee looked hard at Senator Wigfall. "The immediate fruits of our success were the relief of Richmond from a state of siege and the rout of the great army that so long menaced its safety!"

When General Lee's words trailed off, first a clamor then applause broke from the gallery. A sustained ovation poured out upon the exhausted witness.

In the back row of the gallery, only one officer did not clap. Major General Daniel Harvey Hill sat dourly. He remembered his division being slaughtered at Malvern Hill. General Lee could not have heard Harvey Hill when he leaned toward the spectator of rank by his side to whisper, "We attacked just when and where the enemy wished us to attack!" At the moment, Hill had no command, having been relieved. His promotion to lieutenant general had been recommended but never formally confirmed following a bitter political clash with General Braxton Bragg in the fall of 1863, only two months ago.

"There will be order!" Chairman Wigfall called over the pounding of his gavel. "Ladies and gentlemen, unless this session of the Joint Military Affairs Committee retains appropriate decorum, we shall adjourn and go into executive session from which each and every one of you shall be barred!"

The gallery hushed.

"It is 5 o'clock. I believe we have covered sufficient ground to adjourn for today. Our thanks to General Lee and counsel. This Committee stands adjourned until 9 o'clock tomorrow morning."

The gallery rose as the committeemen climbed down from their raised platform and walked somberly to the double doors which the sentries opened. The gallery followed them quickly out of the stuffy chamber into the cool December air of the capitol hallway. Mother Lee lingered in the front row where she leaned heavily upon the arm of Walter Taylor.

"Mother," Robert Lee smiled. "Would you object if the good colonel saw you home? I would like to see sweet Charlotte before dark."

"Of course, Robert. I shall have dinner waiting for you—with the girls and Martha."

The general nodded toward Taylor and took a step backward to make room for Mary Lee to pass. The frail woman shuffled on swollen ankles.

"You did fine, General," Judah Benjamin smiled.

"Well," was all General Lee could say.

"After you, Sir," Secretary Benjamin said as he gestured toward the open door. No one but the sentries were with Judah Benjamin and Robert Lee in the chamber.

"You go on, Mr. Secretary. I shall be right along. Perhaps you could summon a carriage for me at this late hour?"

"Certainly, General."

Lee turned and stood quietly facing the deserted platform for a long moment before he retrieved his slouch hat from the table. At the door, he returned the salutes of the sentries.

★   ★   ★

"We have him," Louis Wigfall smiled behind a blue cloud of cigar smoke in the Capitol Square darkness. His coat was pulled up tightly around his neck behind his salt and pepper beard.

"I don't know," Henry Foote shook his head. "Lee was right about one thing: he did push the Federals back from Richmond's doorstep last year."

"That he did, Henry. But he did it with shoddy organization on the field and he did it with total disregard for Southern blood. Malvern Hill, especially, was nothing but a slaughter of his own people. I shall get him to admit the same waste at Sharpsburg and then at Gettysburg with that useless charge of Pickett and Pettigrew."

"Yes, Senator. And then we can count on Reade and one or two of the others to vote to remove him. Hunter will side with the Virginian no matter what."

"Probably. But even without a majority, we shall have our leverage to force King Jeff to make a choice: relieve his friend Lee and assign Johnston, or keep Lee in the east and send Joe west to Tennessee. Either way, Davis is crippled."

"Well, it only took twenty years," Henry Foote smiled in the cold darkness.

When the two men walked off for a late drink, they did not see General Lee's carriage disappear into the night.

★   ★   ★

Richmond was bitter cold by the time Robert Lee reached the home where his daughter-in-law remained in bed. Lee entered the sleeping woman's bedroom. He left the door open and quietly eased a chair toward the bed.

Charlotte Lee opened her eyes and blinked.

"Papa?" the wasted woman smiled.

"I'm here, child."

"Papa, is it morning or night?"

"Just past suppertime."

"Oh. Is it cold outside?"

"A little."

Charlotte closed her eyes in the yellow lamp light. Her face was the color of the linen beneath her head.

"It must be very cold up North," she stammered as a tear rolled down the angular ridges of her cheek bones. Her mind wandered to a faraway prison camp beyond the northern horizon where her Rooney lay wounded, if the reports were true that he had been or would be transferred to the prison camp at Johnson's Island, Ohio.

"Our friends across the way will give our men what blankets they need," General Lee said softly. He squeezed the clammy hand lost in his large hands.

The faintest smile crossed the woman's blue lips.

Chapter Ten

Tuesday Morning, December 15, 1863

Let us die here, boys!
General Maxcy Gregg, CSA, Second Manassas

*T*he bright and pleasant sunrise promised a perfect Virginia day of clear skies with only slight chill.

General Lee stood alone on his front porch. On the curb of the dirt road, a solitary sentry continued his measured pace as steam rose from his face in the crisp air. No snow was left on the hard ground.

When the general exhaled a cloud of steam, a sudden pain jabbed at his left side. His right hand rubbed his chest.

"Your heart, Cousin Robert?" Martha Williams asked softly from the doorway.

"It's only the cool air, Markie. It makes my old bones talk to me sometimes."

Martha walked outside into the sunshine.

"I do worry about your heart," she said gently at the soldier's side.

"Now Markie," Lee smiled, "I have been for more than a month a great sufferer from rheumatism in my back." He looked momentarily serious. "There is no reason to worry Mrs. Lee."

"I won't, Cousin Robert. But I worry, you know."

The general turned his ruddy face away from Markie. He could not hide the pain in his eyes.

"The rheumatism in my back has given me great pain and anxiety. If I cannot get relief, I do not see what is to become of me."

"It's your heart, Cousin Robert. I know that. How much more of this court martial business can your heart take?" Martha's voice cracked.

General Lee looked sideways at the woman wrapped in a shawl. He smiled and laid his hand upon her arm.

"So long as that heart beats," General Lee said softly, "it will be full of affection and gratitude for you."

For an instant, Martha's hand touched his. They stood side by side and watched the sun glint off the fixed bayonets carried by the guards keeping watch on the frozen mud of Leigh Street.

"Being here with you and Mother Lee brings back so many memories of Arlington, happy and sad."

The war grief of the Lees was deeply entwined with Martha's own personal loss of war. Agnes still mourned for Martha's dead brother Orton. After the first shots of the terrible revolution in April of 1861, it was Orton Williams—still wearing the blue on General Winfield Scott's Washington staff—who had rushed to Arlington house overlooking the Potomac River. He warned Mother Lee of imminent invasion by the Yankees. With this alarm, Mrs. Lee had time to carefully pack her treasures of George Washington relics for shipment to safety in the deep South. Orton and Arlington were both lost to war.

"I remember Arlington," Martha whispered, unable to stop the single tear which rolled down her clear cheek. "Every room; every path; every bud in Mother Lee's wonderful garden....And how all of us would wait anxiously for your return from some frontier outpost." She could not look up at her cousin, the object of 20 years of her love.

"One of the pleasures I always anticipated enjoying there was the sight of you, Markie."

"So many memories, Robert," she sighed. She shivered inside her shawl, but not from the comfortable chill.

"I know, Markie. Having all of us together—except for our Rooney—brings back such memories of friends and family. How empty our table has become."

"Yes."

"Even the weather gives rise to memories. It was almost a year ago, on a day much like today, that I visited my father's grave on Cumberland Island."

General Lee raised his hands and he hugged his own upper arms as if to ward off the chill borne of painful memories. "Yes, it was on a clear winter day like today," General Lee said softly. "It was my first visit to the house and I had the gratification at length of visiting my father's grave. The spot was marked by a plain marble slab, with his name, age, and date of his death. The garden was beautiful, enclosed by the finest hedge I have ever seen. It was wild olive."

The general's sadness was interrupted by the slamming of the front door. Tiny squirrel claws scratched at the wooden floor planks as the ball of brown fur dived from the porch and scurried up a leafless tree. Mildred Lee flew through the door. The youngest Lee daughter plowed into her startled father.

"Good morning, Papa," Mildred smiled breathlessly.

"And to you, Life."

"I'm afraid Custis Morgan got loose."

"Does the Mim know?"

Mildred said nothing. She lowered her eyes from the tall soldier's face.

"How would you like a little squirrel soup?" General Lee's deep voice was serious, but his eyes twinkled. "Custis Morgan would show in such a position! If not required by you, I know it would be beneficial to the poor sick and wounded in the hospitals. It would be most grateful to his feelings to be converted into a nutritious aliment for them...." The general sounded grave indeed. "...and to devote his life to the good of the country!"

General Lee saw the sudden hurt in the teenager's eyes. He laid his hand upon her shoulder and he smiled broadly.

"Oh, Daddy!"

"Good morning, Precious Life."

The girl kissed her father's whiskered cheek and she ran down the steps. She stood at the base of the tree where her pet perched. She tried to entice the little animal down.

"She is a dear girl," Martha smiled beside her cousin.

"I know, Markie. But I fear that one day soon we really will have to feed ourselves with squirrel meat. Food is growing scarcer by the day."

"Yes," the woman nodded. "Poverty is now everywhere. Even in Richmond. No one will escape if this war lasts another year."

General Lee shrugged as he turned to face Markie.

"I am content to be poor and to live on cornbread the rest of my life if a gracious God will give us our independence."

Before Martha could respond, Mother Lee appeared in the doorway. Mary Custis pushed her mother's rolling chair.

"Molly," General Lee smiled. "We seem to have had an escape of Mildred's little prisoner." He chuckled with a cloud of steam in the chilly, clear air.

"Not escaped enough," Mother Lee laughed as she watched Mildred pull Custis Morgan from a low branch.

"Maybe next time," the general smiled.

"Oh, Papa!" Mildred said bravely.

"Let's get out of the cold," Martha said. The general followed Mildred and Martha into the house.

"It's only seven-thirty," Mother Lee said from her chair. "We have time for a hot biscuit and some corn coffee."

With the Yankee blockade of Southern ports stopping the supply of imported coffee, Confederates had learned to brew grain into a warm but tasteless broth. Out in the field, Rebel soldiers routinely traded Southern tobacco for Yankee coffee beans.

After a warm gathering of the Lee clan at Mother Lee's table, General Lee rose to leave for the capitol building. When Mrs. Lee asked Agnes to help her with her heavy coat, General Lee protested his crippled wife's determination to accompany him to the hearings.

"Now, Molly," the general said gently, "there is no need for you to risk catching a draft in this weather."

Mrs. Lee knew when her husband's mind was made up.

"Alright, Robert. But only for today. I would rather be present at the capitol."

General Lee gathered his greatcoat from Mildred's arms. He looked down into Mrs. Lee's pale face.

"You are always present with me," the husband smiled, "in my prayers and thoughts."

★   ★   ★

As the gallery filled for the second day of testimony, General Lee and Judah Benjamin greeted Walter Taylor, James Longstreet and A.P. Hill.

"I trust you left someone behind to mind the store?" General Lee smiled at Walter Taylor.

"You know I did, General," Colonel Taylor said gravely.

Robert Lee squeezed Taylor's arm to break the unintended tension.

When Senator Louis Wigfall led his committeemen to the front of the chamber, General Lee and Secretary of State Benjamin took their places at the witness table.

"Ladies and Gentlemen, General Lee, Secretary Benjamin," Chairman Wigfall said without preliminaries, "we are now on record."

Judah Benjamin nodded.

"General Lee, yesterday we had reviewed the Battle of the Seven Days. Kindly continue your narrative."

"Yes, Senator. After Malvern Hill on July 1, 1862, the Federals concentrated on the shore of the James within range of protecting fire from their gunboats. On July 8th, I pulled our forces back from the river toward our works near Richmond."

"On July 12th," General Lee continued, "I learned that Major General John Pope had occupied Culpeper, 35 miles northwest of Fredericksburg. This movement placed the Virginia Central Railroad at risk. On the 13th, I dispatched General Jackson's two divisions to Gordonsville, where he arrived on the 19th. That left some 69,000 troops defending the Richmond sector." The witness reviewed his pile of notes and records. "On July 27th, I also deployed Major General A.P. Hill's division to Gordonsville, arriving July 29th. That left 56,000 men in our Richmond line."

"General, the disputes arising between the late General Jackson and the very able General Hill are documented in other files of this committee. When you detached General Hill to join General Jackson, did you foresee any of the ill will which developed between these two officers?"

"Senator, let's just say that I foresaw the need for General Jackson to lessen his desire for secrecy in order to take General Hill into his full confidence."

"Can you be more specific, Sir?"

"May it please the chair," Secretary Benjamin said as he rose beside General Lee. "I must object to this line of questioning in that it is not material to General Lee's conduct in the field. First, this is a rather private, administrative matter. And second, such communication between General Lee and his field subordinates is clearly privileged."

"Overruled, counselor," Senator Wigfall said firmly. "General Lee's handling of his subordinates is clearly relevant to his fitness for command. Your exception is noted, of course."

Judah Benjamin nodded and sat down.

"You may continue, General Lee."

The witness turned to his letter book for the summer of 1862 where copies of his dispatches were recorded.

"Senator Wigfall, I wrote to General Jackson the following dispatch on July 27th." General Lee read from his records: "*A.P. Hill, you will, I think, find a good officer with whom you can consult, and by advising with your division commanders as to their movements, much trouble can be saved you in arranging details, as they can act more intelligently.*"

"So, General, you seemed to predict the—shall I say—diplomatic strains between Generals Hill and Jackson?"

"I knew my officers, Senator."

"But you left General Jackson to resolve for himself a potential problem which matured into a real problem during the Maryland campaign when General Jackson arrested General Hill."

Robert Lee did not look over his shoulder toward the gallery and A.P. Hill whose face reddened. Hill never forgave Stonewall for arresting him on the march to Sharpsburg and Antietam Creek.

"I have always left my general officers wide discretion in the field, especially regarding administrative matters within their own commands."

"You delegated wide discretion to General Jackson, did you not?"

"Of course, Senator. Major General Jackson was in the field and I was not. Accordingly, I sent a dispatch to General Jackson on August 7, 1862, granting him the latitude he required—and deserved. May I enter that dispatch into the record, Mr. Chairman?"

"Certainly, General."

The witness adjusted his steel-framed spectacles before he read from his letter book.

"*Make up your mind what is best to be done under all the circumstances which surround us and let me hear the result at which you arrive.*" General Lee removed his glasses. "General Jackson engaged General Banks at Cedar Mountain two days later."

"And, General," Senator Wigfall interrupted, "began the breach with General A.P. Hill which never healed. Is that not also correct, Sir?"

"The record, Senator, would speak for itself."

On August 7th, Stonewall pulled out of Gordonsville to harass General Pope's Federals. The divisions in butternut brown arrived at Orange Court House the same day, 20 miles from Pope's position near Culpeper. That evening, Jackson issued the order of battle for the next day: (1) Baldy Ewell's division would lead the attack upon the Union line; (2) Hill's division would follow Ewell; and, (3) General Charles Winder, age 33, would lead Stonewall's old division. But before dawn on the 8th, Jackson changed his orders by sending General Ewell on an alternate route through Liberty Mills along the Rapidan River toward the Orange-Culpeper Road. Hill was never informed of that change in plan.

"So, General Lee, Jackson had already violated your suggestion of July 27th that he should take A.P. Hill into his confidence?" Senator Wigfall looked over his spectacles at the witness.

"I was not there, Senator."

At daybreak on August 8th, General Hill saw Confederate troops leaving Orange and he assumed that these were General Ewell's division as Jackson had ordered only the evening before. When Hill learned that the division was Winder's due to the change in plan, he delayed moving out until Winder's division had cleared the roadway. By evening, Jackson's three divisions were jumbled in a traffic bottleneck at Barnett's Ford on the Rapidan. Winder had managed to cover eight miles while Hill had moved only one mile. The delay in the march began Stonewall's simmering feud with A.P. Hill. The only reason General Winder was leading Stonewall's men at all was that their regular leader, General Richard Garnett, was still under arrest at Stonewall's orders after the fiasco at Kernstown in the Valley last March.

Jackson's command did battle at Cedar Mountain against his old Valley adversary, General Nathaniel Banks, on August 9th. Cedar Mountain was also known as Slaughter Mountain.

With first light on the 9th, Jackson's three divisions were on the road toward Culpeper, Virginia. Stonewall's command numbered 24,000. Stonewall and General Ewell were on the field by 11:30. Jackson deployed his troops with Ewell to hit the Union left while General Jubal Early with Winder's division marched north on the Culpeper Road to get behind the Federal right flank.

In his haste to engage, Jackson failed to send scouts westward to look for Yankees west of the fork in the dirt road.

In dusky shadows at 5:45, the men in blue attacked the Rebel left flank and drove the Confederates back in ferocious fighting hand-to-hand. Jackson's command was in very serious trouble.

Toward 6 o'clock, three Rebel brigades collapsed and fled from vicious combat. Yankees swarmed through the Confederate line. Only General Jubal Early's gray brigade held its ground.

Stonewall Jackson, as was his way, rode into the thick of the fight. For the first and last time during the war, Jackson drew his sword. He shouted above the din of musketry, "Rally, brave men! Jackson will lead you! Follow me!"

Stonewall's flashing saber stopped his retreating boys who turned on their heels and returned to the action. Fearless North Carolina troops sealed the gap in the Rebel left while Ewell's brigades advanced on the Confederate right in gathering darkness where cannon flashed against the gray sky. Hill's division advanced up the road to drive the Yankees. Jackson's divisions collected themselves and pressed forward under a Confederate artillery barrage. Hill chased the bluecoats until darkness ended the fight. Firing stopped an hour before midnight when two Federal corps of reinforcements arrived.

On August 10th, Sunday's Sabbath peace descended upon the little road where 229 Confederates lay dead and another 1,047 moaned in pain from wounds. General Winder lay among the dead. The Yankees left 2,400 men upon the bloody road—one-third of the Federal command.

All day long, the guns were silent under truce flags as the armies tended their dead and wounded. Jeb Stuart mingled among blueclad enemies who had been his friends two years earlier. Jeb bumped into Union cavalry General George Bayard and the two friends chatted quietly about old times and better days.

The dashing Stuart also found another chum from the Old Army: Union General Samuel Crawford, now a prisoner of war. The laughing Stuart bet General Crawford a new hat that Yankee newspapers would call Cedar Mountain a Federal victory, especially the

New York *Herald.* General Crawford was soon paroled and returned to Federal lines. Seven days later, Jeb Stuart found a package waiting for him at General Lee's headquarters at Orange Court House. The package contained a new hat with General Crawford's compliments: the *Herald* had reported Cedar Mountain as a Union victory.

"Well, General," Congressman Foote interrupted the testimony, "it would seem that Stonewall Jackson abused your discretion and was nearly routed at Cedar Mountain by poor deployment of his troops and by failing to provide adequate intelligence to his field commanders."

"Perhaps, but General Jackson did carry the field."

By August 11th, Jackson's command had returned to its former campsite at Gordonsville. General Lee detached Longstreet's division to Gordonsville where General Lee intended to take personal command of the field. General Pope's Federals were now in a difficult position, sandwiched between the converging branches of the Rappahannock River and Rapidan River.

"I arrived at Gordonsville," General Lee testified, "on August 15th to take command of the assault against General Pope who was camped twelve miles from Fredericksburg. I planned the offensive to affect our crossing of the Rapidan on the 17th and to engage General Pope on the 18th. The cavalry brigades of Jeb Stuart and Fitzhugh Lee were camped at Hanover Court House."

"You took the war council of your field commanders at Gordonsville, General?"

"Of course, Mr. Chairman. I conferred at length with Generals Jackson and Longstreet on August 15th upon my arrival there."

On the 18th, Jeb Stuart was attacked by a cavalry patrol near Verdiersville. There was one prisoner taken: the Yankees captured Jeb's new hat in the fray. Due to Fitz Lee's slow progress in his mounted march from Hanover to Raccoon Ford, the commanding general delayed the attack upon General Pope until August 20th. But General Pope made good his escape from the trap between the two rivers.

On August 20th, the day General Lee had planned to destroy General Pope, George McClellan's massive army evacuated its Virginia beachhead at Harrison's Landing on the James River. While Little Mac was trying to keep his boots dry, the divisions of Stonewall Jackson and A.P. Hill were crossing the Rapidan River in pursuit of Pope's bluecoats. Within 24 hours, General Lee met with Stuart, Longstreet, and Jackson to discuss a new development: General Pope was being reinforced by General Ambrose Burnside's division coming up from Fredericksburg.

"I knew that we had to hasten after General Pope before he could be strengthened by Burnside's division."

On the 22nd of August 1862, Stonewall's division crossed another river, the Rappahannock, in a march to outflank Pope's troops.

While Jackson's division rolled up its trousers at Beverly Ford to cross the Rappahannock, Stuart took 1,500 troopers from camp at Stevensburg on a mission to destroy General Pope's line of communications: the railroad bridge over Cedar Run creek at Catlett's Station. During the afternoon, the Confederate cavalry rested for an hour at Warrenton before pressing on. At nightfall in blinding rain, Stuart attacked the sleeping Yankees.

Although the Federal commander was absent from his tent, the grayclad cavalrymen seized his private trunk, Pope's new coat and hat, and a Federal payroll of $350,000 in Yankee script. After the daring nighttime adventure, Stuart took time to send a note to General Pope proposing an exchange of prized prisoners of war: Jeb's new hat for Pope's cape. When the Federals rejected the parole of wardrobes, Stuart sent Pope's hat and coat to Richmond as a war trophy for the Virginia governor.

On August 24th on General Pope's trail, General Lee joined Stonewall Jackson at Jeffersonton, five miles south of Warrenton

Springs and nine miles north of Culpeper. Pope's command camped east of Warrenton. Stonewall was ordered to march northward to get behind the Federals to seize the Orange and Alexandria Railroad line which supplied the Yankee division and to exit the Bull Run Mountains at Thoroughfare Gap. This march would place Stonewall between Pope and Washington. General Longstreet's command would rendezvous with Jackson at Manassas Junction.

At dawn on the 25th, Jackson's wing left Jeffersonton with General Baldy Ewell's division leading. Stonewall's old division followed with Brigadier General William Taliaferro in command. Powell Hill's division brought up the rear. Late in the morning, the three divisions crossed the Rappahannock at Henson's Mill. Toward sunset near Salem, Jackson was wildly cheered by his passing divisions beneath an orange twilight sky. As darkness descended upon Jackson's 23,000 men, they pitched camp beside the Manassas Gap Railroad, five miles west of Thoroughfare Gap. The three dusty divisions had walked 25 miles since daybreak.

Also on August 25th, General Lee wired a daring and risky request to President Jefferson Davis. Lee wanted Richmond stripped of its military garrison and the home guard detached to Lee in the field for the assault upon General Pope.

"I am pleased to note that the President granted my request," General Lee stated softly.

"That request was granted by the President," Senator Hunter at Chairman Wigfall's right noted, "out of deference to you, General. The troops were detached from Richmond to your command on the 26th. If the chairman will permit, I should like to read into the record the President's reply dispatch wired to General Lee?"

Senator Wigfall looked to his right. The burly chairman seemed irritated.

"Although the President's reply is in the documentary evidence already in the record, your request, Senator, is granted. You may proceed."

The Virginian at Louis Wigfall's side raised a sheet of paper and read slowly.

"*Confidence in you overcomes the view which would otherwise be taken of the exposed condition of Richmond, and the troops retained for the defense of the capital are surrendered to you.*" The Senator lowered the document. "Those were the President's words to General Lee."

While General Lee arrived at Orleans, Virginia, on August 26th, Stonewall's columns pressed northeastward. Jeb Stuart's cavalry arrived at Gainesville on the Warrenton Turnpike by early afternoon, six miles west of Manassas Junction. The mounted troopers rode southeast toward Bristoe Station five miles away and four miles southeast of the Junction. By the time Stuart's horse soldiers made camp there, they had ridden 54 miles in 48 hours without food.

August 27th nearly marked the end of Robert Lee's military career. The general and ten officers rode along a narrow dirt road to survey the terrain. General Lee and his aides rode straight into a detachment of John Buford's Yankee cavalry. The startled bluecoats thought the officers were the head of Jeb Stuart's entire cavalry. Taking no chances—and no prisoners—the Federals fled.

By the time of General Lee's near miss, Stonewall's weary divisions had been in motion for hours. Jackson's command broke camp at 3 o'clock in the morning and headed for Manassas Junction. By daybreak, Jackson's divisions had captured tons of Federal supplies sitting in 100 railroad cars abandoned by General Pope. Although the starving Confederates were permitted to fill their knapsacks with Northern delicacies such as canned lobster, Jackson ordered kegs of Yankee whiskey poured onto the ground to prevent a drunken riot. A mid-morning counterattack by Federals was beaten back along the railroad.

By 8 o'clock on the morning of August 28th, Generals Baldy Ewell and Hill had mustered their divisions at Manassas Junction while General Pope's Federals marched hard to recover their important railhead. Two hours later, Jackson sent Hill's division to hold the strategic fords along Bull Run creek against approaching Yankees. After finding a lost Federal dispatch confirming that the Federals were headed straight for the Junction, Hill disobeyed Stonewall's orders and turned his division toward Manassas to meet the enemy. By noon, the bluecoats were advancing for the attack.

As the Virginia sun set on the 28th, Stonewall rode along a ridge line overlooking the divisions of the Federal Army of Virginia under General Pope's command. At 7:30, Jackson looked down upon 34 Federal regiments and calmly gave General Taliaferro the order he longed to hear: "Bring up your men, gentlemen." For the next two hours, Confederates from Stonewall's old division and half of Ewell's division fell upon the Yankees in a vigorous attack. Baldy Ewell's men did battle against the heroic Iron Brigade: John Gibbon's one Indiana and three Wisconsin regiments of farmboys from the midwest. General Gibbon was from North Carolina and three of his brothers wore Rebel gray.

As darkness ended the engagement in a stalemate, Baldy Ewell's leg was blown off at the knee and General Taliaferro was seriously wounded.

Firing continued until after 9 o'clock. Young John Pelham, revered as "the boy major," saved Stonewall's right flank with his horse artillery. Jeb Stuart would say, "Pelham is always in the right place at the right time."

At daybreak on the 29th, Stonewall's command was exhausted. The 23,000 weary Rebels had marched 54 miles in two days. Now they looked down upon 50,000 Federals and waited for the arrival of Old Pete Longstreet's fresh troops who were somewhere in the Bull Run Mountains. Stonewall deployed his regiments along a two-mile front. By 10 o'clock in the morning, the Yankees were in place below. Stonewall sent Jeb Stuart to ride hard into the mountains to find Longstreet's five divisions before the Federals pushed Jackson from his ridge. Stuart found Longstreet with General Lee and they arrived at Jackson's side by 10:30.

A.P. Hill's division deployed on the Confederate left. The extreme left flank was held by General Maxcy Gregg's South Carolina men. The Yankee assault came at 11 o'clock, concentrating against Hill's left. When a 100-yard wide gap opened in Hill's line, the Federals nearly crushed him. General Gregg had to fall back around 2 o'clock in the afternoon under ferocious fire. He finally stopped the rout by drawing his saber and shouting above the cannon fire, "Let us die here, boys!" The Confederate line held, but not until Maxcy Gregg had lost 600 men, including 10 officers killed and 31 wounded. Fighting was hand-to-hand along the Rebel line. As darkness settled upon the bloody field, General John Hood's Southerners pushed the Yankees back. Among the Confederate dead lay Jeb Stuart's 21-year-old cousin, Captain Hardeman Stuart, along with the son of Stonewall's brother-in-law. The 21st Georgia regiment lost 242 of 311 men killed or wounded.

After dark on the 29th, Longstreet's divisions dug in on Jackson's left flank, bringing the Confederate strength up to 55,000 tired and hungry men.

On August 30th, the battle resumed by 1 o'clock in the afternoon when three Federal lines attacked. When Stonewall's line was hotly engaged, Old Pete Longstreet ordered up his artillery batteries which opened a murderous cannonade at 2 o'clock. Under Longstreet's guns, the Federals attacked Jackson's right flank with devastating power. But the mauled bluecoats had to fall back as Longstreet's cannon cut them into bloody heaps.

Upon General Lee's orders, Longstreet sent his entire command into action at 4 o'clock and the Federal line collapsed. A thunderstorm put an end to the bloodbath. Yankees fled for their lives, wading into the chilly water of Bull Run Creek. The all-night rain fell upon the Yankees who did not make it to the river: 10,000 men killed and wounded with 4,000 captured. The Army of Northern Virginia lost 9,197 men but gathered 30 Federal cannon and 20,000 small arms from the field.

On a soggy August 31st, Stonewall Jackson ordered A.P. Hill's division to march north from the Manassas battlefield. By nightfall, Hill's troops had walked 18 miles to Chantilly.

August 31st also marked a rare injury to General Lee. While pursuing the fleeing Yankees across the Bull Run River, General Lee stood beside his beloved mount Traveller. When Traveller spooked, his master lunged for the gray stallion's reins. General Lee slipped in the mud, fractured his right wrist and badly bruised both hands. The commanding general pursued Pope by horse-drawn ambulance for two weeks.

In violent rain on September 1st, the harried Yankees attacked along the Little River Turnpike near Germantown, between the Chantilly plantation mansion and Fairfax Courthouse. As the battle raged across the pike, 500 Rebels and 1,000 Federals fell to the muddy ground. Before dusk, General Pope escaped across the Potomac, removing nearly all Yankees from Virginia soil.

Among the dead lay Union Brigadier General Phil Kearny, an old friend of General Lee dating back to their military youth in Mexico. Under a flag of truce, Stonewall Jackson sent General Kearny's body and sword through the lines with full military honors. The dead Federal's body was escorted by young Walter Taylor as General Lee's personal guard of honor. Both Taylor and the Confederate ambulance were returned by the retreating Federals.

The Battle of Chantilly (also known as Ox Hill) ended the Second Manassas campaign which cost over 9,000 Rebel casualties and 14,462 Federal casualties. By September 5th, the beaten John Pope would be replaced when General McClellan was returned to command. Pope's troops returned to the Army of the Potomac.

The rainy first day of September also marked the flash point of the simmering feud between the high-strung Ambrose Powell Hill and his taciturn commander, Stonewall Jackson. On the march northward, Hill's division marched not too slowly, but too fast for Stonewall's exacting rules of the road. Jackson had declared that the war-weary men must rest ten minutes of every hour on the march.

When Hill's division did not break to rest beside the dirt road, an angry Stonewall personally ordered the leading regiments to fall out for their ten minute rest. Hill was furious that Jackson would bypass command protocol and bark orders at the men in the ranks instead of relaying orders through the division commander. Hill promptly confronted Stonewall, surrendered his sword, and insisted that Jackson take command of the division if he wanted to order Hill's men around himself. Jackson instantly placed Hill under arrest.

So the Army of Northern Virginia took the war into Maryland with General Lee riding in an ambulance where he nursed broken hands, Major General A.P. Hill walking sullenly under arrest beside his division, some 7,000 Federal prisoners in tow from Manassas, and at least 9,100 Confederate casualties not yet replaced including five Rebel generals killed.

"It would seem, General Lee, that Pope made good his escape across the Potomac?" Senator Reade commented.

"My men had nothing to eat."

"Is it your testimony, Sir, that empty bellies and a little rain derailed your pursuit of General Pope after the victory at Manassas?"

General Lee looked up angrily at Senator Reade.

"Nothing could surpass the gallantry and endurance of the troops who had cheerfully borne every danger and hardship both on the battlefield and march." Lee made a fist on the table. "The history of the achievements of the army from the time it advanced from Gordonsville leaves nothing to be said of the courage, fortitude, and good conduct of both officers and men."

The last of the Yankee wagon trains rumbled out of Virginia behind General Pope's retreating columns on September 2, 1862. The next day, General Lee wrote to President Jefferson Davis and outlined the strategic objectives for taking the offensive into Maryland: (1) Maryland's wavering Union sympathies might be tipped toward the Confederacy once the state was liberated by the Army of Northern Virginia; and, (2) If opportunity permitted, the Rebels might destroy the vital bridge over the Susquehanna River at Harrisburg, Pennsylvania.

On September 4th, the Confederate divisions marched eastward from Manassas with 53,000 men. With the Manassas casualties not yet replaced, at least eight of Stonewall Jackson's brigades were led by colonels instead of brigadiers who were dead or wounded.

On September 5th, the Confederate columns waded the Potomac at White's Ford. As his mighty division crossed the shallow water, Stonewall sat his horse in mid-stream. He raised his hat to salute his passing regiments. The hungry and exhausted men wildly cheered their Stonewall Jackson. They climbed out of the half-mile wide river into Maryland opposite Leesburg, Virginia.

In still another portent of bad luck, on September 6th Stonewall Jackson was violently thrown by his horse. Jackson lay unconscious, flat on his back for several anxious minutes. When he recovered, Jackson was carried to an ambulance. He camped for the night at Best's Grove near Fredericktown, Maryland. Now A.P. Hill was still under house arrest and both Jackson and General Lee were bed-ridden.

Also on the 6th, Jeb Stuart's rowdy cavalry division reached Urbana, Maryland. Stuart ordered a grand ball at a deserted school house on the night of September 7th. While General Lee soaked his swollen hands at Frederick, Jeb's happy cavaliers partied until dawn on the 8th. While the band of the 18th Mississippi infantry played, Jeb interrupted the party briefly for a little skirmish with nearby Yankee cavalrymen in darkness illuminated by flashing carbines and moonlight glinting upon bloody sabers. They returned to dance until dawn.

On September 8th, General Lee supplemented his September 3rd letter to President Davis with a second dispatch. This time, General Lee outlined political objectives for the Maryland invasion.

"You took it upon yourself, General, to render political counsel to the President as justification for the raid into Maryland?"

"Well, Senator, my commission as military adviser to President Davis has never been revoked or even modified. Clearly, all military decisions regarding strategy also have political aspects. This was especially true in September of 1862, only two months before the Federal elections."

"And the gist of your political advice as you marched your men into Maryland?"

"I simply proposed, Mr. Chairman, that the time was right for Richmond to propose a negotiated settlement with Washington, recognizing our independence as a sovereign country....Might I read from my letter of September 8th to the President?"

"Indeed, General."

The witness scanned his letter book through his metal spectacles.

"*Such a proposition coming from us at this time could in no way be regarded as suing for peace, but being made when it is in our power to inflict injury upon our adversary, would show conclusively to the world that our sole object is the establishment of our independence, and the attainment of an honorable peace. The rejection of this offer would prove to the country that the responsibility of continuance of the war does not rest upon us....The proposal of peace would enable the people of the United States to determine at their coming elections whether they will support those who favor a prolongation of the war, or those who wish to bring it to a termination.*"

General Lee removed his reading glasses and handed the letter book to Judah Benjamin at his side.

"Was the result of the campaign an honorable peace, General Lee?"

"Not yet, Mr. Foote."

"Did the Northern Congressional elections two months after your Maryland campaign indicate a shift in Yankee public opinion toward a negotiated peace?"

"No, Mr. Foote."

"Is it fair, General, to suppose that the only result from the Northern national government of your Maryland campaign was Lincoln's proclamation of emancipation of our slaves and the brutal confiscation of our personal property?"

"I am not competent, Congressman, to render judgments about political consequences."

"Seems not, General."

On September 9th, the bruised Generals Lee and Jackson conferred about the immediate raid into half-hostile Maryland—a "border" state with mixed loyalties and with troops fighting on both sides of the war.

General Lee laid out his broad plan for the invasion of the enemy's southern flank and the assault toward Pennsylvania and Harrisburg's vital bridgehead. It was agreed that Stonewall Jackson would climb out of his ambulance to attack the critically important Federal garrison at Harper's Ferry up river on the Potomac. This would prevent a Union assault upon the rear of the Army of Northern Virginia strung out across Maryland. Stonewall's division would attack Harper's from the south, the divisions of Lafayette McLaws and Richard Anderson from Longstreet's wing would attack Maryland Heights north of Harper's, while John Walker's division would lay siege to Loudoun Heights on the western Shenandoah River side.

The complicated marching orders were set down in writing as Special Orders 191, penned by Robert Lee's assistant adjutant general, Colonel Robert Chilton. Colonel Chilton had graduated from West Point in 1837 and saw action in Mexico where he won a brevet commission as major at Buena Vista. Chilton won his laurels when he carried a wounded Mississippi colonel out of the field of fire. That wounded colonel was Jefferson Davis.

The highly secret orders were copied and forwarded to division commanders. General Lee sent a copy to division commander Daniel Harvey Hill. When Stonewall received his copy, he also sent a copy to Harvey Hill. One of Hill's copies was accidently used by someone to wrap up three cigars. When the army pulled out of Fredericktown next day, September 10th, the cigars and Special Orders 191 fell to the ground and were left behind.

On September 10th, Stonewall marched out toward Harper's Ferry. Longstreet headed for the pass through South Mountain and left Harvey Hill as rearguard behind Jeb Stuart's cavalry at Boonsborough. Longstreet continued on toward Hagerstown, Maryland, leaving Harvey Hill's division to fortify the south side of Turner's Gap in South Mountain, 15 miles northeast of Harper's and eight miles east of a tiny town called Sharpsburg beside Antietam Creek.

By September 13, 1862, Stonewall's leading regiments were within sight of Bolivar Heights, east of Harper's Ferry where the Shenandoah flows into the Potomac. Before day's end, General McLaws' division had seized Maryland Heights, northeast of Harper's.

While the cannon were aimed at Harper's by Jackson's wing of the Army of Northern Virginia, Jeb Stuart had his hands full of Yankees in the Catoctin Mountains, between Sharpsburg and Frederick, Maryland, some 15 rugged miles northeast of Harper's Ferry. Young Jeb's cavalry division was driven back toward the west and South Mountain. Stuart sent word to Harvey Hill's division holding Turner's Gap in South Mountain.

At General Lee's order, "the other Hill" was told to hold the vital gap until General Longstreet's divisions (General Lee's other "wing") could march from Hagerstown, Maryland, to Hill's support. By nightfall, Stuart still held onto Turner's Gap and Harvey Hill patrolled South Mountain. The Gap was only five miles east of Sharpsburg.

After the Confederates had pulled out of their camps at Frederick, Maryland, the Federals under re-appointed George McClellan moved into the Rebel camp where the campfire embers were still warm.

Sergeant John Bloss and Corporal Barton Mitchell of Company F, 27th Indiana Infantry, found three soggy cigars on the ground. The cigars were wrapped in dirty paper—Special Orders 191. They took the crumpled paper to Captain Peter Kapulo who sent the paper through channels to general headquarters. When the lost orders were delivered to McClellan, he sent troops to Crampton's Gap between South Mountain and Catoctin Mountain near Harper's.

Although General McClellan could now trap General Lee's divided army in the mountains, he flinched at the thought and he delayed launching his attack for 18 hours.

Thirty minutes after midnight on the morning of September 14th, Jeb Stuart may already have been informed by local spies that

McClellan had found General Lee's battle plans. But as daylight approached on the 14th, blood was already flowing in the beautiful mountains.

First light on the 14th found Harvey Hill's lone division holding Turner's Gap as General Lee's principal line of retreat, if needed. Hill held a three-mile front which the Yankees could attack by five different roads. With 2,300 men under his immediate command until reinforcements could arrive, Harvey Hill faced three Federal divisions of McClellan's IX Corps. At 6 o'clock in the morning, Hill atop South Mountain looked down upon the First Brigade of the blue Kanawha Division. The brigade included the 23rd Ohio regiment commanded by Lieutenant Colonel Rutherford Hayes. Their color sergeant was William McKinley. No other regiment would produce two future Presidents of the United States. The Yankees were already bloodying Samuel Garland's Rebel brigade of Hill's division on the southern slopes of South Mountain.

At 9 o'clock in the morning, the Federals attacked in full fury. At Turner's Gap, General Garland and 1,000 men from North Carolina held off 3,000 bluecoats of Colonel Eliakim Scammon's brigade. When the 23rd Ohio charged Garland at bayonet point, Sam Garland was killed and Rutherford Hayes was severely wounded. After three hours of carnage, the North Carolina troops had to fall back near the crest of South Mountain at Fox's Gap, 3 miles south of Turner's. By 11 o'clock, the Yankees had their beachhead in the mountains. Later they dumped 60 dead Confederates down the well on the Wise farm.

Fox's Gap fell to the advancing Federals just before noon. A trickle of help did little. When General Anderson's Confederate brigade had arrived at 10 o'clock, they were repulsed by the Kanawha Division in desperate combat. Harvey Hill held onto Turner's Gap by his bloodied fingernails until 2 o'clock. At that time, Yankees were pouring into Fox's Gap from Turner's. Reinforced by only three new brigades, Hill faced three Federal divisions commanded by Joe Hooker. At 4 o'clock, a Confederate countercharge failed to dislodge the Federals.

John Hood's Rebel division tried to push the Federals south toward Fox's Gap while Joe Hooker's entire I Corps attacked Turner's Gap from the north. Federal John Gibbon's heroic Black Hat Brigade (also known as the Iron Brigade) of I Corps plowed into Turner's Gap. Gibbon knew Harvey Hill well enough: John Gibbon had been best man at Hill's wedding in another life. Now the old friends labored mightily to exterminate each other.

Gunfire raged through sunset and did not subside until 9 o'clock. The sun setting through the clouds of sulphur cast shadows upon two full Federal corps doing battle at Fox's and Turner's Gaps. Another Yankee corps fought at Crampton's Gap. As daylight faded on the 14th, Major General Jesse Reno, the beloved commander of the Federal IX Corps, was killed in Fox's Gap where General Garland wearing the gray had died earlier. When being carried from the front on a stretcher, the mortally wounded Reno called to old friend Brigadier General Sam Sturgis, "Hello, Sam! I'm dead." He was.

By 8 o'clock on the night of September 14th, the South Mountain passes critical to the Army of Northern Virginia were virtually lost.

In the darkness, General Lee had no choice but to abandon the Maryland campaign and to concentrate upon saving his army from annihilation as Yankee divisions swarmed toward the mountains. Lee ordered Longstreet to evacuate the mountains and to push his way toward the town of Sharpsburg for the retreat back into Virginia. Stonewall's command was still somewhere near Harper's Ferry. During eight hours of ferocious fighting, Harvey Hill's battered division had given Jackson time to capture Harper's Ferry. Under cover of night, the Army of Northern Virginia pulled out of the mountains through Turner's Gap under the guns of three Federal corps of infantry. Lee would make his stand against McClellan at Sharpsburg.

General Lee lost 2,300 men in the bloody mountains. The Yankees lost 1,800. Ahead lay the sleeping town of Sharpsburg beside Antietam Creek.

As General Lee withdrew from the mountains, General Walker's

Rebel cannon were digging in at Loudoun Heights overlooking Harper's Ferry which was surrounded by Confederate arms.

Chairman Wigfall leaned back in his chair and glanced at his pocket watch.

"General Lee, your narrative has taken us to 12 noon. Can you briefly articulate for us your decision to stand at Sharpsburg, with your back toward the Potomac?"

"Yes, Senator. Our position at Sharpsburg, west of Antietam Creek, put our forces on the flank and rear of the Federals if General McClellan attempted to cut off General McLaws' return to us from Harper's. Likewise, Sharpsburg put us close to the Potomac for linking up with General Jackson upon his return from Harper's. Finally, I regarded the high ground at Sharpsburg to be a superior defensive position—a fact confirmed by events on September 17th."

At dawn on September 15th, Stonewall's cannon pounded the Federal garrison at Harper's Ferry from three sides for an hour. Just as Hill's division began to advance against the garrison—Hill had been released from arrest by Old Jack to do what he did best—the Yankees suddenly surrendered. Jackson captured 11,000 prisoners, some 13,000 small arms, 73 cannon, and 200 wagons brimming with desperately needed supplies.

It was all over at Harper's Ferry by 11 o'clock in the morning. Federal prisoners were almost happy at the peculiar honor of having been undone by the mighty Stonewall. Captured Yankees cheered the strangely shy Rebel with the pale blue eyes. Jeb Stuart also dropped by to cheer Jackson.

Jackson enjoyed something of a family reunion at Harper's Ferry this September 15, 1862. Among the Federals were two brothers of his first wife, Ellie Junkin. He visited with George Junkin, the Confederate Junkin who had escaped from a Yankee prison camp, and David Junkin who wore Union blue. The war-divided Junkin brothers would never again see Thomas Jackson alive.

As Stonewall tallied his booty at Harper's on the 15th, General

Lee and 20,000 weary Rebels staggered into Sharpsburg. By 8 o'clock that morning, the Federals were pulling out of the mountains to concentrate along Antietam Creek. By 2 o'clock in the afternoon, blue regiments began to file into camp opposite the exhausted Army of Northern Virginia which was only at half strength with Jackson's divisions still at Harper's Ferry.

"General Lee, before we break for an hour, could you tell us why you did not retreat back into Virginia from South Mountain? After all, you arrived at Sharpsburg on the 15th and the battle there was not until the 17th. Why did you wait two days instead of coming home?"

The witness removed his spectacles before looking up with dark eyes at the chairman.

"Senator Wigfall, I wanted McClellan."

When the Federals built their campfires and lit their pipes on September 15th, they enjoyed a four to one edge in manpower over General Lee's divided army. McClellan at last could avenge the Seven Days. General McClellan had Robert Lee out-numbered, out-gunned, and trapped with the Potomac at Lee's back and Antietam Creek in his front.

While a cadet at West Point, the 19-year-old George McClellan gave the valedictory address for the Point's class of '46. He had declared wide-eyed: "War is the greatest game at which man plays."

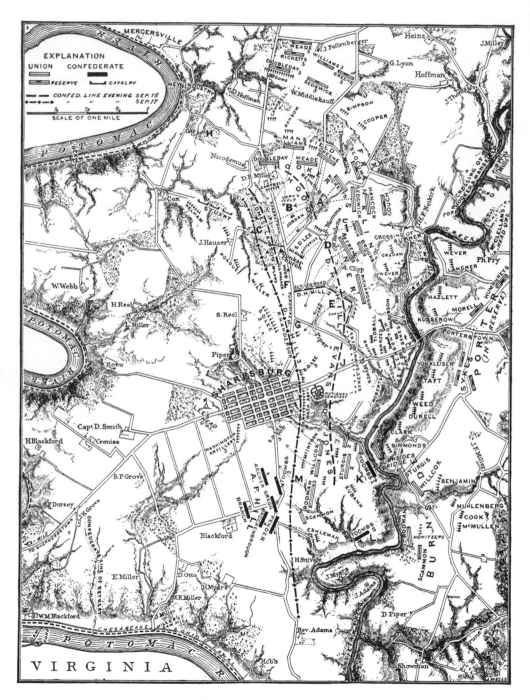

The Battle of Antietam

Chapter Eleven

Tuesday Afternoon, December 15, 1863

They poured out their blood like water.
General Oliver O. Howard, USA,
Sharpsburg (Antietam)

Walking down the capitol hallway after a private lunch in an anteroom with Judah Benjamin, General Lee reached into his gray pocket for his spectacles. His fingers found a crumpled piece of paper which he read silently as he walked toward the Joint Committee chamber. He smiled, gently folded the paper, and returned the scrap to his pocket.

Entering the chamber where the hearths had been restoked, General Lee brushed past a young woman who had pushed her way through the armed guards.

"Papa?" the girl said loudly over the din of the assembling gallery.

General Lee turned to find that he had walked past his daughter Mildred.

"Sorry, Life," the general smiled. "I'm a little pre-occupied. When did you come?"

"Just a few minutes ago. I couldn't bear to leave you here alone without mother or any of us."

General Lee excused himself from Secretary Benjamin and ushered Mildred toward the wall where a fireplace blazed comfortably in the stone chamber.

"Precious Life, you must return to the Mim and your sisters. This is no place for you." General Lee's voice was soft but firm.

"But, Papa," Mildred protested gently. "I want to be with you when mother is not."

"You are with me, Life," the general smiled. "I found your lovely note in my pocket this morning....I love you, too."

"I'm sorry I did not write more. My note was so short. But I could not find a bigger piece of paper."

The soldier smiled and laid his hand upon her shoulder.

"It is, as you state, very short and little. But, in that, it is like you. And like you, it is very sweet. And like you, it has given me much pleasure." The general leaned forward to kiss his child's forehead while the gallery filled behind them. "But you must return to the Mim and serve your country with your sisters by making socks for our poor boys so cold in their tents tonight. Please, Precious Life."

"But, Father! All I ever do is knit, knit, knit."

"Never neglect the means of making yourself useful in the world," General Lee said gravely. "You can do as much as anyone to further our efforts in the field. Please, child. This is no place for you."

"Alright, Papa. If you insist."

"I do, Life. Kiss the Mim for me and I shall be home for supper."

Mildred Lee kissed her father as she turned to leave. At the doorway, she brushed the elbow of Chairman Wigfall who greeted her courteously.

The gallery rose and waited for the Texan to take his place with his silver-haired colleagues.

"Let us resume, ladies and gentlemen. Back on the record." Senator Wigfall gaveled the afternoon session to order.

"To continue from this morning, General Lee....You were reviewing your reasons for the September 1862 raid into Maryland. If you would continue, please."

"The purpose, if discovered, would have had the effect of carrying the enemy north of the Potomac, and if prevented, would not have resulted in much evil." General Lee recited dryly. "The army was not properly equipped for an invasion of the enemy's territory. It lacked much of the materiel of war, was feeble in transportation, the animals being much reduced, and the men were poorly provided with clothes, and in thousands of instances, were destitute of shoes. Still, we could not afford to be idle. And though weaker than our opponents in men and military equipment, we had to endeavor to harass if we could not destroy them."

"So General, you hoped to draw the enemy out of Virginia by threatening Washington, if I understand you correctly?"

"Yes, Mr. Chairman," the witness nodded. "The condition of Maryland encouraged the belief that the presence of our army, however inferior to that of the enemy, would induce the Washington government to retain all of its available force to provide against contingencies....We expected to derive more assistance in the attaining of our object from the just fears of the Washington government than from any active demonstration on the part of the people of Maryland."

"Then, General, you did not expect that your raid into Maryland would somehow encourage that border state to leave the Union and cast its lot with us?"

"Notwithstanding individual expressions of kindness that had been given and their general sympathy in the success of the Confederate States, situated as Maryland is," the witness sighed, "I did not anticipate any general rising of the people in our behalf."

"But you did have broad tactical objectives beyond worrying Washington, did you not?"

"Yes, Senator," the witness said over his folded hands. "Should the results of the expedition have justified it, I proposed to President Davis to enter Pennsylvania unless the President should have deemed it inadvisable upon political or other grounds."

"I believe from your official report of the Maryland campaign that foraging was also your immediate tactical intent?"

"Yes, Senator, as was the case nine months later with the Pennsylvania raid which ended at Gettysburg. And as was especially the case at Gettysburg, we crossed into hostile country in search of shoes."

Senator Reade leaned forward.

"Shoes, General? You risked your army to requisition shoes?"

"Senator Reade," the general said with the color rising on the back of his neck. "a thousand pairs of shoes and some clothing were obtained in Fredericktown, 250 pairs in Williamsport, and about 400 pairs in Hagerstown, Maryland. And they were not sufficient to cover the bare feet of the army." The hostility in the general's voice faded. "And I would also mention horseshoes for the animals, Senator," General Lee sighed, "horseshoes for want of which nearly half our cavalry is unserviceable!"

"General Lee, all of us sympathize with the commissary problems of this war for our independence. But that is not our subject at this inquiry. I beg to remind you."

"Yes, Senator," General Lee shrugged. "But I hasten to add that lack of shoes, clothing, and food always have a direct impact upon our effectiveness in the field. Our best field officers cannot stop straggling by starving, barefoot troops."

"Yes, General. Was such straggling a concern prior to or during the Maryland campaign last year?"

"Absolutely," General Lee said firmly. "Our great embarrassment was the reduction of our ranks by straggling, which seemed impossible to prevent with our present regimental officers. Our ranks were very much diminished, I fear from a third to a half of the original numbers."

Straggling was so serious even before the Maryland raid that on August 20, 1862, Stonewall Jackson summarily ordered that all stragglers would be shot without benefit of trial or court martial.

"I understand, General. In addition to your problem of stragglers, we all know that your entire battle plan, Special Orders Number 191, had fallen into Federal hands prior to the Sharpsburg battle."

General Lee nodded. "A copy of the order directing the movement of the army from Fredericktown had fallen into the hands of General McClellan and disclosed to him the disposition of our forces."

Major Generals James Longstreet and Daniel Harvey Hill had arrived with their divisions at Sharpsburg on September 15, 1862. General Walker's Confederate division arrived from the siege of Harper's Ferry on the 16th. But Lafayette McLaws' division remained upriver at Harper's as did Stonewall's division until late in the day.

Jackson put his exhausted men back on the dirt road between Harper's Ferry and Antietam Creek at 1 o'clock in the morning on September 16th. Jackson's division marched all night for 16 miles. The divisions of A.P. Hill, McLaws, and Walker stayed behind with 18 brigades to issue the paroles for the disarmed prisoners at Harper's. When Stonewall prodded his bone-tired regiments into Sharpsburg just before noon, his men had tramped 60 miles in three days with no real food except green corn foraged along the way. For three weeks, the Army of Northern Virginia had subsisted on green corn until diarrhea crippled much of the Confederate command. General Lee now mustered only 25,000 men against 80,000 Federals.

Stonewall's division dug in near a small white building known locally as the Dunker Church. His line of 19,000 Confederates and their 40 cannon faced some 30,000 Federals armed with 100 cannon.

By noon on the 16th, only 24 Confederate brigades stood opposite 44 Yankee brigades. Even after Stonewall arrived, the Army of Northern Virginia was at its lowest strength since General Lee had assumed command in June. By late afternoon on the 16th, General Lee held onto a 4 mile front with but 26,500 men and 200 cannon. General McClellan hesitated to engage his superior force of 71,500 supported by 300 cannon.

As men, artillery, and miles of wagon trains streamed into the tiny hamlet of Sharpsburg, Maryland, the long gray line grew to 38,000 men while the Federal rolls increased to 87,000.

The Confederate line ran north and south with the wide Potomac at their backs and Antietam Creek in their front. The two waterways were hardly more than three miles apart with the Army of Northern Virginia wedged dangerously between. The blue divisions dug in on the far side of the Antietam.

McClellan finally began to move his divisions across the Maryland countryside on the afternoon of September 16th. At 4 o'clock, he ordered Joe Hooker's I Corps to cross Antietam Creek westward to camp for the night opposite General Lee's far left flank near the Poffenberger farm. McClellan gave Lee all night of the 16th to strengthen his left flank. General Hood's gray division was moved to the left to await Hooker's dawn assault.

At sunset on the 16th, Joe Hooker's three divisions settled in opposite Lee's weak left flank. A twilight artillery duel killed Colonel Hugh McNeil of the 13th Pennsylvania Reserves. McNeil, a lawyer before the war, had practiced law as a partner of William Seward who was now President Lincoln's Secretary of State.

Chaplain Israel Washburn of the 12th Massachusetts took a Rebel bullet in the chest. The lethal Minie ball was stopped by his pocket Bible. On the north end of the lines, the pickets were so close to each other that they could overhear the nervous chatter of their enemies as they ground coffee in tin pots, wrote last letters to loved ones far away, and slept the fitful sleep of condemned men. The men of the 6th Wisconsin regiment threw away their unholy playing cards so they would die clean come daybreak.

The Battle of Sharpsburg (Antietam) began in an all-night rain at 3 o'clock in the morning on Wednesday, September 17th. Federal artillery opened, lobbing shot across Antietam Creek. The drizzle stopped at dawn and promised a clear and cloudless day.

Twenty-six Confederate cannon opened at 5:30 in the morning, pounding Joe Hooker's I Corps. When 24 Yankee cannon replied, 20-pound shot hissed through the dawn air at the rate of one round every second. The cannonade was heard in Hagerstown, 12 miles away. The artillery duel north of Sharpsburg terrified the little town's 1,300 civilians. Many took shelter in the sturdy old barn on the Nicodemus farm east of the Hagerstown Pike. On either side of the Pike stood stands of trees without names. By nightfall, the forests would be known forever as the North Woods and the West Woods. When 20 women and children fled to the Nicodemus barn, Federal cannoneers held their ferocious fire long enough to permit Captain William Blackford of the Rebel cavalry to lead the trembling civilians out of the field of fire. Several small children rode behind Blackford on the cavalryman's horse. The short truce was the last of the day.

Joe Hooker's I Corps opened the infantry battle at daybreak when his bluecoats stormed Stonewall Jackson's three divisions on the Rebel left in the East Woods. Thirty-six Union cannon covered his attack. Five Pennsylvania regiments under Brigadier General Truman Seymour advanced under fire southward through the East Woods until they met Colonel James Walker's brigade of Jackson's wing: the same Jim Walker whom Jackson had expelled from VMI. Colonel Walker fell wounded in the East Woods north of town.

The blue I Corps attacked the East Woods and the North Woods. The Confederates of Baldy Ewell and Dick Anderson's divisions countercharged northeastward from the West Woods. Between 5:30 and 7:30, the Rebel line was slowly weakening. General John Hood led two Confederate brigades to the rescue of the gray line. Hood charged from the West Woods into a stand of corn which would forever become to survivors the Cornfield. Hood pressed through the Cornfield into the East Woods on the Rebel left near the Miller farmstead. In the North Woods at 7 o'clock, Rebel Brigadier General William Starke was killed along the Hagerstown Pike near the Dunker Church sector held by Jackson. Starke would be buried in Richmond beside his son who was killed at the Battle of Seven Pines three months earlier.

By 8 o'clock, General Hood's counterattack had stalled. A Federal surge pushed Hood back. Daniel Harvey Hill's division came to Hood's assistance. Toward 9 o'clock, General Mansfield's Yankee XII Corps slammed headlong into Harvey Hill's exhausted regiments. Hill fell back slowly toward the West Woods and another obscure no-name landmark. Hill crossed an unremarkable dirt road somewhat depressed by years of erosion and wagon wheels. The little road was known to locals as the Sunken Road near the Mumma farm. When Stonewall moved two brigades into the Cornfield 500 yards north of the Dunker Church, Joe Hooker's I Corps virtually destroyed these two brigades. The whole left flank of General Lee's line collapsed as cheering Federals scrambled toward the church.

Confederate divisions under Generals Hood, Jubal Early, and Harvey Hill could not hold the left at the Cornfield. At the last possible moment, the divisions of Walker and McLaws rallied to Hood's support at the Dunker Church. After ferocious combat, the Federals were pushed back from the church. In the carnage, one of Stonewall's brigades suffered 50 percent casualties and another brigade lost 30 percent. In all, 13 of 15 regimental commanders lay dead or wounded.

By 7 o'clock in the morning, in the East Woods one and one-half miles northeast of town, the 6th Georgia regiment of Harvey Hill's division had already lost half of its men. Also in the East Woods, the brigade of General Alexander Lawton, West Point '39 and Harvard Law School '43, of Baldy Ewell's division had lost nearly every regimental commander killed or wounded. Confederates low on ammunition were taking bullets from the cartridge boxes on the belts of dead comrades. Among the Union wounded in the East Woods was Charlie King, the drummerboy of Company F, 49th Pennsylvania Volunteer Infantry. When Charlie King died three days later, he became the battle's youngest casualty. He was 13 years old.

The Cornfield was a 30-acre field on the David Miller farm. The battle there began at 6 o'clock when three New York regiments and one Pennsylvania regiment stormed the Cornfield. One-third of the bluecoats fell within half an hour, among them the colorbearer of the 107th Pennsylvania who was 14 years old.

By 7 o'clock, John Hood's Confederate division charged the Cornfield on the Miller farm. Within 20 minutes, 80 percent of the 1st Texas regiment had been destroyed, losing 186 men. The 4th Texas regiment lost 107 of 200 men. By 7:30, 60 percent of the entire division had been killed or wounded amid the stalks of corn.

Hood's division had been without real food for three days, having been issued only one-half ration of beef with green corn before the battle for the Cornfield.

When Alfred Colquitt's Rebel brigade of Harvey Hill's division charged the Cornfield near the East Woods, they were assaulted by Union regiments from Pennsylvania and Ohio who quickly annihilated half of the Confederate brigade and all of its officers. The already bloodied 6th Georgia regiment simply ceased to exist when 226 of its 250 men were cut to bloody ribbons. When three color-bearers were wounded in Hampton's Legion of Hood's Texas troops, Major J.H. Dingle picked up his regimental colors and shouted above the thunder, "Legion, follow your colors!" Major Dingle led his Texans to the edge of the field where he was killed. General Wofford's brigade of Hood's division lost 560 of 854 Confederates, among whom were 101 casualties of the 176 troops in the 18th Georgia regiment.

When Hood's division charged, they were met by the 6th Wisconsin regiment which left 152 of 314 men face down in the bloody dirt. When Captain Werner Von Bachelle of the 6th fell dead, his dog refused to leave its master's body. (Two days later, the burial parties found the bullet-riddled dog beside his captain. Man and dog were buried together.) The Cornfield cost the 12th Massachusetts regiment 224 of 334 troops for the highest Federal loss rate of the battle along Antietam Creek. The 12th Massachusetts accounted for a 61 percent casualty rate in the Louisiana Tigers brigade of General Alexander Lawton of Baldy Ewell's division. The Tigers lost 323 men in 15 minutes in the Cornfield.

In the Cornfield, Joe Hooker's 8,600 Federals did mortal combat with Stonewall's three divisions of 7,700 hungry Confederates. By 7:30 in the morning, Hooker's I Corps had already lost 2,600 men and John Hood's Rebel division had lost 1,380 of 2,300 troops. When the 1st Texas regiment of Hood's division lost 186 of 226 men in the Cornfield, there were two sets of brothers. In each set, one brother was wounded and one killed. General Ricketts of the blue I Corps sent 3,150 men into the Cornfield and brought 300 of them out alive. The 21st New York lost 40 percent of its men in 15 minutes. The 3rd North Carolina lost 323 men including 23 of their 27 officers. There were only 66 men in the 1st North Carolina who left the Cornfield without wounds.

At 8:30, Brigadier General George Greene led two Federal brigades into the Cornfield and on southward toward the Dunker Church sector where the battered Yankees captured a Rebel artillery position. General Greene and Robert Lee shared ties of friendship extending back to the Revolution. General Lee's impoverished father who could not afford his own grave was buried in the garden of George Greene's Revolutionary ancestor, Nathaniel Greene.

Late in the horrific morning, the 27th Indiana regiment's Corporal Barton Mitchell and Sergeant John Bloss who had found General Lee's Special Orders 191 were wounded. Captain Peter Kapulo to whom they had taken the lost orders was killed in the bloody corn.

By mid-morning, the lines of blue and gray had swept the Cornfield at least 15 times. When a ferocious Rebel fire forced the 3rd Brigade of the 1st Division of Joe Hooker's I Corps from the Cornfield, the brave Federals retired to a protective rocky knoll where they set to brewing their morning coffee under the hail of hot lead passing over their sweating heads.

While farmer Miller's field was being christened forever by the blood of thousands, the woodlot directly across the turnpike was becoming the West Woods by 9:15 in the morning. Edwin Sumner (the war's oldest commander of a corps) sent Uncle John Sedgwick's division of bluecoats across the bloodied Cornfield over the Hagerstown Turnpike toward the West Woods. In furious fighting, Brigadier General Oliver Howard of Maine (cadet Jeb Stuart's closest friend at West Point) suffered 545 casualties in minutes. The year before, Howard had lost his right arm fighting Rebels. In the utter confusion of the smoky holocaust, the 59th New York regiment fired a volley into the obscured blue backs of the 15th Massachusetts ahead of them. The New Yorkers cut down 344 men from Massachusetts. Company H of the 15th lost 52 of 62 men. Lieutenant Sam Fletcher's brother James died in his arms in the West Woods.

During 20 minutes in farmer Poffenberger's West Woods, John Sedgwick's division of Sumner's II Corps lost 2,210 men. The 42nd New York regiment lost half its men. General Sedgwick himself was wounded three times. Among the bloody Union boys lying face down in the woodlot was a gravely wounded young captain of the 20th Massachusetts: Oliver Wendell Holmes, Jr. The captain's father wrote poetry for a living. (The young soldier, shot through the neck, recovered to become Chief Justice of the Massachusetts Supreme Court at the turn of the century and then went on to sit with distinction on the Supreme Court of the United States for 30 years.)

General Sedgwick had done battle in the West Woods with Lafayette McLaws' division of James Longstreet's wing of the Rebel army. General Semmes' gray brigade of McLaws' command had been nearly destroyed: The 53rd Georgia lost 30 percent of its men; the 32nd Virginia lost 45 percent; the 10th Georgia lost nearly 60 percent as did the 15th Virginia regiment. The battle flag of the 10th Georgia left the West Woods with 46 bullet holes and the flag staff had been split twice by bullets in the bloodied hands of the color-guard.

Private Willie Hood of the 35th North Carolina stumbled upon a gravely wounded, Yankee officer. The teenage Rebel called out to the blue pickets to come over to fetch their shattered officer. Grateful Yanks picked up their man, handed Hood a knapsack of precious Federal coffee in tribute, and let the boy pass through the blue line toward the Rebel side of the West Woods.

A desperate lull settled upon the Antietam battlefield by 9 o'clock in the morning. Since dawn, nearly 8,000 men and boys had already fallen in the West and East Woods and in the Cornfield. The momentary respite found the Miller field held by the exhausted Federals. A farmhouse east of the Cornfield was pressed into service as a Federal field hospital. The pile of amputated arms and legs outside reached up to the window sill.

With General Lee's left flank weak but hanging on, the Yankee offensive abandoned the Rebel left and slammed headlong into the Confederate center. Harvey Hill of Stonewall's command held the

Dunker Church sector and the Sunken Road. By noon, the Sunken Road would be forever renamed Bloody Lane.

Uncle John Sedgwick's Federals swept the Dunker Church area in Jackson's front from 9 o'clock to nearly noon. The Yankees fired 40 rounds per man and the blue division suffered 355 men killed, 1,577 wounded. The 15th Massachusetts, 34th New York, and 82nd New York regiments each lost half of their men. At 10 o'clock, Colonel Van H. Manning, leading John Walker's Rebel brigade, charged the Federals east of the Dunker Church. Yankee cannon opened on the brigade with canister from 70 yards. The rounds of lead marbles swept the Southerners from the field. The 30th Virginia regiment was exterminated, losing 160 of 236 men.

Within 30 minutes, the 7th North Carolina lost 140 of 268 troops. The 111th Pennsylvania lost 110 of 300 and their comrades in the 125th Pennsylvania left 229 men behind. Federals fell at the rate of one every four seconds.

Fighting raged near the tiny, white-washed church for two hours. Among the Rebels was Robert E. Lee, Jr., the commanding general's 20-year-old son. He shoved powder and shell down the cannon of the Rockbridge Artillery. When General Lee passed his son's unit in the smoke and horror, the general did not recognize his own be-grimed son. Exactly six months earlier, General Lee had written Mother Lee about young Rob: "I hope our son will do his duty and make a good soldier."

In the Sunken Road depression in the Rebel center, Daniel Harvey Hill had only 2,500 men from the brigades of Robert Rodes, George Anderson, and Howell Cobb. Nearly 6,000 bluecoats from General William "Old Blinky" French's division of II Corps at-tacked Harvey Hill at 10 o'clock. Led by Brigadier General Max Weber, the Federals were massacred. In the first volley from Hill's men under cover of the embankment along the Sunken Road, the 4th New York lost 150 men. Within five minutes, 450 Federals in the 1st Delaware, 5th Maryland, and 4th New York regiments fell.

The 1st Delaware regiment of the blue 3rd Brigade, II Corps, lost one-third of its men and eight company commanders. Many of the

1st Delaware casualties were struck from behind by a volley from the 14th Connecticut. The 132nd Pennsylvania, 1st Brigade, lost 386 of 750 troops. The 1st Brigade of 3rd Division fought for four hours along Bloody Lane and lost 639 men. Blinky French lost 1,750 bluecoats within half an hour. Dead and dying Federals dropped within 20 yards of Harvey Hill's grayclads where one-third of French's division would fall within an hour.

General Weber's attack was beaten back. At 10:30, Israel Richardson's blue division of II Corps sent in the hard-fighting Irish Brigade to take Harvey Hill's Sunken Road. Before the Irish Brigade of four regiments went in, Father William Corby granted absolution to all but cowards. There weren't any. The Irishmen lost 540 of 970 men before pulling back. General Richardson's 1st Division assaulted Bloody Lane with 4,000 Federals for 90 minutes.

Before the Irishmen of the "Fighting 69th" New York withdrew after sustaining 60 percent casualties, they had exterminated the 16th Mississippi regiment in the sunken roadbed. Colonel John Gordon of the 6th Alabama, Rodes' brigade, was wounded four times. Private Joe Johnson of the 6th's Company G lay dying in Bloody Lane beside the corpse of Sergeant Edward Johnson, his son.

When Captain John Strickler of the 130th Pennsylvania was being carried off the field with wounds in his shoulder and both legs, he was hit a fourth time. "My God!," the bleeding Federal pleaded, "I'm being killed by inches."

By noon, the Federals were overrunning the Sunken Road. The 61st and 64th New York regiments broke through the Rebel center. At the same time, General Longstreet unleashed a vigorous counter-charge out of the West Wood toward the Dunker Church sector. Three Rebel brigades fought ferociously in the Mumma farm cornfield between the church and the sunken road. One brigade was led by Jeb Stuart's brother-in-law, Colonel John Cooke. Cooke's Confederates fell back after losing half their men in the bloodbath. Howell Cobb's brigade of Rebels from McLaws' division lost 200 of 250 men. The 14th North Carolina lost 213 men.

At least 224 Federals also fell on the Mumma farm. Two Union divisions were pounding Hill's men along Bloody Lane. Along the Confederate center at the little church and the Sunken Road, the Federals were pouring into the collapsing Confederate line. By 1 o'clock, 2,600 Confederates and 3,000 Federals lay along Bloody Lane. General Richardson's Union division lost 1,163 men. At the last victorious moment in the Sunken Road, General Richardson was gravely wounded and died six weeks later.

By 1 o'clock in the afternoon, the Confederate left was teetering and the center had collapsed with Federals pouring across Bloody Lane. General Lee was completely out of reserve troops to plug the breech in his line. With the center disintegrating, Longstreet brought up Rebel cannon. Longstreet serviced one cannon with his own hands so he could mow down the 20th New York. South Carolina cannoneers fired point-blank into the faces of the blueclad teenagers. One more thrust and General McClellan could have pushed past Bloody Lane and the church to cut Robert Lee's crumbling line in half. Only mopping up of the two shattered Rebel flanks would have been required by nightfall. But Longstreet's artillery convinced McClellan that Lee had reinforced the Rebel center. McClellan abandoned the assault against the weakened middle of the gray line.

By Longstreet's big guns, the Rebel center was saved as the Confederate's second pitched battle of the day slowly petered out. The Federal attack moved southward for the third contest of the Battle of Sharpsburg. The Yankee offensive shifted to the Rohrbach Bridge across Antietam Creek.

General McClellan's attack against the extreme right of the Rebel line began at 10 o'clock in the morning. The blue IX Corps stormed the Rohrbach Bridge which spanned the 125-foot width of Antietam Creek. The bridge was the southernmost of three which crossed the Antietam. Steep hills rose at each end of the bridge and the western Confederate side was defended by only 400 men under the command of Colonel Henry "Old Rock" Benning of General Robert Toombs' brigade. Brigadier General Toombs was a United States senator before the war and Henry Benning had been an associate justice of the Supreme Court of Georgia.

The 11th Connecticut was driven back in their bloody charge against Rohrbach bridge by four Georgia regiments. Colonel Henry Kingsbury of the 11th was killed on the Bridge fighting against Confederate Brigadier General Daniel Jones—Kingsbury's brother-in-law.

The Union's IX Corps was commanded by General Ambrose Burnside, West Point 1847 (and classmate of A.P. Hill), the son of a South Carolina slaveowner. When General Burnside launched four separate charges against the bridge, the bridge soon became "Burnside Bridge." General Burnside sent 3,200 of his 12,500 men well south of the bridge to cross Antietam Creek at Snavely Ford to get on Robert Lee's far right flank, two-thirds of a mile downriver from the bridge. The expedition to the ford was led by General Isaac Rodman. The first Yankee charge against Burnside Bridge was repulsed at 10 o'clock. The second assault at noon also failed and cost the blue 2nd Maryland regiment 44 percent casualties. The Rebel cannon were firing 15-inch lengths of railroad track iron.

By 1 o'clock, General Burnside's suicide charges made it to the Rebel side of Antietam Creek across the bridge. The advancing Federals slugged their way over the bodies of 500 dead and dying bluecoats who lay on the bridge in pools of Northern blood. The victorious Yankees pushed the 3,000 Confederates on General Lee's far right flank back half a mile from Antietam Creek. When General Rodman's force fought their way across Snavely Ford, General McClellan now had three divisions on the Confederate side of the creek.

General Rodman sent Harrison Fairchild's Union brigade across Snavely Ford. Fairchild lost one-fourth of his Federals within minutes. Rodman's troops pushed inland two miles. Fairchild's brigade lost 455 men in hand-to-hand fighting on the Rebel far right flank. After IX Corps had suffered 2,222 casualties on and around Burnside Bridge, the Confederate right evaporated. The Army of Northern Virginia was crumbling.

Where was A.P. Hill's division when General Lee needed it most? By the time the Yankees poured across the bloody bridge, some

18,500 men in blue and gray had already fallen in three separate battles on the left, the center, and the right of the Rebel line.

General Lee's right flank was down to 2,000 men since so many brigades had been pulled off the line earlier in the morning to shore up the shattered center of the Confederate line. Only David Jones' division held the right when Burnside's Federals broke through. In the center, Stonewall Jackson was down to 6,500 men. Meanwhile, 8,500 Federals dragging 22 cannon were fighting their way around General Lee's right. The Yankee line of attack was now three-quarters of a mile wide. Only 2,800 Rebels defended the town of Sharpsburg.

As his right flank folded under the Federal assault, General Lee nervously looked toward the west at a rising cloud of dust churned up by running feet. The Yankees were swarming to the high ground east and west of Sharpsburg, within half a mile of the Confederate rear and General Lee's only line of retreat toward the Potomac. Could the dust be still more divisions in Union blue?

Spyglasses strained to pierce the suffocating clouds of sulfur to make out the distant flags approaching on the run from the west. Were they Stars and Stripes? Or Stars and Bars?

The battle flags snapping in the western breeze at 3:30 were the leading regiments of A.P. Hill's division.

Hill had marched 17 miles in eight hours from Harper's Ferry. Hill deployed his exhausted division of 3,300 men on the run. They plowed into the 15,000 Federals south of Sharpsburg on the Otto farm. Hill saluted Robert Lee who was so overwhelmed with relief that he hugged his red-shirted commander. He had taken the field at the last possible second. In the firestorm on the Rebel right, General Rodman was gravely wounded and Rebel Brigadier General Lawrence Branch was killed. The blue 2nd Brigade of 3rd Division of IX Corps lost 285 men and the 1st Brigade of the 3rd Division lost 235 men.

By 4:30, Burnside's shaken IX Corps was falling back from Hill's sudden attack. Burnside left the field littered with 2,350 dead and wounded Federals. Hill's division, outnumbered nearly 5 to 1, pushed Burnside's corps from the field. At West Point, Hill and Burnside had been very close friends and were roommates their senior year in 1847.

By twilight, the Federal assault was over and the Army of Northern Virginia remained a fighting force still holding the horrific field.

When darkness ended the day-long slaughter, Old Pete Longstreet arrived for a meeting of Robert Lee's general staff. When General Lee saw Longstreet, he greeted Longstreet warmly with "Here comes my old warhorse!"

The Battle of Sharpsburg was over. The toll was stupefying to both bloodied armies.

In a single day, the Federals had lost 2,010 men killed, another 9,416 wounded, and 1,043 missing or captured, for 12,469 total casualties. This does not include the 11,000 Federals who surrendered to Stonewall Jackson at Harper's Ferry. The Army of Northern Virginia had lost between South Mountain, Harper's Ferry, and Sharpsburg, at least 1,567 killed, another 8,725 wounded, and 2,000 missing or captured, for a total of 12,292 casualties. McClellan suffered 25 percent casualties and Lee suffered 31 percent losses in 12 hours. Harvey Hill lost half of his division which held Bloody Lane. He suffered 2,316 casualties.

Each army's command structure had been severely hurt. The Federals lost two major generals mortally wounded and three wounded, five brigadier generals wounded, thirteen colonels wounded and eight killed. General Lee lost three generals killed and six wounded, and ten colonels killed and 25 wounded at South Mountain and Sharpsburg.

The casualty lists for George McClellan were personal. Among the Federal dead was Private Harrison White of the 28th Pennsylvania Volunteer Infantry, a 19-year-old nephew of George McClellan's wife.

Among the piles of dead and dying men in the darkness was a great warhorse. Near the East Woods on the Smoketown Road lay the gray charger of Colonel Henry Strong of the 6th Louisiana regiment. Old men would remember how the dead horse lay peacefully reposing on its forelegs as if asleep. Somewhere nearby, Colonel Strong lay dead.

Beside Antietam Creek on September 17, 1862, the Army of Northern Virginia could have been destroyed—it should have been destroyed. But General McClellan was reluctant to commit his entire army to the job. The Federals had fresh troops available for the attack while General Lee had no rested troops to hold them off.

During the battle, General Lee had committed all available Confederate infantry to saving his divided army. There simply were no fresh troops. On the far side of the bloody field, only two-thirds of the Federals had seen action on the 17th. By the next day, General McClellan had 50,000 Yankees ready for duty, of whom 32,000 were fresh, rested, and unbloodied from the day before. The Federal reserves alone were equal to all of the Confederate forces on the field.

All day on a rainy September 18th, General Lee waited for George McClellan's attack which never came. While he waited, the stretcher-bearers gathered their shattered loads. Somewhere between the lines that Thursday, a wounded Yankee boy took off his bloody boot and used it to catch rain water to pour down his parched throat while he waited for rescue or for merciful death.

Under cover of wet darkness late on the 18th, the Army of Northern Virginia gathered its dead and wounded and began the retreat back into Virginia on the other side of the Potomac. While the Confederates waded the river, Jeb Stuart's cavalry held the pursuing Federals at bay on the Maryland side until nightfall of the 20th. Baldy Ewell's division was still crossing at Boteler's Ford at daybreak on the 19th. When a Rebel wagon full of moaning wounded came under Yankee fire in the middle of the river, the wagoneer jumped off for his life. Brigadier General Maxcy Gregg waded into the Potomac and drove the horses toward Virginia himself. General Gregg had three months to live. On the Virginia shore, a Rebel brass band sadly played "Carry Me Back to Old Virginy" as the army limped to safety.

When the roll was called on September 20th, the battered Army of Northern Virginia could count only 36,418 heads. The rest were dead, dying, some left to the Yankees on the field beside Antietam Creek—or had simply laid down their heavy muskets and gone home. "My army is ruined by stragglers," General Lee would complain bitterly.

With the Confederate army withdrawn from Maryland and the Union garrison at Washington City safe from invasion, President Lincoln seized the occasion to change the entire face of the war and the legitimacy of the Federal cause. On September 22nd, the President showed the Emancipation Proclamation to his cabinet secretaries. The Proclamation was made public the next day. Henceforth, either the Union or slavery would be destroyed forever.

"So, General," Chairman Wigfall continued with great fatigue in his voice, "you elected to stand at Sharpsburg against almost overwhelming odds and with your command severely reduced by desertions?"

The witness removed his spectacles and rubbed his eyes.

"The arduous service in which our troops had been engaged, their great privations of rest and food, and the long marches without shoes over mountain roads, had greatly reduced our ranks before the action began. These causes had compelled thousands of brave men to absent themselves and many more had done so from unworthy motives."

"Then why, in God's name, General, did you not retreat back to Virginia before doing battle at Sharpsburg? After all, you had to wait there for General McClellan to attack you!"

The witness looked up at Senator Louis Wigfall. The general spoke bitterly.

"Although not properly equipped for invasion, lacking much of the materiel of war and feeble in transportation, the troops poorly provided with clothing and thousands of them destitute of shoes, it was yet believed to be strong enough to detain the enemy upon the northern frontier until the approach of winter should render his advance into Virginia difficult, if not impossible."

"Then, General, you were satisfied with the performance of your command in Maryland?"

The general bristled. As his neck reddened, he clenched his left fist which he covered with his right hand atop the table.

"This great battle was fought by less than 40,000 men on our side, all of whom had undergone the greatest labors and hardships in the field and on the march. Nothing could surpass the determined valor with which they met the large army of the enemy, fully supplied and equipped. The result reflects the highest credit on the officers and men engaged."

A murmur briefly swept the restless gallery.

As the two weary armies like wounded animals went into winter camp in late 1862, General McClellan was relieved of command by President Lincoln on November 7th and was replaced by Ambrose Burnside, Hill's old roommate from the Point. Meanwhile, over 100,000 Federals advanced toward Fredericksburg, Virginia.

"I hated to see McClellan go," General Lee smiled. "He and I had grown to understand each other so well." The witness shook his head. "I feared that they might continue to make changes till they found someone whom I didn't understand."

The gallery chuckled.

General Lee did not laugh. Instead, he bowed his white head. The memory of Sharpsburg brought back pain which went beyond the field strewn with men in butternut brown and gray. When the Army of Northern Virginia settled into camp to regroup in October 1862, General Lee learned of the October 20th death of his daughter Annie, at age 23. The father still grieved.

★　　　★　　　★

General Lee rode Traveller homeward in the dark. He could not push memories of his dead Annie from his mind. Only the company of children would ease the pain. Children had always comforted the soldier who spent most of his adult life in lonely bivouacs far from family.

With two mounted guards riding discretely behind, Lee steered Traveller toward the corner of Clay and 12th Streets. Every window in the old Brockenbrough House was illuminated. The darkness made the old gray bricks eerily gloomy. He reined Traveller toward sentries on the street who guarded the Executive Mansion of the Confederate States of America.

Before Lee could dismount, a little crowd on the street broke into a cheer. The rider raised his hat to the citizens before he climbed off Traveller's back. The Confederate gray animal shook his long, black main and swished his black tail.

Every Tuesday night, Jefferson and Varina Davis opened their borrowed home to the Richmond public who could freely pay their respects to the First Family. Jefferson Davis made a point to greet everyone who dropped by.

Lee was half way to the doorway when the tall frame of the President filled the door. He met Robert Lee outside. The President held a child's hand with another little boy perched on his hip. A tiny dog ran between the President's legs and yelped at General Lee's spurs.

"That's my dog, Nicky," a small boy said happily. Jeff Davis, Jr., would be seven years old in January. He released his father's hand and skipped toward the weary general who patted the boy's head and then his dog.

"Good evening, General," the President said warmly. His breath came in clouds of steam. He wore no overcoat.

"It's a little chilly, Excellency."

"Nonsense, General. Do come in. Varina would love to see you."

"Thank you, Sir, but you appear to have a full house already."

Armed sentries had pushed the 20 citizen visitors away from the President and his general. The two famous men spoke out of the crowd's earshot.

"Just came by to wish Billy a happy birthday."

The tiny boy in the President's arms pulled closer to his father. On December 16th, William Howell Davis would be two years old.

Two more Davis children came to the doorway, Joseph, 4, whom Lee had met at the capitol, and Margaret, nearly 9.

General Lee removed his gray slouch hat. He smiled broadly behind his white beard. His eyes lingered on dark haired Margaret. He thought of Annie as a girl.

"Children."

"Margaret, Jeff, this is General Lee," their father said.

"Mrs. Davis," General Lee nodded when the First Lady appeared.

"General, won't you come in? We have real tea tonight."

"No ma'am. I have a house full of ladies waiting for me. Just wanted to pay my respects to the little ones."

"That's very kind, General," the rather round and dark woman smiled.

The Davises were deeply committed to each other. But that was not always the case. Jefferson Davis and Varina had hard years early in their marriage when the head-strong husband could not understand the independent ways of the child bride 18 years younger than himself. It took Varina years to forgive him for going off to Mexico to fight. They separated for nearly two years in December 1847. When Davis first went to Washington and the United States Senate, he refused to take his rebellious wife with him. She stayed behind in Mississippi until November 1849. Now they worked together and their love was well healed.

"Well," the general said, "happy birthday, Billy. I must get home now."

Varina and her husband nodded.

"Good night, General."

"Excellency. Mrs. Davis."

Lee placed his hat firmly on his head and turned toward Traveller. When the men in the crowd nearby called out questions about secret peace talks and armistice by Christmas, Robert Lee lifted his hat to them and said nothing.

Chapter Twelve

Wednesday Morning, 16 December 1863

I had never seen fighting like that....There was no cheering on the part of the men, but a stubborn determination to obey orders....And then the next brigade coming up in succession would do its duty and melt like snow coming down on a warm morning.
General Darius N. Couch, USA, Fredericksburg

*T*he general paced the floor. Robert Lee's breath fogged the frosted window at the end of the hallway. The warm embers in the bedrooms' small hearths did not warm the hall. He stood with a heavy housecoat closed over his long woolies. Mother Lee still slept as did his daughters and Martha Williams an hour before dawn.

General Lee stood shivering in his carpet slippers. He had slept fitfully and finally awoke at 4 o'clock.

All night long, his mind had walked along Antietam Creek. Lying in bed, behind his eyelids he had seen and smelled the carnage recalled by Henry Douglas, Stonewall's aide: "It was a dreadful scene, a veritable field of blood. The dead and dying lay as thick over it as harvest sheaves. The pitiable cries for water and appeals for help were much more horrible to listen to than the deadliest sounds of battle."

In his tortured memory where midnight demons haunted the rest he craved, Lee had felt for his troops what his nephew, General Fitz Lee, would remember of Sharpsburg: "The picture of the private soldier of Lee's army at Sharpsburg as he stood in the iron hail: If he stopped one of the enemy's bullets, he would be buried where the battle raged, in an unknown grave and be forgotten—except by comrades, and possibly by a poor old mother who was praying in her Southern home for the safe return of her soldier boy."

Beside Antietam Creek 15 months ago, even General McClellan had known that there was something special about Sharpsburg, something that would make the ancient gods of war turn away. While the battle raged at Burnside Bridge, McClellan telegraphed President Lincoln: "We are in the midst of the most terrible battle of the war, perhaps of history." Major Orrin Crane of the 7th Ohio regiment would remember of Lee's Confederates that "the enemy fell like grass before the mower." General Lee had dreamed of that bloody reaper.

Major General "Fighting Joe" Hooker of McClellan's I Corps had looked into the sea of teenage blood in the Cornfield: "The slain lay in rows precisely as they had stood in the ranks a few moments before. It was never my fortune to witness a more bloody, dismal battlefield."

General Lee grimaced. In his exhausted mind, he could see the enemy charge his lines before evaporating into clouds of sulfur. Longstreet remembered the Yankees dropping, dropping, dropping into bloody heaps before the Rebel cannon "like the steady dripping of rain from the eaves of a house."

In the cold hallway, Robert Lee shivered with a small convulsion of red-stained memory. He thought of the twilight meeting on the dreadful battlefield among his field commanders. General Shanks Evans had asked John Bell Hood, "Where is your division?" General Hood replied, "Dead on the field."

Lee turned his grieving face from the fogged window when the wooden floor creaked behind him. Mother Lee stood in her dressing gown at the bedroom doorway.

"Molly," the husband whispered in the darkness. "You'll catch your death."

"Are you alright?" she asked.

"My pulse is still about 90. The doctors say too quick for an old man." He was angry with his failing body. "I am weak, feverish, and altogether good for nothing at the very time I require all my strength."

Mother Lee shuffled painfully to her husband's side. The eastern sky was just beginning to show pink. The husband opened his ankle-length housecoat and held it open. Mary Lee stepped under his upraised arm. Robert Lee pulled the heavy robe around himself with Mrs. Lee under his arm like a protective wing.

"It will be morning soon, Robert. Martha and I will make you a hot breakfast of corn bread and milk before you leave. We will make you well again."

"Yes, Mother." He squeezed her shoulder. "That would solve half my problems, anyway."

"I know," Mary Lee said. "God will still give us our liberty."

"Without some increase of our strength," the general said softly, "I cannot see how we are to escape the natural military consequences of the enemy's numerical superiority."

"Then," Mother Lee said slowly, "we shall go home to one of my father's farms and we shall become farmers."

"I expect to die a pauper," he sighed. "I see no way of preventing it."

Mother Lee studied the terrible weariness in the wind burned face which looked aged beyond his 56 years.

"Robert, you could retire now. You have done all and more than the President has requested of you."

General Lee pulled Mother Lee closer.

"I should like to retire to private life, if I could be with you and the children. But if I can be of any service to the state or her cause, I must continue."

"I know." Mother Lee touched her husband's face.

"I suppose that today we shall discuss Fredericksburg...and Chancellorsville."

"Yes, Robert." Mrs. Lee had used the same tone with daughter Agnes when word came of her Orton's execution six months ago.

"I looked for our tree at Fredericksburg, Molly."

"Did you find it?"

"No, Mother."

★   ★   ★

"The troops displayed at Fredericksburg, in a high degree, the spirit and courage that distinguished them throughout the campaign, while the calmness and steadiness with which orders were obeyed and maneuvers executed in the midst of battle evinced the discipline of a veteran army."

"Yes, General Lee," Co-Chairman Henry Foote nodded. "There can be no doubt that Fredericksburg marked a clear victory for our forces in December of '62. Fredericksburg also clearly demonstrated the wisdom of the so-called 'tactical defensive' in which our forces chose the superior, defensive position and awaited suicidal attack by our enemies. Fredericksburg proved that we have no need to invade our enemy's country with the associated ocean of Southern blood. We should simply wait for him to invade our country. We want to be separate from him; he wants to conquer and enslave us. Let his blood flow like water, not ours. That, General, is what Fredericksburg proved to mc. And, so did Gettysburg."

After the Sharpsburg retreat from Maryland back to Virginia, Stonewall Jackson's wing of the Army of Northern Virginia went into camp near Shepherdstown along Opequon Creek. Stonewall's divisions were joined by new recruits and by thousands of the stragglers lost along the way to and from Antietam Creek. The ranks grew from 24,000 to 35,000 men. On September 28th, Jeb Stuart settled in at his winter quarters at The Bower, the Dandridge plantation eight miles from Martinsburg, Virginia. By the second week of October 1862, the army was scattered around Winchester with 64,000 veterans. By November 10th, recruits and repatriated stragglers brought the muster rolls up to 71,000 men.

As General Lee recounted the army's winter encampment a year ago, Jeb Stuart took his place in the packed gallery of the Joint Committee. Jeb was not about to miss the telling of another of his famous expeditions which left Yankee cavalrymen choking on the dust of Jeb's horses.

On October 8, 1862, General Lee had ordered Jeb Stuart to burn the Cumberland Valley Railroad bridge at Chambersburg, Pennsylvania. The vital rail bridge was a Federal lifeline south. The raid was also to capture hostages from Pennsylvania to exchange later for Rebel officials held by the Federals. General Stuart resolved to make the raid with 1,800 of his best troopers, including Rooney Lee. Wade Hampton also led a cavalry detachment. Stuart held a ball at The Bower estate on the 8th and danced until nearly midnight.

When he was not oiling his saddle, shining his saber, or cleaning his revolver, Jeb Stuart on October 8th had one more little errand to run. He gave Stonewall his first formal and elegant uniform with shiny brass buttons and gold sleeve echelons.

Until that day, Jackson did battle in the Valley and along Antietam Creek wearing his tattered and mothholed uniform left over from the Mexican War. His only headgear had been a cadet's ragged cap from Virginia Military Institute.

Next day, Jeb Stuart moved out at noon from Darkesville with his cavalry contingent and four horse-drawn cannon commanded by Major John Pelham.

On October 10th at dawn, Stuart crossed the Potomac at McCoy's Ford, ten miles west of Williamsport, Maryland. Then Jeb's command divided into three wings each with 600 troopers. One wing was charged with rustling Yankee horses to take back home. At sundown, they reached Chambersburg and the tiny town surrendered without a shot. But the Confederates failed to burn the railroad bridge: it was made of iron.

Jeb Stuart's cavalry band took horse early the next day, October 11th. They rode hard for Virginia with alerted Federals galloping behind them and racing ahead of them to cut them off at the Potomac. Before noon, the Confederates seized priceless Yankee supplies and 5,000 rifled muskets still desperately needed to replace the Confederacy's antiquated smoothbore muskets which were inaccurate and short-ranged compared to the new Union issue rifles. Jeb's chilly troopers also captured piles of Union blue winter overcoats.

To avoid the pursuing Federals, General Stuart chose to take the long way home by heading for the Potomac ford well south of Williamsport. He rested at Cashtown, seven miles from a tiny, unknown, and utterly unimportant, Pennsylvania hamlet called Gettysburg. Riding hard for Emmitsburg, Maryland, they came within three miles of Gettysburg. Near Emmitsburg, they captured a Yankee courier whose documents confirmed that 800 Federal cavalrymen were in pursuit only four miles away. Jeb spurred his five-mile long column forward all night on the 11th. By dusk, they were still 40 miles from the Potomac where 5,000 Federals waited for him.

By midnight on the 11th, Stuart was 15 miles from the river crossing. By dawn on the 12th, the Rebel cavalry reached Hyattstown, Maryland, where Federal forces were closing in from the east and west. At 7 o'clock in the morning after riding all night, the gray column was 35 miles south of Emmitsburg and 12 miles from the river. With Rooney Lee leading, they rode south toward Poolesville, Maryland, so Yankee spies would think they were headed well south toward the Potomac. At noon, they left the dirt road and cut westward to Poolesville and rode into a forest near Sugar Loaf Mountain at Beallsville. They then continued west for five miles toward White's Ford across the river.

Young John Pelham's mounted artillery held off pursuing Federals nipping at Rebel heels. Rooney Lee demanded and received the surrender of the Yankee force. Dragging 1200 captured horses and

30 Federal hostages, the Confederates crossed the Potomac at mid-day. Jeb Stuart's exhausted command had covered 130 miles in three days, doing 80 miles in the last 24 hours of non-stop galloping. Jeb had to mourn only one lost prisoner of war: his favorite horse Skylark was captured at the river.

"May it please the Chair," a crusty old Senator droned at Senator Wigfall's side, "I should like to read into the record General Stuart's official review of his daring Second Ride Around McClellan. If there is no objection."

"You may read the excerpt, briefly," Chairman Wigfall nodded.

"Thank you, Mr. Chairman." The old lawmaker adjusted his spectacles and read in a voice like dry leaves underfoot. "*The results of this expedition, in a moral and political point of view, can hardly be estimated. The consternation among the property-holders of Pennsylvania was beyond description....My staff are entitled to the highest praise. I marched from Chambersburg to Leesburg, 90 miles, with only one hour's halt in 36, including a forced passage of the Potomac—a march without parallel in history.*"

This time, Chairman Wigfall suffered the gallery's applause which rang in Jeb's ears.

"Mr. Chairman," General Lee said after the demonstration behind him, "I cannot add to the spirit of General Stuart's report, except to note his efforts during the entire Fredericksburg campaign." The witness removed his spectacles and spoke warmly of his cavalry leader. "To the vigilance, boldness, and energy of General Stuart and his cavalry is chiefly due the early and valuable information of the movements of the enemy. His reconnaissances frequently extended within the Federal lines, resulting in skirmishes and engagements in which the cavalry was greatly distinguished. In the battle, the cavalry effectively guarded our right, annoying the enemy and embarrassing his movements by hanging on his flank and attacking when opportunity occurred."

After his harrowing expedition to learn the whereabouts of Federal forces, Stuart recuperated the only way he knew: On October 15th, he held another grand party at The Bower.

On October 26, 1862, two blue divisions crossed the Potomac at Harper's Ferry and pushed on the next day toward Gordonsville, Virginia. Jeb Stuart broke camp at The Bower never to return when his cavalry pulled out on the 29th in freezing weather. During the first three days of frigid November, young Pelham's cannon held off the Yankees for 72 hours at Mountsville. With the entire Army of the Potomac hot on his trail, Stuart's cavalry withdrew into the Blue Ridge Mountains while John Pelham's artillery blazed away behind the Confederate cavalry. Jeb headed for a rendezvous with Stonewall's divisions arriving November 4th. It was there that Jeb received the crushing news of the death of baby Flora, named for her mother.

With all of his divisions in motion, General Lee tied up the loose ends of his army's command structure. On November 6th, Jackson and Longstreet were promoted to lieutenant general, dating back to mid-October. As lieutenant generals, their "wings" could be officially designated "corps." James Longstreet was given command of I Corps composed of the infantry divisions of Major Generals Dick Anderson, John Hood, George Pickett, Lafayette McLaws, and Brigadier General Robert Ransom, Jr., representing 31,000 men in 22 brigades.

Jackson received command of II Corps and the divisions of A.P. Hill, Harvey Hill, Baldy Ewell (under the temporary command of Brigadier General Jubal Early while Ewell recovered from having his leg blown off at Second Manassas during the summer), and the old Stonewall Division (under Brigadier General William Taliaferro), composed of 19 brigades and 34,000 footsoldiers.

While Robert Lee was reorganizing his division commands to compensate for the terrible loss of officers at Sharpsburg, Mr. Lincoln was still trying to find a commander who could destroy Lee. On November 5th, President Lincoln fired McClellan for the second time and replaced him with General Ambrose Burnside.

General Lee hated to see McClellan sacked, and not merely because George McClellan suffered from terminal hesitation on the battlefield. Lee also nursed a peculiar respect for McClellan since the Young Napoleon of the North was a consummate gentleman, "always and everywhere a gentleman" Major General Fitz Lee would one day say of him. Robert Lee was personally acquainted with McClellan's graciousness.

George McClellan had "captured" Mother Lee twice. In May of 1862, McClellan had captured Rooney Lee's farm at White House plantation. Among the prisoners were Mother Lee, Rooney's wife Charlotte, and Rooney's infant. General McClellan provided the civilian Lees with a Yankee escort south to Charlotte's family homestead at Hanover, Virginia. Mother Lee was again caught behind enemy lines in early June of '62. This time, Mrs. Lee was captured along with daughters Mildred and Annie. McClellan personally escorted Mother Lee and her daughters into the custody of Major Roy Mason of the Rebel army. Major Mason accompanied the Lee women south until they were delivered into the open arms of Robert Lee on June 10th behind A.P. Hill's lines. This was the first time in 14 months that Mother Lee had seen her husband and her first sight of his new beard.

So McClellan was out and A.P. Hill's closest friend at the Point, Ambrose Burnside, was in as commander of the Army of the Potomac. On November 17, 1862, General Edwin Sumner's corps of Federals occupied Falmouth on the Rappahannock north of the elegant Virginia town, Fredericksburg. Jeb Stuart's cavalry scouts confirmed the Yankee position the next day. On the 19th, Longstreet's I Corps arrived at Fredericksburg. Not less than 6,400 of Longstreet's men were barefoot with winter approaching. General Lee arrived at Fredericksburg along with a rainstorm the day after Longstreet.

Lee's first order of business during his first full day at Fredericksburg was the evacuation of the town's civilian population as two massive armies converged there. It was one of the great mass exoduses of the terrible war.

"I believe, General," Chairman Wigfall said as he looked over his spectacles, "that Fredericksburg was evacuated during the night of November 21st."

General Lee nodded sadly and spoke with deep emotion.

"Directions were given for the removal of the women and children as rapidly as possible. Almost the entire population, without a murmur, abandoned their homes. History presents no instance of a people exhibiting a purer and more unselfish patriotism or a higher spirit of fortitude and courage than was evinced by the citizens of Fredericksburg. They cheerfully incurred great hardships and privations."

While the homeless women and children of Fredericksburg walked away from their dearest possessions, Stonewall Jackson was suddenly very aware of hearth and home. On November 23rd, Jackson became a father. His daughter was born while her soldier-father trudged down the dirt road toward Fredericksburg. The baby was named Julia for Jackson's dead mother. Stonewall went into camp at Fredericksburg on November 26th. As General Lee's arrival had brought torrential rains, Stonewall Jackson's brought snow.

The snow turned to sleet and ice. When A.P. Hill led his division into bivouac at Fredericksburg on December 3rd, Hill had marched 175 miles in 12 days through the Blue Ridge Mountains. Frozen roads covered with sleet left a trail of bloody footprints behind Hill's barefoot division.

While the divisions shivered beside the freezing Rappahannock, General Lee learned of the death of the baby daughter of his son Rooney and Charlotte Lee.

Two vast armies glared at each other across the river: 78,000 grayclads and 117,000 Federals. On the night of December 10th, the Confederates strained to listen to the music rising from a Yankee brass band across the Rappahannock. They heard sweetly familiar sounds carried on the bitter wind. The Federal musicians were playing "Dixie."

The late-night concert ended with the opening skirmish of the Battle of Fredericksburg.

At 2 o'clock in the morning on December 11th, General Burnside began building pontoon bridges for crossing the river to assault General Lee's lines. Evacuated Fredericksburg was held by William Barksdale's Rebel brigade from Longstreet's I Corps. They opened fire on the bridge-builders in the dark at 4 o'clock. By noon, ten Federal attempts to lay bridges across the river had been beaten back with Barksdale's firepower. Burnside called upon his artillery to destroy the Confederates holding the town. From the Federal side of the Rappahannock, 181 cannon bombarded Fredericksburg for three hours. The fireworks were the greatest cannonade since the war began.

By 4 o'clock in the afternoon, the cold Yankees completed their bridges across the river south of the city. By evening twilight, the Federal fire had pushed General Barksdale out of Fredericksburg. Barksdale's brigade left 116 dead Confederates on the frozen ground as he pulled back to the long gray line at the base of Marye's Hill. The Federals lost 97 men when the 7th Michigan and 19th Massachusetts regiments crossed the river and were followed by the 42nd and 27th New York.

The Federal cannonade of Fredericksburg lobbed at least 5,000 shells into the town. General Lee watched the town burn from his field headquarters atop a little rise which would forever be "Lee's Hill" when the armies were long gone. Burnside did more than level part of Fredericksburg. His cannon damaged up the tomb of George Washington's mother buried there in 1789.

"These people delight to destroy the weak and those who can make no defense," General Lee recalled of Fredericksburg. He was still haunted by the memory of the civilians walking away over the army's trail of bare footprints in the snow. "Women, girls, children, trudging through the mud and bivouacking in the open fields!"

Morning of December 12th dawned with fog so dense that visibility was no further than 60 yards. The Confederate army was entrenched on the high ground above and west of the bombed out city. Sixty-eight thousand Rebels held a six-mile long line.

Through the fog, General Lee strained to see through his

fieldglasses a great and ancient tree on the Chatham plantation once owned by Mother Lee's family. Under the shade of the old tree, Lieutenant Robert Lee of the Corps of Engineers had courted Mary Custis during the summer of 1830. But river fog and sulfur clouds obscured the frozen lawn where Robert Lee had made memories which lasted 32 years.

New memories were also made this cold December 12th. Stonewall Jackson, always shy and of few words, appeared wearing his fresh, new uniform with the gold braids and new hat given to him by Jeb Stuart. Stonewall's corps held the Confederate right flank, a 2,600-yard line manned by 30,000 troops. Jackson even wore a new saber and new spurs.

Shining in his new uniform, Stonewall was still Stonewall. As he had done beside Antietam Creek, Jackson issued orders to his Provost Marshal, Major D.B. Bridgford, to shoot on sight all stragglers from the front lines once the battle started.

During the night of December 12th-13th, Federals poured across the pontoon bridges into Fredericksburg beneath the looming Confederate entrenchments. At least 306 Rebel cannon frowned down upon the cold Union men along the riverbank. When the sun came up on the 13th, the Army of Northern Virginia looked down upon 50,000 Federals deployed not more than one and one-half miles away—the largest array of men in blue ever seen at one time by General Lee's command. Another 75,000 blueclads milled about the town as reserves.

The Confederate line began directly above and west of the town. This was the Rebel left flank held by James Longstreet's I Corps. The gray line then stretched southeastward some five miles, parallel to the Richmond-Fredericksburg-Potomac Railroad line, down toward the riverbank and Hamilton's Crossing. The Crossing was a mile inland from the icy Rappahannock and it represented the extreme right of General Lee's lines. This far right flank was held by the division of A.P. Hill. Hill's front was one and one-half miles long and was manned by two lines. The front line was secured (left to right) by the brigades of Dorsey Pender, James Lane, and James Archer.

Four hundred yards behind this line, A.P. Hill placed (left to right) the brigades of Maxcy Gregg and Edward Thomas. But Hill's double line of battle was fatally flawed: Due to a stand of trees and swamp, there was a 600-yard gap between the brigades of Lane and Archer. Just south of Hill's division, Jeb Stuart's cavalry anchored the Rebel right flank to the river.

The Saturday sun rose at 7:17. Stonewall Jackson pressed General Lee hard for a Confederate attack upon the Yankees deploying below in the ruined town. But the commanding general cautioned Jackson about such an offensive. He urged, instead, that the dug-in gray line simply sit tight and await a Federal charge against the Confederates' superior position on the high ground.

"Tell us, General," Chairman Wigfall said coldly, "is this not precisely the exchange you had with General Longstreet at Gettysburg when General Longstreet urged a defensive strategy and you, Sir, insisted upon assaulting the superior position of the fortified, high ground of the enemy's position?"

"Mr. Chairman, Gettysburg was not Fredericksburg. At Fredericksburg, we could have waited for the enemy to attack us forever. But at Gettysburg, we were 150 miles from our nearest supply base. We could not sit there and wait for General Meade to attack us in Pennsylvania."

"We shall get to that," Senator Wigfall frowned.

The Rappahannock's cloud of dense fog was as thick as it had been on Friday. Neither side could see the other across the river until 9 o'clock in the morning. Then, Yankee cannon opened to pound Stonewall's II Corps only 1,000 yards away. The Rebel right was pounded by 25 cannon for 90 minutes. At 10:30, the whole blue line opened with a wall of cannon fire. Federals were dressing their lines for the push against Robert Lee's right flank. As the fog lifted, Jackson squinted his pale blue eyes toward the east. Below him, he saw 55,000 Federals.

By noon, the Federals had formed three battle lines of infantry supported by ten batteries of perhaps 35 cannon. In perfect parade-ground order, the men and boys in blue walked calmly up the slope toward Stonewall's front.

As the Federal lines approached A.P. Hill's front near Hamilton's Crossing, 24-year-old Major John Pelham and only two Rebel cannon tweaked 18,000 Yankees covered by 32 Federal cannon. "The Boy Major" caused mass disarray for several minutes as his lone battery peppered the onslaught of bluecoats. General Lee peered into his fieldglasses atop Lee's Hill. He watched Pelham take on the entire Federal line.

"It is glorious to see such courage in one so young!" the general had said as Pelham knocked the first wave of Federals off balance. Major Pelham only pulled back after one of his guns was hit and Jeb Stuart ordered him to withdraw.

In March of 1863, Pelham fell mortally wounded at Kelly's Ford. General Lee promoted the dead Pelham to lieutenant colonel.

"If only we had more like him," Chairman Wigfall nodded sadly.

"I mourn the loss of Major Pelham," General Lee said with emotion welling up in his black eyes. "I had hoped that a long career of usefulness and honor was still before him. He had been stricken down in the midst of both."

The first Yankee assault by George Gordon Meade's Pennsylvanians pitched into Hill's line at Hamilton's Crossing. Hill's cannoneers held their fire until the blue lines were within 800 yards. The Federals assaulted the one quarter-mile wide gap in Hill's line. Hill's cannon roared in the sweating faces of the Northerners. James Lane's gray brigade was outflanked at the railroad and 535 Rebels went down. The Confederate line on the far right in the gap was pushed back 100 yards as the bloodied Yankees advanced ferociously. In the melee along Hill's defective line, John Gibbon's 2nd Division of the Federal I Corps lost 1,249 men. Colonel Adrian Root's 1st Brigade of Gibbon's division lost 478 men in the swampy woodlot.

Maxcy Gregg managed to rally his disarrayed brigade to plug the gap through which the Federals poured on the far right of the Rebel line. By 2 o'clock, General Gregg's men had closed the hole in A.P. Hill's line. When a Yankee bullet shattered Gregg's spine, he held his paralyzed body erect by hanging onto a tree limb. He cheered on his men by waving his bullet-riddled hat.

By early afternoon, A.P. Hill had his battered line under control. In three hours of slaughter, General Meade's 4,500 Pennsylvanians lost 175 men killed, 1,241 wounded, and 437 missing: a 41 percent loss. Holding off the determined Federals, Hill lost 231 men killed, 1,474 wounded, and 417 missing.

At 12:30, Edwin Sumner's blue division of 27,000 Federals threw themselves against the Confederate center at the base of Marye's Heights. The Yankees marched in elegant formation to within 50 yards of James Longstreet's I Corps. Then Longstreet's rifles and cannon decimated them. Ambrose Burnside threw brigade after brigade at the Rebel center.

Burnside stormed a sunken road at the base of Marye's Hill called Telegraph Road. Brigadier General Tom Cobb's Confederates held the sunken road. General Cobb, age 39, was dead within 15 minutes. Major General Lafayette McLaws sent South Carolinian Joe Kershaw, a lawyer, down to replace Cobb. To get to the roadbed, Kershaw had to ride on horseback between the opposing lines. The Yankees were so impressed with the Rebel officer's rash bravery that they held their fire until General Kershaw reached the depressed road. Once behind his own line, Joe Kershaw stood in his stirrups and waved his gray hat at the men in blue who had spared his life.

The blue line assaulted a stone wall at the foot of Marye's Hill. By dusk, the Stone Wall would enter the soldiers' lexicon along with Burnside Bridge, Bloody Lane, and the Cornfield.

Federals stormed across 1,700 yards of open ground toward the stone wall where Confederate riflemen took careful aim. The Federal 1st Division of II Corps lost 2,013 men out of 5,006 at the Stone Wall. The 5th New Hampshire regiment lost 182 of 303 men and four successive regimental commanders. By 2:45 after 90 minutes of slaughter, Longstreet's line pushed back the Yankee assault.

Between 3 o'clock and 4:30, waves of doomed men charged the Stone Wall every 15 minutes, covered by Federal cannon firing 50 rounds per minute. Between 5 and 6 o'clock in lengthening shadows, the Yankees came in continuous waves of walking dead men, some being blown to pieces within 30 yards of the Stone Wall.

During the fearful slaughter, Robert Lee looked down from Lee's Hill, peered into the maelstrom of death, and said softly to General Longstreet, "It is good that war is so terrible—we should grow too fond of it."

By 7 o'clock, the killing stopped.

Of 12,653 killed, wounded, or missing Federals, at least 9,000 lay dead and dying on the frozen ground at Marye's Hill. At the sunken road, 1,100 Federals fell on a single acre of ground where blood and disemboweled viscera froze over night into dirty, red clods. The Union dead were piled eight bodies deep at the foot of the hillside. Of 113,687 Federals on the field from sunup to sundown, 1,284 lay dead, 9,600 groaned with wounds, and 1,769 were missing. Of 72,497 graybacks engaged, 595 were dead, 4,061 were wounded, and 653 were missing.

General Burnside's suicide charges against Marye's Hill accounted for most of his terrible casualties. From the high ground, the Confederates fired some 55 bullets per man. The gray cannoneers lobbed 2,400 shells and rounds of canister down the hillside into the upturned faces of the dying Union men. Upon the bloody slope, the Federal II Corps lost 4,114 men, V Corps lost 2,175, and IX Corps lost 1,330. Of the 5,300 Confederate casualties, Stonewall's II Corps lost 3,500 on the right flank as A.P. Hill plugged the gap in his line at Hamilton's Crossing. Among the shivering wounded within General Lee's lines was General John Cooke, the brother of Jeb Stuart's wife. John Cooke was grievously wounded in the head.

The night of December 13th along the Rappahannock was clear, cold, and fitting for a Christmas card. The starry sky was brilliant with a display of Northern Lights which old soldiers would remember on their deathbeds in the next century. Without cloud cover, the air quickly became brittle and freezing. So cold was the night after the dreadful battle that the shattered bodies of the dead froze solid. Expecting renewed battle come daylight, shivering men rolled the rigid bodies across the frozen ground and used their frozen comrades as breastworks for the morrow.

In the darkness, Stonewall buttoned his new coat and his boots crunched on the frozen earth. He trudged to the Yerby house where General Maxcy Gregg lay dying. General Gregg, 49, was a lawyer, astronomer, botanist, and gentleman from Columbia, South Carolina. It was General Gregg who had rallied his men at Second Manassas with "Let us die here, boys!" Maxcy Gregg had driven an ambulance wagon across the Potomac under fire during the retreat from Sharpsburg.

General Gregg had been one of the many subordinates of Stonewall who had managed to get on Jackson's wrong side. In the cozy warmth of the Yerby house, Thomas Jackson held Maxcy Gregg's dying hand. Each forgave the other for past, petty slights. "Thank you," Maxcy Gregg wept. His spine shattered and in utter agony, General Gregg would be dead in two days.

Somewhere behind the bloodied Yankee lines, a Confederate prisoner was being questioned by his blueclad captors. "How far to Richmond?" they inquired. "Well," said the Southern boy in his very best, down-home drawl, "First, you have to go over two Hills, then get over a Stone-wall, go through a Long-street, and by that time, you should end up on a Lee shore."

Sunday, December 14th, was quiet along the Rappahannock. The field between the lines heard only the murmuring of the wounded. When 19-year-old Richard Kirkland of the 2nd South Carolina regiment climbed over the Stone Wall, he walked between the lines to give water to the Yankee wounded. The Federals by the river held their fire.

All day Monday, a formal truce between Lee and Burnside allowed the stretcher-bearers to do their ghastly work. The pickets on both sides well in front of the main lines laid down their weapons in an informal peace between the cold and weary infantrymen. The hungry men far from home traded Virginia tobacco for Yankee coffee.

During the icy night of December 15th, the Federals withdrew from Fredericksburg and pulled back across the freezing Rappahannock River.

From across the river, the Yankees broke out their brass band which had brazenly played "Dixie" before the battle. This time, the music drifting across the water and up the slope to the Rebel line was the sad, sweet sounds of "Home Sweet Home." So many men cried when "Home Sweet Home" was played that the Federal high command banned it from the Yankee entrenchments during the winter of 1862-1863.

Slowly, the Confederate command retired to winter quarters for Christmas in the field. On December 16th, Stonewall Jackson left the Fredericksburg front for the Corbin home, Moss Neck plantation, 12 miles downriver from Fredericksburg and one mile inland from the Rappahannock. There, Old Jack would teach Janie Corbin, age 6, to make paper dolls. Neither the mysterious warrior with the pale blue eyes nor the child with the golden ringlets would have another Christmas.

"To Generals Longstreet and Jackson great praise is due," Robert Lee testified with emotion in his tired face. "Their quick perception enabled them to discover the projected assaults upon their positions, and their ready skill to devise the best means to resist them. Besides their services in the field, I am also indebted to them for valuable counsel, both as regards the general operations of the army and the execution of the particular measures adopted."

"General," Senator Wigfall inquired wearily, "the battle was not continued after December 13th, I believe."

"That is correct, Mr. Chairman," General Lee nodded. "The attack on the 13th had been so easily repulsed, and by so small a part of our army, that it was not supposed the enemy would limit his efforts to an attempt which, in view of the magnitude of his preparations and the extent of his force, seemed to be comparatively insignificant."

"You expected General Burnside to resume his attack on the 14th?"

"Yes, Mr. Chairman," the witness said with disappointment in his voice. "Believing, therefore, that he would attack us, it was not deemed expedient to lose the advantages of our position and expose the troops to the fire of his inaccessible batteries beyond the river by advancing against him. We were necessarily ignorant of the extent to which he had suffered and only became aware of it when, on the morning of the 16th, it was discovered that he had availed himself of the darkness of night and the prevalence of a violent storm of wind and rain to recross the river. The town was immediately reoccupied and our position on the river bank resumed."

"And, General, no attempt was made to pursue the retreating Yankees after Fredericksburg?" Senator Wigfall's round face radiated contempt.

Robert Lee glared hard at the chairman. He spoke through clenched teeth.

"No one knows how brittle an army is."

With the withdrawal of the bloodied Federals from the Rappahannock, the Battle of Fredericksburg ended and the campaigns of 1862 ended in the eastern theater of operations.

Robert Lee had named and had commanded the Army of Northern Virginia for seven months. Since the first day of June 1862, Lee's army had suffered 48,000 casualties. But they had also inflicted 71,000 casualties on the enemy. The hungry, gray divisions had captured 75,000 muskets and 155 cannon. They had given up only eight cannon and not one square inch of Virginia—General Lee's country.

"General," Senator Wigfall sighed, "let us adjourn for the noon hour. We shall reconvene at 1 o'clock to review your magnificent victory at Chancellorsville."

Robert Lee winced at the word. Chancellorsville was Stonewall

Jackson's day of glory—his last. How gratefully would the exhausted witness trade that day for having Stonewall at his side again.

Chapter Thirteen

Wednesday Afternoon, December 16, 1863

I always wanted to die on Sunday.
> Stonewall Jackson, Chancellorsville,
> Sunday, May 10, 1863

Robert Lee stood sullenly in the statehouse hallway. He had lunched with President Davis and Judah Benjamin. The President had seemed irritable as his facial spasms caused him discomfort.

"It was a hard spring, General."

Robert Lee turned to see Jeb Stuart.

"Yes, Jeb."

"Pelham and Jackson: gone within two months."

Robert Lee nodded silently.

John Pelham would have graduated from West Point in the summer of '61. At the Point, the slim youth was affectionately known to his classmates as "Sallie." But he had resigned from the Academy in April to join the Confederacy. In December 1861, he joined Jeb Stuart's horse artillery in the cavalry. Pelham was only five years younger than Stuart. But the sandy-haired, almost feminine cannoneer was more like a son to Stuart than a brother.

On March 16, 1863, Pelham was with Jeb at Culpeper, a bivouac

Pelham had requested so he could be close to his sweetheart, Bessie Shackelford. Next day, young Pelham joined Fitz Lee's cavalry squad for a daybreak skirmish with the Yankees at Kelly's Ford on the Rappahannock. Pelham took a Federal bullet in the brain. On March 18th, John Pelham was dead at Bessie's home where he had been carried to die. Jeb Stuart kissed the dead forehead when he said good-bye.

"I want my son, Jimmy, to be like Pelham, Sir," Jeb Stuart whispered with his voice cracking. "We still mourn him in camp."

The chamber doors creaked open to make room for the Joint Committee.

★　　★　　★

"Learning that the enemy had crossed the Rapidan and were approaching in strong force, General Anderson retired early on the morning of April 30th to the intersection of the Mine and Plank Roads near Tabernacle Church and began to entrench himself." General Lee spoke about events eight months ago. "The enemy in our front near Fredericksburg continued inactive. It was now apparent that the main attack would be made upon our flank and rear. It was therefore determined to leave sufficient troops to hold our lines, and with the main body of the army to give battle to the approaching column. At midnight on the 30th, General McLaws marched with the rest of his command toward Chancellorsville. General Jackson followed at dawn the next morning with the remaining divisions of his corps."

"So you divided your own force to meet the enemy's superior force, General?"

"Yes, Mr. Chairman. I left a force to hold the Fredericksburg line and retired westward toward Chancellorsville with the bulk of the army. As you know, General Burnside had been replaced by General Joseph Hooker in command of the Federal army. I resolved to assume the tactical offensive in the field."

"You ruled out a frontal assault against the enemy's superior force?" Chairman Wigfall was thinking of the Yankee battlements at Gettysburg.

"It was evident," Robert Lee testified firmly, "that a direct attack upon the enemy would be attended with great difficulty and loss in view of the strength of his position and his superiority of numbers. It was therefore resolved to endeavor to turn his right flank and gain his rear, leaving a force in front to hold him in check and conceal the movement. The execution of this plan was entrusted to Lieutenant General Jackson with his three divisions."

"General Lee," Senator Hunter next to Wigfall interrupted, "much has been said regarding the magnificent victory over General Hooker at Chancellorsville, and especially the role played there by the lamented Jackson. But I am curious about one point: Was the brilliant flank attack which devastated the Federal XI Corps the idea of General Jackson or of yourself?"

The entire gallery seemed to lean forward to hear General Lee's answer which came slowly and carefully.

"In the operations around Chancellorsville, I overtook General Jackson who had been placed in command of the advance. As the skirmishers of the approaching armies met, I advanced with the troops to the Federal line of defenses and was on the field until the whole army recrossed the Rappahannock. There is no question as to who was responsible for the operations of the Confederates...or to whom any failure would have been charged."

"If I might continue, General," Senator Wigfall said, "what are your recollections of the condition of the Army of Northern Virginia during the period immediately following the December 1862 Fredericksburg campaign?"

Robert Lee's eyes flashed.

"While the spirit of our soldiers was unabated, their ranks were greatly thinned by the casualties of battle and the diseases of the camp. Losses in battle were rendered much heavier by reason of our being compelled to encounter the enemy with inferior numbers. Victory, if attained, could only be achieved by a terrible expenditure of the most precious blood of the country. This blood will be upon the hands of the thousands of able-bodied men who remain at home in safety and ease."

"Your protest is well founded, General," said the co-chairman who seemed to back up into his tall chair. "Did your troops fare any better by the spring campaign which culminated at Chancellorsville? Say about April of this year?"

"Their ration consisted of one-fourth pound of bacon, 18 ounces of flour, 10 pounds of rice, to each 100 men about every third day, with a few peas and a small amount of dried fruit occasionally as they could be obtained."

"Yes, General. But your forces did prevail. And the victory might have been even greater had General Jackson lived."

General Lee grimaced at the mention of Thomas Jackson, now seven months dead.

"Could I have directed events," Robert Lee mourned aloud, "I should have chosen for the good of the country to have been disabled in his stead."

Ambrose Burnside retreated with his bloodied Federals from the Fredericksburg front on December 16, 1862. Stonewall Jackson went into winter camp in Caroline County, Virginia. Jackson fell under the spell of six-year-old Janie Corbin. When Janie took sick in the spring with scarlet fever, she was tended by Dr. Hunter McGuire, the chief surgeon of Stonewall's II Corps.

On December 26, 1862, Jeb Stuart split his cavalry command into three wings: Fitz Lee headed for Quantico, Rooney Lee took his troopers toward Dumfries, and Wade Hampton led his contingent north to Occoquan. They rode all day but saw no action. They fought a brief skirmish with bluecoats on the 27th.

On December 28th, Stuart seized a Yankee telegraph at Burke's Station. Jeb sent a wire straight to Washington and the Union Quartermaster Corps: "Quality of mules lately furnished me very poor. Interferes seriously with movement of captured wagons." He signed the dispatch to the Yankees, "Jeb Stuart."

On January 25, 1863, Joe Hooker replaced Ambrose Burnside as commander of the Army of the Potomac.

Along the frozen Rappahannock near Fredericksburg during the winter of 1862-1863, Lee's divisions suffered. During January and February 1863, the ranks were wracked by smallpox and scurvy. "We have mud up to our eyes," Lee wrote home.

Things were no better in the cavalry as horses starved and supplies were short. During January 1863, if a sick horse starved to death, the cavalrymen would hack its legs off so the camp blacksmith could remove the horseshoes to use them on the living animals.

Throughout the dreadful winter, there was no serious contact between the two armies. General Lee spent the winter fortifying his 25-mile long line extending from Fredericksburg to Port Royal on the Rappahannock River.

Just after Stonewall broke winter camp in March, he learned of Janie Corbin's death. While Stonewall wept for the dead child, the ragged men of his old Stonewall Brigade used fence rails to fashion a coarse coffin for the little girl whose curls were tied with the gold braid from Stonewall Jackson's hat.

As Stonewall mourned a dead child, General Lee mourned for a fallen enemy. He had been close to Yankee General Edwin Sumner in the Old Army before the war. In late March 1863, Joe Hooker personally sent Lee word that Major General Sumner was dead of pneumonia at age 66. Robert Lee wrote home to Mother Lee: "General Hooker sent me yesterday the account of the death of General Sumner." Old Sumner's daughter in 1860 had married Armistead Long who was now Robert Lee's field secretary and the artillery chief for Stonewall's II Corps.

On April 20th, a buoyant General Jackson went over to Guiney's Station to happily greet his wife Anna, his beloved "esposita," and their infant daughter Julia, whom Jackson had never seen. Mother and five-month-old child were put up at the Yerby house where Maxcy Gregg had died after the Battle of Fredericksburg. For nine glorious days, Stonewall was a father. When baby Julia slept, Stonewall sat beside her cradle to watch her sleep.

When Julia was baptized on April 23rd at the Yerby house by II Corps' chaplain, Rev. Tucker Lacy, General Lee stood at the proud father's side.

Also during April 1863, there was an addition to Jeb Stuart's staff. Henry B. McClellan joined Jeb to serve as adjutant. Henry was a first cousin of General George McClellan and he had three brothers wearing Union blue.

While Stonewall enjoyed his family, "Fighting Joe" Hooker was busy planning a grand strategy for exterminating the Army of Northern Virginia in the countryside west of Fredericksburg. Major General Hooker knew that General Lee's main supply depot was at Hanover Junction, 20 miles north of Richmond and 25 miles south of Fredericksburg. So Hooker decided to execute a grand march and turning movement to outflank Robert Lee, get behind the Confederates between the Rappahannock and their lines of supply, and crush them.

Hooker would send 60,000 men west and then southeast to get behind Robert Lee near Chancellorsville. Another 60,000 bluecoats would march due west from the Fredericksburg front to trap the Army of Northern Virginia from the west and from the east. Yankee cavalry would block the Rebel avenue of retreat southward by beating the graybacks to Hanover.

Hooker assumed that Lee would do the only logical maneuver: he would back away from the obvious trap. This withdrawal would ensnare the Confederates when they ran into the Yankee cavalry on the only Rebel route of retreat toward Hanover Junction.

The Federal plan called for Hooker's "right wing" of V, XI, and XII Corps, under the command of General Henry Slocum, to cross the Rappahannock westward, then march southeast across the Rapidan River to get behind the Army of Northern Virginia. John Sedgwick would lead the blue "left wing" across the Rappahannock at Fredericksburg and would march I, III, and VI Corps into General Lee from the east.

On April 28th, the three Yankee corps of the right wing crossed the Rappahannock at Kelly's Ford where young Pelham had fallen the previous month. The blue divisions took two days to make the crossing.

The Army of Northern Virginia was concentrated at Fredericksburg, east of a dense thicket of scraggly trees and wild underbrush called the Wilderness. Jeb Stuart's scouts reported the massive Federal advance to General Lee on the 28th. When Jeb reported the crossing, he estimated that 14,000 Federals were on the move. In fact, some 42,000 bluecoats were crossing the Rappahannock.

When Joe Hooker divided his 138,000 men into two separate wings, he did indeed confuse General Lee. Robert Lee fell for the ruse and thought that the Fredericksburg crossing of only three Federal corps was a diversion with the real assault planned for further up river. Lee resolved to leave Stonewall at Fredericksburg to watch the action while Richard Anderson's gray division marched northward.

Early on April 29th, a courier awoke Stonewall and Anna at the Yerby house. Jackson was advised of Hooker's sudden movement and was summoned to the Fredericksburg front. Thomas Jackson kissed his wife and his baby and went off to the war.

The whole front bristled with bluecoats on April 29th. Yankee pontoons were heavy with General Sedgwick's armed divisions crossing the Rappahannock south of Fredericksburg. The Federals were crossing over a 25-mile long front. Three Federal corps were also advancing to the Rapidan River where the corps of Generals Meade, Howard, and Slocum were crossing. General Lee sent Lafayette McLaws' gray division to bolster the Fredericksburg lines. In all, the Federals had 139,000 men available. General Lee's entire force was down to 60,000 men since much of General Longstreet's I Corps had been dispatched to North Carolina.

By the end of April 29th, General Lee knew that he was about to be surrounded by the entire Army of the Potomac. Half of Hooker's force was heading toward Lee's rear and another large force was crossing in his face at Fredericksburg. General Lee anguished over the massive, blue snake poised to wrap around his depleted army. He rejected the traditional rules of war and decided that he would not withdraw. He would divide his already divided army and attack. He would take on Joe Hooker toward the west in the Wilderness while leaving a skeleton force to face Sedgwick on the Rappahannock. Then he would return to the river to deal with John Sedgwick.

In the gathering darkness, General Lee ordered McLaws to abandon Fredericksburg and to dig-in on the heights above the town. General Anderson's division was ordered to hold United States Ford on the Rapidan River since Yankees were already near Germanna Ford there. The next day, Lee would order Anderson to build strong field fortifications, the first of the war anywhere.

Stonewall's three divisions of II Corps were ordered to march westward away from Fredericksburg to assault Hooker in the dense Wilderness. Meanwhile in Lee's rear, the Federals began crossing the Rapidan River at 3 o'clock in the afternoon and continued to pour across the river until 4 o'clock in the morning on April 30th at Ely's Ford. With 2 to 1 odds already against him in his front and rear, the last thing General Lee needed were the 10,000 Yankee cavalrymen crossing the Rapidan near Culpeper and riding hard for Hanover Junction, Lee's only line of retreat.

"God have mercy on General Lee, for I shall have none!" Fighting Joe Hooker bragged on April 30th.

This Thursday the 30th, General Lee still was not entirely certain of Joe Hooker's designs. Lee was genuinely surprised by Hooker's bold flank march which put 60,000 Yankees in his rear, well west of Fredericksburg. Lee's entire army (less Longstreet) was boxed into a sector only ten miles by 14 miles. The tangled Wilderness woods was nearly impassable southwest of Fredericksburg toward Chancellorsville.

Jeb Stuart's scouts reported the splitting of Hooker's vast command. Lee then ordered Jubal Early's division of 10,000 men to hold Fredericksburg against Union General Sedgwick. Lafayette McLaws and Richard Anderson were backtracked with their divisions toward Chancellorsville while Jackson's corps (without Jubal Early) of 30,000 men also marched toward Chancellorsville.

Then General Hooker made his fatal mistake, either of judgment or of courage: he hesitated. His grand strategy with nearly 140,000 men on the march ground to a halt. He gave Robert Lee only 24 hours while the Federals cooled their heels. The son of Light Horse Harry needed no more of a breather than that. At 2:15 on the afternoon of April 30th, Hooker sent word to his five corps commanders to stack arms and wait. By the time the blue right wing stopped in their tracks, they had four corps with ten divisions and 54,000 men resting at Chancellorsville.

During the 30th, General Lee still felt that Hooker's Federals might be upriver to attack the Rebel far left flank near the Wilderness at Spotsylvania. Lee sent Stonewall's II Corps further north. Jubal Early's division would continue to hold at Fredericksburg while Anderson's division moved along the Plank Road, six miles west of Fredericksburg and halfway to Chancellorsville.

By his Special Orders 121 of April 30th, General Lee laid out his final plan of battle: Lafayette McLaws would move his division out of the Fredericksburg line toward Tabernacle Church on the Plank Road to reinforce Richard Anderson's division. McLaws left one brigade at Fredericksburg. Stonewall was to leave one division at Fredericksburg with the rest of II Corps marching toward Anderson and McLaws.

On April 30th, the Battle of Chancellorsville began at noon. Richard Anderson's division tangled with a Yankee cavalry detachment east of the Wilderness jungle. At 2:30, General Lee ordered Anderson to entrench southeast of Chancellorsville while General Early's 10,000 Confederates looked down from the heights of Fredericksburg toward the east and 40,000 Federals down the slope by the Rappahannock. During the night of the 30th, Sedgwick sent one division across the river toward Jubal Early's line at Scott's Ford.

Stonewall's II Corps and McLaws' division marched all night on the 30th toward Chancellorsville. Darkness and dense morning fog covered their movement from nearby Yankees. At midnight on the 30th, Stonewall appeared wearing his new uniform from Jeb Stuart. At 8 o'clock in the morning on May 1, 1863, Jackson arrived at Chancellorsville—really only a great clearing around the Chancellor plantation. A large Federal force was already marching to cut them off. By 11 o'clock in the morning, Stonewall's corps was divided along the turnpike and the Plank Road near Tabernacle Church. Lafayette McLaws' division was spread out between Old Mine Road and the Plank Road. Jackson and the Yankees moved along the same roads. By 11:30, the armies' advanced picket lines made contact and opened fire. Jackson arrived at the scene of the action by noon.

Joe Hooker ordered General Sedgwick at Fredericksburg to launch a heavy "demonstration" but not an all-out attack against the Confederate line. General Hooker wanted only to feel the Rebel line by 1 o'clock in the afternoon of May 1st. He still thought that General Lee's position above the town was held by 40,000 Confederates instead of Jubal Early's paltry 10,000.

Also at noon on May 1st, General Slocum's blue XII Corps was moving southeast from Chancellorsville, down the Plank Road toward the Rebel brigades of Brigadier Generals Carnot Posey and Ambrose Wright of Anderson's division. General William Mahone's brigade of Anderson's division was moving west toward General Slocum along Orange Turnpike. Stonewall's II Corps headed north on Mine Road toward Tabernacle Church, three and one-half miles southeast of Chancellorsville. General Sykes' division of the Federal V Corps slammed into Mahone's brigade on the turnpike.

Major General George Sykes was caught between the gray divisions of A.P. Hill, Lafayette McLaws, and Richard Anderson. The blue and gray lines pounded each other from 1:30 till 5 o'clock in the afternoon. Soundly outnumbered, Sykes was ordered by Joe Hooker to pull back. Heavy Yankee fire stopped any Rebel pursuit at dusk.

While fighting raged up and down the Orange Turnpike near Chancellorsville on the first of May, Robert Lee was making his way to the battlefield from Fredericksburg. He arrived by late afternoon and joined Stonewall Jackson. By 4 o'clock in the afternoon, Stonewall was so close to the fight that he and Jeb Stuart found themselves in the middle of a Yankee artillery barrage two miles south of

Chancellorsville near Catherine Furnace. An aide to the two generals was mortally wounded.

General Lee at 4 o'clock still did not know for certain the location of two-thirds of General Hooker's legions. So he wrote to Jeb Stuart to scout the thorny countryside for the Federals' whereabouts. This is why young Stuart and Jackson were in the thickets at Catherine Furnace, an old iron works, looking for bluecoats. Stonewall and Stuart escaped the Yankee cannonade and found a hill overlooking the Federal position. They saw three lines of Federals milling about their campsite. The Wilderness tangle of vines and saplings crawled with Yankees.

In the darkness on the night of May 1st, Confederate engineers confirmed that the massive blue line was too strong to risk a Rebel, frontal assault. Generals Lee and Jackson met in the dark at the Decker farm near the intersection of the Plank Road and Furnace Road, one mile southeast of Chancellorsville. Jeb Stuart arrived, saluted, and reported that his scouts had grand news: the Federal right flank was "in the air" instead of "anchored" on the Rapidan River. The empty countryside between the river and the blue right flank might allow the Confederates to snake past the Federals to get behind Joe Hooker's lines—the very trap which General Hooker had intended for Robert Lee. General Lee proposed making the daring and risky maneuver.

Jeb Stuart took the first step in executing General Lee's bold plan by sending his scouts back out into the dark to search for a hidden path around the Federal lines west of Chancellorsville. It was Fitz Lee who sent back the happy report that such a path through the Wilderness existed. General Lee conferred with Stonewall between 11:30 and midnight. The plan was discussed and affirmed: Jackson would take some troops south past Hooker's exposed flank, then double back northward on the Brock Road toward Plank Road. Stuart's cavalry would screen the maneuver from Federal scouts. Lee gave Jackson authority to work out the details in the darkness with a division or two of II Corps set to march on May 2nd at 4 o'clock in the morning with first light.

With troop movements drilling inside his exhausted mind, Jackson caught some shuteye after midnight. In the chilly, spring night, Sandie Pendleton gave his overcoat to Stonewall for a blanket. When Jackson awoke well before dawn on May 2nd, he laid the greatcoat over the sleeping Sandie Pendleton.

At 4 o'clock in the morning on the 2nd, Jackson sat on a cracker box beside a low fire and drank his morning coffee. His sword which had been propped against a tree suddenly fell over and clanked loudly to the ground. Men would tell their grandchildren that this must have been an omen of things to come.

Before dawn this Saturday, Generals Jackson and Lee met again beside the little fire. They sat close together on cracker boxes. Their foreheads nearly touched as they spoke softly. They were joined by Reverend Lacy who had baptized Jackson's daughter the week before and by Jed Hotchkiss, Jackson's map-maker.

General Lee asked Stonewall if he had slept on the details of the proposed flank march around Joe Hooker? Jackson nodded.

"Which divisions will you take with you?" Robert Lee asked.

"My whole corps," Jackson said softly.

Robert Lee sat back on his cracker box. If Stonewall moved out with all of II Corps, some 28,000 men, Lee would be left with only the divisions of Anderson and McLaws. Should II Corps meet with disaster in the tangled Wilderness, Lee would have only 17,000 men and 24 cannon to hold off between 60,000 and 70,000 Federals armed with 182 cannon.

Under a brilliant moon, General Lee looked hard into the pale blue eyes of the warrior once known as Tom Fool Jackson.

"Well, go on," the chief said to the Stonewall of the Valley.

Robert Lee and Thomas Jackson never saw each other again.

At 7:30, three hours behind schedule, Jackson mounted and rode off with 15 brigades toward Catherine Furnace. II Corps' three divisions were strung out over ten miles along the narrow dirt road found by Jed Hotchkiss and Jeb's scouts. For half an hour, dense morning fog concealed the great march as they waded Lewis Creek near the old ironworks.

But at 8 o'clock, Jackson's divisions were spied by Yankee scouts perched atop a hill called Hazel Grove, 1-1/4 miles away. Since the first leg of Jackson's march to Hooker's rear headed southward, the Yankees assumed that General Lee was marching away from Hooker and was headed southward toward Hanover Junction right into Hooker's perfect trap.

Marching quietly through the thickets of the Wilderness, II Corps marveled that Stonewall still managed to find a lemon to suck.

At noon, II Corps rested within the protection of the Wilderness. While his divisions stretched out among the saplings for an hour, Stonewall and Fitz Lee rode across the Plank Road to Germanna Ford Road. Beyond the trees, they saw the entire army of Joe Hooker relaxing and eating. Their rifles were peacefully stacked. All day long, Federal scouts continued to report to Hooker that the Rebels were moving south and retreating.

At 1 o'clock, the rearguard of Jackson's column was attacked by Federals near Catherine Furnace. The blue III Corps was chewing at Jackson's heels. He sent two brigades to the rear to defend the gray column. The 23rd Georgia infantry regiment of Harvey Hill's division of II Corps fought for their lives. In an hour-long firefight, the 23rd lost 276 men before withdrawing back toward Jackson.

At 2 o'clock, Jackson's forward units reached the Orange Plank Road three miles west of Chancellorsville. In Joe Hooker's rear, General Lee now had three divisions concealed by the Wilderness.

By 3 o'clock, Jackson deployed his II Corps perpendicular to the Old Turnpike Road in the Wilderness. Ten Rebel brigades formed three lines facing eastward. Their lines ran north-south and stretched two miles. Stonewall sent a courier back to Lee confirming that one gray division was ready and that two others were falling in.

The Yankees were arrayed along the turnpike with their exposed right flank running west to east, a line for which Stonewall's corps crossed the "T" in the woods. The end of the vulnerable Federal line was held by the blue XI Corps with 8,600 men and 16 cannon. The five brigades of Harvey Hill's gray division commanded by Robert Rodes formed Jackson's first assault line, close enough to hear the peaceable chatter from the Union position on the far side of the Wilderness. Much of the conversation was in German since many of Oliver Howard's XI Corps were immigrants. A.P. Hill's division stood ready in reserve.

Somewhere behind the Rebel lines, General Elisha Paxton, commanding the old Stonewall Brigade, gently told young Kyd Douglas, Sandie Pendleton's friend on Stonewall's staff, that he expected to die tomorrow. General Paxton, a 35-year-old lawyer, asked Douglas to kindly send his private papers, his Bible, and his body to his wife at Lexington, Virginia. His premonitions proved accurate.

At 5 o'clock in the evening, May 2, 1863, Stonewall's II Corps was loaded, cocked, and ready.

Fifteen minutes after 5 o'clock, Brigadier General Rodes from Harvey Hill's division approached General Jackson.

"Are you ready?" Stonewall inquired softly.

"Yessir."

"Well," nodded the hero of the Valley, "you can go forward then."

As Robert Rodes went back to his division, Oliver Howard's Yankee Germans cooked dinner next to stacks of rifles propped against each other. The Federals were quite confident that Robert Lee's divisions had hightailed it south where General Stoneman's blue cavalry would devour them at Hanover.

Without warning, the Federals were suddenly in the middle of a stampede of rabbits, deer, and foxes, all stirred from their nests and burrows by 20,000 pair of marching feet. When the Yankees looked up, the air exploded with Rebel bugles and the terrifying Rebel Yell.

Oliver Howard's XI Corps did not know what hit them. The Germans were overwhelmed and swept away.

While II Corps was overrunning Jeb Stuart's old chum from West Point, Oliver Howard of Maine, General Lee launched a full attack by Generals McLaws and Anderson against Joe Hooker's center sector (General Hancock's II Corps) to keep Hooker from sending reinforcements to the Federal right. General Winfield Hancock held on and deflected the Confederate assault.

Back on the Federal right flank, Jackson drove Howard's XI Corps in vicious fighting. The Rebels pushed to within 30 yards of the 25th Ohio regiment of the First Division of XI Corps which lost 135 of 349 men. The blue First Division suffered 24 percent casualties with 61 men killed, 477 wounded, and 432 missing.

By 6 o'clock, barely an hour of fighting had driven the Federals back a full mile east along the turnpike. By moonrise, at least 6,000 men from both sides had fallen. Jackson rode along the smoky battlefield and stopped Little Sorrel at small piles of Rebel dead. Stonewall would stop and silently raise his arms over the dead men as if in benediction.

In the twilight at 7:15, the Confederates on Joe Hooker's collapsing right flank had advanced over the Federal dead another three-fourths of a mile eastward along the turnpike, one and one-half miles west of Chancellorsville. In the dark, Yankee resistance stiffened as fresh Federals joined the fight. Federal cannon atop Hazel Grove one-half mile to the southeast laid down an artillery barrage which slowed the Rebel assault.

The firefight continued in the dark until 9 o'clock. Exhausted and bloodied by three hours of battle, Robert Rodes' division charged the rise called Hazel Grove around 8 o'clock. At least 22 Federal cannon fired the merciless canister rounds for 20 minutes. The cans of lead marbles swishing through the air tore Rodes' division into bloody shreds.

At 9 o'clock, darkness put a damper on the musketry. Stonewall Jackson and Sandie Pendleton rode among the gray line. Jackson ordered Sandie to ride off to find A.P. Hill to direct him to continue pressing the Federals. Hill sent six brigades to General Rodes' assistance at Hazel Grove.

As Sandie Pendleton rode off into the darkness, Stonewall rode along Plank Road with Lieutenant Joe Morrison (the brother of Jackson's wife Anna). Jackson and his brother-in-law were accompanied by Lieutenant Wynn and Captain Wilbourn.

In a combat lull, General Jackson and his party rode close to Confederate positions. In the darkness, their hoof beats were heard by Rebel troops who could not see if the riders wore blue or gray.

The 18th North Carolina regiment of A.P. Hill's division took no chances: they opened fire on the unseen riders.

A hail of gunfire thudded into Stonewall Jackson. He raised his arm to deflect the bullets. A Minie ball went through the palm of his right hand and another Rebel bullet shattered his left arm. When Jackson dropped his mount's reins, the spooked horse bolted. A tree branch slapped Stonewall in the face and knocked him from the saddle. As the general hit the ground, his horse plunged into the darkness toward the Federal lines.

The firing stopped when Lieutenant Morrison shouted.

Shortly after Jackson tumbled to the ground, A.P. Hill rode up in the darkness. Despite his ill feelings toward Jackson's, Hill dismounted and cradled Stonewall's grimacing face in his lap. He tore away Stonewall's shredded, new uniform sleeve and helped to dress the gushing wound. Two litter-bearers emerged from the darkness and General Jackson was laid on the stretcher. The two aides, Hill, and Morrison each took a corner and carried the litter toward Confederate lines. When enemy fire filled the air, one of the aides fell wounded and Jackson tumbled moaning to the ground.

A Yankee artillery shell burst nearby. A shrapnel fragment struck Hill in the back of his legs and he fell, stunned. Robert Rodes took momentary command of II Corps with Jackson and Hill both down. Word went out to find Major General Stuart, the ranking Confederate officer on the field. Jeb was off holding Ely's Ford Road when he was told of Jackson and Hill's wounding. Jeb was on the field and in command of II Corps by midnight.

Jeb relied heavily upon the administrative help of Sandie Pendleton. Stuart collected II Corps to storm the excellent artillery position of Hazel Grove which he assaulted at midnight. Riding tall, Jeb sang above the rattle of muskets and cannon, "Old Joe Hooker, come out of the Wilderness!"

Under a bright moon during the night of May 2nd, a Federal counterattack at midnight became disoriented in the dark tangle of the Wilderness. The Union III Corps fired into the ranks of the blue XII corps. Near Hazel Grove, Yankee cannon fired on their own infantry columns. Union losses were heavy. Slowly, the dry brush of the Wilderness began to burn from the spray of hot lead and cannon shot. The jungle caught fire and burned hundreds of wounded men alive.

An hour before midnight, Jackson was carried from the field of fire toward the field hospital at Old Wilderness Tavern. Corps surgeon Dr. Hunter McGuire examined Stonewall's wounds. At 2 o'clock in the morning, Dr. McGuire assisted by Dr. Harvey Black, amputated Stonewall Jackson's shattered left arm at the shoulder.

With the Wilderness burning and the midnight war going on sporadically around him, General Lee was informed of Stonewall's wounds and surgery. "He has lost his left arm," the general grieved, "but I have lost my right."

Before dawn on May 3rd, Stonewall Jackson awoke from the chloroform anesthesia. Barely lucid, he did not inquire about his empty sleeve or the bullet hole in his remaining, right hand. Instead, he sleepily asked about II Corps. When he was told that his men had the Yankees on the run, Jackson wept. "They are a noble body of men," Stonewall whispered hoarsely.

Joe Morrison took horse to fetch his sister, Mrs. Thomas Jackson, and her child Julia.

"Tell him" Robert Lee ordered an aide en route to Stonewall's bedside, "that I wrestled in prayer for him last night as I never prayed, I believe, for myself."

The Battle of Chancellorsville resumed at first light on May 3rd. By 5 o'clock in the morning, the Federal line had reformed, running north-south through the Chancellorsville clearing, running north-ward for six miles from the Rapidan. Federal General John Reynolds had arrived from the northern sector bringing with him I Corps to give the stunned Joe Hooker a total of 86,000 men with 244 cannon on the field. Four of the blue corps had not yet fired a shot. They faced 45,000 men and 132 cannon in General Lee's divided command.

With half of his Army of the Potomac on the battlefield, Joe

Hooker called for help from the other half which still waited back at Fredericksburg.

At 5:45 in the morning, an artillery duel broke the spring calm along the Rappahannock. John Sedgwick's Federals stormed the Fredericksburg heights at 7:30. At 10:30, Sedgwick tried a direct, frontal assault up the hill where Ambrose Burnside's divisions were massacred five months earlier. Sedgwick figured that Burnside had failed because his men had hesitated in their attack while they reloaded their one-shot muskets. Sedgwick would not risk that fatal delay: He ordered his men to charge the heights with empty rifles. There would be no stopping to reload until the high ground was taken at bayonet point.

Jubal Early was so stunned by the tidal wave of blue which came yelling up the hill that Early's weak line was overrun in 15 minutes. Sedgwick lost 1,500 bluecoats when he swept Early's line and captured 15 Rebel cannon.

It was sweet victory for General Sedgwick. He and Jubal Early had been classmates at West Point in the Class of '37, along with Joe Hooker. Sedgwick's 26,000 men swarmed through Early's line held by only 10,000 Confederates.

At dawn back at Chancellorsville, II Corps under Jeb Stuart's command launched an assault eastward, beginning 1 mile west of Chancellorsville. The critical target was Hazel Grove near Scott's Creek. The quarter-mile long hill commanded the entire field. General Archer's gray troops captured the hill and silenced 29 Federal cannon.

Somewhere behind the retreating blue lines, Colonel Robert Riley of the 75th Ohio shouted to his troops: "If there is a man in the ranks who is not ready to die for his country, let him come to me and I will give him a pass to go to the rear! I want no half-hearted, unwilling soldiers!" No man in blue stepped forward. Among the 75th Ohio's dead this day would be Colonel Riley.

Jeb Stuart drove Stonewall's II Corps eastward along the turnpike. By 7:30, the Confederate divisions of Anderson and McLaws were marching northward toward Stuart. Major General Hiram Berry of the Yankee III Corps fought A.P. Hill's division. General Berry became the first division commander to die at Chancellorsville. Gray cannoneers manned between 30 and 50 cannon atop Hazel Grove and pounded the blue brigades below. Forty Federal cannon fired back. By 9 o'clock, the last Federals were pushed eastward out of the Chancellorsville clearing. At the same time, a Confederate artillery shell exploded at Joe Hooker's headquarters. Fighting Joe was knocked senseless although he was not wounded. In his stupor, Hooker turned command of the field over to Major General Darius Couch of II Corps.

By 9 o'clock in the morning on the 3rd, the fighting was creeping toward the main Chancellor house which gave the widening in the road its name. The mansion stood at the intersection of the turnpike and Ely's Ford Road. The Yankee line, well contracted now, was wedge-shaped with the point on the north side of the mansion. Rebel infantry and artillery were on both sides of the blue wedge. An hour later, Jackson's command under General Stuart on the Confederate left flank finally joined the right flank divisions of McLaws and Anderson. Together, the massed brigades of the Army of Northern Virginia swept the Federals from the Chancellor house which had been Joe Hooker's field headquarters.

Flames engulfed the old mansion. Against the backdrop of burning pillars, air heavy with sulfur clouds, and the earth littered with the dead and dying, Robert Lee rode onto the field at 10:30.

The powdered blackened faces of 20,000 Confederates dressed in blood stained rags looked up at General Lee mounted on Traveller. The men and boys saw their Uncle Robert, their Marse Robert. They erupted into one continuous cheer, at once joyful and terrifying in the smoke rising from the ashes of the Chancellor home. The men in gray and butternut brown cheered and cried.

By 11 o'clock, the crumbled blue lines were pushed back from the Chancellor estate toward the Rappahannock River and United States Ford.

At noon, General Lee learned that General Sedgwick's Federals had pushed Jubal Early's little command off the heights above

Fredericksburg. Now Robert Lee divided his outnumbered army for the third time in as many days.

General Lee detached McLaws' division and one of General Anderson's brigades to the east to give support to the retreating Jubal Early. This separated wing of the Rebel army gave Sedgwick battle at Salem Church the next day, Monday, May 4th. Until the gray division could rendezvous with General Early, only the Rebel brigade of General Cadmus Wilcox at Banks Ford stood between Joe Hooker's reeling but massive force and the other half of the Yankee host under General Sedgwick marching hard to Hooker's aid.

During the night of Sunday, May 3rd, the retreating Federals began hacking a three-mile long road through the forest toward U. S. Ford across the Rappahannock.

Monday afternoon while General Lee mopped up at Chancellorsville, Lafayette McLaws' division reached tiny Salem Church at 3 o'clock, some five miles southeast of Chancellorsville. General Wilcox had fought a desperate delaying action which slowed John Sedgwick's advance until McLaws could deploy along the Plank Road. The blue and gray lines fought vigorously until 5:30 when the Federals were finally driven back. The lines fired at each other, separated by only 80 yards of bloody ground. General Wilcox' brigade suffered 495 casualties.

As the fighting raged at Salem Church, Old Jube Early recaptured the heights overlooking Fredericksburg and trapped the Yankees by blocking their line of retreat to Fredericksburg and the river.

During the last fighting at Chancellorsville and the pitched battle at Salem Church down the turnpike on May 4th, Robert Lee took time to order the wounded Jackson transferred further behind the lines to protect the precious patient from stray gunplay. Stonewall was moved painfully over 27 miles of rutted, dirt roads to the Chandler house at Guiney's Station. Jackson had gone to meet his wife and baby there two weeks earlier. He arrived at 10 o'clock Monday night.

In the darkness of the night of May 4th-5th, Joe Hooker recovered his bearings sufficiently to hold a council of war with his general staff. Over the objection of his corps commanders, Fighting Joe resolved to retreat.

Tuesday, May 5th, the Confederate divisions were busy before dawn. General Early was entrenching into his old line at Fredericksburg and General McLaws' division was returning to Chancellorsville. General Lee prepared to make his final assault against the contracted Federal lines. But the Yankees were in full retreat. Joe Hooker had fled across the Rappahannock well ahead of his six infantry corps. The corps commanders had not been informed that their leader had evacuated the field ahead of them.

Lee learned that his quarry had left the field on May 6th. The Federals had crossed the river during the storm swept night of May 5th. They were all gone by 9 o'clock in the morning of the 6th.

On Wednesday, May 7th, Anna Jackson and baby Julia arrived at the Chandler house where Stonewall lay at Guiney's Station.

Pneumonia had already set into Stonewall's feverish chest. In moments of lucidity, he mumbled to Anna, "My darling, you are very much loved."

Thursday, Stonewall told Anna and his physicians, "I am not afraid to die."

May 9th found Anna and her brother Joe Morrison at Stonewall's bedside. The dying deacon asked for a hymn and the little company sang "Show pity, Lord; Oh, Lord, forgive; and let a repenting rebel live." The singing revived the patient. "I think I will be better by tomorrow," he whispered.

May 10th was Sunday. "I always wanted to die on Sunday," Jackson sighed to Sandie Pendleton. Then he asked Sandie who was preaching at today's Sunday services in the field. Young Sandie walked outside to weep alone. At the general's side, Dr. McGuire softly told Anna that the end was near. Stonewall whispered to Anna that he wanted to be buried back at Lexington in his beloved Valley.

By Sunday afternoon, Stonewall was fading fast. At 1 o'clock his failing mind walked again the terrible fields beside Antietam Creek where A.P. Hill had saved the Army of Northern Virginia. "Tell A.P.

Hill to prepare for action!" Stonewall called from his delirium. Anna and six-month-old Julia were at the bedside.

At 3:15 on Sunday afternoon, May 10, 1863, Jackson said softly, "Let us cross over the river and rest under the shade of the trees." Then the pain stopped.

Stonewall Jackson, Old Blue Light, and plain Old Jack to the barefoot boys who worshipped their lemon-sucking chief, was dead. Thomas Jonathan Jackson, raised by an old bachelor uncle, was 39 years old.

Sandie Pendleton wiped his face and stumbled to the telegraph tent to wire Richmond that the eerie blue light had gone out for good.

The man whom Robert Lee eulogized as "this great and good soldier" was washed and dressed in civilian clothing by Sandie Pendleton for burial. The body was wrapped in a Union blue military greatcoat. May 12th, Stonewall lay in state in President Jefferson Davis' home. The casket was covered by the first Confederate flag ever made. Honorary pallbearers included Generals Garnett (whom Jackson had once arrested), George Pickett, James Longstreet, and Baldy Ewell.

Stonewall Jackson was buried in Lexington, in the Valley of Virginia. (In 28 years, his body would be moved to a new tomb. His casket would be opened. Only bones and a Federal blue greatcoat would be found.)

The Battle of Chancellorsville ended with the ritual of tallying the mothers' sons who felt the sting of hot lead. The Federals, on the defensive, lost 15,818 men for a 15 percent loss with 1,575 dead, 9,559 wounded, and 4,684 missing. General Lee, on the offensive, suffered 26 percent casualties of 12,299 men with 1,581 killed, 8,700 wounded, and 2,018 missing. The Army of Northern Virginia lost five colonels killed, five generals wounded, and two generals, including Stonewall Jackson, dead.

As he had done after the Seven Days, Manassas, Antietam, and Fredericksburg, General Lee now had to replace lost officers and find replacements for another division worth of lost troops. On May

20th, he submitted another reorganization plan for his army to President Davis, to be effective on June 1st. Lee proposed to promote the recovered Richard Baldy Ewell to lieutenant general to replace Stonewall as chief of II Corps. A new III Corps was proposed with its commander to be the fiery A.P. Hill promoted to lieutenant general. Old Pete Longstreet, Lee's senior and most reliable commander, would retain I Corps.

Each corps would be allotted three divisions. The divisions of McLaws, Pickett, and John Bell Hood went to Longstreet. Baldy Ewell and II Corps were assigned the divisions of Jubal Early, Robert Rodes, and Edward Johnson, who would command the old Stonewall Division. A.P. Hill's III Corps would contain the divisions of Dick Anderson, Dorsey Pender, and Henry Heth.

In II Corps, only seven of 17 generals had any experience with large commands. In the new III Corps, only 8 of 13 brigades would be led by experienced brigadier generals. Hill's 13 brigades contained troops from 8 states. Half of Hill's brigades had never worked with the other half. In the entire army, only four of nine divisions would be commanded by well experienced major generals. A.P. Hill and Richard Ewell had no experience leading corps-size commands. At least seven brigades would be led by newly minted brigadier generals. Six brigades would have to be led by colonels until new generals could be promoted. One-third of Jeb Stuart's cavalry would be led by new officers. And there would be no Stonewall Jackson.

Robert Lee was physically weakened by his recitation of the Chancellorsville campaign and the death of General Jackson.

"I do not propose here to speak of the character of this illustrious man, since removed from the scene. I nevertheless desire to pay the tribute of my admiration of the matchless energy and skill that marked this last act of his life, forming as it did, a worthy conclusion of that long series of splendid achievements which won him the lasting love and gratitude of his country."

"Yes, General," Senator Wigfall nodded with emotion in his

voice. "The entire Government mourned the death of General Jackson last May."

General Lee looked up at Louis Wigfall. The witness's eyes were moist when he spoke softly.

"I am sure no one can feel the loss of General Jackson more deeply than I do. No one has the same reason."

★   ★   ★

The night of December 16th was chilly and overcast, promising a Thursday of rain.

General Lee had enjoyed dinner with Mother Lee and the girls. Jeb Stuart and his wife Flora had dropped by to join the Lees. The day of testimony had been hard for both Robert Lee and Jeb who listened patiently in the gallery.

Jeb missed seeing the Lees' middle son, Custis, who could not escape from his military duties. "He was the most intimate friend I had in my class," Jeb said of Custis and their West Point days together.

After his dinner guests had left for their own quarters, at 9 o'clock on this cold Wednesday night, Robert Lee was stirred from the front room hearth by a knock on the door.

At the door, General Lee found one of the sentries from the streetside guard post. The youth in gray greatcoat informed his general that a delegate from Richmond City Council wished a brief audience with him.

"You may bring up our guest, young man."

"Yes, General."

Agnes wrapped a shawl around her shoulders as she stood one step behind her father at the open doorway. A distinguished, gray-haired man walked up the front steps of the rented house on Leigh Street.

"General Lee."

"Sir. Do come in from the cold."

The guest introduced himself as a member of the town council. With great dignity in his politicians' voice, the man informed Lee that the council was aware of General Lee's week in the capital city for secret consultations with President Davis. The council was also aware that the Lees did not own any property in Richmond. So, the man said happily, council had voted to donate a home to the Lees as a gift.

"I am deeply touched," General Lee said slowly.

Robert Lee had never owned a house in his 30-plus years as a soldier. Their Arlington home belonged to Mother Lee from her father's estate. The Lee sons' farms were also bequests from their Grandfather Custis.

Mother Lee's rolling chair creaked across the wooden floor into the front room. General Lee told his wife about the council's kind gift. Mary Lee nodded toward the councilman.

The general walked toward the blazing fireplace. For a moment, he stood with his head bowed and he gazed into the orange flames. When he turned to face their guest, Mother Lee already knew what her husband would say.

"I assure you, Sir, that no want of appreciation of the honor conferred upon me by this resolution—or insensibility to the kind feelings which prompted it—induces me to ask, as I most respectfully do, that no further proceedings be taken with reference to the subject." Mother Lee smiled as General Lee continued. "I trust that whatever means the City Council may have for this purpose may be devoted to the relief of the families of our soldiers in the field who are more in want of assistance, and more deserving it, than myself."

Mother Lee nodded. Agnes Lee's wet eyes glistened in the cozy fire light.

Chapter Fourteen

Thursday Morning, December 17, 1863

Our success at Gettysburg was not as great as
reported.
        Robert E. Lee

*A*n all-night drizzle had washed the dirty snow away. December
17th would be gray and wet.

Martha Williams met Robert Lee before daylight in the narrow
kitchen of the rented house. They shared a quiet cup of corn coffee
beside the potbellied stove. Mother Lee and the girls were still
upstairs.

"I have missed your letters from the field, Cousin Robert. Your
letters have always meant so much to me through the years, going all
the way back to Mexico and my father's death there."

"I regret, Markie, that I have so little time for writing these days.
And I can hardly send mail to the North."

Lee did not raise his dark eyes from his steaming cup. The corn
broth tasted like starch soup.

"I understand," Markie said. "I know you have more pressing
business."

"But, oh!" the general smiled with his voice almost a whisper,

"What lengthy epistles have I composed to you in my mind! Had I any means to send them, you would see how constantly I think of you. I have followed you in your pleasures and your duties, in the house and in the streets." He swallowed hard. "...and accompanied you in your walks to Arlington and in your search for flowers. Did you not feel your cheeks pale when I was so near you? You may feel pale, Markie. You may look pale. You may even talk pale!"

Martha silently studied his face.

★   ★   ★

Two hours after breakfast with Markie, General Lee sat in yellow light cast by the lamp which glowed on Charlotte's nightstand. Outside, the first light of daybreak was gray and dismal. Charlotte Lee's strength was nearly gone, having been squandered on mourning.

Downstairs, Fitzhugh Lee sat sleepily. He had escorted his uncle from home and would ride with him to the capitol for the day's hearings. Major General Fitz Lee of the Rebel cavalry slowly rubbed a sore knot in his breastbone. Four years earlier, Fitz had been wounded by a Comanche arrow while fighting Indians in Kansas. He still carried the flint arrowhead in his chest. The cold and damp morning made the old wound throb.

When the Generals Lee arrived at Charlotte's quarters, a young sentry riding with them intercepted a townsman who rushed over to Robert Lee. The guard accepted the man's message and relayed it to the commanding general. The man was one of Richmond's thousands of able-bodied men who evaded military service by paying some poor laborer to take his place in the ranks under the Bounty and Furlough Act which allowed for paid substitutes. The man had wanted Robert Lee's autograph for his daughter. General Lee turned to the sentry and motioned toward his colorful nephew who rode brilliantly with Jeb Stuart. "You can give Fitzhugh's autograph to those persons desiring mine," General Lee smiled. "It is worth more."

General Lee sat at Charlotte's bedside. Like a father with a little child, he gently fed the woman from a wooden bowel of oatmeal, hand-ground from horse feed. The general reached over with a cloth napkin to wipe the blue lips and white chin.

"My dear daughter," Robert Lee sighed.

She did not chew the warm oats in her mouth but waited with closed eyes for the gruel to trickle down her throat.

"At least you got to see my Rooney at Brandy Station before he was wounded," the woman whimpered between spoonfuls of oats shoveled into her thin face.

"Though I scarcely ever saw him," the father said softly, "it was a great comfort to know that he was near and with me."

Charlotte closed her wet eyes.

When the last of the cereal was gone, General Lee laid the empty bowl beside the oil lamp.

"Papa?"

"Yes, child."

"Thank you."

General Lee turned his face away and wiped his eyes.

★   ★   ★

Senator Louis Wigfall began the morning session of closed hearings with a review of General Lee's thoughts and actions immediately following Chancellorsville when thousands of casualties had to be replaced, including General Jackson. As Robert Lee in mid-May 1863 had labored to muster recruits to his depleted ranks, he had to deal with administrative burdens within his own command. Brave and devoted division commander Major General Daniel Harvey Hill—Stonewall's brother-in-law—had been detached to southern Virginia. When Robert Lee's request went out for replacements, Harvey Hill had suggested sending only his raw recruits back to the Army of Northern Virginia while keeping for his own the tested veterans of the Seven Days, Sharpsburg, Fredericksburg, and Chancellorsville. General Lee had protested.

"It would have increased my army numerically," Lee remembered, "but weakened it intrinsically by taking away tried troops under experienced officers and replacing them with fresh men and uninstructed commanders. I would therefore have had more to feed but less to depend on."

"Nevertheless, General Lee, with greatly reduced ranks and with another reorganization among your division and corps commanders, you still elected to conduct the June '63 Pennsylvania raid. You invaded the enemy's country with the Fredericksburg lesson of the virtues of tactical defense so fresh. Do share with us the basis for taking the offensive into the North so soon after the near disaster at Sharpsburg and your serious losses at Chancellorsville."

"In a line, Senator," General Lee replied with measured cadence, "if I could get in a position to advance beyond the Rappahannock, I should certainly draw their troops from the southern coasts and give some respite in that quarter." The witness paused to collect his thoughts. "And more than that, I greatly feared that doing nothing would invite another invasion into Virginia such that Richmond would be reduced to standing a siege."

"A siege, indeed, General. But the risks of your Pennsylvania offensive seem, in retrospect, to have been overwhelming." Chairman Wigfall sounded hostile. "In your mind, Sir, is there no limit to the well of Southern blood and manhood?"

"As far as I could judge," the witness already sounded tired, "there was nothing to be gained by this army remaining quietly on the defensive, which it must have done unless it could be reinforced. I was aware that there was difficulty and hazard in taking the aggressive with so large an army in its front, entrenched behind a river where it could not be advantageously attacked. Unless it could be drawn out in a position to be assailed, it would have taken its own time to prepare and strengthen itself to renew its advance upon Richmond and force this army back within the entrenchments of that city. This might have been the result in any event, but I still thought it worth a trial to prevent such a catastrophe."

"So, General, you continued to lobby Richmond for additional troops for your command to effect this invasion five months ago, at least as an inspiration for the Federal government to refrain from sending another force into Virginia?"

"Yes, Mr. Chairman," Robert Lee nodded as if finally getting through to the big man from Texas. "I thought that a part, at least, of the troops in North Carolina and of those under General Beauregard could be employed at that time with great advantage in Virginia. If an army could have been organized under the command of General Beauregard and pushed forward to Culpeper Courthouse threatening Washington from that direction, it would not only have effected a diversion most favorable for this army, but would have, I think, relieved us of any apprehension of an attack upon Richmond during our absence. The well-known anxiety of the Northern government for the safety of its capital would have induced it to retain a large force for its defense and thus have sensibly relieved the opposition to our advance."

"But General Beauregard was not dispatched to Virginia by the President as you had proposed?"

"No Sir, he was not."

"And you invaded Pennsylvania anyway, General?"

"It seemed to me," the witness said coldly, "that we could not afford to keep our troops awaiting possible movements of the enemy. Our true policy was and is, as far as we can, to employ our own forces to challenge his at points of our selection."

Between May 14 and 17, 1863, General Lee went to Richmond to share his offensive strategies with President Davis and the Confederate cabinet. Everyone except Postmaster John Reagan (a Texas judge and former U.S. Congressman) agreed to the Pennsylvania raid designed to secure forage to feed the army and to draw Federals out of Virginia. On May 18th, General Lee returned to his Fredericksburg headquarters. Among his general staff, only Lieutenant General Longstreet had serious reservations about invading Pennsylvania. Longstreet suggested that the Confederates assume strong defensive positions on the raid which would invite Federal suicide attacks like Fredericksburg.

The Pennsylvania raid slowly came together during the third week in May. Jeb Stuart's grand cavalry corps was in motion first. As he had done ten days before Sharpsburg, young Jeb thought that the best way to begin a campaign was with a party.

Jeb Stuart's cavalry corps moved from Culpeper on May 20, 1863. General Stuart decided to treat Robert Lee whom he loved to a grand review of the mounted legion of cavaliers. Over 9,500 horsemen were scheduled to parade in formation on June 5th near Fleetwood Hill by Brandy Station on the Orange and Alexandria Railroad. A dress rehearsal was staged on May 22nd by 4,000 riders.

The June 5th weather was perfect. At 10 o'clock in the morning, three brass bands accompanied the parade of 10,000 horsemen in gray. Their column of horses was one and one-half miles long. Unfortunately for Jeb, General Lee was unable to attend the mock cavalry charges and the booming of cannons firing blanks. So Jeb scheduled still another review for June 8th. Of course, the June 5th review ended with another all-night party.

The cavalry show with 22 mounted regiments and 9,536 riders was repeated with General Lee in attendance on the 8th. General Longstreet was at his side. When Fitz Lee of the cavalry told General John Bell Hood to bring along a few of his Texans to the show, General Hood dropped by with his entire division. When the review ended, the tired horsemen made camp in a nine-square-mile clearing north of Brandy Station.

General Lee could not make the June 5th review since armies of blue and gray were in motion all along the countryside. On June 3rd, the Yankees along the Fredericksburg front were quiet, so the Army of Northern Virginia was put in motion. Five gray divisions headed toward Culpeper. A.P. Hill's III Corps and part of Jackson's II Corps now under Baldy Ewell remained at Fredericksburg. During June 4th and 5th, three more Rebel divisions pulled out of the riverfront for Culpeper. Only III Corps remained behind.

General Lee broke camp at Fredericksburg and joined his gray columns on June 6th and arrived to enjoy the June 8th display of men and horse-drawn artillery. "I reviewed the cavalry," General Lee wrote to Mother Lee. "It was a splendid sight. Stuart was in all his glory."

But the Yankees had planned a little cavalry review of their own for June 9th.

At 2 o'clock in the morning on the 9th, haze and river fog covered the formations of a Federal cavalry force east of the Rappahannock near Fredericksburg. By dawn, the blue riders crossed the river at Beverly Ford. At noon, the Yankees rode quietly toward Brandy Station to hit Stuart's camp from two sides. General Alfred Pleasonton led four blue divisions of horsemen.

The Yankees swooped down upon Stuart's camp at noon. Within an hour, the Federals had outflanked Fleetwood Hill which overlooked the bloodied field. It was the largest cavalry clash yet in the war and lasted until darkness. Advancing Confederate infantry saved Stuart's cavalry from disaster. In the dark, the Federals pulled back.

The Confederate horseman suffered 523 casualties to the 936 Federal losses. General Wade Hampton's brother was among the Rebel dead. Wade Hampton's cavalryman son, Frank, would die wearing the gray on the Petersburg front in October 1864.

Captain William Farley, Stuart's trusted scout, lay with the wounded. The 27-year-old captain from South Carolina had been with Jeb since late 1861. Farley's leg had been blown off. When he was carried from the bloody battlefield, the cheerful Farley asked if he could carry the severed leg in his arms. "It is an old friend," he whispered. Bill Farley never saw the sun set.

Also counted with the bleeding was William Henry Fitzhugh "Rooney" Lee, the general's stout son. At 5 o'clock in the evening, General Lee saw his son carried from the battlefield. In 17 days, the recovering Rooney would be carried from his hysterical wife's arms by Yankee raiders at Hickory Hill farm.

Writing to the fragile Charlotte on June 11th about her wounded husband required a gentle pen. General Lee wrote carefully. "I am so grieved, my dear daughter, to send Fitzhugh to you wounded. But I am grateful that his wound is of a character to give us full hope of a speedy recovery. With his youth and strength to aid him and your tender care to nurse him, I trust he will soon be well again....Lift up your whole heart in praise to Him for sparing a life so dear to us."

By June 12th, the creeping gray divisions sent shock waves through Pennsylvania. Governor Andrew Curtin issued a warning to be on the alert for a Rebel invasion. Next day, the advancing Confederate army stretched for 100 miles from Fredericksburg to Winchester, Virginia. By the 14th, A.P. Hill could advise General Lee that the Federals were abandoning their lines at Fredericksburg.

General Lee's invasion route was through the cover of the Shenandoah Valley. The Blue Ridge Mountains to the east would conceal the marching columns of armed men.

On June 16th, General Lee broke camp at Culpeper and followed I Corps toward Manassas Gap. He joined Longstreet the next day at Markham, ten miles east of Front Royal in the shadows of the Blue Ridge. Most of the Army of Northern Virginia was now hidden within the Valley. The I Corps guarded Ashby's and Turner's Gaps through the mountains.

General Lee's bold plan to take the war to Pennsylvania required two critical elements. First, the Blue Ridge Mountains on the eastern rim of the Shenandoah Valley would shield the advancing army from Yankee eyes and cavalry. The army would march northward "down" the Valley with the Federals on the far eastern side of the Blue Ridge. Second, Jeb Stuart's cavalry would stay between General Lee's legion and Joe Hooker's Army of the Potomac.

Between June 17th and 21st, Jeb Stuart was ordered to screen the northward march of I and III Corps through the Shenandoah Valley to deflect probes into the Valley by Yankee cavalry east of the Blue Ridge.

On June 19th, General Lee met with Stuart and Longstreet at Markham near Front Royal. Lee explained to Stuart the need for the cavalry to stay on the right flank (the east side) to keep Joe Hooker's blueclads well separated from the Confederates. Lee then headed for Millwood by Ashby's Gap in the Blue Ridge. By June 20th, General

Lee's headquarters tent was pitched at Berryville, ten miles southwest of Harper's Ferry.

On June 21st, a serious cavalry clash occurred at Ashby's Gap where General Wade Hampton managed to rally his disarrayed Confederate horsemen. The same day, with the Confederates safe in the Valley and Joe Hooker outside the Valley, General Lee ordered Baldy Ewell and II Corps to march northward to Pennsylvania with I Corps to follow. Ewell's target was an impressive one of strategic and political importance: Ewell was to capture Harrisburg, the Pennsylvania capital.

Jeb Stuart's cavalry was active. Since June 18th, Jeb had suffered 510 casualties (65 dead) while inflicting 800 Yankee killed and wounded. On the 22nd, Stuart camped at Rectortown where he began receiving two days worth of conflicting, written orders from General Lee and from General Longstreet.

By June 22nd, Monday, Jeb Stuart was near Ashby's Gap. Baldy Ewell and II Corps were already at Greencastle, Pennsylvania. Jeb opened his orders from General Lee who spoke of the likelihood that Joe Hooker's Federals were following the Confederates northward:

"If you find that he is moving northward, and that two brigades can guard the Blue Ridge and take care of your rear, you can move with the other three into Maryland and take position on General Ewell's right, place yourself in communication with him, guard his flank, keep him informed of the enemy's movements, and collect all the supplies you can for the use of the army." General Lee's order came from Longstreet who had attached a coverletter stating: "Lee speaks of your leaving via Hopewell Gap in the Bull Run Mountains and passing by the rear of the enemy. If you can get through by that route, I think you will be less likely to indicate what our plans are. You had better not leave us, therefore, unless you can take the proposed route in rear of the enemy."

Thus, Longstreet's orders suggested that Stuart could cross the Potomac behind Joe Hooker's Federals. What no one knew was that Hooker was actually between the Confederate infantry and Jeb Stuart.

At his rain-swept camp at Rectortown on June 23rd, Stuart received another set of written orders from General Lee: "If General Hooker's army remains inactive you can leave two brigades to watch him and withdraw the three others. But should he not appear to be maneuvering northward, I think you had better withdraw this side of the mountains tomorrow night, cross the Potomac at Shepherds-town next day, and move over to Fredericktown. You will, however, be able to judge whether you can pass around their army without hindrance, doing them all the damage you can and cross the river east of the mountains. In either case, after crossing the river, you must move on and feel the right of Ewell's troops, collecting infor-mation and provisions."

Now Jeb held at least three sets of orders within 24 hours. Crossing the Potomac at Shepherdstown meant passage west of the mountains; but going around Hooker's rearguard meant crossing east of the range. What was Jeb to do?

By the week ending June 22nd, the Rebel cavalry brigade of Albert Jenkins had already seized a quarter million dollars worth of forage and property from the lush, southern Pennsylvania farmland. While Brigadier General and former U.S. Congressman Jenkins was round-ing up booty, Jeb Stuart, his commander, pondered his conflicting orders.

Young Jeb studied his orders in the rain on June 23rd. Then he smiled. General Lee had given Jeb discretion for his third ride around the Yankees!

Jeb probably still smarted from the licking he suffered at Brandy Station when he had been surprised and bloodied—right under Lee's nose.

What better way for the 30-year-old major general to redeem himself than by another dashing ride clean around the Yankees?

General Stuart resolved to interpret General Lee's orders as authority to pass behind Hooker's Federals by crossing the Potomac east of the Blue Ridge Mountains. Brandy Station would be outdone by another breath-taking raid which would leave Fighting Joe Hooker blinking in disbelief, just like McClellan in '62.

Stuart's cavalry reached Salem, just down the dirt road from Manassas Gap in the Blue Ridge, on June 24th. Jeb selected his three best brigades: Fitz Lee's troopers, Wade Hampton's, and Rooney Lee's men who were now led by 30-year-old Colonel John Chambliss until Rooney's Brandy Station wounds mended.

At 1 o'clock in the morning on June 25th, Stuart's brigades left Salem for the Bull Run Mountains. They found a strong Yankee column near Haymarket just east of the Blue Ridge. General Lee was duly advised by courier before Stuart pushed the bluecoats aside and headed southeast over wet and muddy roads. He was informed that Stuart had fought with elements of General Hancock's corps which was moving northward on Lee's heels.

Also this Thursday, the Army of Northern Virginia began crossing the Potomac River. Rebel bands played "Dixie" as the divisions rolled up their trousers to wade the river. The year before, the band had played "Maryland, My Maryland" when Antietam Creek lay ahead.

Friday, the 26th, Stuart's cavalry reached Bristoe Station in the morning. By nightfall, they camped at Wolf Trap Shoals, still in Virginia. They had covered only 34 contested and bloody miles in 50 hours, although General Lee had told him to move quickly. Meanwhile, General Lee had passed Hagerstown, Maryland, and had entered northern soil in Pennsylvania. He met A.P. Hill in the town square of Chambersburg while his absent cavalry commander pitched camp back in Virginia.

While Jeb burned daylight to catch his army, Albert Jenkins' Rebel cavalry brigade was busy foraging in Pennsylvania. Jenkins scoured Chambersburg for "Negro contrabands." He rounded up free Northern blacks and ex-slaves at gunpoint for shipment south. Free blacks, many born in Pennsylvania, were herded by Jenkins' Confederates at Mercersburg. At least 50 of the terrified civilians woke up free and went to sleep in slavery across the river.

As Jenkins terrorized Pennsylvania blacks, Old Jube Early of Ewell's corps on the 26th made merry by setting fire to the Caledonia Iron Works because it was owned by Yankee Republican fire-brand Thaddeus Stevens.

Most of the Rebel army concentrated in Chambersburg by the 27th. Baldy Ewell was at Carlisle, well on his way to Harrisburg. General Lee spent the pleasant Saturday drafting General Orders Number 73 protecting Yankee private property. While Thad Stevens' foundry smoldered and Albert Jenkins hammered ankle irons onto his black prisoners, the Army of Northern Virginia read General Lee's new orders promoting civility:

"The Commanding General considers that no greater disgrace could befall this army, and through it our whole people, than the perpetration of the barbarous outrages upon the unarmed and defenseless and the wanton destruction of private property that have marked the course of the enemy in our own country....It must be remembered that we make war only upon armed men. We cannot take vengeance for the wrongs our people have suffered."

General Orders 73 did not stop Baldy Ewell from seizing 3,000 Pennsylvania cows for ramrodding back to Virginia to feed the army. As many as 26,000 cattle were collected from Pennsylvania farmers, many of whom were Amish and spoke little English. The Rebels called them Dutchmen. Ewell marveled at the vast richness of the springtime Yankee pastures. He wrote home that "It's like a hole full of blubber to a Greenlander."

But Robert Lee by the 28th still had received no firm word from Jeb Stuart on the whereabouts of Joe Hooker's 115,000 Yankees. Without Stuart's reports, General Lee's 37 infantry brigades, each brigade trailed by 20 wagons of supplies, were blind in the enemy's country. When he had marched north through the Valley, General Lee left his railroad supply lines far behind. The army's most advanced supply depot was at Winchester, Virginia, 90 miles from the railhead at Staunton.

While General Lee paced anxiously at Chambersburg, Jeb Stuart pressed his weary horsemen to the breaking point. At 1 o'clock in the morning on June 28th, Jeb's mounted brigades splashed across the Potomac at Rowser's Ford, 10 miles east of Leesburg, Virginia. The crossing took three hours. Jeb arrived in Maryland three days behind schedule and pounded northward to find Ewell and II Corps. By noon, they trotted into Rockville, Maryland, hardly ten miles north of Washington—the enemy's heart. Down the dirt road at Cooksville, Jeb and his boys attacked a startled Yankee wagon train and captured 125 wagons piled high with food and supplies. The wagon train was eight miles long. Some 400 Yankees were also captured.

General Lee at 10 o'clock in the morning had received news from a scout with I Corps: Joe Hooker had been sacked and replaced with Major General George Gordon Meade. And the scout brought other stunning news: the whole blue Army of the Potomac was north of the Potomac and hot on Lee's trail. This was General Lee's first firm report of the enemy's location.

General Lee had known of General Meade when they soldiered together during the Mexican War 16 years earlier. "General Meade will commit no blunder on my front," Lee said dryly, "And if I make one, he will make haste to take advantage of it."

Monday morning, June 29th, at 7:30, General Lee issued emergency orders to General Ewell to abort his Harrisburg raid and to return to Lee's army. While still at Chambersburg, Lee ordered Ewell to bring II Corps down to a Pennsylvania area nearby where several highways converged for easy access. Ewell was to pull back to the sleepy college town called Gettysburg, where all the roads came together like spokes on a wheel. A.P. Hill's III Corps at Cashtown was also summoned to rendezvous at Gettysburg.

Ewell with his wooden leg and with pockets full of bird seed had already detached Rodes' division to Harrisburg and had already captured 4,000 Federal prisoners, 28 cannon, and 5,000 barrels of flour. Three thousand captured cattle also trudged beside II Corps. It took two notes from General Lee to get Ewell to recall Robert Rodes and head down to Gettysburg for arrival on the 30th.

While Robert Lee spent an anxious Monday gathering his forces and concentrating them at Gettysburg, Jeb Stuart was still down in Maryland on June 29th. At dawn, he skirmished with Federals at

Cooksville, 22 miles west of Baltimore. At noon, he stopped to destroy a stretch of the Baltimore and Ohio Railroad. Not until 5 o'clock in the evening did Jeb finally pitch camp in Pennsylvania at Westminster on the Maryland border. He had to stop for the night. His exhausted horses could not trot another step. Although only 15 miles east of Gettysburg, Jeb still did not know where to find Ewell or General Lee. So he continued north, past Gettysburg, and had to circle back some 50 extra miles.

Tuesday the 30th, Jeb Stuart was on the road by daybreak. He reached Hanover, Pennsylvania, by 10 o'clock in the morning and fought a serious skirmish. More than one hundred Federals were captured. Without stopping and still searching for his missing army, Stuart rode all night toward Dover. He was now surrounded by Yankees: 41,000 Federal troops stood between Jeb and General Lee, and another 41,000 were between Jeb and Washington. On Wednesday morning, July 1, 1863, Jeb reached Dover and sent Fitz Lee's cavalry brigade toward Carlisle in search of Baldy Ewell and II Corps. By late afternoon, Fitz found that Ewell had already left Carlisle for Gettysburg.

While Stuart searched for his army on Tuesday, General Lee had Longstreet's I Corps moving eastward toward Gettysburg with the divisions of Generals Hood and McLaws. George Pickett's division remained behind at Chambersburg as rearguard. General Ewell's II Corps marched south from Carlisle to Gettysburg, and A.P. Hill brought III Corps eastward from Cashtown.

Much of the Army of Northern Virginia was still barefoot. So Brigadier General Johnston Pettigrew, a 35-year-old lawyer and former professor at the U.S. Naval Observatory, volunteered to take his brigade from Heth's division of III Corps into Gettysburg to collect shoes. Because of inflation, shoes cost a private in the Rebel infantry seven months' pay.

Division commander General Henry Heth, of Hill's corps, sent Pettigrew's brigade into town for shoes on the 30th. Instead of shoes, General Pettigrew found the tiny town crawling with Yankee cavalry. The cautious lawyer turned back when he saw the bluecoats. He went back to A.P. Hill and proposed sending Henry Heth's entire division to Gettysburg the next day to clean out the little Yankee command. General Heth would head for town Wednesday, July 1, 1863, opening day of the Battle of Gettysburg.

Tuesday night, General Lee pitched camp at Greenwood, near Gettysburg. Maybe young Jeb would show up the next day and Wednesday would be a better day.

"The record of the Pennsylvania raid, General Lee, speaks clearly regarding your dependence upon General Stuart's cavalry for locating the Army of the Potomac. But I must ask: Wasn't there other cavalry available for intelligence gathering on the march into Pennsylvania?"

"Yes, of course, Senator." General Lee shrugged. "I had Beverly Robertson's cavalry holding Ashby's and Snicker's Gaps in the mountains. Likewise, General Jenkins was operating with II Corps in Pennsylvania."

"Then why didn't you detach these other mounted regiments to find General Hooker when word was lost with Stuart?"

Jeb Stuart sat impassively in the last row of the gallery. He enjoyed a front row seat close to General Lee earlier in the week. But with the coming of Gettysburg testimony, Jeb retired toward the back.

"Mr. Chairman, I depended upon General Stuart. I still do. The thought of enlisting other cavalry in his stead would not have crossed my mind. Not then; not now."

"Nevertheless, General, you cannot deny that you were effectively crippled by the failure of General Stuart to keep you informed of the precise location of the Federal forces last June?"

"That, Sir, is correct."

"So you did not know when General Hooker crossed the Potomac River in your rear until it was too late—until you more or less stumbled upon the Federals now under General Meade at Gettysburg on June 30th?" Chairman Louis Wigfall leaned forward and his eyes were locked upon the black eyes of the witness.

"It was expected that as soon as the Federal army should cross the

Potomac," Robert Lee said wearily, "General Stuart would give notice of its movements. Nothing having been heard from him since our entrance into Maryland, it was inferred that the enemy had not yet left Virginia. Orders were therefore issued to move upon Harrisburg. The advance against Harrisburg was arrested by intelligence received from a scout on the night of the 28th to the effect that the army of General Hooker had crossed the Potomac and was approaching the South Mountains." The voice of the witness was suddenly cold and dry. "In the absence of the cavalry, it was impossible to ascertain his intentions. To deter him from advancing farther west and intercepting our communications with Virginia, it was determined to concentrate the army east of the mountains."

"But General Lee, your second set of orders to Stuart on June 23rd did give him discretion to go around the Federals and to harass their rear and supply lines. That cannot be denied."

"And I do not deny it, Mr. Chairman," the witness replied firmly.

"And, General, is it not a fact that General Stuart's—shall I say 'tendency'—to seize the moment was well known to you?"

"General Stuart has always been a brave and most valuable asset to our national cause."

"Of course, General, but I speak of General Stuart's tendency to exceed prudent caution when opportunity to strike the enemy has arisen in the past."

Robert Lee simply shrugged.

"General Lee," Henry Foote said acidly, "might I refer you to your orders to General Stuart prior to Stuart's June 1862 Ride Around McClellan? Do you have that document at hand, Sir?"

"I do not, Congressman."

"Then the clerk will find it for you....The clerk will hand to the witness General Lee's orders to General Stuart dated 11 June 1862."

The thin clerk nervously shuffled his stacks of documents. He retrieved a single sheet of paper and handed it to General Lee. The witness put on his metal spectacles and examined the document.

"Mr. Co-Chairman, this is my letter to General Stuart as noted. It is hand written. Some segments are underlined, but not by me."

"Kindly read to us, General, the underlined portion of your orders to Jeb Stuart fully one year before the Pennsylvania campaign. The emphasis was inserted at my request."

General Lee read his own handwriting.

"*You must bear constantly in mind while endeavoring to execute the general purpose of your mission not to hazard, unnecessarily, your command or to attempt what your judgment may not approve; but be content to accomplish all the good you can, without feeling it necessary to obtain all that might be desired.*"

"So, General Lee, you had demonstrated your awareness that Major General Stuart's exercise of discretion and independent command carried certain risks inherent to that officer's peculiar courage."

"Perhaps," General Lee said gently, "but," his voice became hard, "General Stuart was directed to hold the mountain passes with part of his command as long as the enemy remained south of the Potomac, and with the remainder to cross into Maryland and place himself on the right of General Ewell. Upon the suggestion of the former officer, that he could damage the enemy and delay his passage of the river by getting in his rear, he was authorized to do so. It was left to his discretion whether to enter Maryland east or west of the Blue Ridge." Now the voice became chilly. "But he was instructed to lose no time in placing his command on the right of our column as soon as he should perceive the enemy moving northward."

"Then, General, you do not dispute that the absence of Major General Stuart, to a degree, precipitated the engagement on July 1st of this year?"

Robert Lee looked up at the man from Nashville. Behind the witness, Jeb Stuart lowered his bearded face.

"The movements of the army preceding the battle of Gettysburg had been much embarrassed by the absence of the cavalry."

Chapter Fifteen

Thursday Afternoon, December 17, 1863

The armies rested without pleasant anticipations
of the morrow, knowing well that at roll call next
evening many would not respond. The pickets
alone were on duty; the surgeons alone at work.
General Fitzhugh Lee, CSA, Gettysburg

*R*obert Lee shared a private lunch with his President and Judah Benjamin.

The President's blind left eye and occasional facial tic caused him immense pain as did his chronic migraine, peptic ulcer, and nausea. But The Cause and the country where never far from Jefferson Davis' thoughts. The President always thought himself a warrior by birth: his father had fought in the Revolution and his three older brothers fought under Andrew Jackson at the Battle of New Orleans during the War of 1812.

President Davis took lunch without the company of little Joseph who so often followed in his tall father's shadow in the capitol. The boy remained at home.

The First Lady was still uncomfortable in the third month of her pregnancy with their daughter, Varina Anne, who would be born next summer and called Winnie by her father. The other small member of the Davis family was a freed black child who called himself Jim Limber. Little Jim was about 4 years old and had been virtually adopted as another Davis child.

"You were rather gentle in your testimony regarding the absence of Major General Stuart in Pennsylvania," President Davis said over his pale soup.

"Well, Mr. President, I am quite fond of young Stuart. He has never failed to devote all of his energies to our country. If he has any fault, it may be his application of too much energy to the cause of our independence. If he has any disagreeable trait, it may be the battle reports he sends us," General Lee smiled. "The General deals in the flowery style, as you will perceive if you ever see his reports in detail."

"Frankly," Judah Benjamin said, "I am more concerned about the strength of your army in the coming spring campaigns than I am about this inquiry. The returns from the field confirm that your forces are being depleted daily during the winter encampment."

"Let the state authorities take the matter in hand," General Lee said firmly, "and see that no man able to bear arms be allowed to evade his duty."

"Well, General," the President offered, "I do not imagine that we can sustain many more invasions of the North." The President sounded weary.

"We are not in a condition and never have been, in my opinion," the General shrugged, "to invade the enemy's country with a prospect of permanent benefit."

"Can your army meet the enemy come spring, General?" President Davis leaned forward.

"I am not in the least discouraged. My faith in the fortitude of this army is not at all shaken." The general spoke confidently, but his voice was tired.

"Well, Mr. President," Judah Benjamin smiled gamely, "our government surely must equal General Lee's resolve. The Congress just convened has much to do. Much, indeed."

Robert Lee frowned.

"Your thoughts, General?" the President asked patiently.

"My thoughts should be confined to military matters only, Mr. President. I am not a statesman. Never claimed to be." Robert Lee looked uncomfortable. His avoidance of unsolicited political advice was one of his many qualities admired by his President.

"Understood, General. But I am asking for your good counsel on matters of state." The President smiled through his facial pain.

General Lee laid his silverware aside, wiped his lips upon a cloth napkin, and spoke slowly and carefully. He paused to select each word and to restrain his passion.

"You see the Federal Congress has put the whole power of their country into the hands of their President. Nine hundred millions of dollars and three million men! Nothing can arrest during the present administration the most desolating war that was ever practiced except a revolution among their people. Nothing can produce a revolution except systematic success on our part." General Lee paused and carefully examined the grave face of his President before he continued.

"And what of the Conscription Acts? Among the thousand applications of Kentuckians, Missourians, Marylanders, Alabamians, Georgians, South Carolinians, etc., etc., to join native regiments out of this army, who ever heard of their applying to enter regiments in it when in the face of the enemy? I hope Congress will define what makes a man a citizen of a state! For some apply for regiments of states in which they were born when it suits their purpose, while others apply for regiments of states in which they live, or have married, or visited, or where they have relatives when it suits their purpose, but never when the regiments of these states are in active service!"

The President's sore face softened as he leaned toward Lee.

"Have you given any more thought to going to Tennessee?"

"Some. But I cannot bear to leave my army, Excellency. Besides, I truly doubt if I have the stamina anymore for a new command, especially one so full of discord and poor morale."

"That part is true enough." Davis shook his head in despair. "I am left with Johnston and Beauregard. Maybe General Longstreet."

"Yes, Excellency. Johnston and I are old friends, you know. And I am dependent upon Longstreet in the field. It is hard for me to be objective in making recommendations for General Bragg's command."

Davis nodded.

"I have always counted on your candor, General. Thank you. So...Longstreet signed the circular of the general staff asking me to relieve General Bragg during his recent mutiny. Perhaps you were not aware of that?"

"No, Excellency. I am rather surprised that my sturdy Longstreet would have participated in so sorry an affair."

A dozen of Braxton Bragg's generals begged Davis to relieve their commanding officer October 4th. Davis stuck by his old friend and refused. Longstreet and his I Corps of the Army of Northern Virginia were detached to Tennessee at the time.

"Beauregard is out, Sir. Out. Period." The President was seething and his good eye twitched out of control. He nursed an abiding distaste for Old Bory, the hero who had captured Fort Sumter what seemed like a lifetime ago. Pierre Beauregard was a good soldier but full of himself. He committed what to Davis was the greatest military sin next to disloyalty: he took his case to the newspapers. Joe Johnston shared that fault.

After the first Battle of Manassas, Beauregard filed his formal battle report with the War Department. That report criticized President Davis for not unleashing the victorious Beauregard to continue his assault straight down Pennsylvania Avenue. After Davis wrote Beauregard a confidential letter challenging his political counsel, Beauregard deliberately leaked his frustrations with Davis to the press in October 1861. Davis saw red with his one good eye.

Davis never forgave the popular Creole with his dyed black hair for evacuating the garrison at Corinth, Mississippi, without a shot. He retreated May 30, 1862, to Tupelo. Within a month, Beauregard was sending editorials to the Mobile, Alabama, newspapers defending his withdrawal. When he left his command in the field without permission to take a little vacation near Mobile in June, Davis pounced on the opportunity to sack him for being AWOL while his hungry brigades were still exposed to enemy fire. The President relieved him and appointed poor Braxton Bragg to the command which he lost six months later in the clouds atop Missionary Ridge, Chattanooga.

"Mr. President, General Beauregard is a good soldier when properly motivated by strong superiors."

"Don't talk to me about Beauregard," the exhausted President snapped. "I'm sorry, General. Forgive my tone. But I have no use for that man."

Lee paused and waited for Davis to collect himself.

"Then that would leave Joe Johnston, Excellency."

Davis winced.

Lee had a lifetime of ties with the 56-year-old Johnston. A great-nephew of Patrick Henry on his mother's side, Johnston's father fought in the Revolution in the command of Light Horse Henry Lee. Johnston was Lee's classmate at the Point and was a groomsman at Lee's wedding 32 years ago.

Johnston's simmering bad blood with Jefferson Davis began when the Confederacy was only weeks old.

When war came, Johnston was a brigadier general in the Old Army and was quartermaster general of the United States Army. But when Jefferson Davis nominated the first class of Confederate generals, he refused Johnston's plea to become senior to all the others since he had held the highest Old Army rank before the war. Robert Lee, only a lieutenant colonel in March 1861, was ranked above Johnston. Confederate law required seniority to be based upon Old Army seniority. Johnston was outraged at the slight by Davis.

When Johnston wrote a letter of protest to the new Confederate President, Davis replied that he was making a distinction between Old Army "field" ranks and "staff" ranks. Lee's colonelcy was a field rank while Johnston was a staff general. Johnston's hurt feelings never healed and Davis never forgave his arrogance.

Johnston compounded his poor relationship with Davis during the days before the June '62 Seven Days campaign. Johnston steadily retreated toward Richmond as McClellan's Federals pressed inland. Davis had little use for generals who marched backwards. Johnston's other bad habit was to keep Davis uninformed of his field decisions. When Davis in Richmond would beg Johnston for field reports, Johnston would ignore his commander-in-chief. And when Johnston in command of the western theater refused to pound General Grant on the doorstep of Vicksburg, Davis held Johnston accountable for Vicksburg's fall five months before this lunch with Robert Lee.

"I still have confidence in General Johnston, Excellency."

Davis smiled in a strangely sinister way.

"General Lee, I cannot help but feel that your friend Johnston is one of the reasons why you are here before Wigfall's grand inquisition."

"I heard rumors, Mr. President."

Davis was surprised.

"Oh? Well, General, I can confirm that General Johnston has shared with Wigfall and Foote his field reports on Vicksburg and my personal correspondence with him. He is working to shift the responsibility for Vicksburg's collapse from his shoulders to mine. That, Sir, is unforgivable. Unforgivable!"

Lee was stricken by his President's ill temper in the small cubical where they ate.

"Mr. President, General Johnston was wounded for our country last year. You were there, Sir. You saw him carried from the field at Seven Pines."

Davis softened.

"Yes. Yes. You're correct, of course. At least he never deserted his command like Beauregard. I do owe him that much."

Lee nodded.

"Well, my friend, is there any hope that you will reconsider and go west for me and for your country."

"Excellency, I don't think the question is whether or not I should assume command in Tennessee. The real issue—this court martial's real issue—is whether or not I am fit to command at all."

General Lee rocked back slightly in his chair. His face was grim. He sat for a long moment in stony silence before he spoke toward his plate.

"The general remedy for the want of success in a military commander is his removal." The general paused and looked Jefferson Davis in his good eye. "I have been prompted by these reflections more than once since my return from Pennsylvania to propose to Your Excellency the propriety of selecting another commander for this army. I have seen and heard of expression of discontent in the public journals at the result of the expedition. I do not know how far this feeling extends in the army."

Jefferson Davis smiled and laid his napkin upon the table. "Suppose, my dear friend," he said warmly, "that I were to admit, with all their implications, the points which you present, where am I to find that new commander who is to possess the greater ability which you believe to be required?"

General Lee looked down at his rough hands folded upon the table. He spoke softly with his head lowered.

"I sensibly feel the growing failure of my bodily strength. I have not yet recovered from the attack I experienced this past spring. I am becoming more and more incapable of exertion, and am thus prevented from making the personal examinations and giving the personal supervision to the operations in the field which I feel necessary. Everything, therefore, points to the advantages to be derived from a new commander." General Lee's voice cracked. "A younger and abler man than myself can readily be attained. I know that he will have as gallant and brave an army as ever existed to second his efforts. It would be the happiest day of my life to see at its head a worthy leader: one that would accomplish more than I could perform and all that I have wished."

General Lee looked up, blinking.

Jefferson Davis laid his hand upon Lee's gray sleeve. He spoke gently as to a life-long friend.

"To ask me to substitute you by someone in my judgment more fit to command," the President smiled warmly, "or who would possess more of the confidence of the army, is to demand an impossibility."

★   ★   ★

His President's support and their breakfast were barely sufficient to fortify General Lee for three hours of grueling inquisition. The President's confidence seemed pale compared to the witnesses' memories of the surgeons' tents after the first day of Gettysburg. A.P. Hill sent III Corps into Gettysburg to forage for shoes at daybreak Wednesday, July 1, 1863.

The Federal cavalry of Brigadier General John Buford had deployed June 30th along the Chambersburg Pike, four miles west of Gettysburg. Next day, Henry Heth's division from III Corps started down Cashtown Pike for Gettysburg at daybreak. Ahead of them went a butternut skirmish line one and one-half miles wide. Shopping was on the mind of A.P. Hill's men. Even "Stonewall's man," Sandie Pendleton, in Baldy Ewell's II Corps, found time in Chambersburg, probably on June 25th, to buy cloths for his mother, sisters, and for his sweetheart Kate Corbin.

As Hill's troops headed toward Gettysburg, Jeb Stuart's cavalry was still near Dover, 20 miles northeast of Gettysburg. Jeb had no idea where to find three Confederate corps of infantry. Not until late in the day at Carlisle did Jeb receive word from General Lee to hasten back to the little college town. Major General Stuart would not arrive until Thursday, and his mounted brigades would not reach Gettysburg until Friday.

General Heth's division had eight miles to march from Cashtown to Gettysburg. They had set out at 5 o'clock in the morning. Hill sent Dorsey Pender's division behind Heth as support.

At 5:30 in the first light of day along the Chambersburg Pike, Lieutenant Marcellus Jones of the 8th Illinois Cavalry fired the first shot of the Battle of Gettysburg. Henry Heth's men fought a two-hour running skirmish west of town with 1,600 of General Buford's cavalrymen.

By 8:30, Brigadier General Johnston Pettigrew engaged his brigade against the main Federal line posted one mile west of Seminary Ridge just west of town. The Yankees deployed a battery of six cannon. Pettigrew drove the Federals toward the town which awoke to the crash of artillery and the crack of rifles. Behind Pettigrew, Hill's III Corps was strung out along the Chambersburg Pike.

By 10 o'clock Henry Heth's division was churning the rich ground near a little stream called Willoughby Run. Heth's brigades of Generals James Archer and Joseph Davis then charged along the Chambersburg Pike. The left of the line advanced through a depression in the ground where a railroad bed had been cut beside the pike. Within 45 minutes, Davis was hotly engaged near the McPherson farm where Federals from New York and Pennsylvania stubbornly hung on. Yankee cannoneers from the 2nd Maine Battery fired 635 rounds of canister into the troops of General Davis, the nephew of the Confederate President. The bluecoats had to fall back along McPherson's Ridge.

From Herr Ridge, 20 Rebel cannon exchanged fire with the six Union cannon which pounded the railroad bed. General Lee was back at Cashtown with A.P. Hill where they could hear the artillery duel eight miles to the east. Longstreet's I Corps and Johnson's division of Ewell's II Corps clogged the Chambersburg Pike with six Rebel divisions. Near Willoughby Run, where Hill's III Corps bloodied the Yankee I Corps of General John Reynolds, teenage Amelia Harmon and her aunt huddled in the old McLean house as Confederate bullets clattered against the wooden shutters.

As the bloodshed along the Chambersburg Pike rolled eastward toward the awakening town, the Federal Iron Brigade led by Solomon Meredith was deploying in McPherson's Woods at 10 o'clock. Command of the Federals fighting for their lives fell upon Major General John Reynolds, a 32-year-old West Pointer, who commanded three blue corps in Pennsylvania. General Reynolds had been born just up the road at Lancaster. As the ferocious fighting swirled in the trees west of town, General Reynolds stood in his stirrups and shouted to the Federals around him, "Forward men, forward for God's sake!" John Reynolds' last word was drowned out by the peculiar whooshing sound made by an ounce of Minie ball lead which spun from a Rebel sharpshooter's rifle. The bullet plowed into the young general's brain. He toppled from the saddle and hit the forest floor.

John Reynolds was a superb soldier and an intellect. Robert Lee knew him well. They had soldiered in Mexico together. When Lee was superintendent at West Point, young Reynolds taught philosophy at the Academy. Writing to Mother Lee during the first summer of the War Between the States, General Lee called John Reynolds "our old friend of West Point memory." The Confederate chieftain reflected upon better days when he continued in his 1861 letter home: "You may recollect him as the assistant professor of philosophy and lived in the cottage beyond the west gate with his little, pale-faced wife." That army wife became a war widow during the first hours at Gettysburg.

The gunplay which cut down General Reynolds swirled along McPherson's Ridge and the adjacent Herbst's Woods west of town along the Chambersburg Pike. The gray brigades battled the 76th and 147th New York and the 56th Pennsylvania regiments of the Army of the Potomac. The Rebels pushed them back. Within 30 minutes, the 147th New York lost 207 of its 380 men, the 76th New York lost 169 of 375, and the 56th Pennsylvania sacrificed 79 of 252 men who fought for their own soil.

In the trench of the unfinished railroad bed beside the Chambersburg Pike, the 6th Wisconsin counter charged the attacking Confederates. The railroad cut was perpendicular to McPherson's Ridge. Three Federal regiments caught three Rebel regiments in the sunken, railroad bed. The Yankees had trapped the Mississippi and North Carolina troops of Joe Davis. The desperate Federal assault of the Iron Brigade captured 1,000 exhausted Confederates. The 6th Wisconsin lost 180 men in the firestorm.

Shortly after noon the battle spread to the north along Oak Ridge.

The rise overlooked the little village from the northwest. The Mummasburg Road, coming into Gettysburg from the northeast, ran across it. Blue and gray drew blood along the ridge from 1 o'clock to 4 o'clock. General Robert Rodes' Rebel division of Dick Ewell's II Corps clashed with two brigades of bluecoats from the Federal I Corps. The gray brigade of Alfred Iverson of Rodes' division attacked a strong Yankee position. Iverson's boys in butternut were slaughtered. General Iverson saw on the bloodied farmland that "500 of my men were left lying dead and wounded on a line as straight as a dress parade."

General Iverson lost 900 of 1,384 men within 15 minutes. In the bloodbath along Oak Ridge, the Second Division of the blue I Corps lost 1,667 of 2,500 men, 124 of whom were officers. When the Confederate brigade of Stephen Ramseur engaged northwest of town along the Mummasburg Road, the Federals were pushed back. The Yankee rearguard was held by the 16th Maine regiment which lost 232 of its 298 Mainers.

By 2 o'clock in the afternoon as fighting raged west and north of town, Robert E. Lee arrived on the field. General Lee from the Chambersburg Pike watched General Pender's Confederate division deploy.

In the early afternoon, fighting opened a third front northeast of town. Here General Oliver O. Howard brought forward two divisions of his XI Corps and posted them north of the town at almost a right angle to the Federal I Corps line. Much to his bad luck, Jubal Early's fresh Confederate division arrived at the same time and was poised to fall upon Howard's far right. Early's attack, supported by part of Rodes' division, bowled back the XI Corps at about 3:30.

As the afternoon fighting raged north of town, one of the war's elegant vignettes of soldiering occurred. Brigadier General John Gordon's Confederates vigorously engaged the Federal brigade of General Francis Barlow near Rock Creek. General Gordon found the 28-year-old Barlow grievously wounded and close to death. General Gordon carried Barlow out of the field of fire, gave him water, and received General Barlow's "last words" which Gordon sent through to Federal lines.

But young Barlow did not die in the shade of a tree along the Harrisburg Road at Gettysburg. And before war's end, he heard that John Gordon who had saved his life had been killed in action. Francis Barlow mourned for 20 years—until he accidently met John Gordon on a postwar speakers' platform. Each soldier had thought the other dead on a long-ago battlefield. They would become friends for life.

While the XI Corps was driven through the town of Gettysburg, the fighting was renewed in earnest on McPherson's Ridge. Slowly the Federal lines fell back before the onslaught. Along the ridge, the 26th North Carolina regiment fired at the bloodied Iron Brigade from a range of barely 20 yards. Fourteen Rebel colorbearers went down dead or wounded. The Federal flag carriers also suffered. Sergeant Samuel Pfiffer, the colorguard of the 150th Pennsylvania, defiantly waved the tattered Stars and Stripes at the Confederates. Pfiffer hit the red earth, dead. The North Carolina men were decimated by the loss of 600 of their 800. Company F of the 26th North Carolina was exterminated to the last of its 90 men.

The Federal withdrawal began about 3:30. The bluecoats were pushed eastward from McPherson Ridge toward Seminary Ridge southwest of town. By 4 o'clock, the Federals I Corps had lost 6,000 men in the retreat to Seminary Ridge. The 2nd Wisconsin lost 233 of it's 302. Along the Cashtown Road, Lieutenant James Davison of Battery B, 4th U. S. Artillery, fired his cannon eastward beside Willoughby Run to slow the assault of Dorsey Pender's gray division. Davison was twice wounded. His cannoneers held the bleeding lieutenant upright so the wounded Davison could rally his men by shouting above the cannonade's din, "Feed it to 'em! God damn them, feed it to 'em!" But the Confederates continued to drive the exhausted Yankees.

The Federals were being pushed from Seminary Ridge toward town by 4 o'clock in ferocious combat. By 4:30, General Lee stood beside A.P. Hill atop Seminary Ridge. They watched the Yankees retreat in orderly discipline to take positions on the opposite Cemetery Hill southeast of town. The withdrawing Federals were cheered on by Colonel Lucius Fairchild of the 2nd Wisconsin. Fairchild stumbled through town and nursed a bloody stump where his arm had just been amputated. He waved his remaining arm and shouted to the boys in blue, "Stick to them, boys! Stay with them!"

By 5 o'clock, Wednesday, July 1, 1863, Gettysburg fell to Jubal Early's Confederate division. Old Jube captured the town and 2,000 XI Corps prisoners who were cornered and could not flee eastward to Cemetery Ridge where General Winfield Hancock rallied his bleeding and wounded divisions.

As the village became a Rebel garrison on Pennsylvania soil, Longstreet rode up to join Generals Lee and Powell Hill upon Seminary Ridge. General Longstreet promptly urged an immediate flank march southward to mass the Rebel army between Washington City and the remnants of the battered Army of the Potomac which now huddled across the valley atop Cemetery Ridge.

In the last hours of daylight, among the acres of dead lay the bodies of the 11th Pennsylvania regiment who fell fighting for their own soil. The 11th's mascot was a scruffy little dog named Sallie. When nightfall brought temporary peace to the shattered farmland, Sallie returned to stand guard beside her dead friends. Sallie would wait patiently for her men in blue to awaken for the next three days.

When the Federals found Sallie half starved on July 4th still guarding the bloated dead, they took the dog back to the 11th's survivors. Sallie followed the regiment for another two years. She died at the Battle of Hatcher's Run in Virginia in February 1865 and was buried with full military honors. Sallie's own statue reposes forever at Gettysburg at the foot of the 11th Pennsylvania Memorial.

When James Longstreet met Robert Lee on Seminary Ridge, he had arrived before his I Corps. Most of July 1st, I Corps camped at Greenwood, 17 miles west of town on the Chambersburg Pike. The corps was strung out along the road. When Longstreet and Lee conferred at 5 o'clock, the bulk of I Corps was still seven hours away.

The roar of battle died out by 5 o'clock in the evening with

General Lee atop Seminary Ridge and the bluecoats atop Cemetery Ridge under the eye of General Hancock, the ranking Federal on the field. Lee would have been proud of Hancock. The 39-year-old Pennsylvanian had been a cadet at the Point when Robert Lee was superintendent. Lee sat on the examination board which heard Cadet Hancock's oral final exams.

The witness shuffled his field reports and dispatches into a pile atop the table.

"So you and General Longstreet met on the field toward evening on Wednesday, July 1st?"

"We did, Senator."

"Do you recollect the time?"

"Between 5 and 5:30." General Lee glanced sideways at the graying shadows beyond the chamber's high and dirty windows. It was evening in Richmond.

"Do you recall General Longstreet's alleged proposal to shift your forces to the right flank and to move southward to get around and behind the Federals?"

"I do, Mr. Chairman. General Longstreet suggested that we make the stated maneuver on the evening of the first of July. Our line was concentrating along Seminary Ridge, the elevation running north and south with the town of Gettysburg on the northern end of the ridge. The Federals concentrated on the opposite ridge, Cemetery Ridge, slightly more than a mile to the east. Seminary and Cemetery Ridges were rather parallel, with the separation spreading to almost two miles at their widest points. Running between the ridges was the Emmitsburg Road. General Longstreet proposed the shift southward as would place us between Cemetery Ridge and Washington. He felt that this would alarm the Washington government and would force the Federals, now commanded by General Meade, to attack us. We would stand on the defensive and meet their assaults with vigor as we did so successfully at Fredericksburg last year at this time."

"And you rejected Longstreet's proposal, General?"

"I did, Senator. I believe I stated that 'If the enemy is there, we must attack him.'"

"And Longstreet's response to that, if you recollect?" Senator Wigfall knew the answer; he just wanted to hear it again.

"Senator, General Longstreet stated, 'If the enemy is there, it will be because he is anxious that we should attack him.'"

"But you rejected the flank maneuver in spite of General Longstreet's counsel?"

"I did, Senator. You know that." General Lee's neck reddened. "I did not believe we could delay the engagement, assume the defensive instead of the offensive, and then await a Federal siege at some other position. First, Senator, we could not have lived off the land for a protracted defense. Second, we could not have abandoned the vital gaps in the mountains west of Gettysburg in order to maneuver to the southeast.

"We needed those gaps to return to Virginia. And third, on the evening of July 1st, I still had not heard from General Stuart—the very eyes of my army. Stuart was still perhaps 30 miles north of Gettysburg and he did not arrive on the field until late on the next day. I was not about to launch another movement of three corps of infantry without Stuart's cavalry to screen the maneuver and to scout the enemy movements."

"I believe you testified, General Lee, that during the evening of July 1st, after the Federal evacuation of Gettysburg, Brigadier General Gordon asked General Ewell for permission to attack Cemetery Hill on the northern end of the Federal line, and that General Ewell declined."

"That is correct, Senator."

"It would seem, General Lee, that Ewell's failure to attack the still weak Yankee position on the north end of Cemetery Ridge on July 1st was a serious error." Louis Wigfall scowled.

"Senator," Robert Lee said firmly, "General Ewell is an honest, brave soldier who has always done his duty well." The chairman had to look away from the fire in the black eyes of the witness.

"But General Ewell was ordered by you to take Cemetery Hill at the northern end of the Yankee line on July 1st, was he not?"

"Not quite, Senator," Lee shrugged.

"Oh?"

"After my 5 o'clock meeting at Seminary Ridge with General Longstreet, I directed my adjutant, Walter Taylor, to ride immediately to General Ewell posted on the far left flank of our line, well north of my position, and opposite Cemetery Hill. By Colonel Taylor, General Ewell was instructed to carry the hill occupied by the enemy if he found it practical, but to avoid a general engagement until the arrival of the other corps of the army. Remember, Mr. Chairman, Longstreet's I Corps was still camped miles to the west."

"No attack was made by General Ewell on the first of July?"

"No, Senator. I remind you that General Ewell only had two of General Early's brigades in fighting condition. General Rodes' division had been too badly hurt during the day to engage the enemy again on the high ground with only two hours of good daylight remaining. Edward Johnson's division of Ewell's II Corps was still on the march from Cashtown. Finally, II Corps was burdened with 2,000 Federal prisoners."

"Did you meet with General Ewell on the evening of July 1st, General?"

"I did, Senator. Perhaps by 6 o'clock, I rode to General Ewell's headquarters north of town on our far left flank at the Blocker house. I found General Ewell conferring with his division commanders, Jubal Early and Robert Rodes. It was there that Major General Rodes informed me that his division was unfit for further action after the full day of combat. Major General Early advised me that he felt Cemetery Hill and Culp's Hill, north of Cemetery Hill, were too well fortified by nightfall for our assault. He suggested an attack further down the Federal line, in the vicinity of the two prominent rises known locally as The Round Tops at the southern end of the Federal position. I agreed—for the moment—to extend our line southward to our right."

"So you agreed—temporarily, as you say—to shift southward for an assault against the middle or the southern end of the Federal line atop Cemetery Ridge?"

"Yes, Senator. When I returned to my headquarters well south of General Ewell's position, I prepared to draft orders for Ewell's II Corps to maneuver around our line to take position on our right flank to the south. Sometime later, General Ewell rode to my headquarters on the Chambersburg Pike. He informed me that new reconnaissance reports had confirmed that Culp's Hill on the far right Federal flank, opposite our far left, was rather lightly defended after all. General Ewell withdrew his opposition to an attack on our left. The assault against Culp's Hill would be made the next day, Thursday, July 2nd.

"I then drafted orders for General Longstreet with two of his I Corps divisions to attack from our right against Cemetery Ridge. On our left, General Ewell's II Corps would make a simultaneous assault against Cemetery Hill. Our III Corps, under General A.P. Hill with two divisions, was to threaten the center of the Federal line. Hill's third division under Richard Anderson was to assist Longstreet's assault. The attack was set for Thursday morning, once all dispositions had been completed."

"General Lee, was there an exact time set for the Thursday assault?"

"None, Senator."

During that bloody Wednesday, the Federals lost 10,000 men killed, wounded, and captured. Among the Yankee dead was General John Reynolds. The battered Federal XI Corps suffered 40 percent casualties and their I Corps took 65 percent losses. At McPherson's Ridge, the blue Iron Brigade left 1,153 of its 1,829 men behind on the red ground and the 24th Michigan regiment lost 363 of 496 men. Henry Heth's gray division lost 1,500 of its 7,500 men on the ridge. John Gordon's Confederate brigade suffered 30 percent casualties. Seven Rebel brigades took 35 to 50 percent losses.

As July 1st ended, some 23,000 Confederates and nearly 19,000 Federals were mustered on the field. During the night, the Yankees would receive another 6,000 men supported by 85 cannon. Federals poured into the cauldron as George Meade's Army of the Potomac converged upon the little town. Once Longstreet's Confederate I Corps came up the next day and all of the bluecoats found their way to Gettysburg, some 75,000 grayclads would do battle with 85,500 Federals for three horrific days. General Lee would count 194 regiments and 67 artillery batteries from 12 Southern states. Major General Meade would amass 270 regiments and 65 artillery batteries from 18 Union states. The Federal reserve artillery alone would muster 108 cannon and limbers carrying 23,883 rounds of artillery shells.

"In other words, General Lee," Henry Foote next to Chairman Wigfall inquired, "you chose to end July 1st without further action even though you still had perhaps two hours of daylight left after your evening conference with General Ewell at your headquarters?"

The witness sighed with fatigue. Outside, the Richmond sky was now dark and low clouds dripped cold December rain.

"It was ascertained from the prisoners," General Lee said softly, "that we had been engaged with two corps of the army formerly commanded by General Hooker, and that the remainder of that army under General Meade was approaching Gettysburg. Without information as to its proximity, the strong position which the enemy had assumed could not be attacked without danger of exposing the four divisions present, already weakened and exhausted by a long and bloody struggle, to overwhelming numbers of fresh troops. It was decided not to attack until the arrival of Longstreet, two of whose divisions, those of Hood and McLaws, encamped about four miles in the rear during the night."

"Very well, General," Senator Wigfall interrupted. "If you and counsel have no objection, we shall adjourn at this point. It is approaching 6 o'clock. We shall meet here again tomorrow morning at 9....Ladies and gentlemen."

The gallery stood when the Joint Military Affairs Committee rose. Robert Lee stood up slowly. His knees cracked loudly. Without thinking, he rubbed his sore left chest with his right hand as the committee members filed past the witness table.

★   ★   ★

General Lee stood at the side of his gray horse Traveller. Walter Taylor and Jeb Stuart stood respectfully off to the side near their own mounts.

In the darkness outside the capitol, the general faced the McClellan Military Saddle. A young George McClellan had designed the spill-proof saddle in 1856, ten years after his graduation from West Point. General Lee's right hand held the rear of the deep-dished saddle and his left gloved hand held the front pommel. But the white-haired soldier in his heavy blue greatcoat did not mount. He paused and rested his forehead against the saddle.

Behind General Lee, Colonel Taylor took an anxious step toward his chief. Only the firm hand of Jeb Stuart stopped Taylor from rushing toward his general. Stuart silently nodded to Taylor to wait. Stuart's eyes were full of concern as he watched the old soldier he loved.

The moment Taylor halted upon Stuart's touch, Robert Lee heaved himself with a soft groan into the saddle where he gathered Traveller's reins. The general adjusted his gray slouch hat.

"Gentlemen," Robert Lee said firmly to his young officers who mounted nearby, "I would like to ride home alone tonight, if you have no objection."

Taylor and Jeb nodded.

Without another word, the general closed his heels upon Traveller's sides and the loyal animal walked off.

Upon a silent motion from Jeb Stuart's hand, four mounted sentries spurred their horses to a slow walk well behind General Lee who did not turn around as he disappeared into the damp darkness.

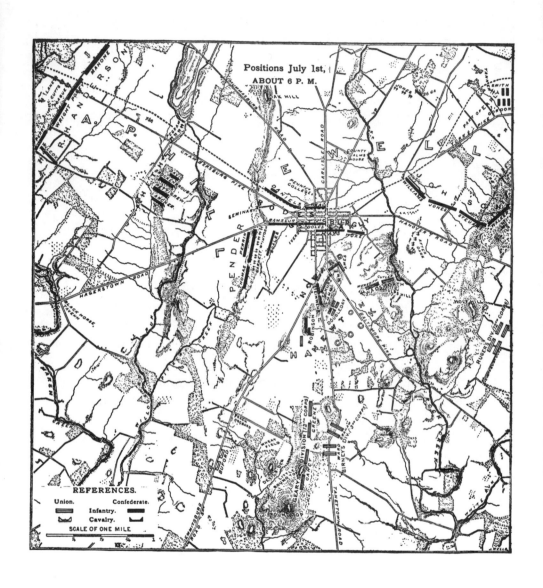

Positions July 1st,
ABOUT 6 P. M.

The Battle of Gettysburg, First Day

342

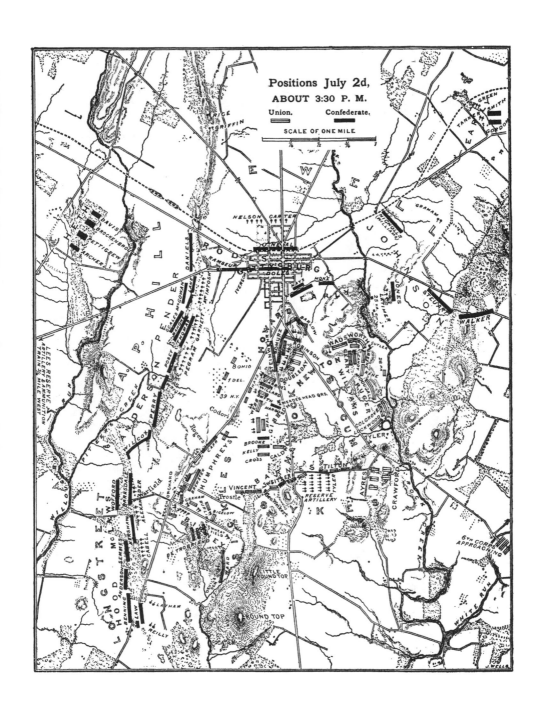

The Battle of Gettysburg, Second Day

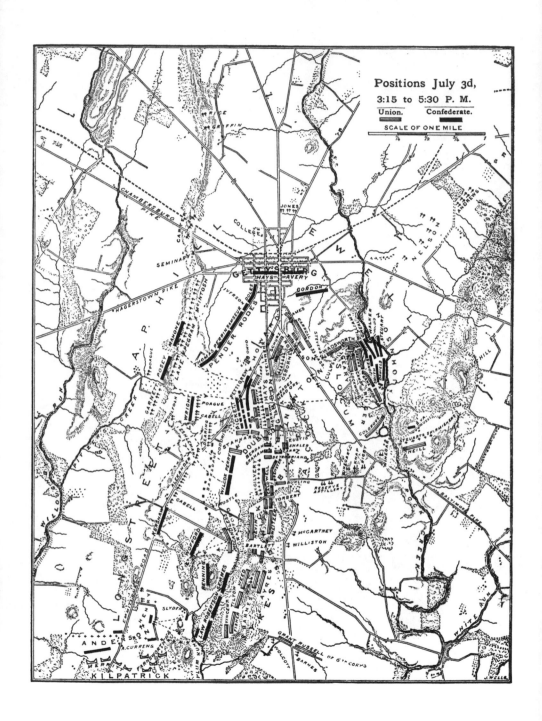

The Battle of Gettysburg, Third Day

Chapter Sixteen

Friday Morning, December 18, 1863

*Upon the open fields, like sheaves bound by the
reaper, in crevices of the rocks, behind fences, trees
and buildings, in thickets where they crept for
safety only to die in agony, by stream or wall or
hedge, wherever the battle had raged or their
weakening steps could carry them, lay the
dead....[A]nd over all, hugging the earth like a
fog, poisoning every breath [was] the pestilential
stench of decaying humanity.*
        Sergeant Thomas Marbaker, USA, Gettysburg

Agnes Lee sat alone at the breakfast table. At daybreak, she was
hunched over her diary which she had kept for half her life.

"Good morning, Papa."

"And to you, Wig." The general smiled and he touched the back
of his beautiful daughter's head.

"I was just writing in my journal, Papa." Her hand moved slightly
to cover the words scrawled across the pages. Her father understood
and moved toward the far end of the table where he could not see
the little book containing his middle daughter's soul.

"Writing military secrets?" he smiled.

"Of course not, Papa!"

"Good, we cannot have you writing secrets which might fall into the hands of the people across the river."

"Papa, you never tell me any secrets!"

"Well, Wig, I know better than to do that when my daughter aspires to be a writer." General Lee worked at his double-breasted brass buttons. He wore new dress grays which had been a gift last year from the ladies of Maryland after the Sharpsburg campaign. The seven rows of shiny buttons bore the seal of the State of Maryland.

"It is so impossible to write unrestrainedly," Agnes frowned, "when you feel someone is going to look over what you have just written."

"Well," the general said merrily, "my order books and your precious diary are both official secrets that will not be shared."

"Thanks, Papa."

"One day, you will share your innermost thoughts and sweet plans with one special man, and with him only. I pray, Wig, to see that day of peace and happiness." The general was suddenly as solemn as the half-dark sky outside.

Agnes Lee bowed her head. She spoke softly toward the crackling hearth.

"I have such longings sometimes, such yearnings for something I know not what. Is it to be loved, to be worshiped by something or someone?"

"Dearest Wiggie," Robert Lee said from the far end of the table, "how much you will be loved by someone. But until he comes along, perhaps you can settle for your old father to love you."

"Oh, Papa!" Agnes rose and walked quickly into her father's open arms. "That will do. That will do."

General Lee stroked the girl's forehead where a dark curl fell upon her temple. He closed his eyes and he imagined the feel of his dead daughter Annie.

Father and daughter separated at the sound of very slow steps upon the staircase. They walked into the hallway as Mother Lee came down while holding tightly to Martha's arm.

"You should have called me, Molly."

"Nonsense, Robert! I can manage just fine."

The soldier kissed his wife on her forehead and smiled at Markie Williams who released her firm grip on Mrs. Lee. Mother Lee sat down hard into her rolling chair.

General Lee pushed his wife across the hard wood floor into the dining room.

"Writing in your diary, Agnes?" Mother Lee smiled as she reached up to touch her daughter's cheek.

"Yes, Mama."

"I'm glad," Mother Lee nodded. "It has been too long since you wrote in your journal."

"A hot biscuit, Molly?" General Lee asked.

"Please."

Robert Lee pushed his wife into the tiny kitchen.

The couple were alone in the cozy kitchen as Agnes and Martha visited at the dining room table. More footsteps bounding down the stairs belonged to Agnes' sisters, Mary Custis and Mildred. The Lee girls and Martha chatted happily around the table.

"What a lovely sound," Mother Lee smiled as she listened to the girls beyond the archway.

"I have missed the company of all my womenfolk," General Lee said. "If I could only have my children around me, I could be happy."

"I know, Robert. It is good to see Agnes writing again. I think it will help her get through the loss of Orton." Mother Lee spoke in a whisper.

"I do hope so, Mother."

"Besides," Mother Lee said gently, "Agnes sets a good example. You should write more—to us, when you return to the army."

General Lee's back stiffened.

"I can write but seldom, so you must not expect letters too often." His voice was weary.

"I know, Robert. But I do long to hear from you more often." The couple were one week from their first Christmas together in four years.

"You must always remember when you do not hear from me that I have no time to write."

"I know. But it would be good for all of us, and for you, if you could try."

General Lee stood off to one side. He turned his back upon Mary Lee and he looked out the back window into the brightening morning.

"I see you are relapsing into your old error: supposing that I have a superabundance of time and have only my own pleasures to attend." The color was rising at the back of his neck. "I am unable even to write to you, though my thoughts are always with you." Robert Lee turned around when he felt his wife's soft and twisted hand touch his own.

"I shall love you anyway," Mary Custis Lee said softly, close to her husband's sleeve. "Always."

"I know, Molly. Will you take the carriage to Charlotte today?"

"If I don't, then Agnes and Mary will go."

"Good," he said. "Tell Charlotte that President Lincoln for special service of General Graham, captured at Gettysburg, has applied for his particular exchange. Fitzhugh has been named by the Secretary of War to be exchanged for him." The grieving father blinked hard at the ceiling. "If it is accomplished, the battle of Gettysburg will at least be of interest to her."

Both of the elder Lees brightened when Martha Williams appeared at the kitchen entrance.

"Cousin Robert, the orderlies have brought your horse around front. Are you leaving so early? It's hardly 7:30."

"Yes, Markie. I am meeting the President before the morning session. I must go, Mother." The general bent low to kiss his wife's forehead. "Don't expose yourself to the weather if it stays cold. The girls can go over to Charlotte's. Give our Charlotte my love."

In the hallway, Mildred helped her father put on his blue great-coat.

"Thank you, Life. I shall be home for supper." He kissed the teenager on her cheek.

"I love you, Papa."

The general smiled. Martha followed him onto the front porch. Down at the street, Traveller pawed the hard earth with his foreleg and he tossed his black mane across his gray shoulder. The cold horse was ready for a warm-up ride to the capitol.

Lee paused at Martha's side on the porch. Mildred closed the door behind them. Martha was wrapped tightly in a thick shawl.

"Mother Lee wants you to write more from the country?"

"Yes, Markie. I do the best I can, you know."

"I know that. And so does Mother Lee."

"But sometimes she does insist about things." The soldier had to smile.

"Maybe, Cousin Robert. But she is a brave soldier in her own way."

"The bravest," he nodded, pulling on his leather gloves which reached to his elbows. "It is hardest for the women we leave behind." He looked down the walk toward his anxious mount.

"If only you could take me with you back to the river when you leave after Christmas. I could write all of your letters for you." The woman smiled up at her cousin.

"I should then have nothing to do," he sighed, "but to look at you, Markie, which would then restore my eyes."

Martha Williams smiled, "Then you won't have to write at all."

"In looking back upon the calamities that have befallen us," he sighed, "I cannot trust my hand to write the feelings of my heart."

"At least," Markie smiled weakly, "the sun has chosen to shine today."

The crisp air and their breath coming in clouds of steam promised a clear cold day.

At the curb of Leigh Street, the youthful sentry struggled to hold Traveller by the restless animal's double reins.

"How are you progressing with Traveller's portrait, Markie? He is getting old like his master and looks to your pencil to hand him down to posterity."

Martha Williams had studied art the year before the war. She had promised her cousin to paint Traveller's portrait.

"I am working on it, Robert. I promise."

"I have never had any hope of his being immortalized except by your brush." General Lee chuckled. "I hope you will not forget to append his tail to his likeness."

"Cousin Robert!" she scolded as she kissed him lightly on his bearded face.

The broad-shouldered man walked down the stone lane toward Traveller. The horse stopped prancing and perked his fine ears toward his master.

★   ★   ★

President Davis, General Lee, Secretary of War James Seddon and Colonel William Preston Johnston sat at a small table in the President's office on the second floor of the old U.S. Customs House across from the capitol, between Bank and Main Streets. The President's office on the east side of the building overlooked 11th Street. The office was adjacent to the Confederate cabinet room. The four men took a light breakfast of biscuits and real coffee.

Robert Lee, still experiencing minor chest pain, looked robust and the picture of health beside his immediate superiors. President Davis' face was emaciated from his collection of physical ailments. His one blind eye was a dull gray in the light from gas lamps around the office which the President shared daily with Judah Benjamin, his closest confidant. The 48-year-old War Secretary Seddon made even Jefferson Davis look healthy.

In November 1862, Seddon became the Confederacy's fifth Secretary of War. A lawyer by training, Seddon looked like death warmed over. His own War Department clerk, John B. Jones, wrote in his diary during General Lee's retreat from Gettysburg that

Secretary Seddon resembled "a galvanized corpse which had been buried two months. The circles around his eyes are absolutely black."

Secretary Seddon had inspired a firestorm of opposition from the Confederate Congress after his recent proposal to meet the South's manpower shortage by "hiring" black slaves for civilian employment so able-bodied white men could leave for the front. Though generally a staunch supporter of President Davis, Secretary Seddon disagreed with President Davis' increasingly personal control over troop movements and field campaigns. Seddon, the legal scholar, vigorously advocated absolute civilian control over the military, but Jeff Davis tended to go too far. James Seddon, as much as anyone, was single-handedly responsible for preservation of the South's civil justice structure when the military emergencies dictated imposing martial law.

The youthful Colonel Johnston was the President's constant companion. To Jefferson Davis, William Johnston was a living ghost. The officer's father was General Albert Sidney Johnston, killed in April 1862 at the Battle of Shiloh Church. Davis and the dead general had been close friends since boyhood at Transylvania University. Then they went to West Point together. When Robert Lee was a lieutenant colonel in the Second United States Cavalry in '55, his colonel was Sidney Johnston. When Colonel Robert Lee, U.S.A. declined President Lincoln's April 1861 offer to take command of Federal armies suppressing the secession rebellion, the post was offered to Albert Sidney Johnston who also refused.

Since May 1862, young Johnston was the President's aide and confidant. They dined together nearly every day. The colonel's bachelor officers' quarters were in the presidential mansion with Varina and the children. The President lovingly called his dead friend's son by his family pet name, Dobbin.

Colonel Johnston looked uncomfortable at table with Lee, his President, and the War Secretary. Dobbin's job was to sit quietly and to stand in for the dead soldier loved by Jefferson Davis. The colonel worked with Lee's son, Custis, as military aides to Davis whom they called "The Chief."

"You still seem confident in military success on the battlefield, General," the cadaverous War Secretary said.

"My only anxiety arises from the present immobility of the army," General Lee responded as he lowered his coffee cup, "owing to the condition of our horses and the scarcity of forage and provisions."

"We are doing the best we can, General," President Davis said firmly. The mutual respect between Davis and General Lee had withstood two years of vicious infighting in the capital city. The two men could exchange sharp military and political differences without doing any damage to their relationship. "You have certainly convinced us, General Lee. If only you could do likewise with the Congress which frustrates our every effort to harvest provisions for your army and the other Confederate forces in the field." The President's twitching face and blind eye showed the terrible strain of the war.

"Short rations are having a bad effect upon the men both morally and physically," General Lee continued. The color slowly rose at the back of his gray collar. "Desertions to the enemy are becoming more frequent and I fear the army cannot be kept together." Robert Lee now gently pounded his right fist into his left palm. "It is absolutely necessary that the army should be properly fed. I recommend, therefore, that the portion of the Army Regulations, Number 1127, which authorizes commissaries to sell to officers for the use of their families be rescinded. Many thousand rations are consumed for officers' families."

"General," James Seddon said sadly, "I concur, Sir, completely. But you, of all people, surely understand our constraints when dealing with Congress. Our hands are tied, both as to feeding the armies of the country and as to conscripting replacement troops." The wasted Secretary shrugged as if his little plea had sapped his last drop of strength.

"More than once," Robert Lee fumed, "have promising opportunities been lost for want of men to take advantage of them. Victory itself has been made to put on the appearance of defeat because our diminished and exhausted troops have been unable to renew a successful struggle against fresh numbers of the enemy."

"What more can we do, General?" the anguished War Secretary asked. "Virtually all non-exempt men under 40 years of age have been mustered for service. Extending the conscription rolls to men between the age of 40 and 45 will only call up another 50,000 men at best. And that would require another six months to get them into the field."

"Let me also assure you, General," President Davis interrupted, "that everything is being done to feed the Army of Northern Virginia. Everything!"

"Everything?" Robert Lee's voice was as bitter as the cold coffee beside his half-eaten biscuit. "I have been mortified to find that when any scarcity existed, this was the only army in which it is found necessary to reduce rations." General Lee's voice softened. "My information not being official and derived from officers of other armies, I may be mistaken. But I have never heard of any reduction in the meat ration issued to the troops in and about Richmond, Petersburg, Wilmington, Charleston, Savannah, Mobile, or in the Southwest. I understand that, at the present time, the army of General Johnston is receiving full rations of meat, bread, rice, molasses, and some whiskey, while in my army only a quarter of a pound of salt and three-quarters of a pound of fresh meat are being issued." The soldier's whiskered face was red to match the back of his neck. "We have also had, in addition, half rations of sugar and coffee, one day's issue of fruit, and some lard." General Lee leaned back in his chair and his face lost its hardness. "I am always glad to hear of troops receiving abundance of provisions at any point, but think all ought to fare alike, if possible."

"Well, General," Secretary Seddon said in his weak voice, "there is still sufficient fight left in our hungry armies. Victory can still be ours."

"If defeated," the General sighed, "nothing will be left for us to live for."

"You sound troubled, General." The War Secretary leaned forward.

"In view of the vast increase of the forces of the enemy, of the savage and brutal policy he has proclaimed, which leaves us no alternative but success or degradation worse than death," Robert Lee looked hard at the wasted face of Secretary Seddon, "if we would save the honor of our families from pollution, our social system from destruction, let every means be employed to fill and maintain the ranks of our armies!"

"Filling the ranks is rendered even more difficult by the number of desertions which is a plague." Secretary Seddon was angry. "We could field a division with deserters, if we could catch them."

"The number of desertions from this army is so great," Robert Lee said coldly, "and still continues to such an extent that, unless some cessation of them can be caused, I fear success in the field will be seriously endangered." The general made a fist on the table. "Nothing will remedy this great evil which so much endangers our cause except the rigid enforcement of the death penalty in the future in cases of conviction."

"That it should come to this necessity: executing our own people!" President Davis shook his emaciated head. "I regretfully agree, of course. Our ruthless enemies will reduce us to their own violent nature. They will take the war into our cities."

"Conceding to our enemies," General Lee said calmly, "the superiority claimed by them in numbers, resources, and all the means and appliances for carrying on the war, we have no right to look for exemptions from the military consequences of a vigorous use of these advantages."

The sunken face of James Seddon leaned toward General Lee. "Is your army up to the spring offensive?"

Robert Lee looked hard at the War Secretary.

"The progress of this army must be forward." The general slammed his open palm upon the tabletop. "Forward!"

"I trust, my friend," the President said warmly, "that you will lead your army when the time comes. I only regret that you have been distracted by this court martial business. If only I could guarantee that all will work out. But Wigfall and Foote are determined to have their way. At your expense, General. I see no way out. I have two painful choices: beg you to go west and send Joe Johnston to the Army of Northern Virginia, or allow this Joint Committee to destroy you. Then Wigfall and Foote can have Congress nominate Johnston or Beauregard for Tennessee or Virginia without much say from us at all. I regret that the unfortunate turn of events in Pennsylvania have given them the opening they have wanted since Vicksburg. I attribute no real malice to General Johnston. He wants a command in the field and will use Wigfall and Foote to get it."

Robert Lee looked past the President toward a window which was full of clear blue sky above Richmond at morning. The general spoke to the December sky.

"The army did all it could. I fear I required of it impossibilities. But it responded to the call nobly and cheerfully." The army's Uncle Robert choked on his last words.

"Well, General," the President said as he rose to his feet, "I presume that means that you remain committed to returning to your command."

"You could order me west, Excellency. I would go then."

"Not yet, General."

With a sentry at each elbow, General Lee walked into the morning sunshine and the cold air outside the old Customs House. He crossed Bank Street and climbed the stone stairway up to Capitol Square and the morning session of the Joint Military Affairs Committee. The morning's closed hearing would begin with the second day at Gettysburg.

★　　★　　★

In the darkness of the Gettysburg night of Wednesday, July 1st, General Lee was still blind without Jeb Stuart's cavalry. But now it did not matter. Robert Lee knew where the blue Army of the Potomac camped: barely one mile across the valley to the east atop

Cemetery Ridge. As the Army of Northern Virginia dug-in behind Seminary Ridge at 1 o'clock in the morning of July 2nd, Jeb Stuart was just leaving Carlisle, Pennsylvania, for the 30 mile ride to the southwest and Gettysburg—over 12 hours away by horseback.

General Longstreet awoke from a midnight nap at 3:30 in the morning. He arrived at Seminary Ridge from I Corps' bivouac by 5 o'clock. An hour earlier, General Lee had sent army engineer Captain S. R. Johnston southward down the length of the Rebel line to scout the Federal positions. Captain Johnston rode by horseback all the way to the extreme right flank of Lee's line, opposite the Yankees' commanding position at Little Round Top, the rocky knoll at the southern apex of Cemetery Ridge. While the Federal lines were being scouted, Longstreet protested to Lee under the trees of Spangler's Woods against making a frontal assault upon the well entrenched Federals across the valley.

Captain Johnston returned from his reconnaissance mission at 7 o'clock and reported that the rocky Round Tops did not appear to be fortified, as of 5:30. The engineer enjoyed a decent view of the area since sunup had been at 4:15. This Thursday promised to be hot. By 7 o'clock in the morning, the temperature was already 74 degrees under a strangely red sun rising above broken clouds.

By the time James Longstreet rode over to General Lee's position before daybreak, the commanding general was already growing impatient to launch an assault by I Corps against Cemetery Ridge. When Longstreet arrived at Spangler's Woods, his divisions were still strung out along Chambersburg Pike. The Old Warhorse of Antietam Creek quietly confronted his chief about an attack. Robert Lee's usual patience was sorely strained by chest pain, a bout of field diarrhea, and profound disappointment at having stumbled into General Meade without scouting intelligence from Jeb Stuart, still missing.

Longstreet argued against a morning attack across the valley. Instead, he advocated to General Lee a sideways shift of the entire army toward the south. General Longstreet recommended the march which would put the Confederates south of the Federal position. By digging-in between General Meade's bluecoats and Washington, the Rebels could sit tight and wait for Meade to attack them. After all, nothing panicked the Federals like a few gray divisions between the Army of the Potomac and Mr. Lincoln's capital city. Then, argued Longstreet, General Lee could pick his ground to make a stand while the Federals threw themselves against Confederate breastworks.

Robert Lee dismissed Longstreet's suggestion.

In the early morning hours, General Lee had watched the Federals digging in along Cemetery Hill. Blueclad reinforcements continued to arrive. Because Captain Johnston had reported at 7 o'clock that the Round Tops were still unoccupied by the enemy, General Lee believed that the left flank of the Federal line (running north and south atop Cemetery Ridge) must end above (north of) the Round Tops. Lee proposed that I Corps attack along the Emmitsburg Road which ran through the valley between the ridges.

The Confederates would push the Yankees back from the road and then advance upon Cemetery Hill. The plan called for I Corps to charge between the southern Round Tops and the Federal left flank. General Longstreet reluctantly accepted his orders. But he requested a delay until George Pickett's division could arrive. "I never like to go into battle with one boot off," Longstreet said.

While Generals Lee and Longstreet debated the course of action at first light, they were joined by Major General Lafayette McLaws, a division commander from Longstreet's I Corps. General Lee proposed deploying McLaws' division perpendicular to the Emmitsburg Road between the ridges. General McLaws first wanted to conduct his own reconnaissance of the ground with engineer Johnston. Longstreet ordered McLaws not to accompany Captain Johnston and to deploy his division parallel to the dirt road. General Lee agreed with McLaws as to the scouting and the deployment. But when James Longstreet repeated his objection, General Lee said nothing more. The exhausted and dehydrated Robert Lee did not have the strength to argue with his hearty warhorse.

While I Corps slowly broke camp behind Seminary Ridge and General Lee paced out of patience and out of sorts, men and boys from yesterday's accidental encounter still lay wounded in fields and hay ripe for its second cutting. Three miles northwest of town where the first shots had been fired, Mrs. Joseph Bayly and her niece carried food and bandages to the wounded. At her request, Confederate soldiers filled water canteens for Mrs. Bayly to put to the parched lips of hurting Federals.

General Lee sent orders to Baldy Ewell on the Rebel left to "demonstrate" during Longstreet's imminent assault along the Confederate right flank. The demonstration would fill the air with cannon balls and bullets to distract the Yankees at the northern end of the blue line. Ewell's II Corps was instructed to attack for real against Culp's Hill north of Cemetery Hill only if General Ewell found Culp's Hill to be lightly fortified.

Between 8:30 and 9 o'clock in the morning, General Lee became impatient waiting for I Corps to form its battle lines behind the protection of Seminary Ridge for the projected assault. After Captain Johnston reported his scouting expedition to his commanding general, Lee tried to prod Longstreet by saying, "I think you had better move on."

To those around him, Lee seemed edgy and not quite himself this morning. Perhaps he was treating his painful dysentery with the government issue remedy used by the Federals: half a cup of castor oil laced with quinine forced down twice daily.

After his 9 o'clock confrontation with James Longstreet, General Lee mounted Traveller for a trot northward behind Seminary Ridge toward General Ewell's field headquarters. General Edward Johnson was deployed at the far left of General Lee's line, opposite Culp's Hill. General Johnson's division of Ewell's corps was actually east of the Federal line. By the time General Lee reached Ewell's headquarters south of Gettysburg, Johnson had already reported to Ewell that Culp's Hill was well fortified with Federals. The Confederate line had assumed a fish-hook shape. The long shank was the north-south line along Seminary Ridge and the hook bent around from the north end of the ridge toward the east and around Culp's Hill at the northern end of the Yankee line.

General Lee found the one-legged Baldy Ewell to be disquieted by the reports that Culp's Hill had been occupied by blueclads during the night. Now Robert Lee had an uneasy corps commander in II Corps to match his balky leader of I Corps, James Longstreet. General Lee calmed Richard Ewell by instructing him again merely to "demonstrate" opposite Culp's Hill unless Ewell became confident that a real assault could dislodge the Federals.

At Baldy Ewell's end of the fish hook, General Lee was a good seven miles away from the Confederate right flank where Longstreet's I Corps was supposed to be massing to assault Cemetery Ridge. By 10 o'clock, General Lee was cocking his ear toward the southwest to hear Longstreet's artillery announcing his advance across the Emmitsburg Road. The impatient Lee turned to Ewell and wondered out loud, "What can detain Longstreet? He ought to be in position by now."

Half an hour later, General Lee was back at Spangler's Woods and Seminary Ridge. He looked impatiently for Longstreet. By 11 o'clock, Lee saw I Corps forming up behind the ridge, but the line had not yet deployed in fighting formation. For perhaps the first time since assuming command of the army, Robert Lee gave Longstreet a direct order to attack.

With the Yankees continuing to dig-in and to reinforce their lines after nearly seven hours of good daylight, General Longstreet was still not ready to engage in a battle he could not endorse completely. When General Lee ordered Longstreet to deploy the divisions of Generals McLaws and John Hood on the right flank of A.P. Hill's III Corps, Longstreet requested one more administrative delay: he wanted to await the arrival of Evander Law's brigade of infantry which was part of Hood's division. General Law's troops were exhausted from an all-night march across 24 miles. Lee consented to another half hour delay.

As Longstreet waited for his divisions to assemble behind Seminary Ridge, General Lee came face to face with the difficulties he had studied 30 years earlier at West Point. From the first hour of Theory of War, he had learned of the tactician's awareness of "interior" versus "exterior" lines concerning infantry. On a battlefield, an army deployed on the inside of a semi-circle has the "interior" line advantage: movement of men and war machines can be executed quickly and safely behind the cover of the arc by moving directly along diagonals. But an army poised along the outside of a semi-circle must move forces along the circumference, the long way. On July 2nd, General Lee's fish-hook-shaped line was the exterior line. But across the valley, the Yankees had essentially a straight line, giving them the shorter route from one end to the other.

The Federals along Cemetery Ridge had the interior line three miles long with an average of over 20,000 men per mile. The Confederates had the longer five-mile long exterior line with only 10,000 men per mile. This tactical aspect of geography and infantry theory partly explained Longstreet's slowness in deploying I Corps. Major General McLaws' division had marched until midnight on July 1st to camp within three miles of Seminary Ridge. General Hood's division marched all night with only one two-hour rest for his dragging brigades.

Once Longstreet lost his pre-dawn argument with Lee about a flank maneuver instead of a direct assault, Longstreet had to move two divisions only three miles. But, he had to march them the long way behind the exterior line to remain concealed from enemy scouts and enemy snipers. What would have been three miles behind interior lines became a six-mile march for I Corps. When General Lee lost patience with Longstreet's apparent slowness in deployment, the weary chief perhaps forgot that even Stonewall Jackson's magnificent deployment at Chancellorsville took over eight hours to execute.

The noon hour came and went with no attack by the gray I Corps. General Lee impatiently rode along the lines behind Seminary Ridge to prod things along.

Not until noon did John Hood's full division assemble with I Corps after nine hours on the dirt roads. The massing of the First Corps of the Army of Northern Virginia produced epic traffic jams. For 90 minutes, the divisions of McLaws and Hood marched behind

Seminary Ridge to take position on the Rebel right flank. While General Lee rode off toward A.P. Hill's III Corps at the center of his long line, Longstreet had to order a march and countermarch of his divisions to avoid enemy scouts.

Lee still thought that the Round Tops on the Yankee left flank were unoccupied, just as Lee's engineer had reported eight full hours earlier. But by the time General Lee arrived at the field headquarters of the ailing A.P. Hill, new scouting reports at 1 o'clock confirmed that the Federals were now fortifying the Round Tops too.

By 2 o'clock in the hot afternoon, Longstreet's I Corps had finally formed up on the Confederate right flank. Hill's III Corps formed battle lines at the Rebel center. But Robert Lee's determination to attack "those people" across the valley continued to unravel for another two hours. General Longstreet's heart was not in it; Hill was having one of his sick days caused by agonizing prostititis left over from his West Point bordello campaigns; and up the line on the far left, Baldy Ewell remained wary of doing battle on his front.

At 3 o'clock, Major General Hood protested to James Longstreet against attacking along the Emmitsburg Road toward the fortified Federal positions in a grove of peach trees near the road and toward a looming rocky formation known locally as Devil's Den. Hood's scouts had found that the left of the Yankee line (the southern end) continued to be extended southward by General Meade. Hood's division was placed opposite the Round Tops to lengthen the Confederate line to match the Federal deployments. At 3:30, General Hood informed Longstreet that Big Round Top and Little Round Top were now well fortified by the enemy. The proposed assault along the Emmitsburg Road would expose the Confederates to flanking fire into their backs when they marched across the fields commanded by the Round Tops.

General Hood argued with Longstreet that he could take his division further south to get behind the Round Tops to take the Federals from behind, Longstreet's original proposal to General Lee ten hours earlier. But now Longstreet's mind was made up: he would follow Lee's orders to the letter. "General Lee's orders are to attack up the Emmitsburg Road."

General Hood begged Longstreet to change the route of the attack at least four times during the hour. Both of I Corps' division commanders on the Rebel right, Generals Hood and McLaws, protested the orders. But Longstreet chose not to relay their objections to General Lee who was two miles up the line. Brigade commanders Joe Kershaw and 27-year-old Evander Law also joined in Major General Hood's protests to Longstreet. Brigadier General Law was so upset that he wrote out a formal protest to General Longstreet which General Hood also signed. While Longstreet listened to his angry subordinates, Federal cannon began to lob shells into the Rebel lines.

By 4 o'clock, the battle lines were finally ready, 14 hours after General Lee set the plans in motion before daybreak. The Confederates now had 22 brigades on the field behind Seminary Ridge with four others in reserve. Across the valley beyond the Emmitsburg Road, 35 blue brigades loaded their muskets with eight more in reserve. Another eight Yankee brigades continued on their hasty march toward Gettysburg.

As I Corps prepared for combat, it was already bloodied by the rain of shell from Federal cannon firing from one mile away. In John Hood's division while they waited to go over the top, a single Yankee artillery round plowed into the 3rd Arkansas regiment. The solid cannon ball killed a Confederate captain, tore the head off a sergeant, continued on to rip off another sergeant's arm, and then crippled a corporal before spending its energy.

At 4 o'clock under a hot July sun, Longstreet passed the word to execute General Lee's orders. I Corps' chief of artillery, Colonel Porter Alexander, gave the nod to his cannoneers and 54 cannon opened to answer the Federal artillery. Major General John Hood's division then moved out on the far right flank, moving uphill toward the Emmitsburg Road. Hood's brigades headed toward Little Round Top, three quarters of a mile away. Within minutes, a Yankee artillery shell burst above John Hood, wounding him seriously.

Young Evander Law took command of the division as it marched into the iron hail.

When Brigadier General Evander Law became acting division commander on the field of fire, he moved Hood's division to the right to assault Big Round Top from the south at the boulder strewn Devil's Den. Hood's division ran into the molten lead teeth of four Federal cannon on the high ground. Devil's Den was the southern end of the Yankee line.

Two of Hood's brigades took fire from 13 Federal cannon. Brigadier General Henry Benning's gray brigade lost 400 men in the attack on Devil's Den. The 49-year-old Benning was an Associate Justice of the Georgia Supreme Court. George Anderson's Rebel brigade (led to the Round Tops by a colonel after Anderson was wounded in Devil's Den) lost 105 men killed, 512 wounded, and 146 missing. In the hailstorm of lead and blood, the gorge between Little Round Top and Devil's Den was given a new name by the bloodied survivors of Hood's assault: the Slaughter Pen.

Hood's division led by Evander Law did battle at Devil's Den with the 20th Indiana regiment. The Hoosiers lost 146 of 268 men within 25 minutes. At Little Round Top, twin brothers in Company K of the 5th Texas regiment died in each others arms. When Captain Henry Brainard of the 15th Alabama in Law's former brigade went down, he whispered in the roar of thousands of muskets, "Oh God, that I could see my mother!" Then he died far from home.

Joshua Chamberlain's 20th Maine and 358 New Englanders defended the vital Little Round Top at the far left end of the Union line. Here Private Phillip Grine of the 83rd Pennsylvania pulled two wounded Johnnie Rebs from the line of fire to safety behind the rocks. When Private Grine crawled back to save a third Confederate, he was shot dead. When Private John Roberts of the 5th Texas was wounded, Yankee teenagers piled a little wall of stones around him to protect him from the iron wind.

Among the Federal heroes at the Round Tops this Thursday was Colonel Strong Vincent of the blue Fifth Corps, First Division. On the way to Gettysburg the day before, Colonel Vincent said to a lieutenant as the colorguard marched by with Old Glory snapping in the breeze, "What death more glorious can any man desire than to die on the soil of old Pennsylvania fighting for that flag?" The 26-year-old colonel was a graduate of Harvard. He fell at the Round Tops and died five days later.

The Round Tops and Devil's Den fighting went on into darkness. Only the men from Maine saved the strategically vital hills from capture by Hood's Confederates.

As the fighting swirled at the Round Tops, Longstreet sent McLaws' division across the Emmitsburg Road at 5 o'clock. They met the Federals in a hand-to-hand bloodbath in a field of peach trees, 150 yards by 100 yards, on the farm of John and Mary Sherfy and their five children. The orchard was the Federal artillery position on the field between the ridges. Forty Yankee cannon mowed down McLaws' brigades. As blood watered the fruit trees, another name was added to the war's geography of gore: the Peach Orchard.

Gettysburg was like a class reunion for Lafayette McLaws. On the field from West Point's class of 1842 were Major General McLaws, James Longstreet, and General Richard Anderson wearing the gray. Federal generals from the Class of '42 included the dead John Reynolds and Generals Abner Doubleday, John Newton, George Sykes, and Seth Williams.

At 6 o'clock, Brigadier Generals Joe Kershaw and William Barksdale led their gray brigades into the Federal line near the Peach Orchard. Kershaw's brigade did battle 300 yards southwest of the Peach Orchard on the slopes of a hill covered with stones. Kershaw lost 600 men. The Confederates battled the 2nd New Hampshire regiment which suffered 193 casualties in 90 minutes.

When General Barksdale rushed the Yankee line near the Emmitsburg Road, the Federal Second Division of III Corps lost 2,088 of its 5,000 men. Barksdale's four Mississippi regiments destroyed the 141st Pennsylvania which lost 149 of its 209 men, including Major Israel Spalding who was mortally wounded. General Charles Graham's brigade of two Pennsylvania regiments lost 740 of its

1,516 men within ten minutes under the weight of Barksdale's charge.

Brigadier General Barksdale led his Mississippi men through the Peach Orchard with a shout of "Brave Mississippians, one more charge and the day is ours!" Within moments, William Barksdale fell mortally wounded. He died in the care of Yankee surgeons who found him on the field the next day. "Tell my wife that I am shot, but we fought like hell," were the Rebel general's last words.

In the lengthening shadows at 6 o'clock, A.P. Hill sent the brigade of General Wilcox from Richard Anderson's division into the Peach Orchard. When the rest of Anderson's division entered the clouds of smoke along Emmitsburg Road, the gray division lost 1,561 of its 4,100 men. Although General Anderson was from South Carolina, his wife was the daughter of the Chief Justice of the Pennsylvania Supreme Court. Anderson's division was cut to pieces partly due to the breakdown of the command structure of the army: corps commanders Longstreet and A.P. Hill each thought that the other was in command of Anderson's division.

When Cadmus Wilcox charged the Peach Orchard, he was pushed back at bayonet point by the 1st Minnesota regiment of the blue Second Division of II Corps. The men from Minnesota counter-charged Wilcox three times and lost 215 of 262 men within 15 minutes. The 1st Minnesota suffered the highest percentage of casualties that day of any Federal regiment during the entire war.

When the 8th Florida regiment of Anderson's division covered the assault of General Wilcox, the men from Florida lost 300 men. When General Wright's brigade from Anderson's division entered the Peach Orchard north of Wilcox, the brigade lost 688 Confederates before being driven back across the Emmitsburg Road.

As the battered Rebels slowly pushed the Federals from the Peach Orchard, the hand-to-hand fighting spilled half a mile eastward to a field of summer wheat. The grain soon became the Wheatfield of Gettysburg.

The 2nd South Carolina regiment of Joe Kershaw's brigade walked calmly into the disemboweling fire of 30 cannon firing from the Peach Orchard. Before the blue Irish Brigade of the First Division, II Corps, went into the molten whirlpool of the Wheatfield, Father William Corby, the brigade's priest, prayed with his Irishmen from three New York regiments. He granted them absolution under the bursting artillery shells whining through the air. The Irish Brigade knelt with rifles in hand. Then they countercharged Kershaw's men and drove them from the Wheatfield.

Somewhere near the Wheatfield where teenage boys died by the hundreds, a private in the 86th New York regiment lay wounded. Cradled in the arms of another Yankee, the boy softly sang to the sky black with gunpowder smoke. He mumbled the favorite refrain dear to every soldierboy's heart, North and South: "Mother Kissed Me in my Dream."

> *Lying on my dying bed*
> *Through the dark and silent night,*
> *Praying for the coming day,*
> *Came a vision to my sight.*
> *Near me stood the forms I loved,*
> *In the sunlight's mellow gleam:*
> *Folding me unto her breast,*
> *Mother kissed me in my dream.*

When Joe Kershaw's Rebels charged the Wheatfield, they met hand-to-hand Colonel Sweitzer's blue brigade. The Yankees were pushed out of the field after losing 427 of their 1,422 men. Major General Winfield Hancock, who had saved the Federal line the day before, sent the brigade of Colonel Edward Cross of John Caldwell's division into the Wheatfield. Hancock told the Yankee colonel, "This is your last fight without a star!" meaning that Colonel Cross's promotion to brigadier general was a certainty. "Too late, General," Colonel Cross smiled, "this is my last battle."

Within minutes of entering the Wheatfield, Colonel Cross was mortally wounded, to die by daybreak Friday. The officer was much loved by his 5th New Hampshire men. In two years, Colonel Cross had been wounded 11 times. "I think the boys will miss me," he said as he slipped away from Gettysburg forever, "Good-bye to all."

> *Comrades, tell her when you write,*
> *That I did my duty well;*
> *Say that when the battle raged,*
> *Fighting in the van I fell.*
> *Tell her, too, when on my bed*
> *Slowly ebbed my being's stream,*
> *How I knew no peace until*
> *Mother kissed me in my dream.*

The fighting swept across the red field until darkness. Brigadier General James Barnes from Massachusetts commanded the First Division of the Federal V Corps there. Thirty years earlier, he had been Robert Lee's classmate at West Point. When Lieutenant Jackson Purman of the 140th Pennsylvania regiment fell wounded in the bloodied wheat, Lieutenant Tom Oliver of the 24th Georgia carried the wounded Yankee to safety.

After much fighting this bloody Thursday, the Confederates pushed the Federals back from Emmitsburg Road, from the Peach Orchard, and from the Wheatfield. Only Joshua Chamberlain's Mainers saved the Round Tops from being overrun by Evander Law's exhausted Rebels.

By evening twilight, Longstreet's assault on the Confederate right flank had bloodied or had annihilated 13 Yankee brigades. The Federal line from the Peach Orchard south to the Round Tops had suffered 30 to 40 percent casualties. Longstreet's boys had knocked out of commission the Federals' entire III Corps, one division from II Corps, and three brigades of V Corps, all too battered to fight again at Gettysburg.

By dark, Confederates had a foothold at the base of both Round Tops. At the base of Cemetery Ridge, a little stream called Plum Run flowed parallel to the Federal high ground. At the western base of Cemetery Ridge near the Wheatfield, the bloodied Confederates knelt by sunset at Plum Run to bathe their fresh wounds in the warm water. The creek turned red with Confederate blood. Men would tell their grandchildren how Plum Run earned its new name on July 2nd, 1863: Bloody Run.

As the action cooled along the Emmitsburg Road, the fighting became hotter far to the north. At 6:30, Baldy Ewell's II Corps began its "demonstration" on the far left of the Confederate line. Ewell sent Edward Johnson's division against Culp's Hill on the northern apex of Cemetery Ridge. In the twilight toward 8 o'clock, Jubal Early sent his division against the Yankee high ground at East Cemetery Hill just west of Culp's Hill.

Jubal Early sent the North Carolina brigade of Colonel Isaac Avery up the hill against General George Greene's lines. Colonel Avery was gravely wounded in the neck. Before his death on the field, Colonel Avery, who could not speak, wrote a note to his comrades in gray: "Tell my father I fell with my face to the enemy." By darkness Early's men had been driven from their foothold on Cemetery Hill and General Johnson's men were digging-in on the slopes of Culp's Hill.

The shooting stopped at nightfall. The Confederate divisions of Hood, McLaws, and Anderson had driven the Yankees one mile toward the east. The Federals still held Cemetery Ridge.

In the darkness, the stillness between the exhausted lines was broken only by the pitiful cries from thousands of wounded who lay along Emmitsburg Road, in the Peach Orchard, upon the wheat freshly mowed by bullet and shell, and along the Round Tops and Devil's Den. At the Rebel right flank, a bloodied foot soldier in Lafayette McLaws' division raised his voice to sing a hymn across the valley of dead and wounded boys in blue and gray. The tired Rebel sang "When This Cruel War Is Over." When he finished, the Yankees atop Cemetery Ridge cheered.

> *Dearest love, do you remember*
> *When we last did meet,*
> *How you told me that you loved me*
> *Kneeling at my feet?*

In the four hours since Longstreet sent Hood's gray division uphill across the Emmitsburg Road, over 6,000 Confederates had fallen dead or wounded. The Federals suffered 9,000 casualties.

> *Oh, how proud you stood before me*
> *In your suit of gray,*
> *When you vowed to me and country*
> *Ever to be true.*

Of course, when the song was song up North, the words became "...in your suit of blue." In the darkness of Thursday night, General Lee saw his army sleeping on their weapons at the base of Cemetery Ridge. The next day, he would finish the job with one more frontal assault. He issued orders for Baldy Ewell to renew the attack upon Culp's Hill on the Rebel left and for Longstreet to launch one last desperate attack against the very center of the Federal line. A.P. Hill's III Corps would support Longstreet's attack. The Friday attack by I Corps would become known as Pickett's Charge.

> *Weeping sad and lonely*
> *Hope and fears how vain!*
> *Yet praying, when this cruel war is over,*
> *Praying that we meet again!*

As the sad sweet song washed over the plain covered with 16,000 dead and dying men, General Lee was stricken with an attack of diarrhea which sorely taxed his ailing heart. His violent cramps continued all night of July 2nd. Exhausted and dehydrated from dysentery, the general did not bother to summon his three corps commanders to headquarters to discuss tomorrow's assaults. Longstreet did not volunteer to ride to Lee. General Longstreet went to sleep at 1 o'clock in the morning on July 3rd.

Robert Lee simply was not in command on Thursday, July 2nd, at Gettysburg. During the four hours of furious killing, he had remained at his field headquarters near the Lutheran Seminary building. He either sat quietly alone or he observed the battlefield through his fieldglasses. All day long, he did not send a single dispatch to his field commanders. He received but one report from the battlefield.

The second day at Gettysburg had ended. Only the surgeons and their bone saws would work throughout the warm night.

The weary witness sat quietly. In his mind, General Lee had walked the bloody Round Tops, the Peach Orchard and Wheatfield for three hours.

"You were satisfied, General, with the results of July 2nd?" Chairman Wigfall's voice sounded colder than the marble columns outside the capitol.

"I believe that I have acknowledged that the advance of our First Corps commenced later that I would have preferred. Likewise, evidently some intelligence regarding the terrain and the dispositions of the enemy was not forwarded to me on the field. However, by the close of operations on that Thursday evening, our lines had advanced well eastward, up to the slight ridgeline topped by the Emmitsburg Road. The raised prominence of the Peach Orchard artillery position was now ours. Our troops had secured a foothold near the Round Tops at the south of the enemy's works and along Culp's Hill at the other end of the Federal line."

"Indeed, General. But there was clearly a shortage of coordination among your divisions on the field."

"The army had labored hard, endured much, and behaved nobly," General Lee said firmly in a low voice heavy with fatigue. "It accomplished all that could have been reasonably expected. It ought not to have been expected to have performed impossibilities."

"You miss my point, Sir," Senator Wigfall interrupted with hostility in his voice. "I argue, Sir, that you failed to exercise a commanding general's authority over that battlefield on July 2nd. General Longstreet's advance commenced hours later than you had anticipated, but never really ordered. You failed to independently secure adequate scouting intelligence on the enemy's troop deployments. And you failed to engage at all in the affairs of the field once the assault began." Chairman Wigfall's voice rose in pitch and he leaned forward. "I ask you, Sir, where were you on the second of July 1863?"

General Lee looked up at the Texan. The wind burned face of the witness was exhausted.

"My leading in battle would do more harm than good. It would be a bad thing if I could not then rely on my brigade and division commanders. I plan and work with all my might to bring the troops to the right place at the right time. With that, I have done my duty. It is my generals' turn to perform their duty."

"Well and good, General. But, before we recess for the noon hour, I suggest that a firmer hand with your subordinates and perhaps some anger toward some of your corps commanders might very well have brought forth more fruit on July 2nd at Gettysburg."

The silent gallery held its breath when the soldier at the witness table spoke softly to Senator Wigfall.

"The manner in which an individual enjoys certain advantages over others is the test of a true gentleman."

Robert Lee looked down at his hands. Louis Wigfall looked away.

Chapter Seventeen

Friday Afternoon, December 18, 1863

It is all over now. Many of us are prisoners, many are dead, many wounded, bleeding and dying. Your soldier lives and mourns. And but for you, my darling, he would rather be back there with his dead, to sleep for all time in an unknown grave.

Major General George Pickett, I Corps,
Army of Northern Virginia, Gettysburg

*A*lexander Pendleton stood awkwardly at the doorway. Looking younger than his 23 years, Sandie hated to intrude into General Lee's private hour. The general had taken a light lunch by himself in a musty anteroom of the capitol.

"Excuse me, General."

"Come in, Colonel." The general rose and returned the officer's courtesy. "I had thought you were on your way to Moss Neck by now. You dare not keep your bride waiting."

Sandie and Kate Corbin were due to be married in 11 days with Sandie's father, a minister and general in Lee's artillery, officiating. The couple were to wed at Stonewall's last winter quarters.

"I have time, General. I did not want to leave you just yet."

"Thank you, Sandie. How might I help you?"

"General, Miss Mildred and Miss Williams are here. In the hall, Sir."

"Well," the general smiled. He wiped his white beard with the cloth napkin beside his plate. "Kindly show them in."

Mildred and Martha entered the little room and Sandie Pendleton stood at the doorway.

"General, ladies," Sandie said as he closed the door and left his general and the women.

"Precious Life," General Lee smiled as he kissed Mildred on her forehead. "Markie," he said as he touched his cousin's hand. "I thought you were to be with Charlotte today?"

"We were, Papa," Mildred smiled. "We were with Cousin Charlotte all morning."

"And?"

"She is so sad, Papa. And so frail. She wouldn't eat a bite."

General Lee sat down slowly at the table. He bowed his head.

"My poor dear daughter. I don't know what will become of her with our Rooney gone." The father sighed deeply.

"We came to be with you this afternoon," Mildred said firmly as she laid her hand upon her father's broad gray shoulder.

"Life," the soldier said gently, "you cannot stay. Neither of you." His black eyes searched Mildred's smooth face, and then Markie's. "Please try to understand, I must do this alone. Both of you can do more for me by staying with the Mim. Both of you should be home making socks with your sisters. Mary Custis and Agnes cannot do it all alone." He smiled as he patted his daughter's hand, still on his shoulder. "My boys are depending on the Lee ladies to keep the snow from their poor bare feet." His smile was hard.

Mildred's face darkened.

"Now, Life, tell me something happy. Please sit down, both of you."

Mildred and Martha took the chairs beside the table.

"Happy, Papa? Maybe for Mama." Mildred pouted.

General Lee raised a gray eyebrow.

"Custis Morgan ran off this morning," Mildred said sadly.

"Absent without a pass?" the general smiled.

"Yes. He escaped. I think he ran away to the Triplett's house." Mildred looked up at her father's merry eyes.

"I would recommend you to restore Custis Morgan to his native woods," the father smiled. "I admire his taste in going to see Miss Mary Triplett, but fear he will bite some of you very severely before you make up your mind to part with him."

"It isn't funny, Papa. I shall have to find him."

"Just be careful, Life."

A knock at the closed door broke the peace of the cozy room. A young voice outside the door called "Five minutes, General."

"Thank you, Sergeant."

"Well, ladies, I thank you for the visit. But you must leave now. The afternoon session should not take too long. I shall be home for an early supper."

Robert Lee rose.

"Can you bring the carriage around, Mildred?" Martha Williams asked.

"Sure, Markie."

Mildred kissed her tall father and she paused in the open doorway.

"See you for supper, Papa."

"I love you, Life."

Then Martha Williams sat down again and the general joined her.

"Markie."

"Mildred is a joy, Cousin Robert."

"I know. From her first day."

"But I worry about dear Agnes. Nothing seems to cheer her anymore." Martha looked sullen.

"Yes. How she still grieves for Orton. There is nothing I can do except to love her."

"Robert, I have decided to go back to New York next week. I would only be another mouth for Mother Lee to feed if I stay after you leave."

The general bowed his head.

"I have never had any trouble getting through the Yankee lines." Martha Williams was more of a Northerner than a Virginian anyway, except for her devotion to the Lees.

"Mary and the girls will miss you, Markie."

"And I them. If you don't mind, Robert, I would like to stop by Arlington on my way through Washington." Markie studied his weary face. He seemed to grimace at the words. "I shall write to you about it, I promise."

General Lee turned his face away from Martha's to gaze at the empty wall.

"Occasionally, at least," he sighed, "visit the spot with which you are intimately associated and where you will always be desired. Your description of the woods, the flowers, and the birds will bring it all plainly before me." He turned and looked into her face. "I wish I could be there with you."

There was a long silence, almost as wide as the 20 years which separated them. Martha laid her hand upon his folded hands. He did not pull his hands away.

"Do you remember, Cousin Robert, when you sent me my father's belt? I have kept it with me for 16 years now."

When Martha's father was killed during the Mexican War at Monterey—young Ulysses S. Grant had nursed the wounded soldier—Captain Lee had sent Markie her dead father's belt.

General Lee looked deeply into his Markie's eyes as he spoke in almost a whisper.

"I was very glad to learn that the belt had reached you in safety and that you recognized it for your father's. I knew it would be a prized relic of one who loved you so dearly and whose fond affection you so truly returned."

Martha Williams pulled her hand from her cousin's so she could touch the corners of her moist eyes.

"Oh, how I shall miss you, dear Cousin Robert," Martha said breathlessly.

Lee smiled weakly as he rose with Martha.

"Little will occur to cheer the sadness that reigns over the house when you depart, Markie."

For an instant, Robert Lee touched Martha's cheek. When the sentry in the hallway knocked on the door a second time, Lee without another word walked into the corridor. Martha walked in the opposite direction to the portico where Mildred waited in the carriage with a boy soldier at the reins.

As she took long strides toward daylight, Martha Williams kept wiping her eyes.

★   ★   ★

Reliving his three days at Gettysburg only caused General Lee anguish. He was quite tired from the morning session where he had detailed the second day of the battle. His pain was physical when he had spoken of Generals Dorsey Pender and Paul Semmes who fell gravely wounded on July 2nd. Brigadier General Semmes was a good soldier who had fought with distinction during the Seven Days, at Antietam, Fredericksburg, and at Chancellorsville. He fell mortally wounded in the Wheatfield.

Friday, July 3rd, began like the second day: a breakdown in command coordination which cost dearly.

General Lee wanted General Ewell on the Confederate left to assault Culp's Hill to advance his foothold won on Thursday. But the attack was to have been timed to coincide with General Longstreet's second frontal assault. At daybreak on the 3rd between 3:30 and 4:30, twenty Federal cannon opened up on the dozing Rebels at the base of Culp's Hill. Yankee regiments from Massachusetts and Indiana attacked the Confederates but were driven back up the hill after losing one third of the men in blue. Baldy Ewell then counter-charged three times. General Lee sent word to Ewell to wait until Longstreet's attack began further down the Confederate line. But the message arrived too late.

Edward Johnson's division attacked Culp's Hill at 8 o'clock in the morning. General James Walker's Stonewall Brigade made the second assault an hour later. At 10 o'clock, the third assault was attempted by brigade leaders Generals George Steuart and Junius Daniel. Before going up the hill, both Steuart and Daniel protested the futility of the charge to division commander Johnson. The brigadiers were correct: their regiments were slaughtered. General Daniel survived to die in battle ten months later. Private Wesley Culp in the 2nd Virginia regiment of Johnson's divison fell dead on Culp's Hill. He had been born on the hill which bore his family name.

By noon, the battle for Culp's Hill was over. The Confederates had been dislodged from their positions. They left 1,200 men behind on the hillside. The 49th Virginia regiment suffered 36 percent losses. The Federal riflemen had ground Baldy Ewell's assault into a bloody heap by laying down a solid wall of fire. The Yankees had fired 277,000 rounds down the hill into the up-turned faces of II Corps.

One of the half million Minie balls fired spun at half the speed of sound into Gettysburg. The thimble-size piece of lead plowed into the McClellan home where it pierced two wooden doors. The 500-grain bullet (slightly more than one ounce of lead) thudded into the breast of 20-year-old Jenny Wade who was helping her sister, Mrs. McClellan, with her three-day-old infant. Jenny was dead when she hit the kitchen floor.

At the center of the bloodied gray line early on July 3rd, General Lee pointed to Cemetery Ridge and a small stand of trees. That point was where he wanted Longstreet's I Corps to attack. The trees at the end of General Lee's finger would forever after be known as the Clump of Trees.

For the second time in as many days, James Longstreet objected to the futility of a direct frontal assault against the Federals' commanding high ground. General Longstreet repeated his argument for sliding the army sideways, toward the south, to get behind the Yankees. Lee's Old Warhorse shook his bearded face and said that no 15,000 men who had ever crossed a battlefield could take that hill. The Yankees still on the two Round Tops south of the clump of trees could hit the attacking Confederates from behind, Long-street added. General Lee remained confident that Porter Alexander's Rebel cannon, upwards of 125 guns, could silence the Round Tops and soften the Federal center before the assault.

General Longstreet also suggested to General Lee that he move the I Corps divisions of Generals Hood and McLaws a little closer to the Confederate center away from the far right flank and the dangerous Round Tops. The commanding general compromised with Long-street by moving Henry Heth's division from III Corps toward the center of the gray line to join Longstreet's I Corps for the assault. Two brigades from Dorsey Pender's division were also added to George Pickett's I Corps division. This troop shift would delay the attack until about 10 o'clock in the morning.

George Pickett's fresh division arrived behind Seminary Ridge between 8 and 9 o'clock Friday morning. General Lee then anxiously awaited Longstreet's imminent attack. But the advance did not come.

At noon, Lee mounted Traveller and trotted down the line to Longstreet's position behind Seminary Ridge. Since silence had been ordered for the forming battle lines, regiment after regiment silently raised their caps to their Uncle Robert. Robert Lee raised his gray slouch hat to return the salute of the doomed division.

While General Lee rode the line, A.P. Hill's III Corps cannon had a 30-minute duel with Yankee cannoneers. Hill's 63 big guns and the Federal cannon fought over a useless barn between the lines. Colonel Porter Alexander directing Longstreet's I Corps artillery ordered his gunners to keep their cannon quiet rather than waste ammunition. Robert Lee had now ridden up and down the line three times awaiting General Longstreet's assault.

At 1 o'clock this hot Friday afternoon, General Lee returned to his post at Spangler's Woods. While he waited for the opening artillery barrage, General Longstreet and Porter Alexander exchanged three written dispatches.

In his first note, Longstreet laid upon young Alexander the burden of deciding if the grand infantry assault would be made at all.

Colonel Alexander was charged with determining if his cannon had sufficiently "demoralize[d]" the enemy to make the charge a likely success. When Alexander objected in writing to bearing the responsibility for sending Pickett's division over the top, Longstreet repeated the order.

At seven minutes after one o'clock, Colonel Alexander opened up. Upwards of 170 Rebel cannon erupted along Seminary Ridge and down along the Emmitsburg Road. Over 200 Yankee cannon across the valley answered. The largest cannonade in human history was heard 140 miles away. The Confederate artillery shells burst among the Federal ambulances and nearly destroyed Federal General George Meade's field headquarters. General Meade—known to his divisions as Old Snapping Turtle—was not hurt. But his chief of staff, General Daniel Butterfield, was wounded.

The deafening cannon barrage thundered between the ridges for over an hour. Shells rained down from the clear blue sky at the rate of six rounds per second.

At 2:30, Porter Alexander ceased fire. He was already low on artillery ammunition. A hasty note from Alexander summoned George Pickett to send his division into the smoky valley immediately, or not at all. Old men would remember Pickett's Charge as a blur of fury, a gray parade of doomed men and boys, and the snapping of regimental battleflags in the summer breeze and hot lead wind. Bouncing great grandchildren on their knees (or on their one remaining knee), or rocking the shortening days away on the porch of some Old Soldiers Home, they would remember...

...George Pickett asking Longstreet if he should attack?

...General Longstreet cannot speak. He can only nod, and look away.

...General Lewis Armistead giving his ring to Pickett for Pickett's young fiancee, Sallie Corbell, before he takes his brigade into the valley.

...Fifty Confederate regiments of 14,000 men marching into the valley of death. Their two battle lines over one mile long.

...Ahead, the Army of the Potomac crouching behind little stone walls on the high ground of Cemetery Ridge.

...The Federals holding their fire until the two battle lines are within 300 yards. Then a wall of fire rolling down Cemetery Ridge into the up-turned faces.

..."Give them cold steel, boys!" General Armistead crying out as he carried his hat atop his saber. General Armistead dying in a cloud of sulfur smoke.

...The North Carolina boy taking his regimental colors to the top of the Cemetery Ridge and the Yankees cannot bring themselves to murder him.

...General Garnett simply disappearing as his body is torn beyond recognition.

...Fourteen thousand men going up the hill. Less than 9,000 coming down.

When George Pickett submitted his official battle report months later, Lee ordered Pickett to destroy the document.

By 2 o'clock in the afternoon, Friday, July 3rd, 1863, the Battle of Gettysburg was over.

While Pickett and Pettigrew's divisions were being destroyed on the slopes of Cemetery Ridge, Jeb Stuart was giving battle east of town.

Stuart had finally found his army on July 2nd. On Friday, he led three brigades into a slashing mounted cavalry battle at Cress Ridge. Jeb's horsemen crossed sabers with George Custer's three brigades. In an indecisive exercise, 181 Confederates and 254 Yankees tumbled bleeding from their horses. The brash Custer was a 23-year-old brigadier general. He had graduated from the Point in 1861—the bottom man in his class. He would rendezvous with his destiny beside the Little Big Horn River in Montana on June 25th, 1876.

Jeb's little joust ended the Gettysburg campaign of the continent's two greatest armies.

In 82 hours, just the Federals had fired 32,781 artillery rounds.

The Army of Northern Virginia suffered at least 20,451 casualties in three days, including six generals killed, three captured, and another eight wounded. The Army of the Potomac lost 23,049. Of the total casualties, some 6,000 were dead.

Throughout the rest of bloody Friday, General Lee rode his lines to encourage his divisions to dig-in for the Federal countercharge certain to follow Pickett and Pettigrew's repulse. But General Meade did not choose to come down from his hill.

When darkness came upon the ghastly valley, a Yankee band behind Cemetery Ridge filled the grim field between the ridges with the sweetly familiar strains of "Home, Sweet Home." In every way, the day was like Fredericksburg seven months earlier. The same mass suicide; the same brass band; even the same music. Only the color of the uniforms on the men who made the hopeless charge was different.

By 1 o'clock in the morning on Saturday, July 4th, General Lee rode Traveller at a walk back to headquarters. He dismounted with great effort near cavalryman Brigadier General John Imboden. When Lee could hardly dismount, Imboden took a step forward to help his exhausted chief from the saddle. But Robert Lee beat him to the ground.

General Lee stood silently beside Traveller. The weary soldier threw his arm across the saddle to hold himself upright. In the darkness under a brilliant moon, he said in a hoarse voice, "Too bad. Oh, too bad."

At noon Saturday, the violent thunderstorm, which seemed to follow every great battle, began. Four hours later in the rain, the gray divisions began the retreat from Pennsylvania. The ambulance wagons led the way home in a train of agony 17 miles long. These were the wounded who could be moved; many were left behind. The rain continued all night as the infantry followed their wounded out of Gettysburg.

For the long march back to Virginia, Jeb Stuart and his cavalry were in their proper position screening the retreat from pursuing Federals. Young Jeb and his sabers were in the saddle for ten continuous days during which they fought five running skirmishes with the Yankees on their heels.

Hill's III Corps left Seminary Ridge first on July 4th in the dark. General Lee left Sunday morning, the 5th, with I Corps. Baldy Ewell's II Corps brought up the rear. They left 6800 wounded Confederates behind to be cared for and imprisoned by the Federals.

As General Lee led his wounded army out of Pennsylvania, Jeb Stuart's cavalry battled the Federals every day from July 5th through the 12th.

When the Army of Northern Virginia evacuated Gettysburg and the Army of the Potomac broke camp to follow their trail southward, both mighty armies left 22,000 wounded comrades behind. Just the amputations required 500 Federal surgeons and their assistants to work around the clock for five gruesome days.

On Monday afternoon, July 6th, General Lee and I Corps arrived at Hagerstown, Maryland. The fords across the Potomac at William-sport were too deep from the continuous rain to permit crossing toward Virginia. Some of the wounded were ferried across on boats as General Meade's Federals were closing in on the retreating South-erners. As the wounded bounced cross the swollen river, the band of the 26th North Carolina regiment piped them back to Virginia while General Imboden's cavalry fought a rearguard action to protect them.

Next day at Williamsport, the grief of war touched Robert Lee personally. He received word that his wounded son Rooney had been carried bodily from his sickbed at the Hickory Hill farm in Hanover County, Virginia.

The wounded General Dorsey Pender died on July 8th and General Paul Semmes died of his wounds on the 10th.

Jeb Stuart's cavalry skirmished daily with the pursuing enemy. General Lee wrote to Jeb on July 12th: "Keep your eye over the field, use your good judgment, and give assistance where necessary."

On July 13th, Major General Johnston Pettigrew, who had com-manded a division during Pickett's Charge, fought a violent skirmish during the retreat across the Potomac at Falling Waters. Pettigrew was gravely wounded. He would die of his wounds in four days: the seventh Confederate general killed during the Pennsylvania campaign.

By Tuesday, July 14th, General Lee and his three infantry corps crossed the makeshift bridge at Falling Waters into Virginia. Gunfire raged behind them as they crossed. The entire Army of the Potomac was no more than one day behind the fleeing Confederates.

On July 15th, the Army of Northern Virginia licked its wounds at Bunker Hill, Virginia. Next day, more news from the captured Rooney Lee was not good. The Yankees served notice that General Lee's prisoner-son would be executed if the Confederate government carried through with its plan to hang two reputed spies. When Richmond relented, Rooney's life was spared.

By late July, the rolls of the once mighty army commanded by Robert Lee numbered only 53,286 soldiers. When the battered army returned to its old camp ground at Orange Court House near Culpeper by August 4th, the Pennsylvania campaign was formally concluded.

"Tell us, General Lee," Co-Chairman Foote sniffed, "if you knew then what you know now, would you have sent the divisions of Pickett and Pettigrew up Cemetery Ridge toward 'the little clump of trees' as you call it?"

General Lee looked up at the committee.

"With my present knowledge, and could I have foreseen that the attack on the last day would have failed to drive the enemy from his position, I would certainly have tried some other course." The weary witness paused. "What the ultimate result would have been is not so clear to me."

"Your faith in those forces remains undiminished?" Senator Wigfall's voice was free of malice.

The witness straightened his back and his dark eyes shone brightly as he spoke firmly.

"I never saw troops behave more magnificently than Pickett's division of Virginians did that day in that grand charge upon the enemy. And if they had been supported as they were to have been—but for some reason, not yet fully explained to me, were not—we would have held the position and the day would have been ours." General Lee lowered his black eyes.

"Nevertheless, General, the Pennsylvania campaign was essentially a failure." Chairman Wigfall was intense, but not hostile. "Have you an overall impression of the engagement?"

"As to the battle of Gettysburg," General Lee said softly, "I must again refer you to the official accounts. Its loss was occasioned by a combination of circumstances. It was commenced in the absence of correct intelligence. It was continued in the effort to overcome the difficulties by which we were surrounded. It would have been gained could one determined and united blow been delivered by our whole line. As it was, victory trembled in the balance for three days. The battle resulted in frustrating the Federal campaign for the season."

"I understand, General. Are you prepared to affix responsibility for the absence of correct information on the location of the Federal army during your march into Pennsylvania? Likewise, as to the failure of General Ewell to take Cemetery Ridge on the first day; or as to General Longstreet's apparent failure to properly scout the Round Tops prior to his assault on the second day or his failure to properly coordinate Pickett's division with General Hill's division under Pettigrew on the third day?" Senator Wigfall leaned forward to hear the answer from the witness. The gallery behind General Lee and Judah Benjamin did the same. A hush fell upon the stuffy chamber.

"No blame can be attached to the army for its failure to accomplish what was projected by me," General Lee's voice rose in pitch. "Nor should it be censured for the unreasonable expectations of the public. I am alone to blame in perhaps expecting too much of its prowess and valor."

"Then, General, the blame is yours?" Senator Wigfall leaned back in his high-backed chair, as if pronouncing sentence.

General Lee raised his face and spoke firmly.

"It's all my fault....I thought my men were invincible."

"General," interrupted one of the old men at Senator Wigfall's side. "If I understand you correctly, are you suggesting that the entire Pennsylvania operation should have been avoided—looking back?"

"No, Senator. I made the only military choice available—with the consent of the civilian administration, I hasten to add," General Lee stiffened his aching back. "I considered the problem in every possible phase, and to my mind, it resolved itself into a choice of one of two things: either to retire to Richmond and stand a siege which must ultimately have ended in surrender, or to invade Pennsylvania."

"Then, General, you still believe in taking the offensive and in attacking the enemy wherever you might find him in the future?"

General Lee's voice was resolute and his eyes flashed. His bearing was again the conqueror at Chancellorsville with the burning Chancellor house reflecting in his dark eyes as his barefoot legions cheered him like Hannibal or Caesar.

"The time has arrived in my opinion," the witness argued, "when something more is necessary than adhering to lines and defense positions. We shall be obliged to go out and prevent the enemy from selecting such positions as he chooses. If he is allowed to continue that course, we shall at last be obliged to take refuge behind the works of Richmond and stand a siege which would be but a work of time. You must be prepared to fight him in the field, to prevent him from taking positions such as he desires!"

Chairman Wigfall's voice was cold.

"But General, after Gettysburg and after all of the futile engagements of the last two months when General Meade escaped your well-laid trap at Mine Run, do you really believe that your ill-clad, ill-fed, and sorely tried army can still engage in offensive operations?"

"Senator," the witness fumed with narrowed eyes, "the privations and hardships of the march and camp were cheerfully encountered and borne with fortitude unsurpassed by our ancestors in their struggle for independence." Robert Lee caught his breath and his words came in measured cadence. "Their courage in battle entitles them to rank with the soldiers of any army and of any time!"

It took Senator Wigfall a full minute to gavel the gallery to silence.

"Ladies and gentlemen," the chairman called, "I know your affinity for this witness. I advise you to control the same. Since it is now 4 o'clock, we shall adjourn until tomorrow, Saturday morning, at 9 o'clock. You may have until that time to regain your composure, or tomorrow's session will be closed to our invited guests!...We now stand in recess until tomorrow."

The buzzing gallery rose as the committee left the chamber.

As the rows of civilians and military brass slowly filed out of the chamber, General Lee stood beside Judah Benjamin.

Robert Lee did not hear Major General George Pickett speak softly to a military aide at his side. General Pickett gestured toward the back of his commanding officer.

"That old man had my division massacred."

★   ★   ★

"There's no turning back," Louis Wigfall said cheerfully through cigar smoke. "We've got him, and Davis, too."

"Yes," Edwin Reade nodded. "But I'm just a little uncomfortable about hanging Lee out to dry like this. There were the Seven Days and Fredericksburg and Chancellorsville. He is the winningest general we have, you know."

The three men were obscured under the capitol pillars by cigar smoke and steam from the cold. The hard air carried the distant clanging from the ironworks down on the river where slaves toiled at smelters night and day.

"I wouldn't worry, Senator," Henry Foote said confidently. "Davis can keep Lee if he wants. The blind leading the half-blind. Lee can return to his army—if Johnston gets Tennessee. Everyone's happy and we have cut King Jeff off at the knees."

Louis Wigfall laughed out loud.

"Well said, Henry."

Chapter Eighteen

Saturday, December 19, 1863

*The day of my death will be better for me than
the day of my birth.*
Robert E. Lee

Saturday, December 19th, dawned cold and bright. A fine frost
glistened on the brown lawn.

Robert Lee stood on the cold front porch beside his daughter,
Mary Custis.

"Then today will be the last day, Father?"

"I suppose so. Secretary Benjamin said last evening that the
committee intends to call only Colonel Alexander and General
Longstreet."

"Isn't he from the artillery?"

"Yes, Daughter. Colonel Alexander is chief of Longstreet's artillery in I Corps. A very able young man."

"What could he offer the committee, Father?"

"I don't really know. Alexander is close to General Longstreet.
Perhaps he can offer some insight into the actions on the field at
Gettysburg."

"Well, Father, at least they will be done with you today."

"Probably, Daughter."

"I worry about you, Papa," Mary said gently. Mary was the prodigal daughter, often absent from home through most of her adult life. It was difficult for Robert Lee to dote on Mary as he had done with Annie, the child-woman Mildred, or the sensitive and grieving Agnes. But Mary's age, 28, gave candor to her relationship with her father.

"The day of my death," Robert Lee said with a sigh, "will be better for me than the day of my birth."

"Father!" Mary Custis protested, "don't be silly!...And don't let Mother hear you say such things!"

General Lee had to smile at the grown woman by his side.

"Yes, Daughter. You are right, of course. There is so much more work for us to do for our poor country."

"That's better, Father."

Mary Custis looked closely at her father.

"There is so little that I can do for you, Papa. All I can do is pray for you and hope that thoughts of us somehow bring you closer to us when you are in the field."

"I think of you all, separately and collectively," the father smiled, "in the busy hours of the day and the silent hours of the night. And the recollection of each and every one whiles away the long nights in which my anxious thoughts drive away sleep."

Mary Custis blinked her moist eyes at her father.

"I do hope so, Papa."

★ ★ ★

Colonel Porter Alexander, 28 years old, arrived at the capitol shortly after General Lee. Alexander rode his trusted mare Meg. Since the beginning of the war, Colonel Alexander had owned two favorite horses, Dixie and Meg. This day, the young artilleryman rode Meg since Dixie was laid up after she had been wounded at both Fredericksburg and Gettysburg.

Porter Alexander was called and sworn in by Louis Wigfall at 9 o'clock. Alexander had known the Lees since West Point. During 1855 and 1856 at the Point, Cadet Alexander had been in cadet company D with General Lee's nephew, Fitz Lee. Robert Lee had been superintendent at the time.

The colonel squirmed uncomfortably in a chair between General Lee's table and the committee's raised platform. Co-Chairman Wigfall introduced each member of the tribunal to the witness.

"Colonel Alexander," Senator Wigfall continued, "we are aware of your impressive record in the First Corps of the Army of Northern Virginia. We commend you, Sir."

"Thank you, Senator, but I still do not understand why I am here. I know that this is some kind of inquiry into the conduct of the war in the east. Am I correct?"

"You are, Colonel. We are simply making inquiry into the leadership of General Lee. More than that need not concern you."

"Then, Mr. Chairman, what could I possibly offer this committee?"

"We anticipate, Colonel, your first-hand impressions of General Lee in the field, especially as to the Pennsylvania campaign."

"Senator Wigfall, my impression of General Lee is quite simple: I think that military critics will rank General Lee as decidedly the most audacious commander who has lived since Napoleon."

The gallery erupted into spontaneous applause. Chairman Wigfall firmly gaveled the gallery to tense silence.

"Indeed, Colonel. Now to the issue at hand: do you have any reservations about General Lee's conduct in the field since he took command of the Army of Northern Virginia in June 1862?" The chairman leaned slightly forward.

Colonel Alexander looked down at his fidgeting hands in his lap.

"Senator, I am a field officer in General Longstreet's artillery. I have utterly no right to entertain public commentary on the commanding general's leadership. My admiration for General Lee is without bounds, Sir. Without bounds."

"Yes, yes, Colonel," the chairman said impatiently. "I shall be more specific. Do you have an opinion on the very first engagement executed by General Lee, the so-called Battle of the Seven Days around Richmond in late June 1862?"

"Senator, my formal military education was in artillery and military engineering. I can entertain an opinion. But I cannot stress how inappropriate that commentary would be." Porter Alexander's voice was pleading with the chairman.

"Colonel, in your presence, I shall ask General Lee for his leave for you to speak freely."

The uncomfortable young officer turned in his chair and looked over his shoulder into Robert Lee's eyes.

"Do speak your mind, Colonel," Robert Lee said with a nod and a trace of a smile which reflected his warm regard for his cannoneer.

"Now, Colonel," the Senator from Texas continued, "the Seven Days, please?"

Porter Alexander took a deep breath.

"Mr. Chairman, I have an opinion—completely inappropriate— as to the conduct of the assault against Malvern Hill, July 1, 1862, I believe."

"Please continue, Colonel."

"Senator," the Colonel said with a deep breath, "I don't think any military engineer can read a description of the ground at Malvern Hill without asking in surprise and almost in indignation, how on God's earth it happened that our army was put to assault such a position." The colonel sighed and his emotions carried along his testimony. "Oh the rivers of good blood that flowed that evening all in vain....Malvern Hill was an utter and bloody failure."

"That's better, Colonel," the chairman nodded as the gallery buzzed and Robert Lee looked hard at his colonel's gray back.

The witness looked down at his wind-burned hands.

"I have no right to say that, Senator."

"You are under oath, Colonel Alexander. I suggest that you might keep in mind that you are here by subpoena and under compulsion of law. You may take comfort from knowing that you are compelled to be here. Now, Sir, I take your remarks to suggest that you have found General Lee's aggressive tactics to be occasionally wasteful of precious Southern blood. Have you other opinions, based upon your professional training, judgment, and experience, as to when General Lee's offensive tactics might have been excessive in the totality of circumstances?"

"Yes, Senator," the witness mumbled self-consciously.

"Please elaborate, Colonel."

"On two occasions, I am quite sure, he will be adjudged to have overdone it. He gave battle unnecessarily at Sharpsburg, September 17, 1862. The odds against him were so immense that the utmost he could have hoped to do was what he did do: to repel all assaults and finally to withdraw safely across the Potomac. And," the witness's testimony now flowed freely, "he probably only succeeded in this because McClellan kept about 20,000 men, all of Fitz-John Porter's corps, entirely out of the fight so they did not pull a trigger. He fought where he could have avoided it, and where he had nothing to make and everything to lose—which a general should not do." The witness sighed and looked down. "Then perhaps in taking the aggressive at all at Gettysburg and certainly in the place and dispositions for the assault on the third day, I think, it will undoubtedly be held that he unnecessarily took the most desperate chances and the bloodiest road."

"In your judgment, Colonel, should the Battle of Sharpsburg beside Antietam Creek have been fought at all? In other words, do you have an opinion as to whether General Lee had any other options open to him in Maryland last year?"

"Our whole army," the colonel said slowly, "was back on the Virginia side of the Potomac except for Longstreet's and Hill's divisions. These could have been easily retired across the river and we would, indeed, have left Maryland without a great battle. But we would nevertheless have come off with good prestige and a very fair lot of prisoners and guns—and lucky on the whole to do this, considering the accident of the lost order. This, I think, will be pronounced by military critics to be the greatest military blunder that General Lee ever made. A drawn battle, such as we did actually fight, was the best possible outcome one could hope for. Even that was only accomplished by the Good Lord's putting it into McClellan's heart to keep Fitz-John Porter's corps entirely out of the battle."

"Colonel Alexander, you seem to be aware now of the lost Order Number 191?"

The witness nodded.

"It was a shabby trick for fate to play us." Colonel Alexander shook his head.

"Mr. Chairman," Judah Benjamin rose beside General Lee, "I choose to ask this witness but one question."

"Mr. Secretary," Chairman Wigfall said coldly, "you are out of order, Sir."

"I am prepared, Senator, to stand here until this war is ended— only to ask one question of this witness!"

The gallery laughed nervously as Senator Wigfall's eyes blazed at the Secretary of State who held his ground.

"Very well, Secretary Benjamin—one question."

"Respondent Lee and I thank the Chairman," Judah Benjamin said courteously. "Colonel Alexander, I ask you one question: were you even at the Battle of Sharpsburg?" The Secretary could not conceal a faint smile.

Porter Alexander turned and looked over his shoulder.

"No, Mr. Secretary. I was detailed to Harper's Ferry with Stonewall Jackson to collect the ammunition and ordnance captured there. I was not beside Antietam Creek during that great battle."

Secretary Benjamin nodded knowingly as he sat down.

"Very well, Colonel," Chairman Wigfall droned dryly. "You were not actually on that field in question. We shall accord your opinions appropriate weight. But you seem to have an opinion as to the overall performance of the army of which you were daily an integral part. Is that correct, Sir?"

"That is correct, obviously, Senator. As a daily participant in that grand army and as a daily observer of it and General Lee, I have a first-hand impression of the Army of Northern Virginia just prior to Sharpsburg when I left the main force to attend to my duties at Harper's."

"Well then, Colonel, share with us your first-hand impression of the army as you observed it under the leadership of General Lee in September 1862."

"Mr. Chairman," Alexander said firmly and clearly, "General Lee's army had acquired that magnificent morale which made them equal to twice their numbers. His confidence in them, and theirs in him, were so equal that no man can yet say which was greatest."

Senator Louis Wigfall did not even attempt to gavel the applauding gallery to silence. He simply let their two-minute ovation expire on its own.

"Very well, Colonel, you were in fact at Gettysburg, were you not? And were you not in the thick of both the combat and the command structure?"

"I was indeed at Gettysburg, Senator. As you know, Colonel Walton was actually General Longstreet's chief of artillery for I Corps. I commanded the 26 cannon in the reserve artillery of I Corps. Not until July 2nd was I placed in overall command of all of the I Corps artillery which covered the charge of Generals Pickett and Pettigrew on the third day."

"Colonel, we have already taken testimony from General Lee on the absence of Major General Stuart from the army as it made its way to Pennsylvania. Do you concur with General Lee's rather guarded opinion that the cavalry's absence from Pennsylvania may have played a part in the Gettysburg setback?"

"Here the absence of Stuart with the bulk of the cavalry does seem to cut some figure. Had they been with us, General Lee would doubtless have been too well informed of the enemy's exact location to have permitted two divisions to blunder into an attack upon two corps and a division of cavalry."

"You refer, I believe to the divisions of Generals Heth and Pender who went to Gettysburg on their ill-fated shoe expedition on July 1st."

"Yes, Senator."

"Thank you, Colonel. General Lee has described the rather difficult line maintained by our forces at Gettysburg from an engineering standpoint. As a military engineer, have you an opinion on the inherent difficulty of our lines there? I believe that General Lee spoke in terms of interior and exterior lines. Do you wish to clarify that discussion?"

"Well, Senator." Returning to engineering matters helped the witness relax markedly. "Our line was like a big fishhook outside the enemy's small one. Communication between our flanks was very long—roundabout and slow, while the enemy were practically all in one convenient-sized bunch. Reinforcements from their extreme right marched across in ample time to repulse our attack on their extreme left. But Ewell's men could hardly have come to our help in half a day—and only under view and fire."

"You refer, Colonel, to General Richard Ewell traversing from our line's left flank to the right flank where you were positioned with General Longstreet's I Corps?"

"That is correct, Senator."

"And on the second day at Gettysburg, July 2nd, you went from commander of the I Corps reserve artillery to commanding the entire line's artillery."

"Yes, Mr. Chairman. By order of General Lee on July 2nd." The witness was again anxious as his testimony returned to naming names with General Lee sitting so close behind him and with General Longstreet pacing the corridor beyond the closed door of the chamber. "In General Lee's presence, Longstreet pointed out the enemy's position and said that we would attack his left flank. He told me to take command of all the artillery on the field for the attack."

"Colonel Alexander, you have already testified today that you felt that General Lee was overly aggressive at Malvern Hill in July 1862, at Sharpsburg last year, and at Gettysburg. Might you elaborate now on your feeling as to Gettysburg? I have to tell you that General Lee is of the opinion that his lines of supply and communication mandated that he not linger long in enemy territory. General Lee has stated here that he had to engage General Meade at Gettysburg rather quickly instead of adopting Longstreet's suggestion that the army wait for General Meade to attack us."

"I am most uncomfortable now, Mr. Chairman. I am hardly qualified to second-guess General Lee."

"Understood, Colonel. But I remind you that this is a fact-finding board of inquiry. Your testimony will be given appropriate weight—or lack of probative weight, as the case may be. With General Lee's generous permission already accorded to you, kindly answer the question: Could General Lee, in your educated judgment, have remained on the field to await attack by General Meade against a superior Confederate position, either at Gettysburg or elsewhere in Pennsylvania?"

The witness squirmed and he spoke softly.

"Now when it is remembered that we stayed for three days longer on that very ground, two of them days of desperate battle ending in the discouragement of a bloody repulse, and then successfully withdrew all our trains and most of the wounded through mountains; and, finding the Potomac too high to ford, protected them all and foraged successfully for over a week in a very restricted territory along the river until we could build a bridge, it does not seem improbable that we could have faced Meade safely on the 2nd at Gettysburg without assaulting him in his wonderfully strong position.

"We had the prestige of victory with us, having chased him off the field and through the town. We had a fine defensive position on Seminary Ridge ready at our hand to occupy. It was not such a really wonderful position as the enemy happened to fall into, but it was not a bad one and it could never have been successfully assaulted." Colonel Alexander looked up at the committee inquisitors. "The onus of attack was upon Meade anyhow. We could even have fallen back to Cashtown and held the mountain passes." The witness looked back down at his hands. "I cannot believe that military critics will find any difficulties in our abstaining from further assault on the following day."

"Thank you, Colonel. I must also ask you: Do you have an opinion as to whether General Longstreet was ordered to attack at dawn on the second day—or could have done so—as many critics in the press are now charging?"

"I don't think General Lee could have ever ordered or expected an attack by our corps at sunrise. The preliminary detail for any attack seems to have been left till morning." The witness shrugged and his voice became softer. "But, by 10 or 11 o'clock at latest, it was entirely practicable for us to have delivered our attack in good shape."

"And, Colonel, the attack was not begun until several hours after the noon hour. Is that correct?"

"That is correct, Mr. Chairman. But I cannot emphasize enough that my only real expertise is limited to surveys of the terrain for artillery placement. I am an artilleryman, not a strategist, Senator."

"I understand that, Colonel Alexander. Let us limit your testimony to artillery for the moment. What was your impression of the Federal artillery at Gettysburg on the second day there?"

"They really surprised me, both with the number of guns they developed and the way they stuck to them."

"Did you observe the ultimate assault by General Longstreet on the Confederate right flank on July 2nd?"

"I did, Sir."

"And based upon your personal observations that day, Colonel, have you an opinion as to the deployment of the attacking divisions of Generals Hood and McLaws on the second day at Gettysburg on your I Corps front on the right of our line?"

"Our method on this occasion struck me as peculiar. I think the best and strongest assault would have been for both divisions, in a decidedly shorter line, to have simultaneously assaulted the Peach Orchard. But, as it was, Hood moved out first and alone and had a long and desperate fight upon Sickles' left flank before McLaws was launched upon the Peach Orchard."

"You refer to Federal General Daniel Sickles who commanded the Federal III Corps positioned in the Peach Orchard on July 2nd?"

"Yes, Senator."

"Do you regard the July 2nd assault by Longstreet as a failure, Colonel Alexander?"

"A failure, Senator? Just the opposite, I would suggest."

"Kindly elaborate, Colonel." Louis Wigfall's eyes penetrated young Alexander's face.

"Our two divisions' 13,000 infantry with 62 guns took the aggressive against a strong position and captured it, fighting successfully for three hours against 40,000 infantry and 100 guns, and holding the ground gained. I think that to be a greater military feat than the partial success gained by Pickett's Charge!"

"Indeed, Colonel. While we are on Pickett's assault, what is your opinion of that operation on July 3rd?"

Porter Alexander looked up. His voice was firm and he spoke with uncommon passion.

"The point selected for Pickett's attack was very badly chosen—almost as badly chosen as it was possible to be. I have no idea by whom it was done. The point we attacked was upon the long shank of the fishhook of the enemy's position and our advance was exposed to the fire of the whole length of that shank, some two miles. Not only that, the shank was not perfectly straight, but it bent forward at the Round Top end so that rifled guns there, in secure position, could and did enfilade the assaulting lines."

Alexander's voice rose in pitch as he continued.

"Now that advance had to be over 1,400 yards of open ground, none of it sheltered from fire and very little from view." The witness sighed and looked down. "I think any military engineer would, instead, select for attack the bend of the fishhook just west of Gettysburg. There, at least, the assaulting lines could not be enfiladed, and, on the other hand, the places selected for assault could be enfiladed."

"Well and good, Colonel. Would you hold General Longstreet accountable for the placement of the assaulting columns or for the location of Pickett's Charge?"

The witness looked most uncomfortable.

"It must be remembered," Colonel Alexander said emphatically, "that the preparations for this charge were made deliberately and under the observation of General Lee himself and all of his staff. From sunrise to 1:30 in the afternoon was nine hours, all devoted to this business and within a few hundred acres of land. It seems to me impossible to believe that General Lee did not know quite accurately the location of every brigade he had upon that battlefield."

"Colonel, there has been some suggestion that General Pickett was not adequately supported in his assault on July 3rd. It is argued that General Richard Anderson's division were supposed to support Major General Pickett with another 8,000 men. But somehow, that support on Pickett's flanks was not forthcoming. Let us assume that this is true. Do you have an opinion as to whether this alleged support would have made a critical difference to the outcome of that disastrous charge by Major General Pickett? General Lee's testimony has suggested as much."

"If Pickett had had the support which General Lee expected, would those five brigades have saved the day? I cannot feel confident of it because of General Meade's ability to use such an immense superiority of force."

"Speaking of whatever support General Lee anticipated for the divisions of Pickett and Pettigrew, we are well aware that the I Corps divisions of Generals Hood and McLaws were not thrown into the assault with Pickett's command. Do you believe that General Longstreet should have also deployed McLaws and Hood to support Pickett on the right flank?"

Porter Alexander did not hesitate.

"It would have been simply impossible to hold the firing line upon which our guns were placed if either Hood or McLaws were taken away to be placed in the column with Pickett."

"Well, Colonel, the fact remains that the so-called Pickett's Charge was launched on the afternoon of July 3rd, perhaps without proper support on its flanks and with inadequate artillery coverage. We understand that the responsibility for actually sending the divisions of Pickett and Pettigrew against the Federal position fell upon you. Did James Longstreet formally give the order to execute the assault?"

"I had communication with General Longstreet all afternoon on the 3rd, Mr. Chairman."

"Yes, Colonel, but did General Longstreet give the attack order to Major General Pickett. Yes or no."

"He, himself, told me afterward that he knew the charge must be made, but he could not bring himself to give the order."

Senator Reade interrupted the chairman.

"So you were placed in command of all Confederate artillery supporting Major General Pickett?"

"Yes, Senator."

"Would you characterize your artillery barrage as merely a demonstration, or more than that, Colonel?"

The colonel bristled and his voice rose in anger.

"My orders were as follows: first, to give the enemy the most effective cannonade possible. It was not meant simply to make noise, but to try to cripple him." The witness paused, collected his thoughts, and restored his reserved dignity. "I could not hope to bombard effectively with anything less than the whole force of artillery at my disposal for my range was to be generally over 1,200 yards and I had not the ammunition to make it a long business. It must have been done inside an hour, if ever. My own good sense made me appreciate that it would be very imprudent not to keep to the last extremity enough ammunition to cover a retreat back to Virginia."

"Yes, Colonel. But how, precisely, did you receive authority to launch this charge? After all, with respect, Sir, you were commanding only the reserve artillery for I Corps prior to that afternoon five months ago at Gettysburg? Suddenly, you were not only commanding all of the field's cannon, but you were evidently also entrusted with sending Pickett off. How is that?" Chairman Wigfall leaned forward and his dark eyes narrowed as he closely regarded the witness.

Colonel Alexander took a moment to pull several pieces of paper from the pocket of his gray waistcoat. He studied the scraps.

"A courier brought me a note from General Longstreet which read as follows: *Colonel: If the artillery fire does not have the effect to drive off the enemy, or greatly demoralize him so as to make our efforts pretty certain, I should prefer that you not advise Pickett to make the charge. I shall rely a great deal upon your judgment and shall expect you to let General Pickett know when the moment offers.* It was no longer General Lee's inspiration that this was the way to whip the battle, but my cold judgment to be founded on what I was going to see."

"Would the clerk please mark the colonel's document as Exhibit Ten....Colonel, have you other documents?"

"I have two others, Mr. Reade."

"The clerk will mark those documents as Exhibits 11 and 12."

The young reporter took the three papers from Alexander's sweating hand. After marking each document, he returned them to the witness.

"Colonel, for the record, can you identify the three documents just handed to you?"

"I can, Senator. They are the notes relayed to me by courier on July 3, 1863, on the field at Gettysburg, Pennsylvania. I believe the handwriting on two of the documents is that of Lieutenant General James Longstreet."

"Very well, Colonel. Did you respond to General Longstreet's memorandum?"

"I did, Senator. My response is here as Exhibit 11."

"Kindly share that document with the committee, Colonel."

Porter Alexander read from the note. His hand trembled slightly.

"I wrote to General Longstreet: *General, I will only be able to judge the effect of our fire on the enemy by his return fire, for his infantry is but little exposed to view and the smoke will obscure the whole field. If, as I infer from your note, there is any alternative to this attack, it should be carefully considered before opening fire. It will take all the artillery ammunition we have left to test this one thoroughly. If the result is unfavorable, we will have none left for another effort. And even if this is entirely successful, it can only be so at a very bloody cost.*"

Chairman Wigfall rocked back in his chair, removed his spectacles, and leaned heavily against the raised table.

"Colonel, are you testifying that you took it upon yourself to advise a corps commander to abort Pickett's Charge if possible?"

"Yes, Mr. Chairman. This is the dispatch I sent directly to General Longstreet only an hour or so before the charge took place."

"Incredible, Colonel! How did your commanding officer, General Longstreet, respond to your suggestion?"

"After a while, there came this reply: *Colonel: The intention is to advance the infantry if the artillery has the desired effect of driving the enemy's cannon off, or having other effect such as to warrant us in making the attack. When the moment arrives, advise General Pickett, and, of course, advance such artillery as you can use in aiding the attack.*"

"So, Colonel, advancing Pickett became your decision?"

"Yes, Senator. And I gave the order to Major General Pickett after our cannonade which lasted well over one hour."

"Colonel, it would seem from this Exhibit 12 that you were also ordered to advance your cannon into the field to follow the divisions of Pickett and Pettigrew. Is that a fair interpretation of Longstreet's dispatch just read?"

"I believe so, Senator."

Robert Hunter of Virginia cut the chairman off.

"Did you send artillery in to cover Pickett's Charge by those brave Virginians?"

"No, Senator, I did not."

"But you were ordered to do so by General Longstreet."

Porter Alexander was uneasy but firm when he replied.

"It must be borne in mind that our Confederate artillery could only sparingly, and in great emergency, be allowed to fire over the heads of our infantry. We were always liable to premature explosions of shell and shrapnel. Our infantry knew it by sad experience. I have known of their threatening to fire back at our guns if we opened over their heads."

"In other words, Colonel, to obey the order to cover the assault with artillery would have put the advancing infantry under your own cannon fire?"

"Precisely, Senator Hunter."

"Well, Colonel, why could you not advance the horse artillery onto the field well to the side of the advancing line of infantry? Wouldn't that have prevented you from firing over their heads?"

"There was not a sheltered foot of ground in the whole expanse we would have to traverse. If any guns were advanced entirely out upon the flank of the assaulting column, they would be exposed not only to the enemy's artillery but also to the rifled musketry of his sharpshooters and infantry line of battle which would bring it to a standstill in a few moments and soon destroy every horse and man."

"And you ultimately engaged your cannon prior to the assault and then gave the order for Pickett to attack?"

The witness paused and spoke softly. He felt General Lee's black eyes close to his gray back.

"I had tried to avoid the responsibility of the decision, but in vain. General Lee had originally planned it and half the day had been spent in preparation. I determined to cause no loss of time by any indecision on my part."

Co-Chairman Foote looked puzzled when he leaned forward.

"You decided before the artillery barrage to send Pickett in?"

"Yes, Congressman."

"Did you so advise General Longstreet?"

"I determined to let General Longstreet know that I intended to put Pickett in. I wrote to him just these words: *General: When our artillery fire is at its best, I shall order General Pickett to charge.*"

"That latter dispatch you are reciting from memory, Colonel?"

"Yes, Mr. Foote. I wrote that to General Longstreet, as well as two other brief notes. I can recite them since it is like yesterday in my mind."

"I understand, Colonel. So you opened your artillery barrage against the Federals along Cemetery Ridge and the enemy cannon replied?"

Porter Alexander spoke softly.

"It was just one o'clock, by my watch, when the double boom of the signal guns from the Washington Artillery broke the silence. It was, indeed, a grand and exciting moment to hear our long line of guns break loose. The whole Federal line from Cemetery Hill to Round Top seemed in five minutes to be emulating a volcano in eruption. Lots of guns developed which I had not before been able to see." Porter Alexander paused. He studied his hands with a long sigh before he looked up toward the raised platform.

"In ten minutes after opening, I had recognized a force of artillery at work on the enemy's line which I thought it madness to send a storming column out in the face of, for so long a charge under a mid-day July sun." Alexander took a final deep breath. "I wrote as follows and sent it to Pickett at exactly 1:25 pm: *If you are coming at all, you must come at once, or I cannot give you proper support, but the enemy's fire has not slackened at all.*"

"And then, Colonel, Pickett went into the valley?"

"No, Mr. Foote." The witness looked the Tennessean squarely in the eye. "I wrote another note to Pickett and sent it at 1:35—ten minutes after the first note: *For God's sake, come quick. Come quick or I can't support you.* I sent two written and one verbal message to that effect."

"So, Colonel, the assault began at that point?"

"Not quite, Mr. Chairman."

"Well then?"

"Some five or ten minutes after sending my last note, General Longstreet rode up all alone. I expressed impatience at Pickett's delay and said I feared the support I could give might not be all I wished and had counted upon. General Longstreet spoke at once and decidedly, 'Go and halt Pickett right where he is and replenish your ammunition.' I said, 'General, we can't do that. We nearly emptied the trains last night. Even if we had it, it would take an hour or two, and meanwhile, the enemy would recover from the pressure he is now under. Our only chance is to follow up now—to strike while the iron is hot.'

"He answered, 'I don't want to make this attack—I believe it will fail—I do not see how it can succeed. I would not make it even now, but that General Lee ordered it and expects it.' He made these statements, with slight pauses in between, while he was looking at the enemy's position through his fieldglasses. I had the feeling that he was upon the verge of stopping the charge and that, with even slight encouragement, he would do it. But that very feeling kept me from saying a word."

"So Major General Pickett launched his offensive?"

"He did, yes, Congressman."

"Did you offer whatever covering fire from the artillery you thought appropriate?"

"I kept up my fire until the cessation of both musketry and artillery around the point of Pickett's attack. Fugitives running back from there showed me that the attack had failed. Then, suddenly, I began to realize more fully than I had before what might happen if the enemy should take a notion to follow up our fugitives from the field with a strong Federal advance. Immediately, I stopped firing, for in that case, every round of ammunition would be worth its weight in gold. I sent orders to all my guns everywhere to hold their positions but not to fire a shot."

"You feared a Yankee countercharge after Pickett had been repulsed?"

"Our ammunition was so low and our diminished forces at the moment so widely dispersed along the unwisely extended line that an advance by a single fresh corps, for instance, could have cut us in two."

"Colonel, I clearly sense your opposition to Pickett's Charge. You said as much directly to General Longstreet in one of your dispatches to him."

"I think it a reasonable estimate to say that 60 percent of our chances for a great victory were lost by our continuing the aggressive."

"Thank you, Colonel. It seems equally clear to me that you vigorously disapprove of General Lee's conduct on the field at Gettysburg. Is that a fair statement?"

A brief murmur swept the gallery.

"Sir," the witness said firmly, "audacity's name was Lee!"

Senator Wigfall touched Henry Foote's sleeve to cut him off so the Texan could continue the questioning.

"I do not quite understand, Colonel. On the one hand, you strenuously object to the conduct of the Gettysburg campaign—then and now—yet, you seem to have no grievance with General Lee. How can that be, Sir?"

"Senator," Porter Alexander said with an outburst of emotion, "there can never have been an army with more supreme confidence in its commander than that army had in General Lee! We looked forward to victory under him as confidently as to successive sunrises."

"But you sent Pickett and Pettigrew into a slaughter which both you and Longstreet clearly opposed at the time. I still do not quite understand you this morning."

Chairman Wigfall and Porter Alexander looked into each other's eyes for a long moment.

"Like the rest of the army," the witness said very slowly with a pause between each word, "I believed that it would all come out right because General Lee had planned it."

"Colonel, we thank you for your cooperation this morning. Secretary Benjamin, have you any cross examination of this witness?"

"No questions, Senator."

"Then you are excused, Colonel."

Edward Porter Alexander rose stiffly. He nodded to the committee and turned to face Robert Lee.

When General Lee nodded with a weak smile, the colonel blinked wet eyes and marched out of the silent chamber.

"Ladies and gentlemen, we shall take a one hour recess and resume at one o'clock with General Longstreet."

The gallery rose until the committee had left the chamber.

After the invited observers had filed out quietly, Judah Benjamin whispered to his client. When Robert Lee shook his head, Secretary Benjamin left the chamber.

Only General Lee remained behind. With head bowed, he looked at his hard hands folded upon the table. In the deserted hall, the two fireplaces crackled and echoed upon the chilly stone walls.

★　　★　　★

Lieutenant General James Longstreet entered the chamber alone. The gallery guests still mingled quietly in the chilly hall. General Lee stood up when he heard Longstreet step behind him.

"General Longstreet."

Lee gestured for Longstreet to take Judah Benjamin's chair at the witness table. The officers sat side by side.

"You look tired," Longstreet said with strained cheer.

"I have been talking for a week to these people," Robert Lee sighed. "I cannot see how this will benefit our army or our country's cause. Had the President accepted my resignation and replaced me with an abler man, at least that would count for something. Maybe I should go quietly to the west, after all."

"Come, General," Longstreet said gently with his right hand resting lightly upon his chief's left forearm. "No one can replace you. I am confident that your testimony here will alert the entire Congress to the critical necessities of our forces. I surely hope so." Longstreet looked away from Robert Lee's brooding eyes. "The Federals will be vigorous in the spring campaign in four months. It is their election year and President Lincoln must press the war in the east before November. Our Congress must be moved by your statements here this week to provision us for spring. The alternative, I dare say, is disaster."

Robert Lee did not face his senior corps commander. Instead, the weary soldier looked up at the empty seats on the raised platform. He spoke to the empty chair of Louis Wigfall.

"I have been up to see the Congress and they do not seem to be able to do anything except to eat peanuts and chew tobacco, while my army is starving!" Robert Lee faced his Old Warhorse of campaigns past. "I told them the condition the men were in and that something must be done at once. But I can't get them to do anything, or they are unable to do anything."

"Well, General," Longstreet said softly, "I have full faith in your ability to move them before we leave here."

"I can only hope that I shall be permitted to return to the field after this inquiry. I fear that this committee has grave doubts about my ability. Colonel Alexander was rather negative this morning. I am advised that I should not discuss his testimony with you before you address the committee. And I know, General, that you have not always shared my tactical judgments." Robert Lee studied Longstreet's intense eyes.

"General Lee, I have not always concurred completely with your tactics on the offensive. You know that. But one thing remains a fact absolute." Longstreet looked his chief squarely in the eye. "Our affections for you are stronger, if it is possible for them to be stronger, than our admiration for you." General Longstreet smiled warmly. "I beg you to believe that, General."

Robert Lee smiled weakly just as the doorway opened and the noisy gallery pushed into the chamber to stake out good seats for Longstreet's testimony.

"What shall I tell these people," James Longstreet said softly.

"The truth," General Lee said firmly as the gallery rose until the committee members filed in, climbed the platform, and took their seats. Longstreet yielded his chair to the rotund Secretary Benjamin who greeted him cordially.

"Ladies and Gentlemen," Louis Wigfall said over the buzzing chatter. "If you will come to order, the clerk will please swear in General Longstreet."

The heavy-set Georgian was sworn before he took the chair formerly occupied by Porter Alexander.

"General Longstreet, you know very well that the purpose of this inquiry is investigation of the Gettysburg affair. From testimony already heard here, some of us believe that you may be accountable for slowness to deploy your I Corps on the second day and for your apparently reluctant cooperation on the third day. As co-chairman of this committee, I invite you to speak in your own defense—if you wish—before we continue further."

Longstreet sat ramrod straight. His healthy and robust race contrasted to the careworn face of General Lee at the table close behind him. He spoke in a clear voice in the gallery's anxious silence.

"As we failed, I must take my share of the responsibility," Longstreet responded firmly. "In fact, I would prefer that all the blame should rest upon me. As General Lee is our commander, he should have the support and influence we can give him. If the blame, if there is any, can be shifted from him to me, I shall help him and our cause by taking it. I desire, therefore, that all the responsibility that can be put upon me shall go there and shall remain there."

The gallery murmured briefly.

"Yes, yes, General Longstreet. Your loyalty is commendable. But is it not a fact, Sir, that you personally told the President and the Secretary of War prior to the Pennsylvania raid that you opposed overtly offensive actions?"

"I did confer with the President and Secretary Seddon on May 6th, I believe of this year."

"And did you not advocate a more defensive strategy than the aggressive one adopted by General Lee in Pennsylvania five months ago?"

"I suggested that after piercing Pennsylvania and menacing Washington, we should choose a strong position and force the Federals to attack us, observing that the popular clamor throughout the North would speedily force the Federal general to attempt to drive us out. I recalled the battle of Fredericksburg as an instance of a defensive battle when, with a few thousand men, we hurled the whole Federal army back, crippling and demoralizing it with a trifling loss to our own troops."

Longstreet paused as if suddenly conscious of Lee's eyes upon his back. "I also endorsed sending General Joe Johnston into Tennessee to attack the Federals there to relieve the pressure on Vicksburg, Mississippi. If he could then have advanced into Ohio, I felt confident that Mr. Lincoln would have to send General Grant northward from Mississippi."

"Did General Lee know of your opposition to aggressive tactics on the Pennsylvania raid?"

"Certainly, Senator. Although General Lee was not in Richmond with me when I expressed my views, he was well aware of my judgment."

"And your candor, indeed opposition, did not compromise your professional relationship with General Lee in the field?"

"Not hardly, Mr. Chairman," Longstreet replied carefully. "General Lee chose the plan adopted, and he is the person appointed to choose and to order. I consider it a part of my duty to express my views to the commanding general. If he approves and adopts them, it is well. If he does not, it is my duty to adopt his views and to execute his orders as faithfully as if they were my own."

"Indeed, General. When did you ultimately learn that General Lee had chosen the offensive policy at Gettysburg?"

"I suppose it would have been toward evening on the first day, July 1st, Senator."

"Would you kindly be more specific." The chairman was growing impatient with the witness's gentility as he had done earlier with Porter Alexander.

General Longstreet spoke slowly and weighed his words with care.

"When I overtook General Lee at five o'clock that afternoon, he said, to my surprise, that he thought of attacking General Meade upon the heights the next day. I suggested that this course seemed at variance with the plan of the campaign that had been agreed upon before leaving Fredericksburg. He said, 'If the enemy is there tomorrow, we must attack him.' I replied, 'If he is there, it will be because he is anxious that we should attack him'—a good reason in my judgment for not doing so. I urged that we should move around by our right to the left of Meade and put our army between him and

Washington, threatening his left and rear, and thus forcing him to attack us in such position as we might select.

"I called his attention to the fact that the country was admirably adapted for a defensive battle and that the heights of Gettysburg were in themselves of no more importance to us than the ground we then occupied. The mere possession of the ground was not worth a hundred men to us, that Meade's army, not its position, was our objective."

"But, General Longstreet, the Federals were attacked the next day—and the day after that by Pickett and Pettigrew—in spite of your counsel."

"The record would speak for itself, Senator."

Robert Hunter continued with the witness.

"Perhaps, General. But that same record may suggest that General Lee anticipated your July 2nd assault by I Corps to begin at sunrise. Was that the case, Sir?"

The witness leaned forward. "General Lee never in his life gave me orders to open an attack at a specific hour. He was perfectly satisfied that when I had my troops in position and was ordered to attack, no time was ever lost."

"Be that as it may," Senator Wigfall said coldly, "your assault was delivered on July 2nd—perhaps against your better judgment, it would seem."

"At half-past three o'clock, the order was given General Hood to advance upon the enemy, and, hurrying to the head of McLaws' division, I moved with his line. Then was fairly commenced what I do not hesitate to pronounce the best three hours' fighting ever done by any troops on any battlefield.

"Directly in front of us, occupying the Peach Orchard, on a piece of elevated ground that General Lee desired me to take and hold for his artillery, was the Third Corps of the Federals commanded by General Sickles. The enemy was tenacious. The fighting had become tremendous."

"And you did carry the Peach Orchard where Colonel Alexander positioned his artillery the next day."

"Yes, Senator. But our progress was less than had been hoped." General Longstreet hesitated and measured his words. "While Meade's lines were growing, my men were dropping. We had no others to call to their aid and the weight against us was too heavy to carry." Longstreet took a deep breath. "No other part of the army had engaged. It was my 17,000 against the Army of the Potomac!"

"Very well, General. And after the long engagement of July 2nd came the so-called Pickett's Charge on July 3rd. Major General Pickett's heroic division was from your I Corps, of course. I presume that you remember July 3rd with equal passion."

Longstreet folded his hands. He spoke into his lap.

"That day at Gettysburg was one of the saddest of my life."

"Your sentiments on the events of July 3rd are shared by many in the Congress, General. Tell us, Sir, did General Lee formalize his orders for Pickett's Charge by written memoranda?"

"Not really, Mr. Chairman," Longstreet said thoughtfully. "He did not give or send me orders for the morning of the third day. In the absence of orders, I had scouting parties out during the night in search of a way by which we might strike the enemy's left and push it down towards his center. I found a way that gave some promise of results and was about to move the command when General Lee rode over after sunrise and gave his orders."

"General Longstreet, did you advise General Lee of your scouting reports and, if you did, what transpired between you and your superior officer on the morning before Pickett's Charge?"

"I said to General Lee, 'General, I have had my scouts out all night and I find that you still have an excellent opportunity to move around to the right of Meade's army and maneuver him into attacking us.' He replied, pointing with his fist at Cemetery Hill, 'The enemy is there and I am going to strike him.' I said, 'General, I have been a soldier all my life, I have been with soldiers engaged in fights by couples, by squads, companies, regiments, divisions, and armies. And I should know as well as anyone what soldiers can do. It is my opinion that no 15,000 men ever arrayed for battle can take that position.' I pointed to Cemetery Hill. General Lee, in reply to this, ordered me to prepare Pickett's division for the attack."

Chairman Wigfall nodded and spoke over Longstreet's head toward the gallery.

"Whereupon the assault by the divisions of Pickett and Pettigrew was subsequently launched. We can tell you, General Longstreet, that Colonel Alexander has shared with us your exchange of notes with him prior to Pickett's attack. Do you agree with Alexander that you placed upon his young shoulders the burden of sending Pickett forward after Alexander's artillery barrage?"

"Mr. Chairman," Longstreet sighed deeply, "never was I so depressed as upon that day. I felt that my men were to be sacrificed and that I should have to order them to make a hopeless charge. I had instructed Colonel Alexander, being unwilling to trust myself with the entire responsibility, to carefully observe the effect of the fire upon the enemy, and when it began to tell, to notify Pickett to begin the assault."

"General, as corps commander, it would seem that you clearly shirked your command responsibilities in that situation. Do you deny, Sir, that during the exchange of notes with Colonel Alexander you did not expressly order General Pickett to launch his assault? I believe this occurred after the note from Alexander to Pickett which began 'If you are coming at all....' What are your recollections?"

"Senator," Longstreet said with emotion in his deep voice, "after I had read the note, Pickett said to me, 'General, shall I advance?' My feelings had so overcome me that I would not speak for fear of betraying my want of confidence to him. I bowed affirmation and turned to mount my horse. Pickett immediately said, 'I shall lead my division forward, Sir.' I spurred my horse to the wood where Alexander was stationed with artillery. When I reached him, he told me that his ammunition was so low that he could not properly support the charge. I at once ordered him to stop Pickett until the ammunition had been replenished. He informed me that he had no ammunition with which to replenish.

"I then saw that there was no help for it, and that Pickett must advance under orders. He swept past our artillery in splendid style. They pressed on until half-way up the slope when the crest of the hill was lit with a solid sheet of flame. When the smoke cleared away, Pickett's division was gone." Longstreet sighed so loudly that he could be heard to the back row of the motionless gallery. "Mortal men could not have stood that fire. In half an hour, the contested field was cleared and the battle of Gettysburg was over."

Silence filled the chamber for one long breath. Then Congressman Foote spoke gravely.

"General Longstreet, forgive a direct question which may sound impolitic at times such as these. But I require of you an assessment of the generalship of General Lee based upon your two years of close observation of him in the field."

The gallery rustled as many guests leaned forward.

General Longstreet chuckled which clearly surprised the Nashville politician.

"Mr. Foote," the large soldier smiled, "you may know that I lost three precious children during the recent outbreak of disease in this city a little more than a year ago. I shall tell you my assessment of Robert Lee—man, soldier, and gentleman: when my wife and I were blessed with another son after our children died, I named my son Robert Lee Longstreet."

A soft murmur swept the gallery. The chairman did not bother to silence the whispers and nods.

"Thank you, General. You are excused."

Longstreet rose and turned his back on the committee. He nodded to his commanding general and left the stuffy chamber late in the Saturday afternoon.

"Ladies and gentlemen," Chairman Wigfall said with fatigue, "I believe that we can adjourn for the day at this point. It is past 4 o'clock. If my learned colleagues have no further comments, I am confident that we have heard during the last six days sufficient testimony to render a judgment on General Lee's fitness for command. We shall reconvene here Monday morning at 9 o'clock."

The Texan's sudden termination of the hearings caught the spectators by surprise. The gallery still sat motionless when Senator Wigfall led his committeemen out of the chamber. One by one, the gallery rose and followed into the dimly lighted corridor of the capitol.

Robert Lee left the chamber close to Judah Benjamin's side. The two men found a secluded corner. Sentries kept the milling crowd from General Lee's conference with the Secretary of State.

"That's it, Mr. Secretary?"

"Apparently, General."

"What next?"

"A verdict by Monday—for want of a better word."

"Well, I suppose we shall see by the day after tomorrow if I shall be returning to my army." General Lee fumbled with his slouch hat.

"I would not worry, General," the round lawyer smiled. "You did better than expected, frankly."

"Thank you for your confidence."

"Yes, General. I shall call on you tomorrow at home."

General Lee shook hands with Judah Benjamin. The advocate left Lee standing alone.

"Traveller is saddled and waiting, General," Jeb Stuart said from the hallway shadows.

"Thank you, Jeb."

"May I escort you outside?"

"Thank you, but I can find my way alone."

Jeb Stuart saluted and walked down the corridor. He left General Lee behind where he waited for the throng to subside. Then Lee walked down the hallway of cold stone. He fetched his blue greatcoat.

Near the capitol's back door, General Lee found Brigadier General Henry Wise. Two weeks past his 57th birthday, Wise had been governor of Virginia up to the year before the war. John Brown had been hanged during the last days of his term. The former governor was one of the officers commissioned by political clout—the kind Robert Lee loathed.

"General Lee," Henry Wise said diffidently.

"Governor," Robert Lee nodded courteously.

"Did it go well, General?" the politician asked gently.

"I don't know, Governor. Either way, I hardly think the army will want to sacrifice for a commanding officer who could be hauled before a Senate board of inquiry, if my men ever found out about this." Robert Lee looked down at the floor. "How could they fight for this country under my command again?"

Henry Wise regarded General Lee carefully. The brigadier general gently laid his hand upon Robert Lee's arm. A warm smile crossed the face of the lawyer-politician. The former governor had been touched by this war among brothers. His own son had died in battle in February 1862 and his brother-in-law was a Yankee major general— George Gordon Meade.

"General," Henry Wise said softly in the empty corridor, "you *are* the country to these men. They fought for *you*."

Chapter Nineteen

Sunday, December 20, 1863

A soldier's heart, you know, is divided between
love and glory.
　　　　　Robert E. Lee

*D*aybreak, Sunday, was still two hours away. But General Lee could not sleep. So in darkness he had dressed. He stood in his greatcoat on the porch. The two freezing sentries, teenagers far from home, paced back and forth on the street.

Robert Lee's breath came in long clouds of steam. Overhead, the Virginia stars burned brightly with little twinkle in the brittle air. When a lone horseman rode slowly toward the sentries, General Lee watched the rider approach through the steam as if in a dream. Each of the guards snapped to attention and raised his massive musket to the present arms, field salute. They recognized the horse Kentucky before they could make out the face of his master.

Kentucky whinnied when a guard took his reins at the curb. President Jefferson Davis landed hard when he climbed down to the frozen street. No escort had accompanied him during one of his all-night rides through the streets of sleeping Richmond. The chronic insomniac was a well known sight to the few citizens who worked all night: the slaves at the Tredegar Iron Works and the military surgeons with their dripping bonesaws who went outside of their butcher shops for a midnight smoke or chew.

There was no danger that Jefferson Davis would get lost during his midnight rides: his McClellan military saddle had a magnetic compass built into the pommel.

So severe was the sickly President's insomnia that his physicians forced him to sniff chloroform anesthesia to induce sleep. For the manic restlessness and intense pain of his facial spasms, they had convinced First Lady Varina Davis to administer twice daily to her reluctant husband a nauseating potion of castor oil and quinine with two grains of opium.

General Lee extended his hand to the President who climbed the steps to the porch. The President nodded and the two men spoke softly so as not to waken the sleeping Lee household.

"How are you feeling, General?"

"My rheumatism I hope is better," the soldier nodded. "But I have had today, and indeed always have, much pain." Robert Lee rubbed his left chest.

Jefferson Davis had left First Lady Varina at home. Mornings were hard for her. She was three months pregnant with the First Family's daughter who would be named for her mother. General Lee missed the company of 5-year-old Joseph, the President's wee shadow in the capitol.

"The Military Affairs Committee has met all night, General," President Davis said softly on billows of steam.

"All night, Mr. President?" Robert Lee faced the tall politician from Mississippi.

"They're with you, General, narrowly I'm afraid. All but two. They voted half an hour ago." Jefferson Davis forced his hollow cheeks to smile in the chill darkness.

Robert Lee studied his chief. The tall President had worked hard to earn his reputation for being intolerant of those he thought to be fools. His scorn could destroy a former friendship forever. Sam Houston, the Texan, had once bristled that "One drop of Jeff Davis' blood would freeze a frog." But Davis could also be warm and kind to his friends—so long as they wore their politics properly.

"Well," the weary general nodded in dawn's first, cold light. "Foote and Wigfall voted against me, I presume? What about Senators Reade and Hunter?"

"Wigfall and Foote are against us, General. Till their last breaths," the President said sourly. "Hunter thinks that I'm a dictator." Davis smiled. "But he and Reade both voted for the country."

The two men stood side-by-side. Robert Lee did not glance over his shoulder when he spoke softly toward the sentries.

"Will I be transferred over to Tennessee?"

"The army will remain yours, so long as you want it and so long as I am President."

"Thank you, Excellency," Robert Lee said with a dry throat. In much of his battlefield correspondence with the Rebel President, Lee addressed Davis as if he were King of the South. "Thank you. What about General Johnston?"

"I had to give Wigfall and Foote their way: Johnston will go west. But anyone is preferred to Beauregard."

Lee shifted his weight and looked toward the dark and frozen earth.

"I feel as if I have made things difficult for you, Excellency."

"Nonsense, General. If at all possible, I want my general officers where they want to be. Except for Beauregard, of course, who would rather take a vacation from harm's way." Davis did not smile.

"All the same, Mr. President, I am truly grateful."

The men stood in silence for a long time.

"Tell me, General, what do you envision for our cause?"

General Lee looked at the brittle sky.

"I fear it may be necessary to abandon all our cities and preparations should be made for that contingency."

"I see. If only I could do more with this Congress and the state governors. The governors think that each state is a separate country. You know how hard it is to get the states to devote their resources to the national good, instead of their own defenses." The President governed a feudal fiefdom in which each of the Confederacy's 11 states was led by a warlord governor who resisted sending local troops to Virginia's defense. The internal conflicts were wearing down the sickly President.

"We have now but one thing to do," Lee said impatiently, "to establish our independence. We have no time for anything else."

"Yes. Might we discuss field matters for a moment? The Joint Committee shared with me their thoughts on your field tactics. If I may, they raised a question regarding your hesitation to destroy civilian property which could be used against us if it fell into enemy hands. The committee mentioned the railroads, specifically those around Fredericksburg during the December '62 contest there."

"The eventuality of our own domestic resources being turned against us never leaves my mind, Mr. President. You know that." Robert Lee continued to speak softly toward the dawn which spread slowly across a clear sky. "I should have commenced breaking up the Orange and Alexandria Railroad from Rappahannock to Gordonsville, as well as that from Fredericksburg to Hanover Junction—but for my reluctance to perpetuate what might prove an unnecessary injury to the community." The general wrapped himself more tightly inside his greatcoat and he sighed deeply. "I instructed the late General Jackson to that effect two years ago. It seems but yesterday."

"I know that remains a painful memory, General. All of us could use Jackson now. But if I might continue, the committee also urged you to reflect upon your opposition to the use of rangers in the field. Our dwindling man-power reserve seems to dictate resort to the use of concealed and rapid-striking forces of small groups of men skilled in partisan warfare. I see little alternative if we cannot better fill the uniformed ranks for the spring campaign in two or three months."

General Lee looked squarely into his President's wasted face. The general's protests against the use of bushwackers was an old soldier's article of faith. Robert Lee still believed that gentlemen can make war. He had admired General McClellan for that.

"Experience has convinced me," General Lee said firmly, "that it is almost impossible, under the best officers even, to have discipline in these bands of Partisan Rangers, or to prevent them from becoming an injury instead of a benefit to the service. And even where this is accomplished, the system gives license to many deserters and marauders who assume to belong to these authorized companies and commit depredations on friend and foe alike." General Lee paused, thought, and continued with passion in his weary voice. "Another great objection to them is the bad effect upon the discipline of the army from the constant desire of the men to leave their commands and enjoy the great license allowed in these bands."

Robert Lee looked away when he continued softly.

"You could, of course, order me to detach such a force. I should then do so immediately, Mr. President."

"Not yet."

General Lee nodded.

"At least, General, on behalf of the committee, and myself, I must respectfully suggest that you give more attention to forcing the men of your illustrious army to stand by their arms at all costs as the need arises. Likewise, the committee expressed its concern about your tendency not to be more aggressive in reprimanding your officers. I hope you can forgive this intrusion into your command."

Robert Lee turned toward his commander-in-chief. He did not suffer lightly the meddling of weaker men into the hearts of his army shivering and starving in winter quarters beside the frozen Rapidan River. The general admired President Davis; it was the Confederate Congress whom General Lee resented.

"These men are not an army, they are citizens defending their country!" The general's voice rose with frustration. "I cannot do things that I could do with a trained army. The soldiers know their duties better than the general officers do, and they have fought magnificently." He paused to control his anger. "When a man makes a mistake, I call him to my tent, talk to him, and use the authority of my position to make him do the right thing next time."

"I understand, General. As an old soldier myself, you know that you and your gallant army have my fullest support. You are all that stand between Richmond and our destruction. But at least on the matter of feeding your hungry troops, surely you can accept the committee's recommendation that forage must be seized in the field from private property. The national Treasury will pay for such impressments of the harvest in the spring as we can. But the whole country can and must do more to provide for our armies. You have said as much on many occasions to me and Secretary of War Seddon."

The general sighed in a cloud of steam.

"Wholesale impressments will give us present relief," the general frowned, "but I fear it will injure our future supplies. It will cause concealment and waste, and deter many farmers from exerting all their efforts in producing full and proper crops. Already I hear of land in Virginia lying idle from this cause. But I think the present law and orders on the subject should be so modified as to authorize the government to impress when necessary a certain proportion of everything produced in the country."

"Excellent, General! At least I can assure the Congress of your support on this vital issue." President Davis' deathlike pallor brightened.

"Most reluctantly, Mr. President. Most reluctantly."

"If only shoes for the men and horses could be likewise impressed, General. I labor night and day to procure shoes for half a dozen armies from the Atlantic to California. And to little avail." President Davis' gaunt cheeks were gray again and his dead eye twitched dully.

"Mr. President, I have already addressed that question. I had requested shoe samples from the commissary department three days ago. The samples arrived late last night. Fortunately for my tired ladies in the house, I was still awake with a pile of Colonel Taylor's latest field returns."

The two men stood in half daylight which glistened upon the frosted windows of Leigh Street.

General Lee pulled his greatcoat tighter about his throat.

"The chief quartermaster of the army brought me a sample of the shoes. One pair was of Richmond manufacture and another from

Columbus, Georgia. They were intended to be fair samples of each lot and were selected with that view." Robert Lee looked hard at his chief. "In the Richmond shoe, the face of the leather was turned in. That is, the side of the skin next to the animal was turned out, which is contrary to the practice of the best makers and contrary to the arrangement of nature." The soldier pounded one fist into his other, open palm. "The leather of the Columbus shoe was not half tanned and the shoe was badly made. The soles of both were slight and would not stand a week's march in mud and water. The army is in great distress for shoes and cloths. The requisitions sent in are unanswered."

"General, I am truly sorry. You know that I do the best for our troops that I can. What would you have me tell the Congress?" The President looked pained to his bones.

"Excellency, you may tell your Congress," General Lee said coldly, "you must not be surprised if calamity befalls us!"

Jefferson Davis stiffened and stood a head taller than his Virginia soldier and friend.

"At least, General, you will fight on, even barefoot."

Robert Lee looked down toward the pacing sentries. The soldier spoke with passion.

"As long as there is one horse that can carry his rider and one arm that can wield a sword, I prefer annihilation to submission!"

"Tell me, General Lee, what can I do for you? Our country owes you so much."

General Lee faced his President and focused upon the one good eye of Jefferson Davis.

"I want for nothing but independence and peace for our distracted country."

The President offered his hand to his friend who accepted the gesture warmly.

"Will you stay in Richmond for Christmas, General?" the President adjusted his riding gloves.

"I think not, Mr. President. I have been away from the army too

425

long already. But I trust that I shall see you at St. Paul's this morning?"

"You will, General."

With a final hand shake, Jefferson Davis walked with long strides to his mount held by the sentry. Kentucky pawed the hard ground as his tall master approached. The two youthful guards saluted their President who mounted and rode slowly away.

"Is he out there, Father?" a girl's sleepy voice called from the doorway.

Robert Lee turned to face Mildred who was dressed and wrapped in a shawl.

"The President just left, Life."

"No, Papa. I mean Custis Morgan. I still cannot find him anywhere. He was gone again when I woke up."

"Sorry, Life. Your furry Custis has not favored me with a visit. Perhaps he has gone ahead to church?" The sadly dark eyes twinkled in the morning sunshine.

"Oh, Papa! Come in before you catch pneumonia."

General Lee entered the front hallway.

"Is the Mim down?" The general hung his greatcoat on a wall peg.

"Mother is in the parlor."

The father kissed his youngest daughter as Mary Custis and Agnes led Markie Williams down the stairs.

"Good morning, Daughter," the general smiled as he kissed Mary Custis, "and to you Wig," as he leaned toward Agnes.

"Morning, Cousin Robert," Martha Williams smiled warmly.

"Dear Markie." He touched the woman's face with his hard hand.

General Lee walked ahead of the Lee women into the parlor where Mother Lee waited patiently in her heavy rolling chair. Her husband took the handles on the back. He always insisted upon being the one to push his crippled wife to the table when he was home from the bloody fields of war.

"Custis Morgan is still among the missing," General Lee said softly as he bent over Mother Lee's ear. "I think the farther he gets from you the better you will be."

"Oh, Papa!" a happy voice called at his back.

"Did I hear voices so early?" Mother Lee asked over her shoulder as the Lees and Markie entered the dining room which smelled delicious from the wood in the kitchen stove and the breakfast fare of hot cornbread and small chunks of fatty bacon.

"Yes, Molly," the general said softly as he pushed toward her place at the head of the table. "President Davis rode over quite early. I had stepped out for some air, or he would not have stopped at all. Sometimes he rides alone all night, you know."

"Well, Robert?" Mother Lee asked impatiently.

"Did he bring news, Papa?" Agnes demanded.

"He did, Wig."

Savoring the sudden suspense, General Lee took his place at the end of the table opposite his wife. There was a vague twinkle in the soldier's black eyes.

"Robert, please!" Mother Lee protested.

"The Military Affairs Committee seems to have spent a long night at the capitol. The indictment against me has been..."—he studied the intense, feminine faces—"dismissed. On all counts."

"Papa!" Mildred cried. She jumped from her chair to hug her father. Agnes and Mary Custis waited their turn. Markie Williams lifted her napkin from the table to wipe her filling eyes.

Only Mother Lee remained perfectly calm among the younger, breathless women who embraced her husband. Mary Lee had never doubted.

"The file is closed," Robert Lee said softly. "The President was kind enough to bring the word himself."

"What about the army?" Agnes asked. Everyone knew that there was only one for Robert Lee.

"I am authorized to return to the Rapidan," the general said gravely. "To my brave boys." He blinked toward the windows full of chilly, morning sunshine. He thought of shivering brigades dressed in rags and living in bark huts. "Our old friend Joe Johnston has won the appointment to the west. Let us now enjoy this food which God

427

has given us and be thankful for His many blessings upon us all. Then I must go to church."

General Lee looked at his chairbound wife.

"I shall be fine, Robert. The girls can stay with me. You go on."

"Thank you, Molly."

★　　★　　★

When General Lee entered St. Paul's Episcopal Church, this Sunday morning, December 20th, President Davis was already in the Presidential Pew, number 63.

Throughout the morning service in the hungry capital city, eyes darted toward Robert Lee. Rumors of a secret court martial had swept the town, but there had been no published confirmation of his week-long ordeal. His tranquil demeanor betrayed no clue of his silent anguish.

After the service ended, the President and Varina Davis left the church first.

When General Lee rose to leave, the entire congregation stood as if at attention. No one moved until Robert Lee had walked up the long aisle. When he realized that the assembly was giving him a silent, standing salute, he acknowledged the quiet ovation with nods of his wind burned face as he walked toward daylight.

Outside St. Paul's at the corner of 9th and Grace Streets, Richmonders stood in threadbare coats. Parents pointed out to children the famous faces of their President, his Cabinet, and the officers in town for the secret conferences of the preceding week. Young girls swooned at the plumed hat and cape of Jeb Stuart, even with his wife, Flora, at his side. Merchants nodded confidently at Robert Lee and his two corps commanders, the towering James Longstreet and the frail green-eyed A.P. Hill. Directly across 9th Street stood the capitol building of the Confederate States of America.

Stuart stepped away from Flora to join General Lee and Generals Longstreet and Hill. The four men softly spoke of the midnight session of the Joint Military Affairs Committee. Lee was not surprised that his subordinates already knew of the committee's decision. Talk touched briefly on when the officers would leave the comforts of Richmond to return to winter camp. Longstreet's I Corps still camped in Tennessee.

When the generals parted with handshakes all around, the decision was made on whether to remain in Richmond with friends and family for the next five days and Christmas 1863.

Robert Lee rode home on Traveller. His nephew, General Fitzhugh Lee, rode at his side. The two Generals Lee were greeted happily by the Lee women.

The Lee daughters shared their warm embraces with their father and their cousin Chuddy. Only they could call Fitz that childhood pet name.

At noon, the Lee clan gathered around the table with Mother Lee at one end and her husband at the other.

The happy girls and Martha Williams planned their first family Christmas in four years. Only their prisoner brother, Rooney, would be missing.

When the general softly announced that he would be leaving for his army before dark, his daughters looked stricken. But Mother Lee only smiled. Without having discussed the matter with her husband, she had known all along where he would spend Christmas: with his other family of 35,000 sons beside the frozen river.

The general's words stifled the good cheer of the Lees' Sunday table. The grief of Rooney's empty chair was now doubled when eyes turned to the old soldier, and again when the Lee women looked upon jovial Fitz Lee who would soon return to Jeb Stuart's command.

Unable to bear the sudden silence any further, Robert Lee looked each woman in the eyes and then at his 31-year-old son Custis. The general spoke firmly to all, but he looked only at his wife. "We must suffer patiently to the end when all things will be made right."

"Yes, Robert," Mother Lee said softly. She alone knew that her husband was not speaking of the end of the bitter war.

General Lee spent Sunday afternoon packing his sparse equipment for the train ride back up the line toward Gordonsville and his winter quarters beside the Rapidan. On the north side of the ice, General George Meade waited for him, too.

One by one they came throughout the chilly afternoon on the last Sunday before Christmas. General Longstreet came first on his way back from the hard sad earth of the cemetery and his dead children. He graciously paid his respects to Mother Lee and the girls. Longstreet would not accompany Lee, Stuart and Hill back to camp. Instead, he would return to I Corps camped near Knoxville, Tennessee.

James Longstreet would do business with his cousin Ulysses S. Grant with the coming of spring to Virginia during the first week of May 1864. Longstreet would stop a bullet with his throat.

Jeb Stuart came by to kiss Mother Lee, make little Mildred blush, and embrace Mary Custis—Major General Stuart's "Marielle" of West Point, only nine years and a lifetime ago. Then Jeb excused himself to spend the Sunday afternoon with his wife. He would accompany General Lee back to the cavalry's winter camp, called the Wigwam by Stuart, at Orange Court House, Virginia.

Young Jeb would return to Richmond to Dr. Charles Brewer's house in five months. He would be carried there to die from a bullet in his belly.

A.P. Hill and his wife Dolly rode over in his carriage. Their tiny children waited behind at the Powhatan with their black nanny. A.P. Hill would put on one of Dolly's handmade, red "battle shirts" to ride the train back to camp at General Lee's side.

Hill was feeble and painfully thin from his recurring venereal disease which had haunted him since West Point. General Hill was a shadow of the former commander who led his Light Division onto the field to save General Lee from annihilation beside Antietam Creek 14 months ago. But Hill's graciousness went to the bone, and he could not leave Richmond without a courtesy call to Mother Lee. Little Powell would lead III Corps until a bullet plowed through his heart seven days before the ragged survivors stacked arms forever.

By 2 o'clock Sunday afternoon, the well wishers had all returned to their Richmond quarters to prepare for their sudden departure back to cold, to starvation, and to death. Fitz Lee waited outside for his uncle. Traveller pawed the cold ground and waited for his master.

Inside 210 East Leigh Street, Robert Lee climbed into his heavy greatcoat and stood awkwardly in the company of weeping women.

Lee buckled on his sash and saber. The steel sword was inscribed on one side "General Robert E. Lee, from a Marylander, 1863." The other side of the shining blade was engraved, "*Aide toi et Dieu t'aidera* (Help yourself, and God will help you)."

Martha Williams stood beside the open doorway.

"Do write sometimes to me," the soldier said to Martha. "It will be a relief to my eyes and a comfort to my heart to discover your hand-writing in the voluminous mail."

Tears streamed down the beautiful and fragile face of 22-year-old Agnes Lee. Her gentle writers' heart had already been broken by the war. Her father held her tightly and the stiff collar of his overcoat scratched her wet face.

"Good-bye, my precious daughter," the general whispered hoarsely. "Remember me in your sweet prayers."

Agnes could only choke back her sobs.

Stepping to 17-year-old Mildred, the father smiled warmly. She had come home only for Christmas from St. Mary's Academy in Raleigh. But the strong-willed teenager had decided to remain in Richmond with her sickly mother and her sisters for the rest of the winter.

"My dear Precious Life." He could say no more as he wiped a tear from his eyes.

"Dear Daughter," he said embracing Mary Custis. "Take care of your mother. God bless you."

"And you, Papa,"

When Robert Lee stood above his chairbound wife, his daughters stepped back and Martha Williams stepped outside onto the front porch.

Robert Lee knelt down and laid his hard hands in the old lady's lap.

"Never forget me or our suffering country," he said with a painful lump in this throat. "God be with you, dearest Molly."

"God go with you, Husband," Mary Lee said into his wet face.

Robert Lee rose with the sound of creaking knees and jingling spurs. He pushed his floppy hat over his white hair until the hat touched his ears. With two long strides, he stood outside in the sunshine. The sad Lee women stayed behind as other wives and children were doing throughout Richmond.

On the narrow porch, Robert Lee coughed and squared his broad shoulders.

Martha Williams walked to his side. He turned his back to the street. He spoke softly to his cousin without removing his hat.

"You know, Markie, how painful it will be to part from you."

"Yes, Cousin Robert," Martha whispered. She could say no more as tears rolled down her cold face.

The weary soldier adjusted his gloves and he spoke into Markie's face.

"A soldier's heart, you know, is divided between love and glory."

Robert Lee turned and marched quickly toward the street. Traveller's gray ears pointed toward his general. The sentries standing beside Fitz Lee came to attention. They held their long rifles erect in front of their chests at the parade salute as their commander mounted.

The two Generals Lee rode slowly away. Behind them, the drapes in the window of the rented house were pulled back and hot breath fogged the windows. Martha Williams stood alone on the porch until her cousin was out of sight.

The two riders stopped first at the browned cemetery where Robert Lee stood quietly for a moment beside his dead grandchildren, Robert E. Lee III and the infant Annie Agnes Lee. Then he and Fitz rode over to say good-bye to their dying mother, Charlotte.

Wearied beyond the effort of his afternoon ride, General Lee arrived at the train station near the James River. Traveller and the other horses were led into the cattle car as the officers took their seats for the long ride back to the war in Virginia. General Longstreet took another train toward Tennessee.

By Monday, December 21, 1863, General Lee was back in his freezing tent beside the Rapidan.

★　　★　　★

Christmas Day 1863 was cold under a low gray sky heavy with the threat of snow.

Sixty miles southeast of Robert Lee's winter camp, Charlotte Lee finally stopped pining for her dead babies and for her prisoner husband. She died on Christmas Day. The general received the news on December 26th. Charlotte would be buried beside her dead children in Shockoe Cemetery.

To Mother Lee, the old man with the broken heart poured out his sorrow in a letter on the 27th. "Thus, dear Mary, is link by link of the strong chain broken that binds us to earth....I grieve for our lost darling as a father can only grieve for a daughter. I loved her with a father's love."

But life went on in the Army of Northern Virginia. On December 29th, Sandie Pendleton returned to the Moss Neck plantation to finally marry his beloved Kate Corbin, his "Katinka." His father, Reverend General William Pendleton, performed his son's marriage.

Until February 3, 1864, Sandie and Kate Pendleton honeymooned in hungry Richmond. Then Sandie joined the staff of General Ewell who had inherited the dead Stonewall Jackson's II Corps. Kate returned alone to Moss Neck. In nine months, Sandie Pendleton whom everyone loved would be killed in action. He would leave behind a pregnant widow.

On New Year's Day 1864, Mother Lee and the girls moved from their rented home on Leigh Street to new quarters at 707 East Franklin Street. Because the brick house had been a bachelor officers' quarters, the home would be forever known as The Mess.

Two weeks after the Lee women had moved, a homesick Robert Lee wrote Mother Lee, "I am glad you are comfortably arranged in your big house....I would rather be in a hut with my family than in a palace with others."

January 19th marked General Lee's 57th birthday. The only presents he coveted were shoes for his barefoot troops. He spent his birthday writing to Richmond pleading for shoes and for reinforcements. To the Quartermaster General he wrote, "I fear that unless great efforts are made, the return of the season of active operations will find a large number of the men barefooted." And to President Davis the same day, he wrote, "It is a matter of great moment that the recruits for this army should reach it in full time for the coming campaign, and whatever is to be done to bring them out should be done without delay."

The trail of bare footprints would lead through a sea of blood to Appomattox Courthouse.

Select Bibliography

- Adams, Richard, *Traveller*, Alfred A. Knopf, New York, 1988.
- Albright, Harry, *Gettysburg: Crisis in Command*, Hippocrene, New York, 1991.
- Alexander, Edward Porter, *Fighting for the Confederacy*, Gary W. Gallagher, Ed., University of North Carolina Press, Chapel Hill, 1989.
- Anderson, Nancy S. and Dwight Anderson, *The Generals: Ulysses S. Grant and Robert E. Lee*, Alfred A. Knopf, New York, 1988.
- Bailey, Ronald H, *The Bloodiest Day: The Battle of Antietam*, Time-Life Books, Alexandria, Virginia, 1984.
- Ballard, Michael B., *A Long Shadow: Jefferson Davis and the Final Days of the Confederacy*, University Press of Mississippi, Jackson, 1986.
- *Battles and Leaders of the Civil War*, Vol. III, Book Sales, Inc., Secaucus, NJ, 1986.
- Bean, W. G., *Stonewall's Man: Sandie Pendleton*, Broadfoot Publishing Company, Wilmington, North Carolina, 1959, 1987.
- Bowers, John, *Stonewall Jackson: Portrait of a Soldier*, William Morrow, New York, 1989.
- Busey, John W. and David G. Martin, *Regimental Strengths and Losses at Gettysburg*, Longstreet House, Hightstown, NJ, 1986.
- Catton, Bruce, *Gettysburg: The Final Fury*, Doubleday, Garden City, New York, 1974, 1990.
- Clark, Champ, *Gettysburg: The Confederate High Tide*, Time-Life Books, Alexandria, Viginia, 1985.
- Coddington, Edwin B., *The Gettysburg Campaign: A Study in Command*, Charles Scribner's, New York, 1963, 1984.
- Connelly, Thomas L., *The Marble Man: Robert E. Lee and His Image in American Society*, Louisiana State University Press, Baton Rouge, 1977.

- Coulling, Mary P., *The Lee Girls*, John F. Blair, Winston-Salem, North Carolina, 1987.
- Craven, Avery, *To Markie: The Letters of Robert E. Lee to Martha Custis Williams*, Harvard University Press, Cambridge, 1933.
- Davis, Burke, *Jeb Stuart: The Last Cavalier*, Fairfax Press, New York, 1957, 1988.
- —, *The Long Surrender*, Random House, New York, 1985.
- —, *They Called Him Stonewall: A Life of Lt. General T. J. Jackson, C.S.A.*, Fairfax Press, New York, 1954, 1988.
- Davis, William C., Ed., *Touched By Fire*, Volume I, Little, Brown, Boston, 1985.
- —, *Touched by Fire*, Volume II, Little, Brown, Boston, 1986.
- —, *Shadows of the Storm: The Image of War (1861-1865)*, Doubleday, Garden City, New York, 1981.
- —, *The Guns of '62: The Image of War (1861-1865)*, Doubleday, Garden City, New York, 1982.
- —, *The Embattled Confederacy: The Image of War (1861-1865)*, Doubleday, Garden City, New York, 1982.
- —, *Fighting for Time: The Image of War (1861-1865)*, Doubleday, Garden City, New York, 1983.
- —, *The South Besieged: The Image of War (1861-1865)*, Doubleday, Garden City, New York, 1983.
- —, *The End of an Era: The Image of War (1861-1865)*, Doubleday, Garden City, New York, 1984.
- —, *Battle at Bull Run*, Doubleday, Garden City, New York, 1977.
- —, *Jefferson Davis: The Man and His Hour*, HarperCollins, New York, 1991.
- deButts, Mary Custis Lee, *Growing Up in the 1850's: The Journal of Agnes Lee*, University of North Carolina Press, Chapel Hill, 1984.
- Douglas, Henry Kyd, *I Rode with Stonewall*, Mockingbird Books, Simons Island, Georgia, 1940, 1961, 1983.
- Dowdey, Clifford, *Death of a Nation: The Story of Lee and his Men at Gettysburg*, Alfred A. Knopf, New York, 1958 (Butternut and Blue edition, 1988).
- —, *Lee*, Bonanza, New York, 1965.
- — and Louis H. Manarin, Ed., *The Wartime Papers of Robert E. Lee*, Da Capo Press, New York, 1961, 1987.
- Drake, Samuel A., *The Battle of Gettysburg*, Broadfoot Publishing Company, Wilmington, North Carolina, 1891, 1988.

- Evans, Eli N., *Judah P. Benjamin: The Jewish Confederate*, The Free Press, New York, 1988.
- Faust, Patricia L. Ed., *Historical Times Illustrated Encyclopedia of the Civil War*, Harper and Row, New York, 1986.
- Flood, Charles B., *Lee: The Last Years*, Houghton, Mifflin, Boston, 1981.
- Foote, Shelby, *The Civil War, A Narrative*, Volume I, Random House, New York, 1958. Cited as *I Foote*.
- —, *The Civil War, A Narrative*, Volume II, Random House, New York, 1963. Cited as *II Foote*.
- —, *The Civil War, A Narrative*, Volume III, Random House, New York, 1974. Cited as *III Foote*.
- Frassanito, William A., *Antietam: The Photographic Legacy of America's Bloodiest Day*, Charles Scribner's, New York, 1978.
- —, *Gettysburg: A Journey in Time*, Charles Scribner's, New York, 1975.
- Freeman, Douglas Southall, *Lee's Lieutenants*, Volume I, Charles Scribner's, New York, 1942, 1970. Cited as *I Lieutenants*.
- —, *Lee's Lieutenants*, Volume II, Charles Scribner's, New York, 1943, 1971. Cited as *II Lieutenants*.
- —, *Lee's Lieutenants*, Volume III, Charles Scribner's, New York, 1944. Cited as *III Lieutenants*.
- —, *R. E. Lee*, Volume I, Charles Scribner's, New York, 1934, 1962. Cited as *I R. E. Lee*.
- —, *R. E. Lee*, Volume II, Charles Scribner's, New York, 1934, 1962. Cited as *II R. E. Lee*.
- —, *R. E. Lee*, Volume III, Charles Scribner's, New York, 1935, 1963. Cited as *III R. E. Lee*.
- —, *R. E. Lee*, Volume IV, Charles Scribner's, New York, 1935, 1963. Cited as *IV R. E. Lee*.
- —, *The South to Posterity*, Charles Scribner's, New York, 1939, 1951. Broadfoot Bookmark edition, Wendell, North Carolina, 1983.
- Furgurson, Ernest B., *Chancellorsville 1863: The Soul of the Brave*, Alfred A. Knopf, New York, 1992.
- Gragg, Rod, Ed., *The Illustrated Confederate Reader*, Harper and Row, New York, 1989.
- Hattaway, Herman and Archer Jones, *How the North Won*, University of Illinois Press, Chicago, 1983.
- Jones, John B., *A Rebel War Clerk's Diary (1866)*, 2 Volumes, Time-Life Books facsimile, Alexandria, Virginia, 1981. Cited as *I Jones* and *II Jones*.
- Jones, J. William, *Life and Letters of Robert Edward Lee*, Neale Publishers,

1906, reprinted Sprinkle Publishers, Harrisonburg, VA, 1986. Cited as *J. W. Jones.*

* Krick, Robert K., *Stonewall Jackson at Cedar Mountain,* University of North Carolina Press, Chapel Hill, 1990.
* Lee, Fitzhugh, *General Lee,* Fawcett Publications, Greenwich, Conntecticut, 1961. Cited as *Fitzhugh Lee.* An elegant, facsimile edition of General Lee was released in 1989 by the Broadfoot Publishing Company, Wilmington, North Carolina.
* Lee, Robert E., Jr., *Recollections and Letters of General Lee* (1904), Broadfoot Publishing Company, Wilmington, North Carolina, 1988.
* Longstreet, Helen D., *Lee and Longstreet at High Tide* (1904), Broadfoot Publishing Company, Wilmington, North Carolina, 1989.
* Luvaas, Jay and Harold W. Nelson, *The U. S. Army War College Guide to the Battle of Antietam,* South Mountain Press, Carlisle, Pennsylvania, 1987.
* —, *The U. S. Army War College Guide to the Battles of Chancellorsville and Fredericksburg,* South Mountain Press, Carlisle, Pennsylvania, 1988.
* —, *The U. S. Army War College Guide to the Battle of Gettysburg,* South Mountain Press, Carlisle, Pennsylvania, 1986.
* MacDonald, Rose M., *Mrs. Robert E. Lee,* Robert B. Poisal Publisher, Pikeville, Maryland, 1939, 1973.
* McLaughlin, Jack, *Gettysburg: The Long Encampment,* Bonanza Books, New York, 1963.
* McMurry, Richard M., *Two Great Rebel Armies,* University of North Carolina, Chapel Hill, 1989.
* McWhiney, Grady and Perry D. Jamieson, *Attack and Die,* University of Alabama Press, University, Alabama, 1982.
* Miers, Earl S., *Robert E. Lee,* Harper and Row, Perennial Library, New York, 1956.
* Miller, Francis T., Ed., *Poetry and Eloquence from the Blue and the Gray,* Castle, New York, 1957.
* Mitchell, Joseph B., *Decisive Battles of the Civil War,* Fawcett Premier, New York, Ballentine Edition, 1989.
* Mitchell, Reid, *Civil War Soldiers,* Viking Penguin, New York, 1988.
* Murfin, James V., *Battlefields of the Civil War,* Crown Publishers, New York, 1988.
* Nagel, Paul C., *The Lees of Virginia,* Oxford University Press, New York, 1990.
* Nevins, Allan, *The War for the Union: The Improvised War 1861-1862,* Charles Scribner's, New York, 1959.

- —, *The War for the Union: War Becomes Revolution 1862-1863*, Charles Scribner's, New York, 1960.
- —, *The War for the Union: The Organized War 1863-1864*, Charles Scribner's, New York, 1971.
- —, *The War for the Union: The Organized War to Victory 1864-1865*, Charles Scribner's, New York, 1971.
- Nofi, Albert A., *The Gettysburg Campaign, Revised Edition*, Combined Books, Conshohocken, PA, 1993.
- Nolan, Alan T., *Lee Considered: General Robert E. Lee and Civil War History*, University of North Carolina, Chapel Hill, 1991.
- Pfanz, Harry W., *Gettysburg: The Second Day*, University of North Carolina, Chapel Hill, 1987.
- Piston, William G., *Lee's Tarnished Lieutenant: James Longstreet and his Place in Southern History*, University of Georgia Press, Athens, 1987.
- Priest, John M., *Antietam: The Soldiers' Battle*, White Mane Publishing, Shippensburg, Pennsylvania, 1989.
- Robertson, James I., Jr., *General A. P. Hill: The Story of a Confederate Warrior*, Random House, New York, 1987.
- —, *Soldiers Blue and Gray*, University of South Carolina Press, Columbia, 1988.
- Sears, Stephen W., *Landscape Turned Red: The Battle of Antietam*, Ticknor and Fields, New Haven, Connecticut, 1983. Cited as *Sears, Antietam.*
- —, *George B. McClellan: The Young Napoleon*, Ticknor and Fields, New Haven, Connecticut, 1988.
- Stackpole, Edward J., *Chancellorsville, Second Edition*, Stackpole Books, Harrisburg, Pennsylvania, 1958, 1988.
- —, *They Met at Gettysburg*, Stackpole Books, Harrisburg, Pennsylvania, 1956, 1989.
- Symonds, Craig L. and William J. Clipson, *A Battlefield Atlas of The Civil War*, Nautical and Aviation Publishing Company, Baltimore, Maryland, 1983.
- Tanner, Robert G., *Stonewall in the Valley*, Doubleday, Garden City, New York, 1976.
- Tapert, Annette, *The Brothers' War: Civil War Letters to Their Loved Ones from the Blue and Gray*, Times Books, New York, 1988.
- Taylor, Walter H., *Four Years with General Lee*, Bonanza, New York, 1962.
- Taylor, Walter, H., *General Lee: His Campaigns in Virginia*, 1906, facsimile edition by Morningside Bookshop, Dayton, Ohio, 1975. Cited as *Taylor, General Lee.*

- Thomas, Emory M., *Bold Dragoon: The Life of Jeb Stuart*, Harper and Row, New York, 1986.
- Ward, Geoffrey C., Ric Burns, and Ken Burns, *The Civil War*, Alfred A. Knopf, New York, 1990.
- Wheeler, Richard, *Witness to Gettysburg*, New American Library, New York, 1987.
- Woodworth, Steven E., *Jefferson Davis and His Generals*, University Press of Kansas, Lawrence, 1990.

References

The following references are limited. The primary purpose of this Appendix is to identify the actual quotations of real, historical characters. General historical citations are limited to either moments which are documented in only one of the author's sources or incidents so important that citations are customary. Citations are not generally provided for incidents or moments so often retold that they have long since passed from historical minutia into American folklore.

Introduction

- "Lee the captain of the host ...". *I Lieutenants*, xxv.
- "The real nature ...". Connelly, 163.
- "A writer of biography ...". *I Lieutenants*, xxix.

Chapter One

- E. Porter Alexander's cannon: McWhiney and Jamieson, 120; Anderson and Anderson, 340; *III Lieutenants*, 154; Coddington, 486. For an excellent essay on the question of the Confederate barrage before Pickett's Charge, see "How Many Guns Bombarded Cemetery Ridge?", Nofi, 165. I have taken an average figure of the sources.
- Federal artillery at Pickett's Charge: McWhiney and Jamieson, 120; *III Lieutenants*, 154; Coddington, 497. I have taken an average figure of the sources.
- Total forces on the field: Stackpole, *Gettysburg*, xxi; Taylor, *Four Years*, 113; Busey and Martin, *Regimental Strengths and Losses at Gettysburg*, 16, 129.
- Robert E. Lee's characteristic of head and neck twitching and redding under stress: Taylor, *Four Years*, 77; Taylor, *General Lee*, 156; Miers, 129; *II R. E. Lee*, 488; *III R. E. Lee*, 243; *IV R. E. Lee*, 145; Connelly, xv, 189, 204; Dowdey, *Lee*, 442.

- Confederate barrage landing long: Dowdey, *Lee*, 387; Coddington, 494-495.
- Pickett and Abraham Lincoln: Dowdey, *Death of a Nation*, 266. During the 1840's, Lincoln and Johnston traded poetry. Abraham Lincoln's verses written to Johnston are found at *Collected Works of Abraham Lincoln*, Rutgers University Press, New Jersey, 1953, Vol. I, Pp. 366, 377.
- Robert E. Lee's physical ailments: Dowdey, *Lee*, 339, 384; Robertson, *Hill*, 220; Clark, 69; Miers, 132; *II R. E. Lee* 502, 504.
- "Load in Nine Times": McLaughlin, 54.
- Robert E. Lee's father and George Gordon Meade's father: Fitzhugh Lee, 258.
- Lewis Armistead, George Pickett and Sallie Corbell: Dowdey, *Death of a Nation*, 272.
- Pickett's Charge: *III R. E. Lee*, 123; Luvaas and Nelson, *Gettysburg Guide*, 178; Coddington, 516; Stackpole, *Gettysburg*, 268; McLaughlin, 155; Anderson and Anderson, 346. Most of the sources use 15,000 as the number of Confederates in Pickett's Charge. I use 14,000 which is the more accurate muster roll according to Busey and Martin, *Regimental Strengths*.
- The death of General Armistead: Stackpole, *Gettysburg*, 27; Dowdey, *Death of a Nation*, 321.
- Casualties of Pickett's Charge: McWhiney and Jamieson, 73; Luvaas and Nelson, *Gettysburg Guide*, 189; Coddington, 526. I use the more accurate accounting at Busey and Martin, 283.
- Total Confederate losses at Gettysburg: *III Lieutenants*, 170, 190, 196; *II Foote*, 578-579; Hattaway and Jones, 409.
- "My heart and thoughts ...". Robert E. Lee dispatch to Jeb Stuart, December 9, 1863. Dowdey, *Wartime Papers*, 642; *III R. E. Lee*, 208.
- "The Marble Model": Miers, 197; *I R. E. Lee*, 68.
- Robert E. Lee's coronary condition and angina: Dowdey, *Lee*, 406; *III R. E. Lee*, 171, 189.
- Bristoe Station: *II Lieutenants*, 222; *III Lieutenants*, 246; *III R. E. Lee*, 180-183, 203; Robertson, *Hill*, 234, 238-239.
- "They must be attacked!" Robert E. Lee at Mine Run, *Ibid.*, 201.
- "I am too old ...". Robert E. Lee at Mine Run, *III R. E. Lee*, 202.

Chapter Two

- Robert E. Lee's new beard: *I R. E. Lee*, 577; Dowdey, *Lee*, 170.
- Train map reference and the street map references for Richmond are gathered from the *Official Military Atlas of the Civil War* (1891). Train map references for north-central Virginia are Plates 87(4) and 100(1). All Rich-

mond, street references are from Plate 89(2): "Map of the City of Rich-
mond, Virginia, 1864."
- Robert E. Lee genealogy: *I R. E. Lee*, 160; Fitzhugh Lee, 12; Nagel, 7-8,
10, 14, 22, 39, 44, 79-80, 159, 161-162.
- Light Horse Harry Lee hangs a deserter: Anderson and Anderson, 10.
- Light Horse Harry Lee, spendthrift: Dowdey, *Lee*, 3-4, 7-8; *I R. E. Lee*, 9;
Nagel, 166, 182.
- "Dark Horse" Harry Lee: Dowdey, *Lee*, 39; Connelly, 177; Anderson and
Anderson, 17, 40, 71.
- Family and early CSA career of Ambrose Powell Hill: Robertson, *Hill*, 4-5,
58-59.
- "My heart aches ...", Robert E. Lee letter to daughter Mildred, 25 Decem-
ber 1862. Dowdey, *Wartime Papers*, 381; J. W. Jones, 211.
- Sketch of childhood of William Fitzhugh "Rooney" Lee: Coulling, 17; *I R.
E. Lee*, 196, 377.
- Sketch of Annie Lee, her childhood and death: Coulling, 17, 108-110; An-
derson and Anderson, 274.
- Deaths of Robert E. Lee's grandchildren: Coulling, 104-105, 112; Dow-
dey, *Lee*, 327.
- Death of Henrietta Hill: Robertson, *Hill*, 160.
- "I have grieved ...sorrows of this world", Robert E. Lee letter to Mrs. Lee,
16 December 1862. Dowdey, *Wartime Papers*, 364.
- Death of Flora Stuart: Thomas, 188-189; Davis, *Stuart*, 245.
- "I have always counted ... must be resigned." Robert E. Lee letter to daugh-
ter Mary Lee, 24 November 1862. Fitzhugh Lee, 225; Miers, 112; Robert
E. Lee, Jr., 80. (Punctuation slightly changed.)
- Lucy Lee Hill named for Robert E. Lee: Robertson, *Hill*, 242.
- Death of James Longstreet's children: Piston, 18.
- Jeb Stuart sketch, and Robert E. Lee and Stuart at Harper's: Stackpole,
Gettysburg, 59; Thomas, 5 7, 31-32, 66
- "... like a mother to me." Jeb Stuart: Thomas, 108.
- Courtship and marriage of Robert E. and Mary Custis Lee: *I R. E. Lee*,
106; Dowdey, *Lee*, 53-55; Fitzhugh Lee, 19; Coulling, 4; Connelly, 7, 165.
- Arthritis of Mrs. R. E. Lee and early arthritis of Eleanor Agnes Lee: *I R. E.
Lee*, 379; Coulling, 57,60; Dowdey, *Lee*, 111.
- "I have no complaints ...", Robert E. Lee letter to Jefferson Davis, 8 Au-
gust 1863. Dowdey, *Wartime Papers*, 590.
- Jeb Stuart at Dr. Charles Brewer's home: Thomas, 293; *III Lieutenants*,
427.
- "Precious Life", Robert E. Lee's pet name for Mildred, "Daughter" for

Mary Custis, "Wig" and "Wiggie" for Agnes, Coulling, 23; Robert E. Lee, Jr., 41. "The Mim" and "Molly" for Mrs. Lee, Robert E. Lee, Jr., 14; Anderson and Anderson, 47; Coulling 8; Dowdey, *Lee*, 60.
- Mrs. Lee's wheelchair ("rolling chair" in the 1800's): *III R. E. Lee*, 210.

Chapter Three

- Sketch of Judah P. Benjamin and career: E. Merton Coulter, *The Confederate States of America 1861-1865*, Louisiana State University Press, Baton Rouge, 1959, 381-382; Max Raisin, *A History of the Jews in Modern Times*, Hebrew Publishing Company, New York, 1930, 278-280; Abram Leon Sachar, *A History of the Jews*, Knopf, New York, 1930, 1964, 306. Spanish ambassadorship: Alan Nevins, *Emergence of Lincoln: 1857-1859*, Scribner's, New York, Volume I, 428. Professor Freeman, at *I Lieutenants* 116, offered a description of Judah Philip Benjamin too lyrical to ruin by paraphrasing: "Short, round, rosy and well groomed, he wore a smile that frowning disaster could dim for a moment only. He always looked as if he had just risen from an enjoyed dinner to greet a friend with pleasant news." Reprinted by permission of Macmillan Publishing Company.
- The statement about the clamor to "Christianize" the Davis cabinet as a euphemism for removing the controversial and Jewish Benjamin is the 10 January 1862 entry in the famous, wartime diary of John B. Jones (1810-1866), clerk in Jefferson Davis' War Department. *I Jones*, 104.
- "I am overwhelmed ...". Robert E. Lee letter to Mrs. Lee, 9 March 1863. Dowdey, *Wartime Papers*, 413.
- "I believe it would be better ...". Robert E. Lee letter to Secretary of War, James Seddon, 9 September 1863. J. W. Jones, 294.
- "I am sorry ...". Robert E. Lee letter to Mrs. Lee, 7 October 1861. Dowdey, *Wartime Papers*, 80.
- Henry S. Foote demands hearings into the loss of Vicksburg and Chattanooga in statement of December 9, 1863. Davis, *Jefferson Davis*, 529.
- "What has our Congress done ...". Robert E. Lee letter to son Custis Lee, 28 February 1863. Dowdey, *Lee*, 335; Dowdey, *Wartime Papers*, 411; J. W. Jones, 227.
- "No man should be excused ... necessity." Robert E. Lee letter to Jefferson Davis, 2 September 1864. J. W. Jones, 338-339.
- "Congress seems to be laboring ... do it." Robert E. Lee letter to his son (unidentified), 12 February 1863. J. W. Jones, 226.
- "Our people have not been earnest enough ... our independence! ...". (Punctuation changed.) Robert E. Lee letter to daughter Annie Lee, 2 March 1862. Dowdey, *Wartime Papers*, 121-122.

- "I have felt very differently ...". Robert E. Lee letter to Mrs. Lee, 28 October 1863. Dowdey, *Wartime Papers*, 616.
- "I am much better ...". Robert E. Lee letter to Mrs. Lee, 4 December 1863. *Ibid.*, 632.
- "I have not the time to be sick." Robert E. Lee letter to Mrs. Lee, 10 June 1862. *Ibid.*, 190.
- "Thousands were barefooted ...". Robert E. Lee letter to Mrs. Lee, 19 October 1863. *Ibid.*, 611.
- "Nothing prevents my advancing ...". Robert E. Lee letter to Jefferson Davis, 24 August 1863. *Ibid.*, 594. (The original letter reads "but for the fear.")
- "The army is in great distress ...are unanswered". Robert E. Lee letter to Lt. General Alexander Lawton, Quartermaster General, 30 January 1864. *Ibid.*, 665.
- "The want of the supplies ... very great". Robert E. Lee letter to Lt. General Alexander Lawton, Quartermaster General, 9 October 1863. *Ibid.*, 610.
- "The Commissary Department proposes ...". Robert E. Lee letter to Jefferson Davis, 19 January 1863. *Ibid.*, 392.
- "Secession is nothing but revolution ...". Robert E. Lee, letter from Fort Mason, Texas, 23 January 1861, to unidentified recipient. Dowdey, *Lee*, 120-121; J. W. Jones, 121.
- "With all of my devotion ...". Robert E. Lee letter to his sister, Mrs. Anne Marshall, who remained loyal to the Union in Baltimore, 20 April 1861. Dowdey, *Wartime Papers*, 10; J. W. Jones, 133. (Verb tenses changed for clarity.)
- "[T]hough opposed to secession ...". Robert E. Lee letter to Reverdy Johnson after the war, 25 February 1868. Robert E. Lee, Jr., 27.
- "True patriotism ...". Robert E. Lee letter to General P. T. Beauregard after the war, 3 October 1865. J. W. Jones, 390. (Syntax slightly changed for clarity.)
- "I could have taken no other course ...". Robert E. Lee comment to General Wade Hampton after the war, June 1868. *I R. E. Lee*, 447.
- "In this enlightened age ... any country." Robert E. Lee letter to Mrs. Lee, 27 December 1856. Dowdey, *Lee*, 108; Fitzhugh Lee, 69; J. W. Jones, 82.
- "He has left me ...". Robert E. Lee letter to son, Custis Lee, 2 July 1859. J. W. Jones, 102.
- Robert E. Lee's slaves, Nancy and her children: Nagel, 247.
- "Considering the relation ...". Robert E. Lee letter to Andrew Hunter, 11 January 1865. Nolan, 21.

- "I think measures ... against us." Robert E. Lee letter to Jefferson Davis, 2 September 1864. J. W. Jones, 338; Dowdey, *Wartime Papers*, 848.
- "I have always observed ... improving." Robert E. Lee quoted by Robert, Jr., 168. Nolan, 145; Dowdey, *Lee*, 639-640.
- "I think it would be better ...". Robert E. Lee at Nolan, 145-146.
- "The three propositions ... all the states." Robert E. Lee letter to son, Custis Lee, 14 December 1860. Nolan, 32; J. W. Jones, 118-119. (Verb tenses changed.)
- "The war may last 10 years." Robert E. Lee letter to Mrs Lee, 30 April 1861. Dowdey, *Wartime Papers*, 15.
- "I shall endeavor ...". Robert E. Lee letter to Mrs. Lee, 21 February 1865. *Ibid.*, 907; J. W. Jones, 347.
- "You have no idea ...". Robert E. Lee letter to his son Custis, written from Mexico, during the Mexican War, 25 April 1847. Fitzhugh Lee, 47. (J. W. Jones, 53, identifies the recipient as Lee son, Rooney.)
- "I am gradually losing ... among the dead". Robert E. Lee letter to Jefferson Davis, 23 September 1863. (Syntax changed.) Dowdey, *Wartime Papers*, 603-604. The General Deshler reference is to General James Deshler, killed during the campaign of the Battle of Chickamauga, Georgia, September 1863, at age 30. General Longstreet's I Corps was detached to Tennessee during the Fall of 1863.
- "My heart bleeds ...". Robert E. Lee letter to Mrs. Lee, 25 December 1862. *Ibid.*, 380; J. W. Jones, 213.
- "Had I had Stonewall Jackson ... victory". Robert E. Lee remarks after the war. Fitzhugh Lee, 142; *III R. E. Lee*, 160; *II Foote*, 596; Robert E. Lee, Jr., 415; J. W. Jones, 259.
- "It had not been intended ...". Robert E. Lee, battle report on Gettysburg written to General Samuel Cooper, 20 January 1864. Dowdey, *Wartime Papers*, 576.
- "Has it ever occurred to you ... undermining his reason." Senator Louis Wigfall letter to C. C. Clay, 13 August 1863. Hattaway and Jones, 428; Piston, 202, note 7; Nevins, *The Organized War: 1863-1864*, 398.
- "His blunder at Gettysburg ...". Louis Wigfall letter to C. C. Clay, 13 August 1863. Piston, 65.
- Jefferson Davis' early feuds with Henry S. Foote and Judah P. Benjamin: Davis, *Jefferson Davis*, 170, 178, 264, 451.
- "If I could take one wing ...". Jefferson Davis, June 1863. *II Foote*, 643.
- "Our maximum strength ...". Jefferson Davis at Nevins, *War Becomes Revolution*, 231.

- "To some men ... My confidence ...". Jefferson Davis, August 1863, with slight change in syntax and punctuation. *II Foote*, 645.
- "I fear ... wives." Robert E. Lee letter to Mrs. Lee, 1 November 1863. Robert E. Lee, Jr., 112.
- "If you have missed me ...". Robert E. Lee letter to Agnes Lee, 3 April 1864. Dowdey, *Wartime Papers*, 690.
- "I think of you ...". Robert E. Lee letter to Mildred Lee, 5 July 1864. Dowdey, *Wartime Papers*, 814; J. W. Jones, 317.
- "I wish indeed ...". Robert E. Lee letter to daughters Annie and Agnes, 22 November 1861. Dowdey, *Wartime Papers*, 88; Robert E. Lee, Jr., 55; J. W. Jones, 154. (Original text lacks the word "more" inserted here for clarity.)
- "You girls have no time to be sick ...". Robert E. Lee letter to Agnes, 25 May 1863. Dowdey, *Wartime Papers*, 492.
- "I think it afforded me ... study". Robert E. Lee letter to Mrs. Lee, 27 March 1863. Coulling, 120; Dowdey, *Wartime Papers*, 420.
- "How unerring is the course ... as sure." Robert E. Lee, letter to Martha Williams from West Point, 26 May 1854. Craven, 46.
- "Our young people ...". General Lee letter to Mrs. Lee, 11 June 1861. Dowdey, *Wartime Papers*, 48. (Slight change in punctuation.)
- "I cannot express ... agonizing in the extreme." Robert E. Lee letter to Mrs. Lee, 26 October 1862. Fitzhugh Lee, 209; Robert E. Lee, Jr., 79.
- "I had not expected ... carried off." Robert E. Lee letter to Mrs. Lee, 7 July 1863. Dowdey, *Wartime Papers*, 542.
- "I saw him the night of the battle ...". Robert E. Lee letter to Mrs. Lee, 11 June 1863. Robert E. Lee, Jr., 96-97; J. W. Jones, 245.
- "Fitzhugh has been sent ... officers are." Robert E. Lee letter to Mrs. Lee, 21 November 1863. Dowdey, *Wartime Papers*, 625. The reference to Butler is to General Benjamin "Beast" Butler.
- "I have no idea ... grievous to me." Robert E. Lee letter to Mrs. Lee, 28 October 1863. *Ibid.*, 615 (Syntax changed.)
- "What a cruel thing is war ...". Robert E. Lee letter to Mrs. Lee, Christmas Day, 1862. *Ibid.*, 380; Robert E. Lee, Jr., 89; J. W. Jones, 213. (Punctuation changed.)
- "How many happy homes ... forever." Robert E. Lee letter to Mrs. Lee, 31 July 1864. Dowdey, *Wartime Papers*, 828.
- "In the quiet hours ...". Robert E. Lee letter to Mrs. Lee, 24 November 1862, writing of the death of his daughter, Annie Lee. Robert E. Lee., Jr., 80; J. W. Jones, 200. The word "quiet" appears only in the Jones version.

- "There is a great God ...". Robert E. Lee letter to Mrs. Lee, 5 April 1863. Dowdey, *Wartime Papers*, 429. (Punctuation changed.)
- "We must make up our minds ...". Robert E. Lee letter to Mrs. Lee, 25 December 1861. *Ibid.*, 96.
- "I begrudge every step ...". Robert E. Lee letter to Mrs. Lee, 23 May 1864. *Ibid.*, 748.
- "I do not think Richmond will be permanent." Robert E. Lee letter to Mrs. Lee, 28 May 1861. *Ibid.*, 40.
- "It is plain ...". Robert E. Lee letter to daughter Annie Lee, 2 March 1862. *Ibid.*, 121.
- "When I reflect ...". Robert E. Lee letter to son, Rooney Lee, 8 May 1861. Robert E. Lee, Jr.0 30.

Chapter Four

- "How great is my remorse ... afforded me." Robert E. Lee letter to Mrs. Lee, 26 July 1863. Dowdey, *Wartime Papers*, 560.
- "I find too late ...". Robert E. Lee letter to former, Confederate General Richard Ewell, 3 March 1868. Connelly, 218; J. W. Jones, 430.
- "All that we have to be proud of ...". General James Longstreet, undated reference at Piston, 68. Reprinted with permission of the University of Georgia Press.
- "the staff of my right hand.". Robert E. Lee, undated reference at Piston, 22.
- "Perfect and true ...". Inscription on grave of Annie Lee. Robert E. Lee, Jr., 81; Coulling, 173, with photo of Annie's grave at Plate 16.
- "I would have wished him ...". Robert E. Lee letter to son, Rooney Lee, 29 January 1861. J. W. Jones, 121. (Verb tenses changed.)
- "Only old people ...". Robert E. Lee letter to Mrs. Lee, 28 October 1863. Dowdey, *Wartime Papers*, 616. (Syntax changed: original letter reads, "old people can ...".)
- "A good man and a good horse ...". Thomas, 72.
- "To die game," Jeb Stuart. *I Lieutenants*, 302.
- "He was an able general ...". Robert E. Lee at Miers, 104.
- Sketch of Lee daughter, Mary Custis: Coulling, 7, 11-12, 15.
- Mary Custis Lee as Marielle: *Ibid.*, 35-36.
- Poetry to Mary Custis Lee by Jeb Stuart and Fitz Lee: *Ibid.*, 100.
- "This war ... see the end." Jeb Stuart at Thomas, 97. (Syntax slightly changed.)
- "A more zealous, ardent ...". Robert E. Lee letter to Mrs. Lee, 16 May 1864. Dowdey, *Wartime Papers*, 731.

- Value of Confederate paper money: *II Jones*, 112; Sallie Putnam, *Richmond During the War*, Carleton and Co., London, 1867, 271.
- Sketch of Martha Custis Williams: Connelly, 174; Coulling, 37; Anderson and Anderson, 78.
- "I have thought of you constantly." Robert E. Lee letter to Martha Williams, 23 June 1855. Craven, 32.
- "The pleasure of your company ...". Robert E. Lee letter from Ft. Hamilton, New York, to Martha Williams, 17 September 1845. *Ibid.*, 13. (Punctuation changed slightly.)
- "With the return of a new year ...". Robert E. Lee, in retirement, letter to Martha Williams, New Years Day, 1868. *Ibid.*, 78. (Slight change of syntax.)
- "Cheer up, Markie ...". Robert E. Lee letter to Martha Williams, 17 September 1845 in the context of Rooney Lee's boyhood visit north. *Ibid.*, 14. (Punctuation and syntax slightly changed for clarity.)
- Sketch of Annie and Agnes Lee as children and at West Point: Coulling, 14-15, 40-41.
- Execution of Orton Williams: *Ibid.*, 66, 114, 123-125; *III R. E. Lee*, 212; Flood, 73-75; deButts, 12. Here, Orton Williams is noted as the son of Mrs. Lee's first cousin which agrees with Mary P. Coulling, at page 37. This would make Orton (and his sister, Martha Williams) a second cousin to Mrs. Lee, and a third cousin to Agnes Lee. However, Mrs. Coulling's family tree for the Lees, at Coulling 201, shows Orton and Martha as third cousins to Mrs. Lee with Orton and Martha's great great grandfather being Mrs. Lee's grandfather. This would make Orton Agnes' fourth cousin. The noted deButts text (by Robert E. Lee's granddaughter) at page 117 contains a photograph of Orton Williams. A different portrait of Orton is found at Coulling, Plate 6.
- "My blood boils ...". Robert E. Lee letter to Martha Williams, 1 December 1866. *III R. E. Lee*, 213; Craven, 71-72.
- "You must not say ... better wife than you, Markie." Robert E. Lee letter to Martha Williams, 14 April 1868. Craven, 81. (Punctuation and syntax changed.)
- "Old age and sorrow ...". Robert E. Lee letter to Mrs. Lee, 9 March 1863. Dowdey, *Wartime Papers*, 413. (Punctuation and syntax slightly changed.)
- "There is nothing ...". Robert E. Lee letter to Martha Williams, 20 June 1865. Craven, 63. (Syntax slightly changed.)

Chapter Five

- A. P. Hill gonorrhea: Robertson, *Hill*, 11.

- Sketch of A. P. Hill education and career: *Ibid.*, 9, 15, 17, 30, 32, 36, 45, 49.
- "I have suffered ... like an old boiler before condemning it." Robert E. Lee letter to Mrs. Lee, 5 April 1863. Dowdey, *Wartime Papers*, 428.
- "The contest must be long ...". Robert E. Lee letter to Mrs. Lee, 8 February 1862. *Ibid.*, 111; J. W. Jones, 159.
- "Our people are so hard ...". Robert E. Lee letter to President Davis, 29 July 1863. Dowdey, *Wartime Papers*, 563. (Syntax changed slightly for clarity.)
- "The Confederacy has lost ...". Robert E. Lee quoted at *II Lieutenants*, 386. (Slight syntax change for clarity.)
- "The loss of Major General Pender ...". Robert E. Lee, battle report on Gettysburg, 20 January 1864. Dowdey, *Wartime Papers*, 585.
- General Scott: the worst decision of Robert E. Lee's life. Dowdey, *Lee*, 133; Miers, 4; *I R. E. Lee*, 437.
- Cadet Jefferson Davis at West Point and early career in Army: Evans, 61-62; Davis, *Jefferson Davis*, 30-37, 63-70.
- "... the struggle it has cost me ... draw my sword." Robert E. Lee letter to General Winfield Scott, 20 April 1861, Dowdey, *Lee*, 134; Dowdey, *Wartime Papers*, 8-9. (Syntax slightly changed.)
- "... [u]nless it is intended ...". Robert E. Lee letter to Jefferson Davis, 7 December 1863. Dowdey, *Wartime Papers*, 642.
- Robert E. Lee knowing Charlotte Wickham Lee since childhood: Anderson and Anderson, 145.
- " ... they are both mere children ...". Robert E. Lee letter to Mrs. Lee, 22 August 1857, Coulling, 66. Reprinted by permission of the Virginia Historical Society, custodian of the original document, manuscript number 1L51c225.
- "... very pretty and sweet." deButts, 59: diary entry by Eleanor Agnes Lee, 17 April 1855.
- "I have a beautiful white beard ... remarked on." Robert E. Lee letter to Mildred Lee, 15 November 1861. Dowdey, *Wartime Papers*, 86. (The word "now" is added to the original document for clarity.)
- "I cannot bear ...". Robert E. Lee letter to Charlotte Wickham Lee, 26 July 1863. J. W. Jones, 278. (Punctuation changed.)
- Custis Lee's failed attempt to changes places with Rooney Lee in Federal prison: Coulling 132; Robert E. Lee, Jr., 117. Robert E. Lee, Jr., puts his brother Rooney's imprisonment during December 1863 at Fort Monroe, Virginia. Clifford Dowdey has Rooney at the Johnson Island, Ohio, POW camp (*Lee*, 411).

- "I can see no harm ... humanity." Robert E. Lee letter to Charlotte Lee, 26 July 1863. Robert E. Lee, Jr., 100-101; J. W. Jones, 277.
- "I was so grateful at her birth ... strength." Robert E. Lee letter to Charlotte Lee, 10 December 1862. Dowdey, *Wartime Papers*, 357. (Syntax slightly changed.)
- "Summer returns ...". Robert E. Lee letter to Charlotte Lee, 22 June 1862. Dowdey, *Wartime Papers*, 197; J. W. Jones, 185.
- "I long for Arlington ... dear home." Eleanor Agnes Lee, diary entry of 26 August 1853. deButts, 21; Coulling 40.
- "Dear, dear Arlington ...". Eleanor Agnes Lee, diary entry of 13 December 1857. deButts, 101; Coulling 68. The original diary entry reads, "Dear, dear Arlington. I cannot bear to leave it."
- "Dear West Point: the beautiful mountains ... and sidewalk." Eleanor Agnes Lee, diary entry of 16 April 1855. deButts, 52.
- "I had no idea ... once more." Eleanor Agnes Lee, diary entry of 20 April 1855. *Ibid.*, 62.
- "I fear he will give some ... be dismissed." Robert E. Lee letter to Mrs. Lee, 23 April 1864. Dowdey, *Wartime Papers*, 705.
- "Keep Custis Morgan out of her [Mrs. Lee's] sight ...." Robert E. Lee letter to Mildred Lee, 5 July 1864. *Ibid.*, 814. [Syntax changed slightly.]
- "You have only always ... with practice." Robert E. Lee letter to Mildred Lee, 10 September 1863. *Ibid.*, 597.
- "Mildred has it in her power ... with glory." Robert E. Lee letter to Mrs. Lee, *Ibid.*, 681. (Syntax changed slightly.)
- "Her illness was short ... dear friend." Robert E. Lee letter to Martha Williams, 22 June 1853. Craven, 31.
- " ... had been to me all a father could." Robert E. Lee letter to Martha Williams. *Ibid.*, 39. (Syntax slightly changed.)
- "Were it not ...". Mrs. Lee letter to General Scott. McDonald, 151.
- "It never occurred to me ...". Mrs. Lee letter to General Sandford. Coulling, 88.
- General McDowell's reply to Mrs. Lee: Fitzhugh Lee, 109; J. W. Jones, 142-143.
- "It is better to make up our minds ... can preserve." Robert E. Lee letter to Mrs. Lee, 25 December 1861. Dowdey, *Lee*, 177; Miers, 49; Dowdey, *Wartime Papers*, 96; J. W. Jones, 153.
- "And particularly for our ... his misery." Robert E. Lee letter to Mrs. Lee, 29 December 1863. Dowdey, *Wartime Papers*, 646. (Syntax slightly changed.)

- "I feel for her all the love ...". Robert E. Lee letter to Mrs. Lee, 25 December 1863. *Ibid.*, 644.
- "I spend many anxious hours ...". Robert E. Lee letter to Mrs. Lee, 9 June 1863. *Ibid.*, 507.

Chapter Six

- Richmond hospitals: Davis, *IV Images of War: 1861-1865*, 247, 254; Davis, *II Touched by Fire*, 228; Robertson, *Soldiers*, 167.
- "It is so solemn ...". Eleanor Agnes Lee journal, 6 August 1853. deButts, 20.
- "Do not grieve for the brave dead ...". Robert E. Lee letter to Mrs. Lee, 27 July 1861. Fitzhugh Lee, 114; Robert E. Lee, Jr., 37; J. W. Jones, 144.
- "I do wish ...". Eleanor Agnes Lee diary entry, 20 July 1853. deButts, 18. The word "better" is added for clarity.
- "I am very happy ...". Agnes Lee letter to Robert E. Lee, 9 April 1857. deButts, 141.
- "I want all the husbands ...". Robert E. Lee letter to Charlotte Wickham Lee, 11 June 1863. Dowdey, *Wartime Papers*, 91; J. W. Jones, 246.
- Martha Williams' violets: Craven, 22
- "If it was not for my heart ...". Robert E. Lee letter to Martha Williams, 10 May 1851. *Ibid.*, 26.
- "Love is all-powerful." Robert E. Lee letter to Martha Williams, 10 May 1851. *Ibid.*, 26.
- Traveller's purchase by General Lee: *I R. E. Lee*, 644-645; Adams, 22, 37.
- "If I were an artist ... comfort he is to me." Robert E. Lee letter to Martha Williams, 22 December 1866. Craven, 73-74. Robert E. Lee, Jr., erroneously cites this letter as one to Lee daughter Agnes at Robert E. Lee, Jr., 83; J. W. Jones, 191-192.
- Fitzhugh Lee known as Chudie: Coulling, 41; deButts, 54.
- "Yes, my son ...". Robert E. Lee to his son at Antietam. Sears, *Antietam*, 275.
- Richmond food prices: *I Jones*, 113-114, 118, 328, 335-336.
- "Our people are opposed ... as labor." Robert E. Lee letter to Jefferson Davis, 5 June 1862. Dowdey, *Wartime Papers*, 184. (Syntax changed.)
- "Colonel Taylor, when I lose my temper ...". Robert E. Lee quoted by Walter Taylor in *General Lee*, 156.
- "I prefer the Bible ...". Robert E. Lee letter to Martha Williams, 20 December 1865. Craven, 65.
- Sketch and career of Judah P. Benjamin: Evans, xiii, 4-5, 8, 13, 15, 17-19, 23-26, 31-33, 110, 116, 121, 138, 152, 215-216.

- Jefferson Davis beats Henry Foote with a crutch: Davis, *Jefferson Davis*, 171-172; Woodworth, 10.
- "I never intimated to anyone ...". Robert E. Lee letter to Reverdy Johnson, 25 February 1868. Robert E. Lee, Jr., 27-28; J. W. Jones, 131. (Syntax changed.)
- "[a]s an American citizen ... of honor." Robert E. Lee letter to son Rooney Lee, 1860. Dowdey, *Lee*, 124.
- "I only see that a great calamity is upon us ... of honor." Robert E. Lee letter to Martha Williams, 22 January 1861. Craven, 58. (Syntax changed.)
- "Now we are in a state of war ...". Robert E. Lee letter to his sister, Mrs. Anne Marshall of Baltimore, 20 April 1861. Dowdey, *Wartime Papers*, 9; Robert E. Lee, Jr., 26.
- "It has occurred to me ... speedy termination." Robert E. Lee letter to Secretary of War James Seddon, 10 January 1863. *Ibid.*, 389. (Syntax changed.)
- "Our army would be invincible ... obtained." Robert E. Lee letter to General John B. Hood, 21 May 1863. *Ibid.*, 490.
- "I am willing to starve myself ...". Robert E. Lee letter to Mrs. Lee, 8 February 1863. *Ibid.*, 401.
- "I can advise no young man ...". Robert E. Lee letter to Martha Williams, 16 September 1853. Craven, 37; Coulling, 42.
- "the indomitable Jackson." Robert E. Lee letter to Jefferson Davis, 16 September 1862. Dowdey, *Wartime Papers*, 310.
- "I am willing ...". Lt. General Thomas "Stonewall" Jackson, quoted at Miers 93; *I Lieutenants*, 662; *II R. E. Lee*, 261.
- "Any victory would be dear ...". Robert E. Lee quoted at *III R. E. Lee*, 1; similar language in letters to Mrs. Lee and son Custis Lee at J. W. Jones, 242 and 288.
- A. P. Hill and George B. McClellan: Dowdey, *Lee*, 434; Thomas, 216; Sears, *McClellan*, 33-34, 42, 60-63; Robertson, *Hill*, 27-29, 63.
- "If it gives you as much pleasure ...". Robert E. Lee letter to Lt. General James Longstreet, 25 September 1863. Dowdey, *Wartime Papers*, 604-605.
- "I am confident ... the service." Robert E. Lee letter to Lt. General James Longstreet, 21 March 1863. Dowdey, *Wartime Papers*, 416.
- "What a glorious world ...". Robert E. Lee letter to Mrs. Lee, 4 August 1861. Dowdey, *Wartime Papers*, 62.

Chapter Seven

- Mary Lee genealogy and Martha Washington: MacDonald, 12-14.
- Sidney Smith Lee: Fitzhugh Lee, 44, 27; Robert E. Lee, Jr., 25, 156;

Hattaway and Jones, 128-129; Davis, *Guns of '62*, 150 (portrait of Sidney Smith Lee).

- Robert E. Lee's largest command before 1861: *I R. E. Lee*, 366-368.
- "I would much have preferred ...". Dowdey, *Lee*, 143.
- "The Constitution was intended ... convention assembled." Robert E. Lee letter to son, Custis Lee, 1859, according to Miers, 27; J. W. Jones, 121, dates the letter 23 January 1861.
- Cadet Robert E. Lee reads *The Federalist* nine times: *I R. E. Lee*, 72.
- "As far as I have been able to judge ... or aid." Robert E. Lee letter to President Davis, 6 July 1864. Dowdey, *Wartime Papers*, 816.
- "I have great consideration ...". Robert E. Lee letter to Mrs. Lee, 18 September 1864. *Ibid.*, 855.
- "As regards the liberation of the people ... impossible." Robert E. Lee letter to Mrs. Lee, 16 December 1862. *Ibid.*, 365 (Syntax changed slightly).
- "Perry is very willing ... take care of him." Robert E. Lee letter to Mrs. Lee, 7 December 1862. *Ibid.*, 354 (Punctuation changed.)
- "That indeed was a glorious victory ... my home." Robert E. Lee letter to Mrs. Lee, 27 July 1861. Robert E. Lee, Jr., 37.
- Death at Manassas of Edward Anderson: Davis, *Jefferson Davis*, 352.
- " ... I directed Mr. Collins as soon as he could get in a small crop ...". Robert E. Lee letter to Mrs. Lee, 11 November 1863. Dowdey, *Wartime Papers*, 622 (Syntax changed slightly.)
- "I much prefer their receiving their free papers ... as others do." Robert E. Lee letter to Mrs. Lee, 1 January 1864. *Ibid.*, 661.
- "The soldiers everywhere were sick ...". Robert E. Lee letter to Mrs. Lee, 4 August 1861. *Ibid.*, 61 (Verb tenses changed.)
- Henry S. Foote calls for relieving officers of command who lose public support. Davis, *Jefferson Davis*, 530.
- "Rain, rain, rain ...". Robert E. Lee letter to son, Custis Lee, 3 September 1861. Dowdey, *Wartime Papers*, 70 (Verb tenses and punctuation changed.)
- "We have a great deal of sickness ...". Robert E. Lee letter to Mrs. Lee, 1 September 1861. *Ibid.*, 68-69; J. W. Jones, 146. (Verb tenses changed.)
- "It had been raining ...". Robert E. Lee letter to Governor John Letcher, Richmond, 17 September 1861. Dowdey, *Wartime Papers*, 76 [verb tenses changed].
- "It rained there all the time ...". Robert E. Lee letter to daughters Annie and Eleanor Agnes, 29 August 1861. *Ibid.*, 67 (Verb tenses changed.)
- "I cannot tell you my regret ...". Robert E. Lee letter to Mrs. Lee, 17 September 1861. *Ibid.*, 74; J. W. Jones, 148.

- "Our greatest loss ...". Robert E. Lee letter to Governor John Letcher, Richmond, 17 September 1861. Dowdey, *Wartime Papers*, 75-76 (Syntax, tenses changed.)
- Col. John Washington and Mount Vernon: Robert E. Lee, Jr., 40 (note).
- "Brigadier Generals Floyd and Wise ...". Taylor, *Four Years*, 16 (Punctuation changed.)
- "Commands were seriously reduced ...". *Ibid.*, 17 (Punctuation changed.)
- "It is useless to attempt ... shivering men." *Ibid.*, 16-17 (Punctuation changed).
- "He never assumed immediate personal command ...". *Ibid.*, 16.
- "I discovered ...". Taylor, *General Lee*, 25.
- "I did not see ...". Robert E. Lee letter to Mrs. Lee, 14 March 1862. Dowdey, *Wartime Papers*, 127-128 (Syntax changed).

Chapter Eight

- "His face was calm ...". Douglas, 109. Henry Kyd Douglas was a Virginia lawyer, educated in Pennsylvania. His friendship with Sandie Pendleton resulted in Douglas' appointment as an aide to Stonewall Jackson in April 1862. Davis, *Stonewall*, 176.
- Sketch of Alexander Swift "Sandie" Pendleton: Bean, 3, 18, 156, 211; *II Lieutenants*, 438.
- "I grieve much over the death of General Jackson ...". Robert E. Lee letter to Lt. Gen. John B. Hood, 21 May 1863. Dowdey, *Wartime Papers*, 490.
- "It is a terrible loss ...". Robert E. Lee letter to Custis Lee, 11 May 1863. *Ibid.*, 484.
- "Poor General Jackson ...". Sandie Pendleton letter to Kate Corbin, 5 May 1863. Bean, 117. (Slight syntax change.)
- "[N]o one was more convinced of his worth ...". Robert E. Lee letter to Dr. A. T. Blesdoe, 28 October 1867. Luvaas and Nelson, *Chancellorsville and Fredericksburg*, 174.
- Sandie Pendleton and Kate Corbin: Bean, 48, 87-88, 97, 99, 110 (note 44), 111, 161, 166, 173, 177, 180-182.
- "God knows ...". Sandie Pendleton, comment to Mrs. T. J. Jackson, May 1863. *Ibid.*, 118.
- "... that enthusiastic fanatic ...", and "... crazy as a March hare." General Richard S. Ewell, letter to sister Lizzie Ewell, 13 May 1862. *I Lieutenants*, 350-351, 355; Davis, *Stonewall*, 22.
- Professor Jackson (VMI) and Cadet James Walker, duel: Tanner, 183, 187.
- "The brave and gallant Federals ...". Stonewall Jackson: Davis, *Stonewall*, 192; Bowers, 239.

- "We must do more than defeat ...". Stonewall Jackson: Bowers, 320.
- Robert E. Lee letter of 21 April 1862 to Stonewall Jackson: Tanner, 155-157; Dowdey, *Lee*, 196, and Dowdey, *Wartime Papers*, 151.
- Battle of McDowell: *I Lieutenants*, 354; Bowers, 192-196; Davis, *Stonewall*, 179; Tanner, 169-174.
- "Richmond must be defended. Richmond shall not be given up!" General Robert E. Lee. Dowdey, *Lee*, 201-202; *II R. E. Lee*, 48; Miers, 67.
- Jackson's "Foot Cavalry" and Front Royal campaign: Tanner, 201-203; Douglas, 58-59; *I Lieutenants*, 379-381; Davis, *Stonewall*, 32, 36-37.
- Stonewall stands watch over his sleeping division: *I Lieutenants*, 394; Davis, *Ibid.*, 50-51.
- Battle of Winchester and Monday Sabbath in the Valley: Douglas, 66-67; Bowers, 218; Tanner, 211, 215, 225-233; Davis, *Stonewall*, 51, 53-57, 61; *I Lieutenants*, 400, 402-403, 407.
- Battle of Cross Keys: Davis, *Stonewall*, 81, 83, 85-87, 190; *I Lieutenants*, 451-461; Bowers, 236-240; Tanner, 296-307; Douglas, 91, 95.
- Stonewall's exhausting ride from the Valley to Robert E. Lee headquarters, June 17-23, 1862: *I Lieutenants*, 462, 470, 494; Davis, *Stonewall*, 200-201, 203-204; Bowers, 244-248.
- Record and Marches of the Valley Army, March-June, 1862: Davis, *Stonewall*, 192-193; Tanner, 319, 358-359; Douglas, 98.
- "Such an executive officer ...". Robert E. Lee, quoted *II R. E. Lee*, 524. (Syntax and verb tenses slightly changed.)
- "Oh, for the presence and inspiration ...". Sandie Pendleton to Henry Kyd Douglas. Bean, 139; Douglas, 239.

Chapter Nine

- "I prefer Lee ...". Major General George McClellan letter to Abraham Lincoln, 22 April 1862. Sears, *McClellan*, 180.
- "... had been to the Chickahominy ...". Major General Jeb Stuart, quoted at *I Lieutenants*, 301. (Pronouns changed.)
- Stonewall Jackson, exhausted by 24 June 1862: *I Lieutenants*, 506; Davis, *Stonewall*, 213.
- "In consequence of unavoidable delays ...". General Lee report to General Samuel Cooper, 6 March 1863. Dowdey, *Wartime Papers*, 213.
- Shortage of CSA military engineers: *II R. E. Lee*, 233; Taylor, *General Lee*, 65.
- "It was not war...". Major General Daniel H. Hill. Miers, 89; Savis, *Stonewall*, 252. (Punctuation changed.)

- "General Jackson was to march ...". General Lee report to General Samuel Cooper, 6 March 1863. Dowdey, *Wartime Papers*, 212. (Syntax changed.)
- "A. P. Hill did not begin ...". General Lee report to General Samuel Cooper, 6 March 1863. *Ibid.*, 213.
- "D. H. Hill's leading brigade ...". General Lee, *Ibid.*
- "It was never contemplated ...". General A. P. Hill: Robertson, *Hill*, 75, 77.
- "Long lines of dead and wounded ...". General Lee report to General Samuel Cooper, 6 March 1863. Dowdey, *Wartime Papers*, 216 (Punctuation changed.)
- "The principal part of the Federal army ... advance of the enemy." General Lee, *Ibid.*, 214-215. (Syntax changed.)
- A. P. Hill's melted cannon: Robertson, *Hill*, 84-86.
- "The arrival of Jackson on our left ... feint on the enemy's left." General Lee report to General Samuel Cooper, 6 March 1863. Dowdey, *Wartime Papers*, 214-215.
- "The enemy were driven ...". General Lee, *Ibid.*, 215.
- "On the morning of the 28th ...". General Lee report to General Samuel Cooper, 6 March 1863. *Ibid.*, 216.
- "Jackson was directed to cross ...". General Lee report to General Samuel Cooper, 6 March 1863. *Ibid.*, 217-218. (Syntax changed.)
- "I regret very much ...". General Lee dispatch to General John Magruder, 28 June 1863. *Ibid.*, 205; Davis, *Stonewall*, 232; *I Lieutenants*, 554.
- Davis, *Stuart*, 139, suggests that the home burned was the home in which George Washington was married. Professor Freeman argues that the actual Washington house had been destroyed some 20 years before Rooney Lee's home stood on the same site. *I Lieutenants*, 634, Note 2.
- "The superiority of numbers ...". General Lee report to General Samuel Cooper, 6 March 1863. Dowdey, *Wartime Papers*, 218-219.
- Exhausted Stonewall Jackson falls asleep at Seven Pines: Davis, *Stonewall*, 237-242; *I Lieutenants*, 576.
- "Huger not coming up ...". General Lee report to General Samuel Cooper, 6 March 1863. Dowdey, *Wartime Papers*, 218.
- Often-told incident of Stonewall Jackson going to sleep with food in his mouth at Frayser's Farm, 30 June 1862: Davis, *Stonewall*, 244.
- "The general conduct ...". General Lee report to General Samuel Cooper, 6 March 1863. Dowdey, *Wartime Papers*, 220.
- "Immediately in his front ...". General Lee report to General Samuel Cooper, 6 March 1863. *Ibid.*, 220.

- "Batteries have been established ...". General Lee at *II R. E. Lee*, 207; Dowdey, *Lee*, 266.
- "Owing to ignorance of the country ...". General Lee report to General Samuel Cooper, 6 March 1863. Dowdey, *Wartime Papers*, 219.
- "For want of concert among the attacking columns ... should have been destroyed." General Lee report to General Samuel Cooper, 6 March 1863; *Ibid.*, 220-221 (Syntax changed.)
- Seven Days, Confederate casualties: *I Lieutenants*, 605-606; *II R. E. Lee*, 230; Robertson, *Hill*, 95.
- Seven Days, Federal casualties: *II R. E. Lee*, 231; Sears, *McClellan*, 223.
- "On Thursday, June 26th ...". General Lee report to General Samuel Cooper, 6 March 1863. Dowdey, *Wartime Papers*, 210 (Syntax changed.)
- "We attacked just when and where ...". Daniel Harvey Hill, quoted at Hattaway and Jones, 194.

Chapter Ten

- "I have been for more than a month ...". General Lee letter to Leonidas Polk, 26 October 1863. Dowdey, *Wartime Papers*, 614.
- "The rheumatism ...". General Lee letter to Mrs. Lee, 4 September 1863. *Ibid.*, 595. (Syntax changed.)
- "So long as that heart beats ...". General Lee letter to Martha Williams, 26 May 1854. Craven, 46.
- Orton Williams warns the Lees at Arlington: MacDonald, 148-149.
- "One of the pleasures I always anticipated ...". General Lee letter to Martha Williams, 1 April 1849. Craven, 23. (Verb tenses changed.)
- "It was my first visit ...". General Lee letter to Mrs. Lee, 18 January 1862. Dowdey, *Wartime Papers*, 103.
- "How would you like a little squirrel soup ... good of the country." General Lee letter to Mrs. Lee, 7 July 1864. *Ibid.*, 816-817. (Syntax changed.)
- "I am content to be poor ...". General Lee letter to Mrs. Lee, 21 November 1863. *Ibid.*, 625.
- "You are always present with me ...". General Lee letter to Mrs. Lee, 29 January 1863. *Ibid.*, 396.
- "A. P. Hill, you will, I think ...". General Lee letter to Stonewall Jackson, 27 July 1862. Davis, *Stonewall*, 270; Dowdey, *Wartime Papers*, 239.
- "Make up your mind what is best to be done ...". General Lee dispatch to Stonewall Jackson, 7 August 1862. Bowers, 268; Dowdey, *Wartime Papers*, 248.
- Stonewall Jackson draws his sword at Cedar Mountain, 9 August 1862: *II Lieutenants*, 26-43; Davis, *Stonewall*, 277, 280-282; Bowers, 270-272.

- Jeb Stuart's reunion and bet with Federal General Samuel Crawford: Davis, *Stuart*, 158, 160-161.
- "Confidence in you ...". Jefferson Davis dispatch to Robert E. Lee: Dowdey, *Lee*, 287.
- "Pelham is always ...". Jeb Stuart at Davis, *Stuart*, 179.
- Robert E. Lee breaks his hands: *II Lieutenants*, 153; *II R. E. Lee*, 340; Dowdey, *Lee*, 296; Davis, *Stonewall*, 309-310; Douglas, 145.
- Death of General Kearny and military honors: Davis, *Stonewall*, 310; Douglas, 146; *II R. E. Lee*, 342-344; *II Lieutenants*, 133.
- Stonewall Jackson arrests A. P. Hill: Davis, *Stonewall*, 314-315.
- "My men had nothing to eat." General Lee quoted at Miers, 98; *II R. E. Lee*, 349; Robert E. Lee, Jr., 416.
- "Nothing could surpass the gallantry ...". General Lee letter to Jefferson Davis, 3 September 1862. Dowdey, *Wartime Papers*, 270. (Punctuation and verb tenses changed.)
- "The history of the achievements of the army ...". General Lee battle report to General Samuel Cooper, Adjutant General, 18 April 1863. *Ibid.*, 285. (Syntax slightly changed.)
- Stonewall Jackson thrown from horse: Davis, *Stonewall*, 316; Douglas, 149.
- "Such a proposition coming from us ...". General Lee letter to Jefferson Davis, 8 September 1862. Dowdey, *Lee*, 299; Dowdey, *Wartime Papers*, 301.
- Loss of copy of Special Orders 191: Dowdey, *Lee*, 303; *II Lieutenants*, 173-174, 715-723; Dowdey, *Wartime Papers*, 301-302.
- Copy of lost General Orders 191 found by Federals: *II Lieutenants*, 173; Davis, *Stonewall*, 323-324; Sears, *Antietam*, 112, 208; Sears, *McClellan*, 280-281; Taylor, *Four Years*, 67; Hattaway and Jones, 242.
- Professor Freeman suggests that General Stuart learned of the Federal discovery of Special Orders 191 in *II Lieutenants*, 173, but rejects this theory in *II R. E. Lee*, 369. Stuart's awareness of the discovery of the lost order is noted at Davis, *Stuart*, 201, and Thomas, 167.
- Stonewall Jackson's reunion at Harper's Ferry with brothers-in-law: Bowers, 298-299.
- "War is the greatest game ...". George McClellan at Sears, *McClellan*, 11.

Chapter Eleven

- "They poured out their blood ...". General Howard. Luvaas and Nelson, *Antietam*, 171.
- "It is, as you state ...". General Lee letter to daughter Mildred Lee, 28 July 1862. Dowdey, *Wartime Papers*, 240.

- "Never neglect the means ...". General Lee letter to daughter Mildred Lee, 6 November 1864. Robert E. Lee, Jr., 139.
- "The purpose, if discovered, ... could not destroy them." General Lee letter to Jefferson Davis, 3 September 1862. Dowdey, *Wartime Papers*, 293. (Verb tenses and syntax changed.)
- "The condition of Maryland ...". General Lee report to Adjutant General Samuel Cooper, 19 August 1863. *Ibid.*, 313. (Syntax changed.)
- "Notwithstanding individual expressions of kindness ...". General Lee letter to Jefferson Davis, 7 September 1862. *Ibid.*, 298. (Verb tenses changed.)
- "Should the results of the expedition ...". General Lee letter to Jefferson Davis, 4 September 1862. *Ibid.*, 294. (Syntax changed.)
- "A thousand pairs of shoes ...". General Lee letter to Jefferson Davis, 12 September 1862. *Ibid.*, 305. (Syntax changed.)
- "... horseshoes, for want of which ...". General Lee letter to Jefferson Davis, 16 July 1863. *Ibid.*, 552.
- "One great embarrassment ...". General Lee letter to Jefferson Davis, 13 September 1862. *Ibid.*, 307. (Syntax changed.)
- Stonewall Jackson orders execution of stragglers: *II Lieutenants*, 149.
- "A copy of the order ...". General Lee report to Adjutant General Samuel Cooper, 19 August 1863. Dowdey, *Wartime Papers*, 315.
- Chaplain Israel Washburn saved by Bible: Priest, 20.
- Death and joint burial of Capt. Werner Von Bachelle and his dog: *Ibid.*, 43.
- Casualties in the Cornfield in 21st New York, 1st Texas, 1st and 3rd North Carolina, and 128th Pennsylvania: *Ibid.*, 66, 77, 82.
- Fate of Sgt. Bloss, Cpl. Mitchell, and Capt. Kapulo: Sears, *Antietam*, 208.
- The Fletcher brothers: Priest, 125.
- Private Willie Hood: *Ibid.*, 175-176.
- "I hope our son ...". General Lee letter to Mrs. Lee, 15 March 1862. Robert E. Lee, Jr., 68.
- Father Corby grants absolution to the Irish Brigade: Priest, 159-160, 335.
- Deaths of Joe and Edward Johnson in Bloody Lane: *Ibid.*, 170.
- Wounding of Capt. John Strickler, USA: *Ibid.*, 145-146.
- "My old warhorse": *II Lieutenants*, 239; *II R. E. Lee*, 403.
- The Antietam casualties figures are slightly different among the secondary sources: Sears, *Antietam*, 295-296, and Appendix III; Luvaas and Nelson, *Antietam*, 212, 302; Frassanito, *Antietam*, 288; *II Lieutenants*, 225, 251-252.
- Pvt. Harrison White cited in Frassanito, *Antietam*, 175. There are undocu-

mented references to the wounding of Robert E. Lee's son, Rooney, at Antietam: Davis, *Stuart*, 240-241; Douglas 166. There are no such comments in Freeman's *II Lieutenants* or *II R. E. Lee*, nor in Dowdey's *Lee*. Robert E. Lee, Jr., did serve at Antietam with the Rockbridge Artillery battalion and was not wounded.

- Colonel Henry Strong, CSA, and his dead horse: Frassanito, *Antietam*, 123-124.
- General Maxcy Gregg drives ambulance wagon: *II R. E. Lee*, 405-406; Davis, *Stuart*, 208-209.
- "My army is ruined ...". General Lee at *II R. E. Lee*, 408, 411.
- "The arduous service ...". General Lee report to Adjutant General Samuel Cooper, 19 August 1863. Dowdey, *Wartime Papers*, 322.
- "Although not properly equipped for invasion ...". General Lee report to Adjutant General Samuel Cooper, 19 August 1863. *Ibid.*, 313.
- "This great battle ...". General Lee report to Adjutant General Samuel Cooper, 19 August 1863. *Ibid.*, 322. (Punctuation changed.)
- "I hated to see McClellan go ...". General Lee letter to Mrs. Lee, undated citation in Miers, 111-112; Hattaway and Jones, 266; Sears, *McClellan*, 340.
- President Davis and Tuesday night, open house at Executive Mansion: Davis, *Jefferson Davis*, 539.
- Jefferson and Varina Davis, early marital discord: *Ibid.*, 168-170, 185, 190.

Chapter Twelve

- "I had never before seen fighting ...". Major General Darius N. Couch, USA, quoted at Fitzhugh Lee, 220.
- "It was a dreadful scene ...". Douglas, 173.
- "The picture of the private soldier ...". Fitzhugh Lee, 203. (Text condensed and syntax slightly changed.)
- "We are in the midst ...". General George B. McClellan. Sears, *McClellan*, 313.
- "The enemy fell like grass ...". Major Orrin Crane, USA, quoted at Sears, *Antietam*, 232.
- "The slain lay in rows ...". Major General Joseph Hooker, USA, quoted Luvaas and Nelson, *Antietam*, 126.
- "... like the steady dripping ...". Lt. General James Longstreet, quoted at Miers, 121-122.
- Exchange between Generals Evans and Hood quoted at *II Lieutenants*, 209.
- "My pulse ... old man." General Lee letter to Agnes Lee, 11 April 1863. Dowdey, *Wartime Papers*, 431. (Punctuation changed.)

- "I am weak, feverish ...". General Lee letter to son Custis Lee, 31 March 1863. J. W. Jones, 287.
- "Without some increase in our strength ...". General Lee letter to Secretary of War, James Seddon, 23 August 1864. Dowdey, *Wartime Papers*, 844.
- "I expect to die a pauper ...". General Lee letter to Mrs. Lee, 21 December 1862. *Ibid.*, 379.
- "I should like to retire ...". General Lee letter to Mrs. Lee, 9 June 1861. *Ibid.*, 46. (Punctuation changed.)
- "The troops displayed at Fredericksburg ...". General Lee report to Adjutant General Samuel Cooper, 10 April 1863. *Ibid.*, 373.
- Stonewall Jackson's new uniform from Jeb Stuart: Davis, *Stuart*, 213; Davis, *Stonewall*, 346; Bowers, 306.
- "The results of this expedition ...". General Jeb Stuart, cited at Davis, *Stuart*, 238. (Punctuation changed.)
- "To the vigilance, boldness, and energy ...". General Lee report to Adjutant General Samuel Cooper, 10 April 1863. Dowdey, *Wartime Papers*, 373-374. (Syntax changed to adjust antiquated idioms.)
- "always and everywhere a gentleman." Fitzhugh Lee, 213.
- Mrs. Robert E. Lee "captured" by Federals: Dowdey, *Lee*, 205, 214; *II R. E. Lee*, 253-254; Anderson and Anderson, 253; Coulling, 103; Miers, 77; MacDonald, 104; Nagel, 272. Some authorities suggest that these two episodes might be a single incident.
- "[D]irections were given for the removal of the women and children ...". General Lee report to Adjutant General Samuel Cooper, 10 April 1863. Dowdey, *Wartime Papers*, 367.
- Federal cannonade of Fredericksburg: *II R. E. Lee*, 446.
- Bombardment of Washington tomb at Fredericksburg: Frassanito, *Grant and Lee*, 70.
- "Those people delight ...". General Lee quoted at *II R. E. Lee*, 446.
- "Women, girls, children ...". General Lee cited as letter to Mrs. Lee dated 22 November 1862 at Miers, 116, and cited as 24 November 1862 letter to daughter Mary Lee at Fitzhugh Lee, 225, and Robert E. Lee, Jr., 86.
- General Lee looks for the old tree on Chatham plantation: *I R. E. Lee*, 99; *II R. E. Lee*, 461. Chatham plantation recollections at Dowdey, *Wartime Papers*, 91, and Robert E. Lee, Jr., 57.
- Stonewall Jackson orders execution of stragglers: Luvaas and Nelson, *Chancellorsville and Fredericksburg*, 66.
- "I mourn the loss...". General Lee cited at *II Lieutenants*, 350, 466.
- General Maxcy Gregg wounded and A. P. Hill's casualties at Fredericksburg: Luvaas and Nelson, *Chancellorsville and Fredericksburg*, 37,

39-40, 52-53, 60, 70-71, 84-85, 88; *II Lieutenants,* 357; *II R. E. Lee,* 467; Robertson, *Hill,* 160, 164-167.
- "It is good that war ...". General Lee: Dowdey, *Lee,* 332; Miers, 120; *II R. E. Lee,* 462; Davis, *Stonewall,* 360.
- Federal casualties and frozen corpses: *II R. E. Lee,* 470-471; *II Lieutenants,* 385; Dowdey, *Lee,* 328-331; Luvaas and Nelson, *Chancellorsville and Fredericksburg,* 116, 349; Alexander, 179.
- Death of Maxcy Gregg and Stonewall Jackson' farewell: Davis, *Stonewall,* 363-364; Bowers, 317-318; *II Lieutenants,* 374-375; *II R. E. Lee,* 466.
- "How far to Richmond?": Tapert, 107.
- Federals play "Home Sweet Home" which is later banned: *II R. E. Lee,* 496; Dowdey, *Lee,* 332; Catton, *Reflections,* 47; Robertson, *Soldiers,* 85-86.
- "To Generals Longstreet and Jackson ...". General Lee report to Adjutant General Samuel Cooper, 10 April 1863. Dowdey, *Wartime Papers,* 374.
- "The attack on the 13th ...". General Lee report to Adjutant General Samuel Cooper, 10 April 1863. *Ibid.,* 373.
- "Believing, therefore, that he would attack us ...". *Ibid.*
- "No one knows ...". General Lee quoted at Hattaway and Jones, 308.
- Recapitulation of General Lee's casualties, June-December 1862: *II R. E. Lee,* 477; Davis, *Stonewall,* 388.

Chapter Thirteen

- Life and death of John Pelham: Davis, *Stuart,* 84, 269-275; Alexander, 173 (reference to nickname "Sallie").
- "Learning that the enemy .... divisions of his corps." General Lee report to Adjutant General Samuel Cooper, 23 September 1863. Dowdey, *Wartime Papers,* 460-461.
- "It was evident ...". General Lee report to Adjutant General Samuel Cooper, 23 September 1863. *Ibid.,* 462.
- "In the operations around Chancellorsville ...". General Lee letter to Dr. A. T. Blesdoe, editor of the *Southern Review,* 28 October 1867. Luvaas and Nelson, *Chancellorsville and Fredericksburg,* 174. (Syntax changed.)
- "While the spirit of our soldiers ...". General Lee letter to Secretary of War James Seddon, 10 January 1863. Dowdey, *Wartime Papers,* 389. (Verb tenses changed.)
- "Their ration consists of ...". General Lee letter, undated, to Secretary of War James Seddon. *II R. E. Lee,* 494. (Syntax and verb tenses changed.)
- "Could I have directed events ...". General Lee note to Stonewall Jackson, May 3rd or 4th, 1863. Dowdey, *Wartime Papers,* 452-453; Bowers, 349; Davis, *Stonewall,* 437. General Lee actually wrote to Jackson: "Could I

have directed events, I should have chosen for the good of the country to have been disabled in your stead."

- "Quality of mules ...". Jeb Stuart telegraph: Davis, *Stuart*, 262.
- "We have mud ...". General Lee letter to son Custis Lee, 28 February 1863. Dowdey, *Lee*, 332, (evidently misidentifying the letter as one to Mrs. Lee), and *Wartime Papers*, 411 (citing Custis as recipient).
- Death of Janie Corbin and hand-hewn coffin: Davis, *Stonewall*, 392, 394; Bean, 110.
- "General Hooker sent me ...". General Lee letter to Mrs. Lee, 27 March 1863. Dowdey, *Wartime Papers*, 420.
- Stonewall Jackson as father: Bean, 112-113; *II Lieutenants*, 519-520, 522.
- Julia Jackson baptized: *II Lieutenants*, 520; Davis, *Stonewall*, 397-398.
- Stonewall Jackson sleeps May 1-2, 1863, and his sword falls to the ground: *II Lieutenants*, 542, 544-545; Stackpole, *Chancellorsville*, 197; *II R. E. Lee*, 522.
- The folklore of Lee to Jackson, "Well, go on.", 2 May 1863: Stackpole, *Ibid.*, 206-207; Davis, *Stonewall*, 410-411; Luvaas and Nelson, *Chancellorsville and Fredericksburg*, 173; Bowers, 332-334; Dowdey, *Lee*, 347-348; *II Lieutenants*, 547; *II R. E. Lee*, 522-524.
- Elisha Paxton's premonition: Douglas, 217-218.
- Stonewall Jackson wounded: Luvaas and Nelson, *Chancellorsville and Fredericksburg*, 226; Bowers, 330, 334, 340; *II Lieutenants* 564, 567-573; Davis, *Stonewall*, 425-426, 430; Stackpole, *Chancellorsville*, 260.
- "He has lost his left arm ...". General Lee at Miers, 141; Bowers, 351.
- "Tell him that I wrestled ...". General Lee at *II R. E. Lee*, 562; Miers, 142. This is the traditional statement. Robert E. Lee, Jr., gives a slightly different version at 94.
- Colonel Robert Riley, USA, exhorts his Ohioans: Robertson, *Soldiers*, 215.
- The death of Stonewall Jackson, 10 May 1863: Davis, *Stonewall*, 442-446; Bowers, 352-355; Bean, 118; Robertson, *Hill*, 148; Dowdey, *Lee*, 355-356; Douglas, 221; *II Lieutenants*, 675, 677, 681-682.
- "this great and good soldier ..." General Lee, General Orders No. 61, 11 May 1863. Dowdey, *Wartime Papers*, 485.
- Chancellorsville casualty figures differ slightly among the various secondary sources. It is likely that some sources do not include the Fredericksburg casualties in the figures for Chancellorsville. These sources would regard the Early-Sedgwick engagement on 3 May 1863 as the separate Second Battle of Fredericksburg. *II Lieutenants*, 644, 649-650; *III R. E. Lee*, 5; Dowdey, *Lee*, 356; Miers, 143; Stackpole, *Chancellorsville*, 374-375; Luvaas and Nelson, *Chancellorsville and Fredericksburg*, 349.

- "I do not propose here ...". General Lee, report to Adjutant General Samuel Cooper, 23 September 1863. Dowdey, *Wartime Papers*, 469.
- "I am sure no one ...". General Lee comment made to Henry Kyd Douglas, 11 May 1863, quoted at Douglas, 221.
- "He was my most intimate friend ...". Jeb Stuart quoted, Davis, *Stuart*, 81.
- "I assure you, Sir ...". General Lee, undated response to Richmond City Council, December 1863. Robert E. Lee, Jr., 116. (Syntax changed.)

Chapter Fourteen

- "Our success at Gettysburg ...". General Lee letter to Mrs. Lee, 12 July 1863. Dowdey, *Wartime Papers*, 547. (Punctuation changed.)
- "But oh ... [W]hat lengthy epistles I have composed ...". General Lee letter to Martha Williams, 10 May 1851. The original letter to Markie Williams used the antiquated word "indited" which is here changed to "composed" for clarity. Punctuation also changed. Craven, 24.
- Fitzhugh Lee's old, Indian war wound: Stackpole, *Chancellorsville*, 40.
- "You can give Fitzhugh's autograph ...". General Lee letter to Mrs. Lee, 19 March 1863. Dowdey, *Wartime Papers*, 415.
- "Though I scarcely ever saw [him] ...". General Lee letter to son Rooney Lee, 10 June 1863. The original letter was dictated to Rooney and was in the second person singular: "Though I scarcely ever saw you ...". *Ibid.*, 509.
- "It would have increased my army ...". General Lee letter to General Daniel Harvey Hill, 16 May 1863. *Ibid.*, 485. (Verb tenses and syntax changed.)
- "If I could get in a position ... in that quarter". General Lee letter to Jefferson Davis, 11 May 1863. *Ibid.*, 483.
- "As far as I could judge ... catastrophe." General Lee letter to Secretary of War, James Seddon, 8 June 1863. *Ibid.*, 505. (Verb tenses changed.)
- "I thought that a part ...". General Lee letter to Jefferson Davis, 23 June 1863. *Ibid.*, 527-528. (Verb tenses changed.)
- "It seemed to me that ...". General Lee letter to Jefferson Davis, 25 June 1863. *Ibid.*, 532. (The word "challenge" is substituted for the original language, "to give occupation to".)
- General Lee's Richmond conference, May 14-17, 1863, and James Longstreet's reservations about the Pennsylvania raid: *III R. E. Lee*, 19-21; *II Foote*, 430-433.
- "I reviewed the cavalry ...". General Lee letter to Mrs. Lee, 9 June 1863. Dowdey, *Wartime Papers*, 507; Davis, Stuart, 305.
- Death of Captain Farley, CSA, Brandy Station, 9 June 1863: Davis, *Stuart*, 309; Thomas, 225; *I Lieutenants*, 280.

- "I am so grieved, my dear daughter ...". General Lee letter to daughter-in-law, Charlotte Lee, 11 June 1863. Dowdey, *Wartime Papers*, 512.
- "If you find that he [General Hooker] ...". General Lee dispatch to Major General Jeb Stuart, 22 June 1863. Davis, *Stuart*, 320-321; Dowdey, *Wartime Papers*, 523.
- "Lee speaks of you ...". Lt. General James Longstreet dispatch to Major General Jeb Stuart, 22 June 1863. Davis, *Stuart*, 322-323. Longstreet cover letter noted at *III Lieutenants*, 55; *III R. E. Lee*, 43.
- "If General Hooker's army remains inactive ...". General Lee dispatch to Major General Jeb Stuart, 23 June 1863. Dowdey, *Wartime Papers*, 526. (Punctuation changed.) Noted at *III Lieutenants*, 57; *III R. E. Lee*, 47; Clark, 26.
- Albert Jenkins, CSA, kidnaps Northern, free blacks: Mitchell, 155; Coddington, 161.
- "The Commanding General considers that ...". General Lee, G. O. 73, 27 June 1863. Coddington, 127; *III R. E. Lee*, 57; Dowdey, *Wartime Papers*, 534. (Punctuation changed.)
- "hole full of blubber." General Richard Ewell: Coddington, 174-175; *III Lieutenants*, 30.
- "General Meade will commit no blunder ...". General Lee: *III R. E. Lee*, 64.
- "It was expected that ... army east of the mountains". General Lee battle report to Adjutant General Samuel Cooper, 20 January 1864. Dowdey, *Wartime Papers*, 574.
- "You must bear constantly in mind ...". General Lee dispatch to Major General Jeb Stuart, 11 June 1862. *Ibid.*, 192; noted, *I Lieutenants*, 278.
- "General Stuart was directed ... enemy moving northward." General Lee battle report to Adjutant General Samuel Cooper, 20 January 1864. Dowdey, *Wartime Papers*, 573.
- "The movements of the army ...". General Lee: *Ibid.*, 580.

Chapter Fifteen

- "The armies rested ...". Fitzhugh Lee, 276.
- Jefferson Davis' health and family: Evans, 127, 150-151; Woodworth, 6, 15-16.
- Jim Limber and Jefferson Davis family: Ballard, 25; Davis, *Long Surrender*, 14, 90.
- "The General deals ...". General Lee letter to Charlotte Lee, 22 June 1862. Dowdey, *Wartime Papers*, 197; Davis, *Stuart*, 172; J. W. Jones, 184.

- "Let the state authorities ...". General Lee letter to Secretary of War, James Seddon, 10 January 1863. Dowdey, *Wartime Papers*, 390.
- "We are not in a condition ...". General Lee letter to Jefferson Davis, 3 February 1864. *Ibid.*, 667; J. W. Jones, 325.
- "I am not in the least discouraged ...". General Lee letter to Jefferson Davis, 8 July 1863. Dowdey, *Wartime Papers*, 544.
- "You see the Federal Congress has put the whole power ... states are in active service." General Lee letter to son, Custis Lee, 28 February 1863. *Ibid.*, 411. (Words and syntax changed slightly for clarity and antiquated idioms.)
- Jefferson Davis controversies with Generals Beauregard and Joseph Johnston over leaking official documents to newspapers or members of the Confederate Congress, and Beauregard's evacuation of Corinth: Davis, *Jefferson Davis*, 368, 537; Woodworth, 76-77, 105-106. Davis-Johnston dispute of rank seniority: *Ibid*, Davis, 356-357 and Woodworth, 176-177.
- "The general remedy for want of success ... I have been prompted by these reflections ... I sensibly feel the growing failure ... It would be the happiest day of my life ...". General Lee, written resignation to Jefferson Davis, 8 August 1863. Dowdey, *Wartime Papers*, 589-590. (Syntax slightly changed.)
- "Suppose my dear friend... To ask me to substitute ...". Jefferson Davis letter, 12 August 1863, to Robert E. Lee rejecting General Lee's resignation. *III R. E. Lee*, 157-158; J. W. Jones, 282. This elegant letter was actually drafted by Judah P. Benjamin: Evans, 239.
- Sandie Pendleton buys cloths for Kate Corbin: Bean, 135.
- Anna Garlach at Gettysburg: Wheeler, 118-119.
- Chambersburg Pike, Willoughby Run, and Amelia Harmon: Dowdey, *Lee*, 366; Luvaas and Nelson, *Gettysburg*, 11; Wheeler, 121; *III R. E. Lee*, 66; Coddington, 280.
- Death of General John Reynolds, USA: Coddington, 261, 269; Clark, 47-48.
- "... our old friend ... You may recollect him ...". General Lee letter to Mrs. Lee, 9 August 1861. Dowdey, *Wartime Papers*, 63.
- "500 of my men ...". General Alfred Iverson, USA. Luvaas and Nelson, *Gettysburg*, 35, 37.
- General Gordon, CSA, and General Barlow, USA: Clark, 60-61; Bailey, 102-103; Dowdey, *Death of a Nation*, 140-141.
- Colonel Lucius Fairchild, USA: Coddington, 294-295, 297, 310; Wheeler, 153.
- At Seminary Ridge, James Longstreet urges a maneuver to get between the

Federals and Washington: *III R. E. Lee*, 74; *II Foote*, 480; Coddington, 360-361.

- Dog Sallie and the 11th Pennsylvania regiment: *Civil War Times Illustrated, Gettysburg!*, Historic Times, Inc., Harrisburg, PA, 1985, page i (inside, front cover frontispiece).
- Sketch of General Richard Ewell, USA: *I Lieutenants*, 347; *II Lieutenants*, 696; Hattaway and Jones, 405; Alexander, 568 (Note 49, Gary Gallagher, Ed.).
- "... honest, brave soldier ...". General Lee letter to Jefferson Davis, 20 May 1863. Dowdey, *Wartime Papers*, 488.
- General Lee agrees, for the moment, to extend his line southward: Dowdey, *Lee*, 370-371; *III Lieutenants*, 101.
- Federal casualties: Stackpole, *Gettysburg*, 143; Clark, 62; Coddington, 305, 307. For the 24th Michigan, I have used Busey and Martin, 239, which contradicts the other sources.
- CSA and USA regimental strengths: Coddington, 249-250, 308, 321; Stackpole, *Gettysburg*, xxi; Pfanz, 77. My regimental figures are drawn from Busey and Martin which contradicts the other sources.
- "It was ascertained from the prisoners ...". General Lee battle report to Adjutant General Samuel Cooper, 20 January 1864. Dowdey, *Wartime Papers*, 576. (Syntax changed.)

Chapter Sixteen

- "Upon the open fields ...". Thomas Marbaker, USA: Clark, 146.
- Robert E. Lee's uniform and buttons: Bailey, 11.
- "It is so impossible ...". Eleanor Agnes Lee, diary entry of 13 July 1853. DeButts, 16.
- "I have such longings ...". Eleanor Agnes Lee, diary entry of 23 March 1856. *Ibid.*, 79. (Punctuation changed.)
- "If I could only have my children ...". General Lee letter to son Custis Lee, 17 March 1858. J. W. Jones, 91.
- "I can write but seldom ...". General Lee letter to Mrs. Lee, 19 March 1863. Dowdey, *Wartime Papers*, 415.
- "You must always remember ...". General Lee letter to Mrs. Lee, 31 May 1863. *Ibid.*, 498.
- "I see you are relapsing ...". General Lee letter to Mrs. Lee, 23 May 1863. *Ibid.*, 491. (Punctuation changed.)
- "Tell Chass that President Lincoln ... interest to her". General Lee letter to Mrs. Lee, 9 August 1863. The text of this letter of Robert E. Lee referencing Gettysburg was generously provided to the author by Mrs. Mary

Coulling, author of *The Lee Girls*, cited here often. This letter does not appear in Dowdey's *Wartime Papers*, in Robert Lee, Jr.'s, *Recollections and Letters*, or in Jones' *Life and Letters*. It is believed that the letter fragment is published here for the first time. The original document is in the custody of the Virginia Historical Society, Richmond, manuscript number Mss.1 L51 c470. Reprinted by permission.

- "I should then have nothing to do ...". General Lee letter to Martha Williams from West Point, 29 June 1854. Craven, 47.
- "In looking back upon the calamities ...". General Lee letter to Martha Williams after the Civil War, 20 December 1865. *Ibid.*, 66.
- "How are you progressing ...". General Lee letter to Martha Williams after the Civil War, 1 January 1868. *Ibid.*, 80.
- "I have never had any hope ...". General Lee letter to Martha Williams after the Civil War, 4 October 1867. *Ibid.*, 76. Avery Craven also notes Markie Williams' art school training at 57, note 2.
- "... a galvanized corpse ...". I, Jones, 380 (16 July 1863).
- Sketch of William Preston "Dobbin" Johnston: Davis, *Jefferson Davis*, 416, 419.
- "My only anxiety ...". General Lee letter to Jefferson Davis, 16 April 1863. Dowdey, *Wartime Papers*, 435.
- "Short rations ...". General Lee letter to Secretary of War James Seddon, 22 January 1864. *Ibid.*, 659-660. (Syntax changed.)
- "More than once ...". General Lee letter to Secretary of War James Seddon, 10 January 1863. *Ibid.*, 389.
- The conscription situation in the South: Nevins, *Organized War, 1863-1864*, 13.
- "I have been mortified ...". General Lee letter to Colonel Lucius Northrop, Commissary General, CSA. Dowdey, *Wartime Papers*, 648.
- "If defeated, nothing ...", General Lee letter to son, Rooney Lee, 24 April 1864. J. W. Jones, 299.
- "In view of the vast increase ...". General Lee letter to Secretary of War James Seddon, 10 January 1863. Dowdey, *Wartime Papers*, 390.
- "The number of desertions ...". General Lee letter to Jefferson Davis, 17 August 1863. *Ibid.*, 591.
- "Conceding to our enemies ...". General Lee letter to Jefferson Davis, 10 June 1863. *Ibid.*, 508; J. W. Jones, 248.
- "The progress of this army ...". General Lee, Special Orders of 9 September 1861. Dowdey, *Ibid.*, 73.
- "The army did all it could ...". General Lee letter to cousin Margaret Stuart, 26 July 1863. *Ibid.*, 561; J. W. Jones, 283.

- James Longstreet again urges a shift southward to threaten Washington and his request to wait for General Pickett ("one boot off"): *III R. E. Lee*, 87-89.
- Mrs. Joseph Bayly nurses the wounded: Wheeler, 174-175.
- Generals Hood and McLaws protest Longstreet's battle plan: *III R. E. Lee*, 98; Dowdey, *Lee*, 378; *III Lieutenants*, 119-122; Coddington, 382; Dowdey, *Death of a Nation*, 198-201, 204, 207; Pfanz, 164-165; Luvaas and Nelson, *Gettysburg*, 62-63.
- The deaths of Henry Brainard and Philip Grine; the wounding of John Roberts: Pfanz, 182, 222, 231, 236, 434.
- Colonel Strong Vincent, USA, "What death more glorious ...": *Ibid.*, 51; Coddington, 396.
- The death of General Barksdale, CSA: Pfanz, 318, 333, 335, 349-350, 435; Clark, 108; *III R. E. Lee*, 99-100.
- Father William Corby grants absolution to the Irish Brigade at the Wheatfield: Wheeler, 200; Pfanz, 255, 268, 285, 288; Robertson, *Soldiers*, 28.
- "Mother Kissed Me in my Dream": Miller, 350 (The boy was wounded in the Wheatfield July 2nd and recited the favorite Civil War poem the next day.)
- The death of Colonel Edward Cross, USA: Luvaas and Nelson, *Gettysburg*, 115; Clark, 100-101; Wheeler, 201-202; Robertson, *Soldiers*, 130.
- Jack Purman and Tom Oliver in the Wheatfield: Pfanz, 434.
- Plum Run becomes Bloody Run: *III Lieutenants*, 122-135; McLaughlin, 108, 112.
- Confederate soldier sings "When This Cruel War Is Over": Pfanz, 428, for incident; Miller, 350, for lyrics.
- General Lee not in command of the field from Lutheran Seminary: Coddington, 444; Wheeler, 183; Anderson and Anderson, 339; Clark, 113.
- "The army had labored hard ...". General Lee letter to Mrs. Lee, 26 July 1863. Dowdey, *Wartime Papers*, 560. (Punctuation and verb tense changed.)
- "My leading in battle ...". General Lee letter to a German, battlefield observer, undated, *II R. E. Lee*, 347. (Punctuation and syntax changed.)
- "The manner in which ...". General Lee, undated, quoted at Connelly, 187, J. W. Jones, 444; *IV R. E. Lee*, 499. Professor Freeman cites the line as part of a long-hand essay written by General Lee during the Civil War. The fragment was found after General Lee's 1870 death.

Chapter Seventeen

- "It is all over now ...". Major General George Pickett, letter to fiancee Sallie Corbell, 4 July 1863. (Punctuation changed.) Clark, 126.
- "I would recommend ... part with him." General Lee letter to daughter Mildred Lee, 28 June 1864. Dowdey, *Wartime Papers*, 810.
- "Occasionally, at least, visit ...". General Lee letter to Martha Williams from West Point, 25 May 1854. (Verb tenses and syntax slightly changed.) Craven, 44.
- "I was very glad ...". General Lee letter to Martha Williams from Mexico City, 21 May 1848. (Verb tenses and spelling changed.) *Ibid.*, 20-21.
- "Little will occur ...". General Lee letter to Martha Williams from Arlington house, 5 December 1857. (Syntax changed.) *Ibid.*, 55.
- Generals George Steuart and Junius Daniel protest attack against Culp's Hill: Coddington, 465, 469-471, 475; Luvaas and Nelson, *Gettysburg*, 144-145, 147, 158; *III Lieutenants*, 143.
- Federals fire 32,781 artillery rounds: Luvaas and Nelson, *Gettysburg*, 177.
- CSA and USA casualties: *Ibid.*, 231; Robertson, *Hill*, 225; *II Foote*, 578; *III Lieutenants*, 190, 196; Coddington, 536, 541.
- Federal band plays "Home, Sweet Home" after Pickett's Charge: Wheeler, 249.
- "Keep your eye ...". General Lee letter to Jeb Stuart, 12 July 1863. Dowdey, *Wartime Papers*, 547.
- "With my present knowledge ...". General Lee letter to Jefferson Davis, 31 July 1863. *Ibid.*, 565.
- "I never saw troops ...". General Lee quoted by General John Imboden, cited *III R. E. Lee*, 133; Dowdey, *Lee*, 390.
- "As to the battle of Gettysburg ...". General Lee letter after the war to Major William M. McDonald, quoted at Robert E. Lee, Jr., 102.
- "No blame can be attached ...". General Lee letter to Jefferson Davis, 31 July 1863. Dowdey, *Wartime Papers*, 565.
- "It's all my fault ...". General Lee quoted at *III R. E. Lee*, 136; Dowdey, *Lee*, 389.
- "I considered the problem ...". General Lee quoted at *II Foote*, 431.
- "The time has arrived ...". General Lee dispatch to Lt. General A. P. Hill, dated June, 1864 (no day noted). Dowdey, *Wartime Papers*, 760.
- "The privations and hardships ...". General Lee report to General Samuel Cooper, 20 January 1864. *Ibid.*, 584. (Syntax changed.)
- "That old man ...". Major General George Pickett. Piston, 62.

Chapter Eighteen

- "The day of my death ...". Robert E. Lee, quoted: Anderson and Anderson, 141.
- "I think of you all ...". General Lee letter to daughter Annie Lee, 2 March 1862. Dowdey, *Wartime Papers*, 121. (Punctuation changed.)
- Colonel Alexander's horses: Alexander, 39, 76.
- "I think that military critics ...". Edward Porter Alexander: *Ibid.*, 91.
- "I don't think ... Malvern Hill was an utter and bloody failure." *Ibid.*, 111-112, 120. (Syntax changed and insertion made for clarity.)
- "On two occasions ...". *Ibid.*, 92. (Syntax changed.)
- "Our whole army ...". *Ibid.*, 145-146. (Syntax changed.)
- "It was a shabby trick ...". *Ibid.*, 141.
- "General Lee's army had acquired ...". *Ibid.*, 139. (Text condensed and punctuation changed.)
- "Here the absence of Stuart ...". *Ibid.*, 231-232.
- "Our line was like a big fish hook ...". *Ibid.*, 242.
- "In General Lee's presence ...". *Ibid.*, 235.
- "Now when it is remembered ... on the following day." *Ibid.*, 233-234. (Syntax changed.)
- "I don't think General Lee ...". *Ibid.*, 237. (Punctuation changed.)
- "They really surprised me ...". *Ibid.*, 239.
- "[Our method on this occasion ...] I think the best and strongest assault ...". *Ibid.*, 238-239. (Syntax changed.)
- "Our two divisions' ...". *Ibid.*, 242. (Syntax changed.)
- "The point selected ...". *Ibid.*, 252. (Syntax and verb tenses changed.)
- "It must be remembered ...". *Ibid.*, 280.
- "If Pickett had had the support ...". *Ibid.*, 282.
- "It would have been simply impossible ...". *Ibid.*, 252.
- "He, himself, told me ...". *Ibid.*, 260.
- "My orders were as follows ...". *Ibid.*, 245-246. (Syntax changed.)
- "A courier brought me ...". *Ibid.*, 254.
- "I wrote to General Longstreet ...". *Ibid.*, 254-255.
- "After a while ...". *Ibid.*, 255. (Text insertions for clarity.)
- "It must be borne in mind ... and soon destroy every horse and man." *Ibid.*, 248. (Syntax changed.)
- "I had tried ...". *Ibid.*, 255.
- "I determined ...". *Ibid.*
- "It was just one o'clock ... slackened at all." *Ibid.*, 257-258. (Syntax changed.)
- "I wrote another note ...". *Ibid.*, 259.

- "Some five or ten minutes ... from saying a word." *Ibid.*, 261. (Syntax changed.)
- "I kept up my fire ...". *Ibid.*, 264. (Syntax changed.)
- "Our ammunition was so low ...". Edward Porter Alexander, quoted at *II Foote*, 577.
- "I think it a reasonable estimate ...". Alexander, 277.
- "[a]udacity's name was Lee." *Ibid.*, 146.
- "[t]here can never have been ...". *Ibid.*, 222.
- "[L]ike the rest of the army ...". *Ibid.*, 254.
- "I have been up to see the Congress ...". General Lee to son, Custis Lee, March 1865, quoted at *III R. E. Lee*, 538.
- "Our affections for you ...". James Longstreet: Longstreet, 78.
- "As we failed ...". Lt. General James Longstreet, letter to Judge Augustus B. Longstreet, Columbus, Georgia, 24 July 1863. Longstreet, 65; *II Foote*, 595; Dowdey, *Lee*, 398; Piston, 125-126.
- "I suggested ...". Lt. General James Longstreet, quoted *III Lieutenants*, 46.
- "General Lee chose the plan ...". Longstreet, 65. (Same letter to Judge Longstreet noted above.)
- "When I overtook General Lee ...". *Ibid.*, 38. (Quoting General Longstreet's 1877 article written for the *Philadelphia Weekly Times*. Syntax and punctuation changed.)
- "General Lee never in his life ...". *Ibid.*, 68. (Same 1877 article as noted immediately above.)
- "At half-past three o'clock ... had become tremendous." *Ibid.*, 40-41. (Same 1877 article noted above. Syntax changed.)
- "While Meade's lines were growing ...". *Ibid.*, 42. (Same 1877 article noted above. Syntax changed with insertion for clarity.)
- "That day at Gettysburg ...". General Longstreet's often-quoted statement noted at Piston, 59, referencing *III Battles and Leaders*, 345.
- "He did not give or send ...". Longstreet, 48. (Insertions for clarity.)
- "I said to General Lee ...". *Ibid.*, 48-49; Coddington, 460. (Syntax changed with insertions for clarity.)
- "[n]ever was I so depressed...". Longstreet, 50-51. (Porter Alexander is noted in the quotation as being a colonel. In the original statement of Longstreet, Alexander is ranked as general, a rank dating after December 1863.)
- "... after I had read the note ...". *Ibid.*, 51-52. (Syntax changed.)
- Birth and naming of Robert Lee Longstreet: *Ibid.*, 109.
- "You are the army ...". General Henry Wise, April 1865, quoted at Connelly, 16.

Chapter Nineteen

- Jefferson Davis' saddle with compass: Davis, *Jefferson Davis*, 339.
- Jefferson Davis' insomnia, pain, and opium medication: Davis, *Long Surrender*, 7.
- "My rheumatism, I hope ...". General Lee letter to Mrs. Lee, 1 November 1863. Robert E. Lee, Jr., 113.
- "... blood would freeze ...". Davis, *Long Surrender*, 8.
- "I fear it may be necessary ...". General Lee letter to War Secretary Breckinridge, 19 February 1865. *IV R. E. Lee*, 4; Dowdey, *Wartime Papers*, 905; J. W. Jones, 355. The Dowdey transcript of this dispatch inserts the word "all" as to "all our cities." Professor Freeman omits the more urgent connotation of "all."
- "We have now but one thing ...". General Lee letter to Jefferson Davis, 19 April 1864. Dowdey, *Wartime Papers*, 704. (Punctuation changed.)
- "I should have commenced breaking up ...". General Lee letter to Stonewall Jackson, 14 November 1862. *Ibid.*, 335.
- "Experience has convinced me ...". General Lee report to Adjutant General Samuel Cooper, 1 April 1864. *Ibid.*, 689.
- "These men are not an army ... right thing next time." General Lee statement quoted as having been made to General A. P. Hill at Spotsylvania Courthouse, 15 May 1864. *III R. E. Lee*, 331; *III Lieutenants*, 449.
- "Wholesale impressments will give ...". General Lee letter to General James Kemper, 29 January 1864. Dowdey, *Wartime Papers*, 663.
- "The chief quartermaster of the Army brought me ...". General Lee letter to Quartermaster General, General Alexander Lawton, 30 January 1864. *Ibid.*, 664-665.
- "[y]ou must not be surprised ...". General Lee letter to War Secretary Breckinridge, 8 February 1865. *Ibid.*, 890; *IV R. E. Lee*, 3.
- "As long as there is one horse ...". General Lee, undated, quoted at Nolan, 149 and Connelly, 201.
- "I want for nothing ...". General Lee letter to Mrs. Lee, 9 April 1864. Dowdey, *Wartime Papers*, 695.
- "Custis Morgan [is] still among the missing ...". General Lee letter to Mrs. Lee, 10 July 1864. Dowdey, *Wartime Papers*, 818; J. W. Jones, 318. (Verb tense changed.)
- General Lee and silent, standing ovation at St. Paul's Church, 20 December 1863: II Foote, 887; MacDonald, 174.
- "We must suffer patiently ...". General Lee letter to Mrs. Lee, 14 August 1864. Robert E. Lee, Jr., 137; Dowdey, *Wartime Papers*, 837.

- "[D]o write sometimes ...". General Lee letter from West Point to Martha Williams, 25 May 1854. Craven, 44-45.
- "Good-bye, my precious child ...". General Lee letter to daughter Eleanor Agnes, 25 May 1863. Dowdey, *Wartime Papers*, 493. ("daughter" substituted for "child" in original document.)
- "Never forget me ...". General Lee letter to Mrs. Lee, 19 June 1864. *Ibid.*, 793.
- "You know, Markie ...". General Lee letter from West Point to Martha Williams, 14 March 1855. Craven, 53.
- "A soldier's heart, you know ...". General Lee letter to cousin Margaret Stuart, 7 April 1864. J. W. Jones, 302.
- The secondary sources disagree on the date of Charlotte Wickham Lee's death. She died either on Christmas Eve or Christmas Day 1863. Anderson and Anderson, 354; Coulling, 132-133. The most likely cause of death was tuberculosis rather than the usual, historians' (and novelists') dramatic claim of succumbing to a broken heart. Nagel, 279.
- "Thus, dear Mary ...". General Lee letter to Mrs. Lee, 27 December 1863. Dowdey, *Wartime Papers*, 645; *III R. E. Lee*, 217; J. W. Jones, 298. General Lee wrote a very similar letter to his cousin Margaret Stuart two days later. J. W. Jones, 297.
- Sandie Pendleton and Kate Corbin marry: Bean, 182, 187.
- "I am glad you are comfortably arranged ...". General Lee letter to Mrs. Lee, 15 January 1864. Dowdey, *Wartime Papers*, 652.
- "I fear that unless ...". General Lee letter to General Alexander Lawton, Quartermaster General, 19 January 1864. *Ibid.*, 653.
- "It is a matter of great moment ...". General Lee letter to Jefferson Davis, 19 January 1864. *Ibid.*, 655.